# Reshaping
# Rogue States

A WASHINGTON QUARTERLY READER

# Reshaping Rogue States

PREEMPTION, REGIME CHANGE,
AND U.S. POLICY TOWARD
IRAN, IRAQ, AND NORTH KOREA

*EDITED BY*
**ALEXANDER T. J. LENNON**
AND
**CAMILLE EISS**

THE MIT PRESS
Cambridge, Massachusetts
London, England

The contents of this book were first published in *The Washington Quarterly* (ISSN 0163-660X), a publication of The MIT Press under the sponsorship of The Center for Strategic and International Studies (CSIS). Except as otherwise noted, copyright in each article is owned jointly by the Massachusetts Institute of Technology and CSIS. No article may be reproduced in whole or in part except with the express written permission of The MIT Press.

François Heisbourg, "A Work in Progress: The Bush Doctrine and Its Consequences," *TWQ* 26, No. 2 (Spring 2003); Anthony Clark Arend, "International Law and the Preemptive Use of Military Force," *TWQ* 26, No. 2 (Spring 2003); Lawrence Freedman, "Prevention, Not Preemption," *TWQ* 26, No. 2 (Spring 2003); Jason D. Ellis, "The Best Defense: Counterproliferation and U.S. National Security," *TWQ* 26, No. 2 (Spring 2003); Gu Guoliang, "Redefine Cooperative Security, Not Preemption," *TWQ* 26, No. 2 (Spring 2003); Pascal Boniface, "What Justifies Regime Change?" *TWQ* 26, No. 3 (Summer 2003); Catherine Lotrionte, "When to Target Leaders," *TWQ* 26, No. 3 (Summer 2003); David B. Rivkin Jr. and Darin R. Bartram, "Military Occupation: Legally Ensuring a Lasting Peace," *TWQ* 26, No. 3 (Summer 2003); Barry Rubin, "Lessons from Iran," *TWQ* 26, No. 3 (Summer 2003); Michael O'Hanlon and Mike Mochizuki, "Toward a Grand Bargain with North Korea," *TWQ* 26, No. 4 (Autumn 2003); David Shambaugh, "China and the Korean Peninsula: Playing for the Long Term," *TWQ* 26, No. 2 (Spring 2003); Derek J. Mitchell, "A Blueprint for U.S. Policy toward a Unified Korea," *TWQ* 26, No. 1 (Winter 2003); Victor D. Cha, "Focus on the Future, Not the North," *TWQ* 26, No. 1 (Winter 2003); Gary Sick, "Confronting Terrorism," *TWQ* 26, No. 4 (Autumn 2003); Shahram Chubin and Robert S. Litwak, "Debating Iran's Nuclear Aspirations," *TWQ* 26, No. 4 (Autumn 2003); Ali M. Ansari, "Continuous Regime Change from Within," *TWQ* 26, No. 4 (Autumn 2003); Mahmood Sariolghalam, "Understanding Iran: Getting Past Stereotypes and Mythology," *TWQ* 26, No. 4 (Autumn 2003); Steven Metz, "Insurgency and Counterinsurgency in Iraq," *TWQ* 27, No. 1 (Winter 2003–04); Daniel L. Byman and Kenneth M. Pollack, "Democracy in Iraq?" *TWQ* 26, No. 3 (Summer 2003); Dawn Brancati, "Can Federalism Stabilize Iraq?" *TWQ* 27, No. 2 (Spring 2004); Jon B. Alterman, "Not in My Backyard: Iraq's Neighbors' Interests," *TWQ* 26, No. 3 (Summer 2003).

Selection and introduction, copyright © 2004 by The Center for Strategic and International Studies and the Massachusetts Institute of Technology.

Library of Congress Cataloging-in-Publication Data

Reshaping rogue states : preemption, regime change, and U.S. policy toward Iran, Iraq, and North Korea / edited –by Alexander T.J. Lennon and Camille Eiss
    p.   cm. — (A Washington quarterly reader)
   Includes bibliographical references.
   ISBN 0-262-62190-8 (pbk. : alk. paper)
   1. United States—Foreign relations—2001- 2. Preemptive attack (Military science) 3. Intervention (International law) 4. United States—Foreign relations—Iran. 5. Iran—Foreign relations—United States. 6. United States—Foreign relations—Iraq. 7. Iraq—Foreign relations—United States. 8. United States—Foreign relations—Korea (North). 9. Korea (North)—Foreign relations—United States. I. Lennon, Alexander T. II. Eiss, Camille. III. Series.

E902.R47 2004
327.73056—dc22

                                                          2004040256

# CONTENTS

## Part IV: Iran

## Part V: Iraq after Saddam

## Alexander T. J. Lennon and Camille Eiss

# Introduction: The Bush Revolution in Rogue Strategy

The precise membership of the club of states that "stand outside the international community,"[1] what they threatened to do to be made part of it, the political rhetoric used to identify and rally support against them, and the various policies proposed or enacted to combat them have evolved from administration to administration. Generally recognized as underdeveloped countries pursuing weapons of mass destruction (WMD) and supporting terrorism, these actors have been called everything from outlaw or pariah states[2] to backlash states[3] to rogue states[4] to states of concern[5] and at various times have included Cambodia, Cuba, Libya, Iran, Iraq, North Korea, South Africa, Sudan, Syria, and Uganda.

The Clinton Department of State's official change in the political lexicon from "rogue states" to "states of concern" in 2000 was the most significant shift as it marked a conscious effort to move away from the ineffective one-size-fits-all strategy that seemed to result from dealing with distinct states collectively as "rogues" and move toward a strategy of "differentiated containment"[6] that treated each potential threat and its unique challenges individually.

After the September 11, 2001, attacks, the new threat perception, rhetoric, and security strategy that emerged swung the political pendu-

Alexander T. J. Lennon is editor-in-chief of *The Washington Quarterly* and a Ph.D. candidate at the University of Maryland's School of Public Affairs. Camille Eiss is the associate managing editor of *The Washington Quarterly*.

lum to the other extreme. In a striking parallel to Ronald Reagan's Cold War reference to the Soviet Union as the "evil empire," President George W. Bush's 2002 State of the Union address candidly redefined the enemy in precisely three parts: "States like [Iran, Iraq, and North Korea], and their terrorist allies, constitute an axis of evil, arming to threaten the peace of the world."[7] The president declared the potential nexus of weapons proliferation and terrorism as the defining criteria: "By seeking weapons of mass destruction (WMD), these regimes pose a grave and growing danger. They could provide these arms to terrorists, giving them the means to match their hatred ... In any of these cases, the price of indifference would be catastrophic."[8] To the alarm of much of the international community, the administration's subsequent National Security Strategy made clear that, in a post–September 11 world, the United States would not tolerate inaction. Defeating the new enemy necessitated a new strategy: in the administration's words, "to forestall or prevent such hostile acts by our adversaries, the United States will, if necessary, act preemptively."[9]

Together these statements not only pinpointed those international actors perceived by the United States to pose the greatest threats to U.S. interests and international stability but also previewed for the world the lengths the United States would go to defeat them. In the two years that have passed since, the United States has preempted and overturned one government, seeks to foster democratic trends while working with the International Atomic Energy Agency and its European allies to root out nuclear weapons in a second, and continues to balance between isolating and multilaterally building incentives with its Asian partners in the third. Thus, despite the candid, collective categorization of the axis of evil, U.S. policy toward Iraq, Iran, and North Korea has varied greatly.

*Reshaping Rogue States* presents a variety of perspectives to begin to analyze the common policy trends and the distinct policy options that can address the unique threats posed by each of the so-called axis members. By presenting international and U.S. perspectives on potential future developments and their implications within each rogue state, among regional players, and in international law in particular, this book encourages you to draw your own conclusion about the recent U.S. policy actions to combat these threats.

Its declared national security strategy of preemption, more than anything, arguably will distinguish the Bush administration from its predecessors in the history books. Whether or not one believes that key players in the administration had visions for preemptively striking and overturning the Saddam Hussein regime prior to the September 11 attacks, the drastic change in the international security context and the emergence of a clear and capable threat to the U.S. homeland precipitated by those attacks set the stage for the United States to shift its foreign policy, along with all of the implications for international law on the use of force.

Although not made quite as explicit or asserted as a doctrine per se, the policy of regime change has emerged as just as central to the Bush administration's overarching rogue strategy in the post–September 11 world. Whether and how U.S. policy should, or legally can, seek a change in the regime—or at least in its behavior[10]—in these axis states has moved to the center of international debate, particularly after being implemented in Iraq.[11] The first two parts of this book grapple with the concepts of preemption and regime change in both real and theoretical terms. Strategists and scholars from around the world examine the underlying implications of states pursuing such policies for international norms on sovereignty and the use of force; ask and begin to answer fundamental questions about what, if anything, justifies such policies; and weigh the benefits of alternative approaches to meeting the new threats indisputably upon us. Parts One and Two therefore introduce a conceptual and global framework for analyzing each of the three case studies that comprise the rest of the book.

The articles in Part One assess preemption's efficacy in deterring the acquisition, distribution, or possible use of weapons of mass destruction; the potential for preemptive threats, as opposed to actual operations, to serve these purposes; and the likely reactions of key international players as well as the axis itself to the United States' bold declaratory policy. Their responses revealed an array of prospective consequences, international priorities, legal definitions, and policy alternatives.

In their attempts to decipher the strategy, both François Heisbourg and Lawrence Freedman deal directly with the real implications of rhetorical semantics at play, specifically elaborating on the international confusion between a declared strategy of preemption and one, when implemented, that actually looks more like prevention. Heisbourg calls the Bush doctrine a "work in progress" that will require further clarification—in definition and scope—before it can converge with other countries' national security strategies or support. Also arguing the need for clearly distinguishing between the two, Freedman advocates an updated notion of prevention, not preemption or deterrence, as an effective strategy to deal with threats as they develop rather than after it is too late. Anthony Clark Arend's discussion of international law and the use of force analyzes preemption in the paradigm of the UN Charter but ultimately concludes that, for all practical purposes, that paradigm is outdated. He calls on the United States to take the lead in improving it. At the center of each of the three strategist's discussions is the question of "imminence" and what, more specifically, defines an imminent threat in the contemporary strategic context?

The rest of the first section presents strategic alternatives. Jason D. Ellis proposes a comprehensive counterproliferation strategy; in a world that has moved fundamentally beyond five nuclear (and few chemical and biological) weapons states, he argues that the United States must move beyond traditional nonproliferation approaches, as the administration did. Gu Guoliang, in contrast, shifts the discussion from preemption to cooperative security, calling on the United States to work cooperatively with other powers to address the threat of WMD terrorism. Guoliang's objections are clear: in practice, preemption will not work and, in principle, it breaks all existing rules.

Part Two is a collection of articles on the various implications of regime change, what some might argue is the logical extension of preemption in dealing with rogue states. The section opens with Pascal Boniface's discussion of what justifies pursuing a policy of regime change in the modern world. Are dictatorship, WMD proliferation, genocide, and/or support for terrorism conditions that obligate the international community to enforce a policy of regime change as a last resort? Who decides, and how?

Catherine Lotrionte as well as David B. Rivkin Jr. and Darin R. Bartram then address two different options for regime change from the international legal perspective. Lotrionte provides a comprehensive analysis of when and under what circumstances targeting regime leaders might provide the best policy option. Her article provides the historical, domestic precedents established by prior administrations and the international legal principles for taking such action in the past as well as the moral, legal, and practical criteria policymakers should consider today. Rivkin and Bartram then defend the international legality of military occupation, maintaining that arguments to the contrary are either misinformed about historical precedent and doctrine or are employed as pseudolegalistic assertions to object to a war opposed for other reasons. In the end, they argue, what matters is to legally ensure a lasting peace. Suggesting that a U.S. policy of regime change might not be all that new at all, Barry Rubin closes the section by drawing lessons from the U.S. experience in Iran in 1953 for U.S. efforts toward changing regimes today, particularly in Iraq. Among other lessons, Rubin warns that the real danger may lie not in the U.S. role in initially changing the regime but rather in a long-standing U.S. presence.

The latter half of the book discusses the political, military, regional, and geostrategic dimensions of U.S. policy toward each of the three axis members. In Parts Three and Four on North Korea and Iran, respectively, authors deal with the threats posed by the two remaining members (what some now call the "axle of evil") vilified by the Bush administration in early 2002, while Part Five examines Iraq after Saddam to shed light on the challenges of yet another phase of U.S. rogue policy: post–regime change. Our goal in each of these sections is to promote awareness—in classrooms, governments, and think tanks as well as among the concerned public—of the unique domestic and regional factors that will have to be addressed to effectively thwart the potential threats posed by each country and the ramifications of pursuing certain policies. At the same time, we hope that you can also discern parallels among the threats and regime behavior of the three as well as international reactions to available policy options to help draw your own conclusions about the direction for future strategy.

The North Korean threat and potential policy responses are the subject of Part Three. Michael O'Hanlon and Mike Mochizuki outline the incentives behind and a plan for striking a grand bargain with North Korea. They explain how coupling carrots that actually entice with tough demands to address North Korea's nuclear program, reduce its conventional forces, and reform its outdated economic system can begin to transform one of the world's most troubled regions. David Shambaugh then elucidates the driving forces behind China's strategy toward North Korean nuclear advancements, arguing that halting North Korea's nuclear program is not the ultimate end that China hopes to achieve. Rather, China's calculations, interest, and goals are more long term and complicated, leading to a longer hierarchy of objectives. Derek J. Mitchell's blueprint for U.S. policy toward a unified Korea provides guiding principles for planning for this contingency today to help ensure regional stability, precisely because policymakers cannot definitively predict when unification might occur. Finally, Victor D. Cha contends that as the U.S.-South Korea alliance steadily approaches a pivotal reassessment, the focus must be on the future, not just North Korea; policymakers need to stop thinking about the alliance in ad hoc terms and start creating a vision for the future U.S. presence in Northeast Asia generally and in Korea specifically.

Part Four on Iran seeks to shed light on some of those aspects of the Iranian threat that appear to have been overlooked in policy circles thus far and their implications for policy responses. Gary Sick draws attention to a shift in Iranian terrorism away from hostage-taking and targeted assassinations and toward support for radical anti-Israeli groups in Palestine that calls for a different and more creative set of responses by the United States. Shahram Chubin and Robert S. Litwak propose moving the debate on Iran's nuclear developments beyond international nonproliferation efforts to include leveraging nuclear politics within Iran, specifically calling for ways to generate real debate among the Iranian public about the state's nuclear future. Both Ali M. Ansari and Mahmood Sariolghalam appeal to U.S. policymakers to move beyond oversimplifications and stereotypes in dealing with this country's complex polity. Ansari's historical analysis suggests that regime change in Iran has been a continuous process and that the democratic tendency introduced during the Constitutional Revolution in 1906 may not have lost its way, while Sariolghalam disabuses misconceptions, including those about the nature of political Islam in the country. Sariolghalam concludes that Washington needs to look beyond 2010, when groups that will compete to advance Iran's national interests, economic prosperity, and political openness will manage the country.

The four final chapters of the book address the challenges the United States continues to face in post-Saddam Iraq. Steven Metz tackles the ongoing insurgency specifically, outlining the intractable dilemma of promoting insurgency if the United States stays or instability if it leaves. He advocates implementing six principles as the basis for a comprehensive counterinsurgency strategy to forestall the threat. Daniel L. Byman and Kenneth M. Pollack then grapple with the strategic possibility of making democracy work in Iraq; they conclude that the transition will be difficult but not impossible and that the stakes make it imperative. Dawn M. Brancati goes one layer deeper into the democratization debate by making her case for establishing federalism in Iraq as the only means to prevent ethnic conflict and secessionism. She explains how and why three principles in particular must shape the development of a specific kind of federalism for peace and stable democracy to prevail. Finally, Jon B. Alterman discusses the U.S. vision for Iraq and the region more broadly from the perspective of Iraq's neighbors. Not only do these Middle Eastern countries find U.S. plans and especially U.S. rhetoric deeply troubling, he argues they also have the means to keep them from coming to pass.

The various chapters of *Reshaping Rogue States* by no means cover all the intricacies and challenges that have arisen thus far or that will continue to emerge as the United States moves forward in its campaign to combat threats posed by states that support terrorism and/or seek WMD now or in the future. It also does not provide any specific insight into potential challenges presented by other states beyond the three axis members branded in early 2002. Moreover, the articles presented here collectively do not advocate any single policy prescription nor do they draw any uniform conclusions about the administration's rogue strategy more broadly.

Rather, the objective is to provide you, the reader, with the background and diversity of international perspectives to be able to come to your own conclusions. In dealing exclusively with the twin policies of preemption and regime change and the three states targeted, at least rhetorically, we hope that this book will encourage readers to identify the parallels and the differences among these three challenges to international order and, where appropriate, draw on historical lessons to help combat their threats without creating new threats in the process.

In the aftermath of the conflict in Iraq, it remains to be seen whether the so-called Bush doctrine of preemption and regime change will be overtly applied to Iran, North Korea, or any future threats. History may record that only Iraq's regime was preemptively changed because of its potential to spread WMD technology to terrorist networks. Nevertheless, that decision has altered the realm of what is considered possible. New calculations are undoubtedly being made within potential rogue targets and among prospective U.S. partners while new policy tools are being considered to help improve the array of options available for combating unprecedented and increasingly complex threats in the future.

Whether you agreed with the decision to overthrow Saddam's regime or not, the policy landscape has forever been redesigned by it. Should Iran's or North Korea's regime be preemptively changed? Under what circumstances would international law allow it? What other options are available? What lessons and new challenges are emerging in Iraq? The goal of *Reshaping Rogue States* is not to answer these questions definitively but to provide a range of expertise that helps all readers begin to understand and improve the policy options available to combat the threats posed by WMD in the hands of terrorists or of these regimes ... whatever you or the U.S. administration chooses to call them.

## Notes

1. Thomas H. Henriksen, "The Rise and Decline of Rogue States," *Journal of International Affairs* 54, no. 2 (spring 2001): 349.

2. Ibid., p. 354; Robert S. Litwak, "What's in a Name? The Changing Foreign Policy Lexicon," *Journal of International Affairs* 54, no. 2 (spring 2001): 377.

3. Anthony Lake, "Confronting Backlash States," *Foreign Affairs* 73, no. 2 (March/April 1994): 45–46.

4. Bill Clinton, "Remarks to Future Leaders of Europe in Brussels, January 9, 1994," *Public Papers of the Presidents, William J. Clinton, Volume 1* (Washington D.C.: Government Printing Office, 1994), p. 11.

5. See U.S. Department of State, "Daily Press Briefing, DPB #61," June 19, 2000, http://secretary.state.gov/www/briefings/0006/000619sb.html (accessed March 18, 2004). See also Steven Muffson, "A 'Rogue' is a 'State of Concern,'" *Washington Post*, June 20, 2000, p. A16.

6. See Zbigniew Brezinski, Brent Scrowcroft, and Richard Murphy, "Differentiated Containment," *Foreign Affairs* 76, no. 3 (May/June 1997): 20–30.

7. Office of the Press Secretary, The White House, "President Delivers State of the Union Address," January 29, 2002, www.whitehouse.gov/news/releases/2002/01/20020129-11.html (accessed March 18, 2004).

8. Ibid.

9. National Security Strategy of the United States of America, September 2002, p. 15, www.whitehouse.gov/nsc/nss.pdf (accessed March 18, 2004).

10. Some statements by administration officials were interpreted to mean that Saddam's disarmament, even if he remained in power, might constitute regime change. See, for example, Joyce Howard Price, "Saddam Could Stay in Power," *Washington Times*, October 21, 2002.

11. For an exceptional discussion of regime change and its potential to be used to prevent proliferation, see Robert S. Litwak, "Non-proliferation and the Dilemmas of Regime Change," *Survival* 45, no. 4 (winter 2003–04): 7–32.

# Part I
# Preemption

François Heisbourg

# A Work in Progress: The Bush Doctrine and Its Consequences

With the attacks of September 11, 2001, in mind, the United States has begun to transform its security strategy—radically altering its postulates but imprecisely reforming its doctrine and operations. As both friends and foes assess the consequences of the new National Security Strategy (NSS) of the United States, it is prudent to remember that this strategic revision remains a work in progress. In particular, the semantics at play—notably the wide use of the words "preemption" and "prevention" interchangeably to summarize this new strategy—require a careful examination, and indeed clarification, of the strategy itself. Such a clarification is needed to attempt to reconcile the new U.S. vision with the strategic choices of allied countries.

## First Impressions

The president's State of the Union address on January 29, 2002, conveyed the gist of the new U.S. defense strategy in two concise sentences: "We must prevent the terrorists and regimes who seek chemical, biological, or nuclear weapons from threatening the United States and the

François Heisbourg is director of the Fondation pour la Recherche Stratégique in Paris and chairman of the International Institute for Strategic Studies (IISS) in London.

Copyright © 2003 by The Center for Strategic and International Studies and the Massachusetts Institute of Technology
*The Washington Quarterly* • 26:2 pp. 75–88.

world. ... I will not wait on events, while dangers gather." Elsewhere in his speech, President George W. Bush singled out Iraq, Iran, and North Korea as constituting an "axis of evil."[1] Later, on June 1, 2002, Bush clarified the implications of the strategic shift in his West Point commencement speech, where he compared today's security situation to the Cold War: "For much of the last century, America's defense relied on the Cold War doctrines of deterrence and containment. In some cases, these strategies still apply. ... If we wait for threats to fully materialize, we will have waited too long. ... We must take the battle to the enemy ... and confront the worst threats before they emerge." Even more explicit language was used in Deputy Secretary of Defense Paul Wolfowitz's speech at the International Institute for Strategic Studies on December 2, 2002: "[T]he notion that we can wait to prepare assumes that we know when the threat is imminent. ... When were the attacks of September 11 imminent? Certainly they were imminent on September 10, although we didn't know it. ... Anyone who believes that we can wait until we have certain knowledge that attacks are imminent has failed to connect the dots that led to September 11."[2]

Despite an abundance of similar wording in the president's, vice president's, and secretary of state's various speeches, the Bush doctrine has yet to be translated into specific new policies. The call for regime change in Iraq, for instance, has been heard before; Bush made it a campaign commitment in 2000, after it had already been put into law during the Clinton administration in the Iraq Liberation Act of 1998.[3] There has been no official word on what the new doctrine means for force postures or for the actual conduct of military operations (at least not yet) beyond those undertaken against Al Qaeda in response to the September 11 attacks.

Alongside such rhetorically radical presentations, it is worth noting that the language contained in the Nuclear Posture Review (NPR), presented to Congress on January 8, 2002,[4] does not appear to depart significantly from a similar report issued in 1995 during the Clinton administration. The 2002 NPR generated controversy throughout domestic and foreign media, however, because of Bush's emphasis on preventive action—not because of the actual content of the publicly available parts of the document. To a large extent, the same can be said about the NSS, issued by the White House on September 17, 2002. Under previous administrations, the very existence of a national security strategy went largely unnoticed by the general public.

The significance of the 2002 NSS document is contained in chapter 5, entitled "Prevent Our Enemies from Threatening Us, Our Allies, and Our Friends with Weapons of Mass Destruction," which fleshes out the concept of preemptive and anticipatory action. Here, force posture and structure implications remain sketchy at best; the document is limited to statements such as building "better, more integrated intelligence capabilities" and continuing "to transform our military forces to ensure our ability to conduct rapid and precise operations to achieve decisive results."[5]

Preemption, on the other hand, is developed in great detail but in a way that both downplays the novelty of the doctrine and appears to set limits on the kind of preemptive action it advocates. Specifically, the document states that the United States has entertained the option of preemption in the past and emphasizes the role that determining an imminent threat plays in the decision to use preemptive force. It calls for a reconsideration of what constitutes such a threat in today's world while never dictating a new definition. Beyond the militant promotion of freedom, democracy, and free enterprise in the president's cover letter, the strategy itself makes no other mention of the anticipatory use of force except to combat imminent and emerging threats:

> For centuries international law recognized that nations need not suffer an attack before they can lawfully take action to defend themselves against … an imminent danger of attack. … [I]nternational jurists often conditioned the legitimacy of preemption on the existence of an imminent threat. … We must adapt the concept of imminent threat to the capabilities and objectives of today's adversaries. … The United States has long maintained the option of preemptive actions to counter a sufficient threat to our national security. … The United States will not use force in all cases to preempt threats nor should nations use preemption as a pretext for aggression.[6]

It is difficult for U.S. partners and allies, and even for an analyst, to equate this classical approach with the one developed, among others, in Wolfowitz's speech.

## You Say Preemption, I Say Prevention

Bush has brought the concepts of prevention, preemption, and anticipatory action to the fore. Although each word has its own semantic meaning reflected in general-purpose dictionaries, the public discussion of the new national security strategy uses them, more or less, interchangeably. For example, chapter 5, intended to define and outline the concept of preemption uses the verb "prevent" in its heading to summarize the chapter's contents. By using both terms, the Bush doctrine can be interpreted in many different ways with the potential to lead to substantial policy adjustments by U.S. foes, partners, and allies. Because Bush's speeches, in general, tend to lend themselves to such broad interpretation as well, potential U.S. adversaries may be led to make worst-case assumptions as they shape their own responses.

Prevention and preemption are rooted in the Latin verbs *praevenire* (to forestall) and *praemere* (to buy before others). According to the *Merriam Webster's Collegiate Dictionary*, two of the meanings of the verb "prevent," relevant to this discussion, are "to deprive of power or hope of acting or succeeding" and "to keep from happening or existing."[7]

This broad set of definitions has had extraordinarily diverse implications in the strategic arena. Until recently, "prevention" was widely used in strategic discourse to refer to crisis prevention or preventive deployment—as an alternative to the use of lethal force. Hence, the widely and accurately hailed deployment of United Nations peacekeepers in Macedonia during the 1990s was an effective measure to prevent (until their withdrawal in 2000) the emergence of an armed conflict in that part of the Balkans. Presumably, this concept of prevention is not what Bush has in mind; in fact, it is the polar opposite of the prevalent interpretation of the Bush doctrine, which assumes that the United States may use lethal force in cold blood to accomplish its objectives.

Simultaneously, however, some analysts have invoked the notion of prevention to combat the root causes of terrorism through economic, social, and political means.

The potential for confusion is even greater when it comes to preemption. Although the noun comes from the original Latin word meaning "the right of purchasing before others," its derived meanings are much broader, spanning even well beyond the derived principle of imminence (as in imminent threat) that largely defines the concept of preemption in international law. "Preemptive" has been taken to mean "marked by the seizing of the initiative: initiated by oneself" (as in, preemptive attack).[8] This broad interpretation has allowed prevention and preemption to be used interchangeably in numerous strategic situations, long before the inception of the Bush doctrine.

For example, the Israeli attack in 1981 against the Osirak reactor, built by the French near Baghdad, has been indiscriminately portrayed as preventive and/or preemptive. An Internet search conducted on November 19, 2002, yielded 145 entries for "Osirak + strike + preventive" and 441 entries for "Osirak + strike + preemptive." The fact that this strike against the Osirak reactor could not be justified as an imminent threat, as described in the NSS, make the results of this search all the more illuminating. The Israelis were not trying to preempt an Iraqi attack but were conducting a preventive operation, designed to keep an Iraqi nuclear weapons capability "from happening or existing" a number of years down the road. Regardless of the extent to which the Israeli strike was justified and successful (and in this author's opinion, the Israelis had ample cause for concern about the military use or misuse of the Osirak facility), the UN Security Council (including the United States) roundly rejected Israel's invocation of the right to self-defense under Article 51 of the UN Charter to justify its anticipatory action.

Conversely, the Six-Day War of 1967 was, in the purest sense, a preemptive attack as described in chapter 5 of the new NSS, based on "an imminent threat—most often a visible mobilization of armies, navies, and air forces preparing to attack."[9] Israel's objective case for striking first in this instance was sufficiently obvious to keep the Security Council from disavowing it at the time. Yet, because the verb "to prevent" can mean "to deprive of power," which the preemptive attack against the Arab states did supremely, the June 1967 war is more often than not portrayed as an act of prevention. An Internet search using "six + day + war + prevention" yielded 301,000 entries, as opposed to only 5,570 entries when "preemption" was substituted for "prevention."

This semantic analysis is more than a purely academic exercise. In strategic debate, a number of practical consequences result from the use and misuse of prevention and preemption. First, an essential distinction in current international law is blurred. If the Bush doctrine strictly boiled down to preemption—in turn, tied to the concept of imminent threat—then the new U.S. national security strategy would not necessarily involve upsetting basic principles governing the use of force in international relations. Conversely, when preemption is used interchangeably with prevention and both are subject to wide interpretation, the legitimization of the use of force may be revolutionized.

Another consequence of misusing the two terms is to confuse the public debate in the international arena, inviting a confluence of strategic worst-case analysis and political anti-U.S. sentiment by both U.S. allies and adversaries. Such confusion can undermine mutual confidence and trust among U.S. allies and partners while also increasing the domestic and international margin for political maneuvering by U.S. adversaries when contemplating radical countermeasures, thus easing the way for all states with which the United States interacts to make dangerous and destabilizing decisions.

At the political and strategic level, the Bush doctrine's loose language may hinder a convergence between the new U.S. national security strategy and those of U.S. allies, which are being redefined at varying rates in the wake of September 11. Combined with questionable characterizations of the security landscape (e.g., the alliance-splitting "axis of evil" formula), such ambiguous language could accelerate, for better or worse, a reshuffling of the U.S. partner network, as old allies such as Germany keep their distance while new partners such as Russia fill the void, forming a would-be "axis of good."

Similarly, unfixed terminology forces U.S. adversaries to make potentially flawed assumptions about the actual scope of the new policy. This is not to say that uncertainty of a strategy's actual scope is necessarily bad; for example, it was the former Soviet Union's strategic uncertainty of what circumstances would lead the United States, Great Britain, or France actually to contemplate the use of nuclear force that largely kept the Cold War cold. Such uncertainty, however, should be the product of a deliberate evaluation of likely outcomes. According to the Cold War theory of deterrence (expressed as "mutually assured destruction" by the United States, "flexible response" by NATO, and "dissuasion du faible au fort" by France), such uncertainty was intended to foster prudence, based on the accurate prediction that Moscow would use worst-case analysis and act cautiously as a consequence. Given today's complex and unstable strategic reality, the question becomes, Will uncertainty lead to worst-case conclusions; and if it does, will such conclusions prove stabilizing or destabilizing in practice, particularly as others are considering the acquisition or the use of weapons of mass destruction (WMD)?

The current ambiguity of the U.S. national security strategy does, however, have at least the saving grace of keeping options open. Semantic confusion leaves room for strategic convergence on military and security implications, particularly since prevention has also, as previously discussed, been invoked to address root causes in a nonmilitary manner and to stop crises from developing.

## Responses from Friends

As U.S. allies attempt to adapt their own national strategies to the challenges presented by the September 11 attacks and the broader reshuffling of America's network of global partnerships, the affirmation of preemption/prevention as the new centerpiece of U.S. defense strategy significantly affects, either positively or negatively, allied political, strategic, and defense interests in at least three ways:

- the international rules and organizations legitimizing the use of force;
- the harmonization of U.S. and allied strategy; and
- the responses to countermeasures taken by targeted states.

## BREAKING OR REMAKING RULES FOR THE USE OF FORCE?

International affirmation of the Bush doctrine could directly challenge the existing rules pertaining to the use of force in the world—how those rules are made as well as what they entail. With respect to how, Europeans have largely maintained their vigorous defense of multilateralism. Bush's pledges to take the battle to the enemy with no mention of international support, therefore, has made the Bush doctrine a contributing if not an essential element of the European perception of U.S. unilateralism (collectively shaped by the Bush administration's approaches to the Kyoto Protocol, the International Criminal Court, and so forth). Furthermore, this reassertion of multilateralism is not exclusively European, as evidenced by Mexico's role in the Security Council negotiations leading to Resolution 1441 concerning Iraq.

The net result of this hardening of the multilateralist impulse among U.S. allies has been the creation of a more polarized situation than was the case, for instance, during the mission in Kosovo. In 1999 the Europeans found it possible to initiate the NATO air campaign alongside U.S. forces without a direct and explicit mandate from the Security Council. They tolerated this exception to global multilateralism precisely because it was understood that it was an exception and therefore would not compromise the more general European tendency toward global action.

In the case of Iraq's WMD acquisition and development, acting with UN authorization was deemed necessary by nearly all U.S. allies, despite the fact that the Security Council had found Iraq in material breach of Resolution 688 more than a decade ago. The legal basis for military action against Iraq without a new UN resolution was arguably as good as, if not better than, that during the Kosovo crisis. In other words, it is precisely because the United States has been asserting a unilateralist posture that the international community has pressed the Bush administration to operate within the constraints of a Security Council compromise or face the political consequences of the kind of unilateral behavior most U.S. allies and partners have traditionally disavowed.

How international rules are made significantly affects what those rules contain. As the NSS accurately states, preemption based on imminent threat has an established place in international law, specifically in Article 51 of the UN Charter. Furthermore, by adopting Resolution 1368 the day after the September 11 attacks (at the initiative of the French), the Security Council's interpretation of Article 51 officially and for the first time made the UN responsive to threats from nonstate actors.

The ambiguities in the language used by the Bush administration could actually hinder further legal innovations and new interpretations of existing international laws, while a perfectly good case might be made for preemption and, with qualifications, for prevention in existing international legal terms. For example, if faced with a challenge such as the ongoing nuclear and ballistic-missile trade between Pakistan and North Korea, the international community may have to consider taking some degree of preventive action; otherwise, immediately or eventually, the existing multilateral nonproliferation regime might collapse.

Action might be required even though nuclear material and missile trade between North Korea and Pakistan appears to be legal, strictly speaking. Because Pakistan did not sign the Nuclear Non-Proliferation Treaty (NPT), it is not prohibited from selling or transferring nuclear technology and material to North Korea. No legal constraints on North Korea's missile transfers to Pakistan exist; and although as an NPT signatory North Korea is acting illegally by "going nuclear," the NPT does not prohibit Pyongyang from buying nuclear technology from third parties.

Yet, the threat posed to the current nonproliferation regime by trade that might facilitate further North Korean nuclear development would make a strong case for the Security Council to adopt a set of measures (including sanctions and embargoes and, if need be, interdiction) to prevent North Korea from pursuing its nefarious nuclear and missile activity. The question remains, however: Is the Security Council more or less likely to adopt such measures in an environment where the United States is promoting an ill-defined and open-ended strategy of forceful prevention? Suspicion of the United States and its intentions might make it more difficult for U.S. allies and partners in the UN to consider such measures.

## CONVERGENT OR CONFLICTING STRATEGIES?

By its very existence, the Bush doctrine affects U.S. allies' strategic interests. By moving prevention and preemption to the fore while pushing deterrence and containment to the sidelines, the United States has, ipso facto, departed from its allies' strategies—whether expressed collectively (as in the case of NATO's strategic concept adopted in April 1999) or individually. Diverging from the strategy of one's allies is nothing novel; in several instances during the Cold War, the United States initiated a national strategy that NATO and most allies only subsequently adopted with varying degrees of tension and difficulty. Massive reprisals (eventually encased in NATO Document MC 14/2) and flexible response (Document MC 14/3) were one example (although France did not endorse NATO's flexible response as a national strategy and withdrew its forces from the integrated NATO commands when the alliance adopted the concept as its official strategy in the 1960s). Putting the United States first, allies second was not necessarily painless, but it has proved effective.

U.S. strategy could still converge with individual allies. Because of the uncertainties about the scope of prevention and preemption, however, such a process could prove intensely problematic. For instance, Germany's public and political debate, exemplified by the success of Chancellor Gerhard Schröder's campaign promise to keep out of military operations in Iraq, does not bode well for incorporating prevention into Germany's national defense strategy. Furthermore, in contrast to Cold War and early post–Cold War precedents, the strong possibility exists that convergence may never be officially established as collective NATO strategy because of the marginalization of NATO's war-fighting role.

Nonetheless, there are signs that preemption and prevention can and have already begun to be incorporated into other countries' national defense strategies. Most prominent in this respect is the new French six-year defense bill, adopted in November 2002. The bill redefines French strategy post–September 11 and lists its four foundations as deterrence (in its traditional mode directed toward other states), prevention, force projection, and protection (including the military aspects of homeland defense). For the French:

> [Prevention] is the first step in the implementation of our defense strategy. ... It is a permanent necessity against the reappearance of large direct or indirect threats, [or] the development of crisis situations or of conflicts liable to involve our security and interests and those of our partners in the [European Union] and Atlantic Alliance. Through intelligence it must have the capability to anticipate and assess any situation autonomously. ... The capacity for surveillance and alert must be coordinated ... at a European level but also at an international level. ... Prevention relies also on maintaining a joint system of permanently or temporarily pre-positioned forces, thus facilitating situation analysis [and an] immediate response.[10]

Moreover, action in response to an imminent threat is today, as in the past, an option that French forces have officially been able to exercise. The French defense bill states that "preemptive action is not out of the question where explicit and confirmed threats have been recognized."[11] The concept of preemption, therefore, as related to "imminent threat," is part of declared French strategy. The contrasts with the Bush doctrine are clear enough but so are elements that have the potential to overlap, at least if one takes the 2002 NSS at face value.

### ALLIED RESPONSES TO ADVERSARIES' COUNTERMEASURES

U.S. allies, like the United States itself, will be affected by any countermeasures (which will be discussed shortly) potentially adopted by those countries that consider themselves threatened by the Bush doctrine. The interests of U.S. Atlantic and Pacific allies would be adversely affected if adversaries are not deterred from developing WMD as anticipated but actually accelerate proliferation, particularly if this in turn leads to a chain reaction of deteriorating confidence in the nonproliferation regime. Such a prospect should lead U.S. allies to engage the United States in substantive discussion to clarify the definitions and implications of the Bush doctrine and to make U.S. strategy congruent with a multilateral approach to prevention and preemption. In a sense, the Security Council's negotiation of Resolution 1441 on Iraq in November 2002 may have served as a successful example of such a process. A case-specific resolution, however, cannot sufficiently substitute for bilateral or multilateral deliberations among the United States and its allies on the terms of the new U.S. national security strategy and their implications.

In military terms, WMD proliferation into Europe's "near abroad" (the Middle East) and East Asia would impose substantial burdens on defense spending, notably homeland defense costs. Strategically, extended proliferation may also affect the very alliance relationships with the United States themselves, depending on the circumstances under which such new proliferation might arise. For instance, if more Asian governments acquired nuclear capabilities, would Japan continue to maintain its security under the U.S. umbrella or would it seek national solutions, either by obtaining a nuclear capability of its own for deterrence or by opting out of its bilateral defense treaty with the United States to appease its adversaries?

## Responses from Actual or Potential Foes

Those countries that are potential or actual targets of the Bush doctrine—most explicitly Iraq; Iran; North Korea; and earlier, Taliban-governed Afghanistan—cannot be expected to remain passive in the face of this new challenge posed by the United States. The countries that comprise Bush's "axis of evil," however, are not alone in this sense; states such as Saudi Arabia or Pakistan may also have cause to fear their potential transfer to the "foe" category. Post–September 11 conditions combined with acts perceived as unfriendly to the United States (such as noncooperation in a war against Iraq) could catalyze such a shift for Saudi Arabia; as for Pakistan, WMD-proliferation misconduct coupled with unchecked Islamic militancy could have the same effect.

## ACCELERATED WMD PROLIFERATION

Such states might be tempted to accelerate their WMD acquisition as well as the means to deliver them. If a country—Iran particularly comes to mind—becomes convinced that it will be the next object of U.S. attempts at regime change, for example, it is possible that it might hasten what is currently a partially developed WMD-acquisition or -development program. In the case of Iran, it is still too early to provide convincing empirical evidence of such moves following Bush's 2002 State of the Union address. North Korea's October 2002 public acknowledgment of unpublicized U.S. accusations that it has been pursuing the production of weapons-grade enriched uranium, however, might be interpreted as an explicit attempt by an adversary to reinforce the deterrent effect of the actual or imminent possession of nuclear weapons.

Indeed, one of the lessons that an overtly targeted country such as Iran might draw from the North Korean case is that possession of a nuclear deterrent precludes the United States from considering military action. Iraq can be attacked precisely because it lacks an existent nuclear deterrent whereas North Korea remains safe by virtue of a combination of geography (10 million South Koreans are within easy range of North Korean artillery) and the possibility of a North Korean nuclear (and/or other WMD) response.

The North Korean case raises another potential response: countries with existing WMD capabilities can implicitly or explicitly threaten to spread proliferation further to deter, or in response to, U.S. military operations. North Korea, which sent missile technology to Pakistan and other states, might be willing to conduct similar transfers to other players in the Middle East. In the end, lessons may be drawn that a target state with WMD capability is safer than one without it.

The conclusion to be drawn from these possibilities is not to "go soft" on potential proliferants. Simply, countries that have not yet crossed the nuclear or WMD threshold—and even more so, those currently uncertain about their future WMD policies—need to know that they are not irreversibly "marked" as irredeemably evil. Although the adoption of Resolution 1441 was useful in this regard, Bush's "axis of evil" formula did just the opposite.

## PRECAUTIONARY PROLIFERATION

Countries not yet there, but that fear finding themselves on the list of targets for U.S. preventive action might also quietly prepare to prevent this prospect. Under certain circumstances, such an option might prove tempting for a country such as Saudi Arabia, which already possesses large medium-range Chinese CSS-2 rockets. Although this idea is currently speculative, such a scenario could be prompted by warfare aimed at regime change throughout the Middle East—in the wake of intervention in Iraq, for instance. Neoconservative discourse on democratizing the Middle East helps fuel such fears. Here again, the United States would do well to clarify the limits of prevention and preemption.

It is worthwhile recalling that covert moves toward proliferation can go a long way without being detected: two years elapsed between the sale of the sizable Chinese CSS-2 missiles to Saudi Arabia and its detection by U.S. intelligence. Similarly, it took several years for U.S. intelligence to discover the transfer of uranium enrichment technology from Pakistan to North Korea, and this was despite the close attention paid to North Korean's nuclear ambitions.

## COMPLIANCE

Naturally, the most desirable consequence of international affirmation of the Bush doctrine would be to convince potential aspiring foes to continue to renounce WMD or persuade existing proliferators to change their ways. Although this possibility may yet come to pass, insufficient time has passed to find evidence of this best-case scenario. If anything,

Pakistan's continued missile tests in 2002—after its nuclear trafficking with North Korea had been discovered—bodes ill for potential target states' willingness to forgo proliferation.

## Shaping Preemption and Prevention

Notwithstanding the enormous amount of controversy caused by the Bush doctrine and the corresponding disagreements among U.S. allies, the potential for convergence among the United States and its allies on preemption and prevention is potentially quite high. To converge national security strategies, the Bush doctrine will need to meet several conditions, as will U.S. public diplomacy within and between the allied countries of Europe, Asia, and North America.

First and most important, the U.S. president's public statements need to clarify the definition and scope of preemption—linking it to and defining the terms of an imminent threat in light of the September 11 attacks—and, even more so, the U.S. understanding of prevention. Such clarification must be manifest to friend and foe alike. The Cold War brand of strategic uncertainty had virtues in its time, but not under existing circumstances.

Second, preemption and prevention need to be managed as tools that can (and should, as a Kantian European would say) be assembled and wielded multilaterally. It is doubtful that the Bush doctrine will be naturally implemented multilaterally in present-day Washington. Yet, the drafting and adoption of Resolution 1441 demonstrates that U.S. partners can exercise substantial influence, with the quid pro quo that allies of the United States understand that some action must be taken.

Finally, intensive consultation is in order between the United States and its allies on the entire range of issues involved in preemption and prevention. Legal, political, diplomatic, strategic, and military consequences should be the object of open discussion, primarily in a bilateral context but also, if possible, within the framework of NATO and the Group of Eight.

If the United States and its allies can accomplish these tasks and together redefine "imminent threat" in the post–September 11 world while consulting to flesh out the doctrinal and operational implications of new strategic approaches, then international law, norms, organizations (including the nonproliferation regime), and alliances can evolve and be preserved to face new challenges rather than be discarded haphazardly.

## Notes

1. This and all quotes by Bush cited in this article have been excerpted from the official White House website, located at www.whitehouse.gov.

2. See www.dod.gov/speeches/2002/s2002/s.20021202.depsecdef.html (accessed January 10, 2003).

3. A war against Iraq on the basis of Security Council Resolution 1441 would belong to the realm of enforcement, not prevention or preemption.

4. See Vice President Dick Cheney, speech to the Veterans of the Korean War, San Antonio, August 29, 2002, www.whitehouse.gov/vicepresident (accessed January 10, 2003).

5. "Nuclear Posture Review Report to Congress" January 8, 2002, as reproduced by John Pikes, www.globalsecurity.org/wmd/library/policy/dod/npr.htm (accessed January 10, 2003).

6. "National Security Strategy of the United States of America," September 2002 (released September 20, 2002) (excerpted from chapter 5).

7. See www.merriamwebster.com (accessed November 19, 2002).

8. Ibid.

9. "National Security Strategy of the United States of America," September 2002 (released September 20, 2002) (excerpted from chapter 5).

10. Government of France, Defense Ministry, "Loi de Programmation Militaire 2003–2008," September 11, 2002, pp. 24–25, www.defense.gouv.fr/english/files/d140/inde.htm.

11. Ibid.

Anthony Clark Arend

# International Law and the Preemptive Use of Military Force

In the wake of the tragic events of September 11, 2001, and a perceived threat from Iraq, the Bush administration promulgated a new national security strategy.[1] One critical element of this strategy is the concept of preemption—the use of military force in advance of a first use of force by the enemy. Long a contentious doctrine under international law, the claim to use preemptive force has been taken to an even more controversial level by the administration. Although traditional international law required there to be "an imminent danger of attack" before preemption would be permissible, the administration argues in its 2002 National Security Strategy (NSS) that the United States "must adapt the concept of imminent threat to the capabilities and objectives of today's adversaries."[2] It contends that "[t]he greater the threat, the greater is the risk of inaction—and the more compelling the case for taking anticipatory action to defend ourselves, even if uncertainty remains as to the time and place of the enemy's attack."[3]

Is this more permissive approach to preemption acceptable under current international law? The answer to this question depends on how one understands the contours of contemporary international law. Un-

Anthony Clark Arend is a professor in the Department of Government and the School of Foreign Service, an adjunct professor of law, and a director of the Institute for International Law and Politics at Georgetown University.

Copyright © 2003 by The Center for Strategic and International Studies and the Massachusetts Institute of Technology
*The Washington Quarterly* • 26:2 pp. 89–103.

der the United Nations Charter paradigm for the use of force, unilateral preemptive force without an imminent threat is clearly unlawful. But if the charter framework no longer accurately reflects existing international law, then the Bush doctrine of preemption may, in fact, be lawful—even if it is politically unwise. This article will assess the lawfulness of the Bush doctrine and then seek to make several policy recommendations in light of international law.

## Before the UN Charter: Necessity and Proportionality

International law is created through the consent of states. States express this consent by two basic methods: treaties and custom. Treaties are written agreements between states; in effect, they are the international equivalent of contracts. Bilateral treaties are concluded between two states, such as the Strategic Arms Reduction Treaty between the United States and Russia; and multilateral treaties are negotiated among many states, such as the UN Charter.

Customary international law is different. Unlike treaties, customary international law is not created by what states put down in writing but, rather, by what states do in practice. In order for there to be a rule of customary international law, there must be an authoritative state practice. In order words, states must engage in a particular activity and believe that such activity is required by law. Diplomatic immunity, for example, began as a rule of customary international law before it was ultimately codified in a treaty. Centuries ago, states began the practice of granting diplomats immunity from local jurisdiction for a variety of pragmatic reasons: they did not wish to cut off a channel of communication; they feared that, if they arrested diplomats of a foreign state, the foreign state would do the same to their diplomats; and so on. As time passed, more and more states began to grant immunity until virtually all states in the international system were giving diplomats immunity. Gradually, these states that had originally begun granting immunity for largely practical reasons came to believe that granting such immunity was required by law. At that point, there was a rule of customary international law—when there was both a near-universal practice and a belief that the practice was required by law.

Under the regime of customary international law that developed long before the UN Charter was adopted, it was generally accepted that preemptive force was permissible in self-defense. There was, in other words, an accepted doctrine of anticipatory self-defense. The classic case that articulated this doctrine is the oft-cited *Caroline* incident.

During the first part of the nineteenth century, an anti-British insurrection was taking place in Canada. At the time, Canada was under British rule while the United States and Great Britain were in a state of peace. There was, however, a ship owned by U.S. nationals, the *Caroline*, that was allegedly providing assistance to the rebels in Canada. On the night of December 29, 1837, while the ship was moored on the U.S. side of the Niagara River, British troops crossed the river, boarded the ship, killed several U.S. nationals, set the ship on fire, and sent the vessel over Niagara Falls. The British claimed that they were acting in self-defense, but after some heated exchanges with Secretary of State Daniel Webster, the British government ultimately apologized. Nonetheless, over the course of diplomatic communications between the Americans and the British, two criteria for permissible self-defense—including preemptive self-defense—were articulated: necessity and proportionality.

First, the state seeking to exercise force in self-defense would need to demonstrate necessity. As Webster explained in a letter to Lord Ashburton, a special British representative to Washington, the state would have to demonstrate that the "necessity of that self-defense is instant, overwhelming, and leaving no choice of means, and no moment of deliberation."[4] In other words, the state would need to show that the use of force by the other state was imminent and that there was essentially nothing but forcible action that would forestall such attack.

Second, the state using force in self-defense would be obliged to respond in a manner proportionate to the threat. In making the argument to the British, Webster explained that, in order for Canada's action to be permissible, it would be necessary to prove that "the local authorities of Canada, even supposing the necessity of the moment authorized them to enter the territories of the United States at all, did nothing un-reasonable or excessive; since the act, justified by the necessity of self-defense, must be limited by that necessity, and kept clearly within it."[5]

Throughout the pre–UN Charter period, scholars generally held that these two criteria set the standard for permissible preemptive action. If a state could demonstrate necessity—that another state was about to engage in an armed attack—and act proportionately, preemptive self-defense would be legal.

## The Effect of the UN Charter

As the Second World War was coming to an end, the delegates from 51 states assembled in San Francisco in the spring of 1945 to draft the charter of the new global organization. Pledging to "save succeeding generations from the scourge of war,"[6] the framers of the UN Charter sought to establish a normative order that would severely restrict the resort to force. Under Article 2(4) of the charter, states were to "refrain in their international relations from the threat or use of force against the territorial integrity or political independence of any State or in any other manner inconsistent with the Purposes of the United Nations." In the charter, there were only two explicit exceptions to this prohibi-tion: force authorized by the Security Council and force in self-defense. Under Article 39, the council is empowered to determine if there is a "threat to the peace, breach of the peace, or act of aggression." If the Security Council so determines, it can authorize the use of force against the offending state under Article 42.

The critical provision relating to the other exception, self-defense, is Article 51, which provides in part:

> Nothing in the present Charter shall impair the inherent right of indi-vidual or collective self-defense if an armed attack occurs against a Member of the United Nations, until the Security Council has taken measures necessary to maintain international peace and security. Mea-sures taken by Members in the exercise of this right of self-defence shall be immediately reported to the Security Council and shall not in any

way affect the authority and responsibility of the Security Council under the present Charter to take at any time such action as it deems necessary in order to maintain or restore international peace and security.

Although the basic contours of Article 51 seem straightforward, its effect on the customary right of anticipatory self-defense is unclear. If one reviews the scholarly literature on this provision, writers seem to be divided into two camps. On one hand, some commentators—"restrictionists" we might call them—claim that the intent of Article 51 was explicitly to limit the use of force in self-defense to those circumstances in which an armed attack has actually occurred. Under this logic, it would be unlawful to engage in any kind of preemptive actions. A would-be victim would first have to become an actual victim before it would be able to use military force in self-defense. Even though Article 51 refers to an "inherent right" of self-defense, restrictionists would argue that, under the charter, that inherent right could now be exercised only following a clear, armed attack.

Other scholars, however, would reject this interpretation. These "counter-restrictionists" would claim that the intent of the charter was not to restrict the preexisting customary right of anticipatory self-defense. Although the arguments of specific counter-restrictionists vary, a typical counter-restrictionist claim would be that the reference in Article 51 to an "inherent right" indicates that the charter's framers intended for a continuation of the broad pre–UN Charter customary right of anticipatory self-defense. The occurrence of an "armed attack" was just one circumstance that would empower the aggrieved state to act in self-defense. As the U.S. judge on the International Court of Justice (ICJ), Stephen Schwebel, noted in his dissent in *Nicaragua v. U.S.*, Article 51 does not say "if, and only if, an armed attack occurs."[7] It does not explicitly limit the exercise of self-defense to only the circumstance in which an armed attack has occurred.

Unfortunately, despite Schwebel's willingness to express his views on anticipatory self-defense, neither the ICJ nor the UN Security Council has authoritatively determined the precise meaning of Article 51. Indeed, in the *Nicaragua* case, the ICJ made a point of noting that, because "the issue of the lawfulness of a response to the imminent threat of armed attack has not been raised ... the Court expresses no view on the issue."[8] As a consequence, the language of the charter clearly admits of two interpretations about the permissibility of preemptive force. Given this state of affairs, it is logical to explore the practice of states in the period after the charter was adopted to determine if recent customary international law has either helped supply meaning to the ambiguous language of Article 51 or given rise to a new rule of customary international law in its own right that would allow for preemptive action.

## Post–UN Charter State Practice

As noted earlier, international law is created through the consent of states. Behind this understanding is the assumption that states are sovereign and, accordingly, can be bound by no higher law without their consent. As a consequence, states can lawfully do as they please unless they have consented to a specific rule that restricts their behavior. As the Permanent Court of International Justice, the predecessor of the current ICJ, noted in the *Lotus* case:

> International law governs relations between independent States. The rules of law binding upon States therefore emanate from their own free will as expressed in conventions or by usages generally accepted as expressing principles of law and established in order to regulate relations between these co-existing independent communities or with a view to the achievement of common aims. Restrictions upon the independence of States cannot therefore be presumed.[9]

This consent-based conception of international law, or positivism, as it is called, has critical significance for an examination of post–UN Charter practice regarding the preemptive use of force. Given that the charter is sufficiently ambiguous on this question and that there was a preexisting rule of customary international law allowing for anticipatory self-defense, it is not necessary to establish that a customary rule has emerged to permit states to use force preemptively in order for such use of force to be lawful. On the contrary, it is necessary rather to establish that there is no rule prohibiting states from using force preemptively. If states are sovereign, under the logic of the *Lotus* case, they can do as they choose unless they have consented to a rule restricting their behavior.

Although there are undoubtedly many ways to explore state practice relating to preemption in the post–UN Charter world, perhaps one of the most useful is to examine debates in the Security Council in cases where questions of preemptive force were raised. Since the charter was adopted, debate has ensued about the efficacy of preemption in three major cases: the 1962 Cuban missile crisis, the 1967 Six-Day War, and the 1981 Israeli attack on the Osirak reactor in Iraq.[10]

## THE CUBAN MISSILE CRISIS (1962)

During the Cuban missile crisis, the United States made a number of formal legal arguments in support of the institution of a "defensive quarantine" in advance of any actual Soviet or Cuban use of force. Most of these official arguments revolved around the role of regional organizations and their ability to authorize force absent a Security Council authorization. Nonetheless, during the course of council discussion of the quarantine, a number of Security Council representatives spoke about preemption. Although there was no clear consensus in support of such a doctrine, there was also no clear consensus opposing it. Indeed, even several states that argued against the U.S. position seemed not so much to reject a doctrine of preemption as to question whether the criteria established under customary law were met in this case. The delegate from Ghana, for example, asked, "Are there grounds for the argument that such action is justified in exercise of the inherent right of self-defense? Can it be contended that there was, in the words of a former American Secretary of State whose reputation as a jurist in this field is widely accepted, 'a necessity of self-defense, instant, overwhelming, leaving no choice of means and no moment for deliberation'?"[11] Then, he responded to these questions: "My delegation does not think so, for as I have said earlier, incontrovertible proof is not yet available as to the offensive character of military developments in Cuba. Nor can it be argued that the threat was of such a nature as to warrant action on the scale so far taken, prior to a reference to this Council."[12] In essence, the delegate was accepting the notion that anticipatory self-defense would be permissible if the criterion of necessity were met. In this case, he concluded that that requirement was not met.

## THE SIX-DAY WAR (1967)

On June 5, 1967, Israel launched military action against the United Arab Republic and quickly won what came to be called the Six-Day War. During the course of the Security Council debates, Israel ultimately argued that it was acting in anticipation of what it believed would be an imminent attack by Arab states. Not surprisingly, support for Israel tended to fall along predictable political lines. The Soviet Union, Syria, and Morocco all spoke against Israel. Interestingly enough, those states arguing against Israel tended to claim that the first use of force was decisive, seemingly rejecting any doctrine of anticipatory self-defense. Supporters of Israel, such as the United States and the United Kingdom, on the other hand, tended to refrain from asserting a doctrine of preemption. Unlike the Cuban missile crisis debates, there seemed to be more speakers who were negatively disposed to anticipatory self-defense; but again, there was no clear consensus opposed to the doctrine.

## THE ATTACK ON THE OSIRAK REACTOR (1981)

Israel was once again the object of criticism in 1981, when it used force to destroy an Iraqi reactor that Israel claimed would be producing nuclear weapons-grade material for the purpose of constructing nuclear weapons that would be used against Israel. As in 1967, Israel claimed that it was acting in anticipatory self-defense. Israeli ambassador Yehuda Blum asserted that "Israel was exercising its inherent and natural right of self-defense, as understood in general international law and well within the meaning of Article 51 of the [UN] Charter."[13] A number of delegations spoke against Israel, with several taking a restrictionist approach to Article 51, including Syria, Guyana, Pakistan, Spain, and Yugoslavia.

Yet, other states that argued against Israel's action took a counter-restrictionist approach. They supported the lawfulness of anticipatory self-defense but believed that Israel had failed to meet the necessity requirement. The Sierra Leonean delegate, for example, claimed that "the plea of self-defence is untenable where no armed attack has taken place *or is imminent.*"[14] Quoting from Webster's letter in the *Caroline* case, he explained that "[a]s for the principle of self-defence, it has long been accepted that, for it to be invoked or justified, the necessity for action must be instant, overwhelming and leaving no choice of means and no moment for deliberation."[15] "The Israeli action," he continued, "was carried out in pursuance of policies long considered and prepared and was plainly an act of aggression."[16] Similarly, the British representative to the Security Council, Sir Anthony Parsons, explained, "It has been argued that the Israeli attack was an act of self-defence. But it was not a response to an armed attack on Israel by Iraq. There was no instant or overwhelming necessity for self-defence. Nor can it be justified as a forcible measure of self-protection. The Israeli intervention amounted to a use of force which cannot find a place in international law or in the Charter and which violated the sovereignty of Iraq."[17] Delegates from Uganda, Niger, and Malaysia tended to take a similar approach. Interestingly enough, the U.S. ambassador to the UN, Jeane Kirkpatrick, while speaking against the Israeli action, did not explicitly rely upon the doctrine of anticipatory self-defense.

Although the Security Council ended up censuring Israel for its action, the most notable aspect of this debate was the willingness to engage in a discussion of the concept of preemptive self-defense. Even though there was no clear consensus in support of the doctrine, there did seem to be greater support than in previous cases—provided that the *Caroline* criteria are met.

## EVALUATION OF POST–UN CHARTER PRACTICE

Given this brief examination of some important indicators of state practice in the post–UN Charter period, it would be difficult to conclude that there is an established rule of customary international law prohibiting the preemptive use of force when undertaken in anticipatory self-defense. If anything, there seems to have been greater support for the doctrine in the most recent case. In all the discussions, however, those who supported the doctrine of anticipatory self-defense continued to claim that the right is limited by the requirements of necessity and proportionality set out in the *Caroline* case.

## The Bush Doctrine and the Law

In light of this examination of international law, it is fairly unremarkable for a U.S. administration to assert a doctrine of preemption. What makes the Bush doctrine different is that it seeks to relax the traditional requirement of necessity. As noted earlier, the 2002 NSS specifically claims that "[w]e must adapt the concept of imminent threat to the capabilities and objectives of today's adversaries." It argues that "[t]he greater the threat, the greater is the risk of inaction—and the more compelling the case for taking anticipatory action to defend ourselves, even if uncertainty remains as to the time and place of the enemy's attack." In other words, the administration is contending that, because of the new threat posed by weapons of mass destruction (WMD) and terrorists, the old requirement of necessity may not always make sense. By the time imminent WMD use has been established, it may be too late to take any kind of successful preemptive action. Although traditional international law would not require certainty regarding time and place, it would suggest near certainty. If an attack is imminent, it is nearly certain that the attack will occur. Given this conclusion, many scholars would be tempted to say that the Bush doctrine is clearly at variance with international law, but is this necessarily the case?

The preceding discussion presupposes two things about the nature of international law. First, it assumes that the threat posed by WMD and terrorism are similar to the threats to use force that existed as the law relating to anticipatory self-defense was developing historically. Second, the discussion assumes that the UN Charter framework for the recourse to force constitutes the existing legal paradigm. I would argue that both these assumptions are not correct.

## The Changed Nature of the Threat: WMD and Terrorism

As international law relating to the recourse to force developed over the centuries and culminated in the UN Charter, the main purpose of the law was to address conventional threats posed by conventional actors: states. Both WMD and terrorism pose threats unanticipated by traditional international law. When the charter was adopted in 1945, its framers sought to prevent the types of conflict that had precipitated World War II—circumstances in which regular armies engaged in clear, overt acts of aggression against other states. As a consequence, Article 2(4) prohibits the threat and use of force by states against states, and Article 51 acknowledges a state's inherent right of self-defense if an armed attack occurs. Even if UN Charter provisions are understood in light of customary international law allowing anticipatory self-defense, the charter's focus is still on states using force the conventional way.

Neither WMD nor terrorist actors were envisioned in this framework. The three main WMD types—chemical, biological, and nuclear—could not have seriously been on the mind of the delegates while they were drafting the UN Charter. Even though chemical weapons had been used during World War I, they had not proven to be particularly militarily useful and, in any case, were not used in any significant way as an instrument of war in World War II. The very idea of nuclear weapons was a carefully guarded secret until August 1945 and thus could not have figured into the deliberations on the charter in the spring of 1945. Indeed, as John Foster Dulles would later observe, the UN Charter was a "pre-atomic" document.[18] Terrorism, although certainly not a recent phenomenon, was not addressed in traditional international law relating to the recourse to force. Prior to the twentieth century, customary international law dealt with state actors. Even major multilateral treaties that related to use-of-force issues, such as the League of

Nations Covenant, the Kellogg-Briand Pact of 1928, as well as the UN Charter, addressed their provisions only to states.

It is precisely in this lacuna in international law that the problem lies. WMD and terrorism can strike at states in ways that customary international law did not address. Underlying international law dealing with the recourse to force is the principle that states have a right to use force to defend themselves effectively. When conventional troops prepare to commit an act of aggression, the basic criteria of *Caroline* would seem to make sense. The soon-to-be victim would still be able to mount an effective defense if it were required to wait for an armed attack to be imminent. The soon-to-be aggressor would be taking enough overt actions, and the attack itself would require mobilization, which would give the victim enough lead time.

Both WMD and terrorism, however, are different. It can be very difficult to determine whether a state possesses WMD, and by the time its use is imminent, it could be extremely difficult for a state to mount an effective defense. Similarly, terrorists use tactics that may make it all but impossible to detect an action until it is well underway or even finished. As a consequence, it could be argued that it would make more sense to target known WMD facilities or known terrorist camps or training areas long in advance of an imminent attack if the goal is to preserve the state's right to effective self-defense.

From a legal perspective, there is great difficulty with this relaxation of the *Caroline* criterion of necessity. Where does one draw the line? If imminence is no longer going to be a prerequisite for preemptive force, what is? With respect to WMD, would it be simple possession of such weapons? Such an approach is especially problematic. Given the current realities in the international system, India would be able to use force against Pakistan, and vice versa; Iraq could target Israel; and many states could target the United States, Great Britain, France, China, and Russia.

What about hostile intent as a criterion? Perhaps it could be argued that, if the state that possessed these weapons had hostile intent toward other states, this would justify preemption. But, a hostile-intent approach could be even more permissive. It could be claimed that preemptive force would be justified if a state were in the early stages of developing a nuclear weapons program—long before actual possession.[19] In a sense, Israel was making this kind of claim when it struck the Osirak reactor in 1981, but this extremely permissive approach was clearly rejected by the Security Council.

What would be the standard for terrorism? If there is a group such as Al Qaeda that has been committing a series of attacks against the United States, preemption is not really at issue. Rather, the United States and its allies are simply engaging in standard self-defense against an ongoing, armed attack. The problem would present itself if there were a group that had not yet committed an action but seemed likely to act at some point in the future. Short of an imminent attack, when would a state lawfully be able to preempt that group?

So, here is the difficulty. Although it is true that contemporary international law dealing with the recourse to force in self-defense does not adequately address the problem of WMD and terrorism, no clear legal standard has yet emerged to determine when preemptive force would be permissible in such cases. Some scholars have suggested standards, but it does not seem that either treaty law or custom has yet come to endorse one.

## THE FAILURE OF THE CHARTER FRAMEWORK

The lack of a new standard for preemptive force may not be the greatest challenge facing international law dealing with the recourse to force. As indicated above, most scholars addressing the current status of international law dealing with the preemptive use of force would argue that the law can be understood as being embodied in the UN Charter paradigm as modified slightly by customary international law. Hence, most scholars would conclude that the use of force is prohibited unless it has been authorized by the Security Council or is undertaken in self-defense. Typically, scholars would claim that Articles 2(4) and 51 have to be read to allow for anticipatory self-defense as defined in *Caroline*, and many would argue that certain other uses of force such as force to rescue nationals and humanitarian intervention would be lawful. Generally, however, these scholars would claim that the core of Article 2(4) is still existing international law and that the charter paradigm describes contemporary international law. Is this correct?

As noted above, international law is created through the consent of states expressed through treaties and custom. Because both treaties and custom are equally the source of international law, if a conflict arises between the two, such a conflict is resolved by determining the rules to which states consent at the present time. This can be determined by ascertaining which rules currently possess two elements: authority and control. First, to have authority, the would-be rule must be perceived by states to be the law; in the traditional language of the law, the rule must have *opinio juris*. Second, the putative rule must be controlling of state behavior. It must be reflected in the actual practice of states.

When the UN Charter was adopted as a treaty in 1945, that was a clear indication that states perceived the norms embodied in that agreement to be law. In the more than 50 years that have transpired since the conclusion of the charter, however, the customary practice of states seems to be wildly at variance with the charter's language. If the charter framework intended to prohibit the threat and use of force by states against the territorial integrity or political independence of states or in any other manner inconsistent with the purposes of the UN, such prohibition does not seem to be realized in practice. Almost since the moment that the charter was adopted, states have used force in circumstances that simply cannot be squared with the charter paradigm.

Although commentators may differ on the precise uses of force that have violated the UN Charter framework, the following list would seem to represent the kinds of force that have been used against the political independence and territorial integrity of states, have not been authorized by the Security Council, and cannot be placed within any reasonable conception of self-defense: the Soviet action in Czechoslovakia (1948); the North Korean invasion of South Korea (1950); U.S. actions in Guatemala (1954); the Israeli, French, and British invasion of Egypt (1956); the Soviet invasion of Hungary (1956); the U.S.-sponsored Bay of Pigs invasion (1961); the Indian invasion of Goa (1961); the U.S. invasion of the Dominican Republic (1965); the Warsaw Pact invasion of Czechoslovakia (1968); the Arab action in the 1973 Six-Day War; North Vietnamese actions against South Vietnam (1960–1975); the Vietnamese invasion of Kampuchea (1979); the Soviet invasion of Afghanistan (1979); the Tanzanian invasion of Uganda (1979); the Argentine invasion of the Falklands (1982); the U.S. invasion of Grenada (1983); the U.S. invasion of Panama (1989); the Iraqi attack on Kuwait (1990); and the NATO/U.S. actions against Yugoslavia in the Kosovo situation (1999).[20] One could add to this list numerous acts of intervention in domestic conflict, covert actions, and other uses of force that tend to fall below the radar screen of the international community. In short, states—including the most powerful states—have used force in violation of the basic UN Charter paradigm.

Given this historical record of violations, it seems very difficult to conclude that the charter framework is truly controlling of state practice, and if it is not controlling, it cannot be considered to reflect existing international law. As Professor Mark Weisburd has noted, "[S]tate practice simply does not support the proposition that the rule of the UN Charter can be said to be a rule of customary international law."[21] "So many states have used force with such regularity in so wide a variety of situations," Professor Michael Glennon echoes, "that it can no longer be said that any customary norm of state practice constrains the use of force."[22] Although I would argue that there is customary prohibition on the use of force for pure territorial annexation, as witnessed by the international community's reaction to the Iraqi invasion of Kuwait in 1990, such minimal prohibition is a far way from the broad language of the charter prohibition contained in Article 2(4). For all practical purposes, the UN Charter framework is dead. If this is indeed the case, then the Bush doctrine of preemption does not violate international law because the charter framework is no longer reflected in state practice.

## Options for Policy

Given the preceding legal discussion, what are the options for U.S. policymakers? At first blush, there seem to be three ways to proceed. First, U.S. decisionmakers could opt to accept the traditional understanding of international law. They could recognize that preemptive force is permissible in the exercise of anticipatory self-defense, but only if the imminence criterion of *Caroline* were met. This approach would have the advantage of being the least controversial approach to the law, but it would require policymakers to make the case that the use of force by an enemy state is indeed imminent before preemption would be permissible. Based on the language of the 2002 NSS, this would require the administration to back away from policy that has already been articulated.

Second, policymakers could claim that, because WMD and terrorism pose a threat that was completely unanticipated in traditional international law, the law must be reinterpreted to allow for a relaxing of the imminence criterion. This tack would be consistent with the administration's public statements. Here, the difficulty would be in establishing a new standard for preemption that would not legitimate a host of preemptive actions from a variety of other states in the international system.

Third, policymakers could declare the UN Charter framework dead. They could admit that charter law is no longer authoritative and controlling. This would be the most intellectually honest approach. It would recognize the current, unfortunate state of international law and create clean ground to build anew. The disadvantages to this approach, however, are legion. If the United States were to proclaim the charter dead, many states would rejoice at the funeral and take advantage of such a lawless regime. U.S. allies, on the other hand, would be likely to condemn such a seemingly brazen rejection of multilateralism and conceivably refuse to give the United States the kind of support it may need to continue the war against terrorism and promote order in the international system.

So, what is to be done? Although I believe that the charter paradigm does not describe contemporary international law relating to the recourse to force, I would recommend the following approach: First, the administration should accept as a matter of policy the notion that preemptive force in self-defense should only be undertaken unilaterally if the *Caroline* criterion of imminence was met. Irrespective of the current status of international law on this question, such a policy would be less destabilizing, and it could contribute to a return to a more rule-based legal regime. Second, the administration should indicate that, as a matter of policy, the use of preemptive force should be undertaken in the absence of imminence only with the approval of the Security Council. Such a policy would ensure multilateral support for such action and would likely prevent the opening of the flood gates to unilateral preemptive action by other states. Third, the United States should acknowledge that existing international law relating to the use of force is highly problematic and seek, through the Security Council, to move toward the development of a legal regime that would be truly authoritative and controlling of state behavior. This may be a daunting task, and the United States might prefer that the law be left "in a fog," as Glennon has said. Nevertheless, if the legal regime for the recourse to force is to return to something more closely resembling a stable order, the United States—as the superpower in the international system—needs to take the lead both in acknowledging the deficiency in the current legal structure and in pointing the way to its improvement.

## Notes

1. The National Security Strategy of the United States, September 2002, www.whitehouse.gov/nsc/nss.html.

2. Ibid.

3. Ibid.

4. Letter from Mr. Webster to Lord Ashburton, August 6, 1842, cited in Lori F. Damrosch et al., *International Law: Cases and Materials* (2001), p. 923.

5. Letter from Mr. Webster to Mr. Fox, April 24, 1841, cited in Damrosch et al., *International Law: Cases and Materials* (2001).

6. UN Charter, preamble.

7. *Case Concerning Military and Paramilitary Activities in and against Nicaragua*

(*Nicaragua v. U.S.*), Merits, International Court of Justice (judgment of June 27, 1986), (dissent of Judge Schwebel).

8. Ibid., (opinion of the Court) para. 194.

9. *The S.S. Lotus*, Permanent Court of International Justice (1927), P.C.I.J. Ser. A, no. 10, reprinted in Damrosch et al., *International Law: Cases and Materials* (2001), pp. 68–69.

10. See Anthony Clark Arend and Robert J. Beck, *International Law and the Use of Force: Beyond the UN Charter Paradigm* (Routledge, 1993), pp. 71–79.

11. Mr. Quaison-Sackey, UN Doc. no. S/PV.1024:51 (1962).

12. Ibid.

13. Yehuda Blum, UN Doc. no. S/PV.2280, June 12, 1981, p. 16.

14. Mr. Koroma, UN Doc. no. S/PV.2283:56 (1981) (emphasis added).

15. Ibid.

16. Ibid.

17. Statement of Sir Anthony Parsons, UN Doc. no. S/PV.2282:42 (1981).

18. John Foster Dulles, "The Challenge of Our Time: Peace with Justice," *American Bar Association Journal* 38 (1953): 1066.

19. I want to thank my colleague Robert E. Cumby for suggesting this approach to me.

20. See Arend and Beck, *International Law and the Use of Force*, pp. 182–183.

21. A. Mark Weisburd, *Use of Force: The Practice of States since World War II* (Pennsylvania State Univ. Press, 1997), p. 315.

22. Michael Glennon, "The Fog of Law: Self Defense, Inherence and Incoherence in Article 51 of the United Nations Charter," *Harvard Journal of Law and Public Policy* 25 (2002): 539, 554.

**Lawrence Freedman**

# Prevention, Not Preemption

It is difficult to argue with the principle that it is better to deal with threats as they develop rather than after they are realized. This may be especially true when those threats originate "at the crossroads of radicalism and technology," as President George W. Bush warned in his June 2002 West Point commencement address. This intersection now affords certain rogue actors in the international system the opportunity to acquire weapons of mass destruction (WMD) and to contemplate their use. Under such circumstances, Bush warned that deterrence, evidently successful during the Cold War against a risk-averse adversary, would prove ineffective. Against stateless and militant terrorist groups who have shown little evidence of cautious decisionmaking, it might be necessary to take the initiative. The much-quoted September 2002 U.S. National Security Strategy (NSS) officially advocated preemption to address these threats.[1] Yet, as this document acknowledges, deterrence still has a role in certain situations while preemption, widely cited as the new fulcrum of U.S. security strategy, was never ruled out in the past. New circumstances may very well call for a new strategy, but this transition is unlikely to take the form of a simple switch from deterrence to preemption. Both concepts harken back to earlier periods in international relations, and although they are not wholly obsolescent, neither can form the basis of a new strategy.

Lawrence Freedman is professor of war studies at Kings College in London.

Copyright © 2003 by The Center for Strategic and International Studies and the Massachusetts Institute of Technology
*The Washington Quarterly* • 26:2 pp. 105–114.

## Distinguishing Preemption from Prevention

Before considering their contemporary relevance, it is necessary to investigate the meaning of these concepts and add a third—prevention—that perhaps better defines what is often currently referred to as preemption. Both preemption and prevention can be considered controlling strategies, that is, they do not rely on adversaries making cautious decisions. They assume that, given the opportunity, an adversary will use force and therefore cannot be afforded the option in the first place. In contrast, coercive strategies such as deterrence assume that an adversary's relevant calculations can be influenced. An actor's readiness to pursue a controlling strategy can, of course, reinforce a coercive one, such as deterrence, by reminding the target of the potential consequences of noncompliance.

Consider country A in conflict with country B. Because of its strength and determination to defend its vital interests, A is confident that it has deterred B. Deterrence works because B cannot foresee any prospect of substantial gains: it would face either tough resistance from A (deterrence by denial) or punitive retaliation (deterrence by punishment). But what happens if A sees that B is getting stronger so that in time B could advance and overwhelm resistance or blunt the impact of retaliation?

Aware of this possibility, A may decide to act to prevent B from reaching this position. This would qualify as a preventive war if it had at least one of two potential objectives. The first, at a minimum, would be to disarm B to keep it unambiguously militarily inferior. The second would be to change the political character of B's state so that, even if allowed to rearm, it would no longer pose a threat. The latter, more ambitious objective would be more militarily demanding, but disarmament without regime change would mean that an embittered victim would just rearm with greater vigor. Prevention exploits existing strategic advantages by depriving another state of the capability to pose a threat and/or eliminating the state's motivation to pose a threat through regime change. Thus, prevention provides a means of confronting factors that are likely to contribute to the development of a threat before it has had the chance to become imminent.

Should A decide not to instigate a preventive war and B acquire that extra strength, then B may come to feel with time that it has acquired the upper hand and can safely take initiative against A. At this point, A may come to regret its past restraint and decide that there is no more time to lose. A preemptive war takes place at some point between the moment when an enemy decides to attack—or, more precisely, is perceived to be about to attack—and when the attack is actually launched. This is where there might be a legal justification for anticipatory self-defense. For A, the challenges lie in both the quality of the evidence of imminent attack and the ability of its forces to disrupt the attack at this stage. If not disrupted effectively, then A's attack is bound to prompt a response from B that otherwise might have been avoided. After all, a favorable balance of power is not the only factor that influences an actor's decision to go to war, and there might have been good reason for B to have eschewed taking advantage of its new military superiority or at least waiting until there was a genuine cause to use it. Thus, preemption, especially if prompted by a worst-case assumption about what an opponent might be planning, could well start a war when there might not have been one otherwise, in the hope that in taking the initiative the balance of power will have been reset in A's favor, whether or not B retaliates and a war continues.

So long as one sets aside larger issues, such as the opinion of the international community or the effect on an actor's ability to form coalitions and alliances, then once an actor supposes that the onset of war is inevitable, it is best to initiate it and to do so with a surprise attack. By knocking aside enemy capability, an actor can gain critical strategic advantage, often measured historically in territory, forcing the enemy into retreat, and buying time to consolidate before the counteroffensive begins. One has to be very certain, however, that the targeted state would otherwise take military action before taking preemptive measures or at least be very anxious that conceding the initiative will result in disaster.

Prevention is cold blooded: it intends to deal with a problem before it becomes a crisis, while preemption is a more desperate strategy employed in the heat of crisis. Prevention can be seen as preemption in slow motion, more anticipatory or forward thinking, perhaps even looking beyond the target's current intentions to those that might develop along with greatly enhanced capabilities. There is, in addition, another important difference. With prevention, A has great advantages in deciding when to attack and doing so while B remains inferior. It should be possible to find an optimum moment when B is quite unprepared and not at all alert. Even if B can fully appreciate what A is planning, it might still be helpless. With preemption, on the other hand, B may no longer be inferior nor unprepared, causing the possibility that A, even if taking only precautionary moves to prepare a preemptive contingency, might be noticed and provoke B's first strike. Preemption requires, at the very least, that A believe it is more likely to win a war it initiates.

An attack that does not cripple the enemy will only succeed if good use can be made politically, as well as militarily, of the extra time gained as the enemy recovers. Preemption is directed specifically at the enemy's most dangerous capabilities and thus sets for itself a very serious but unambiguous test. If B's targeted capability escapes largely unscathed, then it is likely to be used at once. If the concern was serious enough to warrant the attack, then the military consequences of failure must be very severe. With prevention, by contrast, the military test is bound to be milder, because of B's inferiority. As with preemptive action, regardless of the enemy's actual intentions, it will usher in an irreversible move from peace to war, but one in which victory should be assured. The political test, on the other hand, will be much more severe, with the threat more distant and open to subjective interpretation. The superior power can expect to be accused of bullying, acting prematurely, perhaps on no more than a hunch. To the extent that A does not care about international opinion, this may not matter, but without a compelling cause, preventive war can soon look like any other sort of aggressive war and thus provoke a reaction elsewhere—from diplomatic isolation to the formation of alliances among potential victims.

## Deterrence in Hindsight

These political limitations were very evident during the Cold War. Washington considered the possibility of preventive war through the mid-1950s while the United States had, at first, a nuclear monopoly and then clear superiority, even as the Soviet Union was feverishly working to catch up. The possibility of initiating preventive war was serious at times, especially when it became evident that Moscow was close to acquiring a thermonuclear capability during the first year of the Eisenhower administration. In the end, such a move was rejected: it was too risky and potentially illegal as an aggressive war, especially when unleashed by a country still recalling the surprise Japanese attack of December 7, 1941.

Preventive war against China, the rising and revolutionary power of the 1960s, was also discussed. President John Kennedy mused about preventing China from becoming a nuclear power, but as it approached an operational capability, it was the Soviet Union that came to fear the prospect of a nuclear China the most. In 1969, Moscow went so far as to hint that it was planning a strike against Chinese nuclear assets, to the point where the United States felt obliged to make it known that it could not support such a move.

It was preemptive war, however, that was most prominent in Cold War strategic thinking. The reason was simple. The only apparent way to win a nuclear war was to eliminate the enemy's nuclear capability before it could be used. Past theories of strategic airpower provided the conceptual framework. Attempts to knock out enemy airpower were known as blunting missions, tried unsuccessfully by Germany in 1940 and achieved spectacularly by Israel in the June 1967 war against Egypt. The trouble with applying this model to the eradication of an adversary's nuclear weapons was that, if attacks failed to destroy all targeted assets and a few survived, they could be launched in retaliation with catastrophic consequences. Nuclear arsenals became so big, and the needed proportions to inflict terrible damage so slight, that preemption simply risked bringing about the very war that it was supposed to prevent.

Policymakers attempted to address this challenge with the concepts of first- and second-strike capabilities. A first-strike capability was intended to disarm the enemy in a surprise, preemptive attack by destroying as much of its means of retaliation as possible on the ground and intercepting any of its bombers or missiles that might have escaped before the attack was executed. If a target country were able to absorb that first strike and still maintain the capability to retaliate with enough nuclear force to overwhelm any existing enemy defenses, it was said to possess a second-strike capability.

In the Cold War, deterrence was arguably effective because both the United States and the Soviet Union acquired nuclear systems that could withstand attacks or remain hidden, while the planned missile defense always seemed too porous to reduce significantly the other side's second-strike capability. In all the relevant calculations, the awesome power of individual weapons just left too little of a margin for error to contemplate preemption. Under such circumstances, mutually assured destruction was a concept used to describe a terrible reality. It was considered a strategy only because there was no way found around it. Various targeting strategies may have reduced the probability of retaliation, but they could never diminish it to zero and therefore remained at best under certain dire circumstances a theoretical alternative to immediate Armageddon.

Until mutually assured destruction was acknowledged in the mid-1960s, a far greater worry was that of two opposing first-strike capabilities. Such a condition, it was feared, would put a premium on striking first, encouraging preemption at the slightest provocation lest one lose its weapons and suffer annihilation. Mutually assured destruction, by contrast, turned out to be remarkably stable, provided many good reasons not to risk direct military conflict, and enabled the political conflict of the Cold War to be decided by the collapse of one of the two competing ideological systems.

## Addressing Threats in the 1990s

This interpretation of the Cold War is reflected in the 2002 U.S. NSS. It depicts a status quo, risk-averse Cold War adversary as the threat around which national strategy was largely shaped. Yet, at the time, including the early years of the Reagan administration—with numerous officials on the same wave of the political spectrum as current administration officials—talk of an "evil empire" was as prevalent as that of the "axis of evil" today, while deterrence through mutually assured destruction was derided as both immoral and incredible. Its flaws were the main rationale behind President Ronald Reagan's Strategic Defense Initiative to produce nationwide protection against missile attack. It should also be recalled that NATO countries regularly presented the conventional might of the Warsaw Pact as so superior to their own that every effort was made to think of nuclear weapons as more than just weapons of last resort. Although deterrence was elevated into an all-purpose and largely successful doctrine throughout the Cold War years, the exceptions described here convey that confidence in it was never total, especially—but by no means only—among those largely promoting preemption now.

The widespread celebration of the quality of deterrence strategies in retrospect is perhaps most pertinent today for how it illuminates precisely those conditions that no longer exist. Now, instead of symmetrical conflicts, it is asymmetrical ones that haunt policymakers. With great powers less inclined to threaten each other, threats are more likely to come from far weaker powers, which might be inclined to use unconventional means to compensate for their inferior conventional military capabilities. Although asymmetrical conflict was an issue during the Cold War, particularly in Vietnam as regular forces had to cope with guerrilla warfare, its influence was always governed by the bigger picture—a great-power confrontation based on quite a remarkable symmetry: two superpowers, two alliances, two nuclear arsenals. The concept of escalation enabled one side to threaten to shift a conflict from one level (a weapons class or a subregion), where asymmetries favored the side bold enough to initiate it, to another level that might favor the side initially attacked. Nonetheless, the process and thus the de-escalatory pressure for restraint was presumed to be governed by the ultimate symmetry of massive nuclear exchanges.

The Cold War symmetry called for a focus on contingencies that carried enormous risks for both sides. An unwillingness to confront the ideological challenge presented by communism could result in the transformation of the political life and socioeconomic organization of whole continents; a false step in the other direction and civilization itself might be swept away. Not surprisingly, the corresponding conceptual framework that emerged out of academic and policy debates was geared toward steering a middle course between these two potential catastrophes. A conflict that could not be securely resolved either through diplomacy or war required strategies that demonstrated determination but were at the same time infused with caution and restraint: containment, deterrence, stability, crisis management, détente, and arms control. The preferred alternative to escalation was to seek symmetry to avoid fighting, represented by the strategic paraphernalia of hot lines, confidence-building measures, and summits. Such strategies were reinforced by principles of international law, which stressed noninterference in internal affairs and military action strictly for the purpose of self-defense. More radical notions—from appeasement and disarmament on the one hand to rollbacks and arms races on the other—appeared reckless.

With the dissolution of the Soviet Union, asymmetries in raw military power were obvious but were also apparent in political concerns. Western nations, at least, seemed to have few vital interests at stake in the many conflicts that still raged around the world. Their interests lay more fundamentally in establishing and enforcing rules for a more civilized international system, including general respect for minorities and liberal economic practices. Well before the end of the Cold War, a series of tensions and conflicts—only loosely related to the superpower confrontation in Africa, Asia, and the Middle East that occasionally erupted violently and viciously—increasingly began to develop dynamics all their own. Whether or not to intervene in particular conflicts—in Somalia but not in Rwanda, tentatively in Bosnia but assertively in Kosovo—was a matter of choice for those few powers with an expeditionary capability, mainly the United States, the United Kingdom, and

France. Unlike those nations directly involved, which naturally had no choice, in every one of these conflicts the intervening powers were only willing to apply a small portion of their available resources and were wary of enduring excessive human costs for these more limited interests.

The strategic language required to describe and analyze such new situations has only developed slowly. Because contemporary conflicts often involved actual combat, some traditional concepts (e.g., attrition, maneuver, interdiction) were resurrected, but because such terms tended to relate to the application of airpower or the movement of armies, they were tactical, not strategic. The concept of prevention, usually in the form of "conflict prevention," had a place during this period, but more in a diplomatic than a military sense. In certain instances, such conflict prevention could even be considered preemptive, such as the ultimatum against Serbia in a belated effort to prevent the persecution of the local Albanians. By and large, however, the great powers got involved when fighting was already underway, humanitarian catastrophes loomed, or neighboring countries risked getting dragged in. Few of these conflicts even started with a classic military offensive but instead emerged out of intercommunal violence.

The language has been most prominently and controversially used, however, in the context of another asymmetric challenge, posed by radical powers threatening to gain artificial strength through WMD. Iraq, Iran, and North Korea have long been on the list, while China was occasionally presented as an ascendant great power. Unlike discretionary intervention in civil conflicts in remote parts of the developing world, paying attention to WMD proliferation among radical powers did not seem to be a matter of choice. The total nature of the threat made the framework and vocabulary of the past seem appropriate. Although counterproliferation policy under the Clinton administration suggested preemption at times, public emphasis remained on deterring rather than eliminating the rogues so that, for example, policy toward Iraq and Iran was described as "dual containment."

Neither agenda—addressing intercommunal conflicts nor possible rogue proliferation—called for placing a strategy of preemption at the heart of a new U.S. strategic doctrine. Precisely because of their military superiority, the United States and its allies did not need to take military initiative to secure victory. Instead, military operations were geared toward containing conflicts, mitigating their effects, coercing guilty parties, and establishing law and order.

## Defending Prevention

After September 11, an effective U.S. national security strategy became more urgent. Although both the source of the threat and the means of delivery employed were novel, that day's tragic events reinforced long-established U.S. fears of surprise attacks in the form of a bolt from the skies. This fear is the product of geography and history, of Pearl Harbor and the years when the Soviet Union appeared to be forging ahead with intercontinental missile deployments. Other states tend to worry more about land invasions.

If September 11 was a preemptive attack against the United States, it was hardly decisive, and it was possible to deal with the perpetrators in an effort to ensure that such a blow would never be struck again. The United States suddenly found itself in a war that highlighted the two existing asymmetric challenges and their potential intersection. Although a hyperpower without a military peer among states, the United States proved unexpectedly vulnerable to a murky underworld of gangsters and terrorists who might acquire devastating instruments, either by complicity from rogue states or by capitalizing on the anarchy of weak states.

So, as stated in the U.S. NSS, the greatest change in international security since September 11 has been the "nature and motivations of these new adversaries, their determination to obtain destructive powers hitherto available only to the world's strongest states, and the greater likelihood that they will use weapons of mass destruction against [the United States]." Instead of a status quo, risk-averse adversary against whom deterrence might work, the United States now has gamblers for enemies, many of whom embrace martyrdom and prefer weapons of mass destruction—weapons that can be easily concealed, delivered covertly, and used without warning—perhaps to compensate for vast U.S. conventional superiority but also because "wanton destruction and the targeting of innocents" has become an end in itself.

In the strategy document, these two types of threat were combined as a sort of composite enemy, combining the worst features of Saddam Hussein and Osama bin Laden. Saddam, for example, has (at least for the moment) a state, no hint of any personal interest in martyrdom, and a calculating nature, in addition to extreme ruthlessness and an undoubted fascination with all types of destructive instruments. As there is no evidence that the two have yet come together, an argument for action before they do is preventive rather than preemptive. The desire to thwart the emergence of such a hybrid enemy helps to explain the argument, found in the NSS, that the concept of imminence, upon which the grounds for preemption are based, needs to be reconsidered. Recognizing that prevention is at issue here—not preemption—is key.

Preemption as a strategic concept has been introduced in connection with the dangers posed by WMD. Events over the last few months, however, indicate the concept's limited value even in this context. No preemptive action has yet been suggested against North Korea, while the preventive case against Iraq has come to be based, for sound legal and political reasons, on its noncompliance with United Nations resolutions. What either of these states might do in the future is a matter of anxious speculation; but no aggressive action on either of their parts has been shown to be imminent, and to the extent that they have contemplated taking such action, it is difficult to say that existing policies of deterrence and containment have proven entirely inadequate. If the United States attacks facilities and overthrows regimes before these dangers have had a chance to emerge, such action will be described as preemption because that is the language currently in vogue, but this language would be incorrect. The relevant concept here is prevention.

The national security strategy suggests that preemption can be considered not only in terms of military strikes but also in the softer fields of sharper intelligence work; diplomatic attention; and judicious applications of economic assistance, technical advice, and military/police support. As a prudent and effective approach to the war on terror, this makes sense, as it provides sound guidance for dealing with the security problems within and arising from weak states. But again, prevention is the more applicable term in this context rather than preemption—acting early rather than late, while a problem gestates but before it erupts, using all available means. There will, of course, be instances in which a terrorist attack is imminent and a quick, preemptive strike will be appropriate, but deterrence is not necessarily impossible under such circumstances—public warnings about imminent attacks alone have often been used in an attempt to ward off those planning them, and action is more likely to be taken by the police than the armed forces. In cases where traditional preemptive strikes might be justified, the old tests will still apply—making sure that action heads off danger rather than aggravates or instigates it.

The new, dynamic, and unsettled international environment has exposed the limits of a conceptual framework derived from a period in which international politics was dominated by great-power rivalries and international law gave overriding respect to the rights of states, no matter how brutal their internal policies. It is not surprising that the United States and its allies see no reason to wait for problems to develop and wish to tackle them before they reach a critical stage. So long as one is sure of the diagnosis (no small test in and of itself), "an ounce of prevention is better than a pound of cure" is as good a motto for foreign policy as it is for medicine. Under contemporary conditions, this requires paying close attention to what is transpiring in the disadvantaged and disaffected parts of the international system and considering the full range of policy instruments.

When responding to a situation involves the use of force, it can challenge traditional notions of international law, but the greater challenge is likely to be the traditional habits of great powers. The enthusiasm for preemption reflects a yearning for a world in which problems can be eliminated by bold, timely, and decisive strokes. Cases where this can happen today are likely to be few and far between. An updated notion of prevention, by contrast, might encourage recognition that the world in which we live is one in which the best results are likely to come from a readiness to engage difficult problems over an extended period of time.

## Note

1. White House, *The National Security Strategy of the United States of America* (Washington, D.C.: U.S. Government Printing Office, September 2002).

Jason D. Ellis

# The Best Defense: Counterproliferation and U.S. National Security

Neither terrorism nor the proliferation of weapons of mass destruction (WMD) are new phenomena; states in key regions of U.S. security concern have for several years aggressively pursued nuclear, biological, or chemical weapons and missile capabilities or have engaged in or sponsored terrorism. What is new is the prospective conjuncture of these twin scourges that constitutes a combined threat greater than the sum of its parts. The Bush administration's new national security strategy, aimed at refocusing U.S. efforts to deal with proliferant states and nonstate actors, essentially replaces the traditional state-centered U.S. nonproliferation approach with one that—for the first time—privileges counterproliferation and explicitly acknowledges prospective requirements for preemption.

Rather than a recipe for further proliferation or a license to hunt those who would harm the United States, the national security strategy is the product of the existing post-proliferated and terror-prone security environment. It is precisely because nonproliferation efforts have failed to prevent WMD proliferation effectively in the past—and there is no convincing reason to believe that nonproliferation will exclusively be

Jason D. Ellis is a senior research professor at the Center for Counterproliferation Research, National Defense University, in Washington, D.C. The opinions, conclusions, and recommendations expressed or implied within are those of the author and may not represent the views of the National Defense University, the Department of the Army, or any other U.S. government agency.

Copyright © 2003 by The Center for Strategic and International Studies and the Massachusetts Institute of Technology
The Washington Quarterly • 26:2 pp. 115–133.

able to address these increasingly linked threats in the future—that a comprehensive national counterproliferation strategy is needed. In this context, the best defense against proliferation and terrorism is a good offense—backed up by effective deterrent, operational, and mitigative plans and capabilities.

## Why All the Hype about Counterproliferation?

Traditional diplomatic and economic measures, such as sanctions, export controls, international arms control, and technology denial regimes, and their more recently developed nonproliferation counterparts, such as cooperative threat reduction, clearly retain a place in the emergent strategy. But counterproliferation—defined by the secretary of defense as the "full range of military preparations and activities to reduce, and protect against, the threat posed by nuclear, biological, and chemical weapons and their associated delivery means"—is of central importance.[1] Counterproliferation is not the Bush administration's creation. The concept was developed during the last two years of the first Bush administration and officially articulated under Clinton administration secretary of defense Les Aspin.[2] Indeed, in the view of Gilles Andréani, "one finds convincing signs of a gradual shift" toward counterproliferation through the 1990s.[3]

Although that general sense is undoubtedly accurate, the rise of counterproliferation to national stature really begins with the current administration. Relevant counterproliferation capabilities, plans, and programs clearly were developed in Clinton's Department of Defense, but they remained subordinate to a larger national strategy predicated primarily on traditional and more recent nonproliferation measures. Although there were occasions where preemptive or preventive measures were actively contemplated against proliferant states, such as North Korea in 1993–1994, the administration's sustained approach revolved more around diplomatic dissuasion than military operations. (Preemption and prevention are often conflated, but for purposes of this discussion, a preventive attack would be one undertaken to preclude a given actor from obtaining a particular weapons capability, while a preemptive attack would aim to degrade or destroy an existing capability.)

In comparison, for instance, Clinton's national security strategy recognized prospective future requirements for "countering potential regional aggressors" and "confronting new threats," just as Bush's does.[4] But the two documents differ fundamentally in their central policy approaches and specific prescriptions. The Clinton administration defined, in a highly detailed, lengthy section, "Arms Control and Nonproliferation" as the axis around which the U.S. response to WMD and missile proliferation centered, while measures relating to the "Department of Defense's Counterproliferation Initiative" drew just one short paragraph, supplemented with one dedicated paragraph each on deterrence, combating terrorism, and the role of nuclear weapons in the U.S. security posture.[5] The Bush version gives continued importance to "strengthened" nonproliferation efforts but downgrades the prior treaties-and-regimes approach, elevating the status of proactive counterproliferation efforts to deter and defend against WMD and missile threats as well as effective consequence management should such weapons be used.[6] It also issued the first-ever companion *National Strategy to Combat Weapons of Mass Destruction*, an unclassified synopsis of National Security Presidential Directive 17.

Perhaps the most striking distinction between the two strategies—and certainly the one that has drawn the most expert debate—is the Bush administration's avowed determination not to let enemies of the United States strike first, underscoring that the risks of inaction in particular cases may outweigh the risks of action. The new security strategy states that, in the face of a looming threat, the United States "will, if necessary, act preemptively" to "forestall or prevent hostile acts by our adversaries."[7] Even though discussion a decade ago of preemption's potential future requirements, its prospective utility and potential liabilities, the requisite strategic and operational framework, and the military capabilities needed to enact such an approach nearly derailed the Defense Counterproliferation Initiative, issues relating to preemption have once again risen to the forefront of national strategy.[8]

The urgency motivating the current national security team stems from two underlying assumptions: WMD and missile capabilities have and will continue to proliferate; and use of these weapons against U.S. forward-deployed forces, U.S. friends and allies, or even U.S. or allied homelands is increasingly likely. In response, the United States seeks to advance its security along two parallel and mutually reinforcing lines: pursuing a proactive, full-court press against security challenges emerging from the proliferation-terrorism nexus; and strengthening homeland and transforming military capabilities to deter, protect against, and mitigate the effects of an attack. Thus, the administration seeks both to devalue the attractiveness of WMD and missiles and to diminish the adverse consequences to U.S. interests should adversaries execute such attacks.

## A Manifest Threat

WMD capabilities continue to deepen and to spread; particular terror organizations and state actors actively threaten U.S. security interests; and the prospective nexus of proliferation and terrorism is an ascendant security concern. The gravity and urgency of the threats we face today, as well as the inadequacy of both U.S. and international efforts to prevent them, necessitate the new national counterproliferation strategy.

### CLEAR AND PRESENT DANGER

The 1991 Persian Gulf War clearly demonstrated the importance of being prepared to fight WMD-armed adversaries. Although Iraq did not ultimately use chemical or biological weapons in the war, postwar revelations of the scope of Iraqi WMD activities shocked the national security community, surprising even informed observers and highlighting serious potential vulnerabilities in U.S. regional security strategies and war-fighting plans. Had Iraqi chemical and biological weapons (CBW) been employed, U.S. and allied forces would have been inadequately equipped to confront them, and most U.S. coalition partners were even worse off. This Iraqi capacity, coupled with its evident (and largely undetected) technical progress, underscored the emergence of a major post–Cold War defense planning challenge. This development inspired former secretary of defense Les Aspin to declare, while chartering the Defense Counterproliferation Initiative in 1993, that "we are making the essential change demanded by this increased threat ... adding the task of protection to the task of prevention."[9] In his view, although prevention remained our primary goal, the Defense Department had adopted a new mission: developing military capabilities to cope with WMD-armed regional adversaries.

The spread of WMD and their delivery systems poses major strategic and operational challenges to the United States and a crucial political challenge to the international community. In the hands of hostile states, these weapons threaten stability in key regions, put U.S. forces at risk, and undermine the U.S. ability to project power and reassure friends and allies. The possibility of asymmetric warfare—confrontations with actors unable to challenge U.S. conventional military dominance—must now be a central focus for defense planning. WMD not only afford such nations the ability to attack U.S. interests directly but also may afford adversaries a tool of coercion—an opportunity, as the 1997 *Quadrennial Defense Review* concluded, "to *circumvent* or *undermine* our strengths while *exploiting* our vulnerabilities."[10]

Arguably, even a limited WMD capability may afford regional adversaries a significant strategic advantage: the ability to hold friendly cities and other important strategic assets at unacceptable risk. Conceivably, the mere possession of nuclear weapons could embolden a rogue state and encourage risk-taking behavior. Nations with nuclear capacity may be more likely to employ chemical or biological weapons while reserving a nuclear trump card to deter regime change or to use as leverage during war-termination negotiations. Indeed, states such as North Korea or Iraq are likely to integrate developing capabilities fully into their war-fighting plans and may view nuclear or highly lethal biological weapons as part of an escalation-dominance framework. WMD proliferation also fundamentally changes the very theater of operations, making it possible for states with nascent WMD capabilities to at least threaten, if not attack, the United States and/or allied homelands in response to U.S. or allied military engagement in a regional conflict overseas.[11] Indeed, one clear lesson of September 11, 2001, was that geographic locations traditionally defined as "rear area," such as the U.S. homeland, are increasingly at risk.

Nor is the threat of WMD attack confined to state actors. Although states should remain a principal focus, terrorists and other nonstate actors have never before ranked as high among U.S. national security concerns. If Aum Shinrikyo did not sound the clarion call, then Al Qaeda certainly has. According to Director of Central Intelligence George Tenet, intelligence collected in Afghanistan revealed that Al Qaeda was "working to acquire some of the most dangerous chemical agents and toxins, ... pursuing a sophisticated biological weapons research program, ... seeking to acquire or develop a nuclear device, ...and may be pursuing a radioactive dispersal device."[12] The continuing diffusion of technology, the ongoing risk of diversion of weapons-related expertise, and the clear potential for particular actors—whether at the national or subnational level—to contemplate mass destruction collectively foreshadow an ominous future. WMD-equipped states may also share their capacities with terrorist or other subnational organizations that seek to inflict mass casualties. The product: a distinctly dangerous intersection of threats to U.S. security.

## IT'S A POST-PROLIFERATED WORLD

The Bush administration's national security strategy starts with the reality of a post-proliferated international security environment. The intricate network of nonproliferation treaties and regimes established over the past several decades share one key feature: failure to prevent determined states from developing nuclear, chemical, or biological weapons as well as increasingly capable missile and related delivery systems.

South Africa, for instance, successfully developed and produced six nuclear devices despite its purported adherence to the Nuclear Non-Proliferation Treaty (NPT). Similarly, Iraq was well on its way when the Gulf War interrupted its progress, and North Korea also sought clandestinely to develop nuclear weapons in contravention of its international obligations. At the same time, the voluntary and unenforceable gentleman's agreement among supplier states to refrain from exporting ballistic-missile development technologies to aspirant states has hardly kept key states—whether Iran, North Korea, Pakistan, India, or others—from making steady, incremental progress toward such developments. Several additional states also will develop the ability to produce land-attack cruise missiles indigenously over the next several years.[13]

All told, nuclear- and missile-related treaties and regimes have not prevented the acquisition or development of weapon capabilities, although they have arguably served to slow the pace of development in the past. In the years ahead, foreign assistance—the transfer or sale of technologies, material, or expertise with possible weapons-related applications by key suppliers—and the growing phenomenon of secondary supply—exports or cooperative development of WMD or missile delivery systems, their constituent enabling or production technologies, or the requisite expertise necessary to their development or production by nontraditional suppliers—pose severe challenges to the nonproliferation regime. At the same time, the continued insecurity (and large quantity) of fissile material in the former Soviet Union and other regions, evident advancements in indigenous weapons-related technology among less-developed states, and the potential availability of germane technical expertise together suggest that existing multilateral constraining mechanisms are bound to prove even less effective in the years ahead. In this context, traditional supply-side constraints have and will continue to erode.

The challenge becomes even more acute in combating chemical- and biological-weapon development. The U.S. government has assessed that "many [chemical warfare] agents ... are simple to produce. They are often based on technology that is at least 80 years old and sometimes older, putting them well within reach of virtually any Third World country that wants them." Although newer agents, such as the reputed, Russian-developed *Novichok*-class of next-generation nerve agents, may not yet be as readily accessible, the "technology for these agents is widely available in the public domain."[14]

A majority of nations are states-parties to the Chemical Weapons Convention (CWC), which prohibits the development, production, acquisition, retention, stockpiling, transfer, and use of chemical weapons; but it is unlikely that that this treaty has ended potential chemical weapons threats to U.S. or allied equities. In 1999 the intelligence community assessed that, despite the CWC and related supplier-restraint regimes such as the Australia Group, at least 16 states maintained active, clandestine chemical weapons programs.[15] The twin realities of technology diffusion over time and growing interest among particular states and subnational actors suggest that chemical weapons, as well as the infrastructure needed to develop and produce them, will remain permanent features of the international security landscape.

Supply-side controls face even more daunting prospects in the realm of biological weapons. According to the Office of the Secretary of Defense, "[V]irtually all the equipment, technology, and materials needed for biological-warfare-agent research, development, and production are dual use." This makes offensive programs "relatively easy to disguise within the larger body of legitimate commercial activity, as no specialized facilities are required," and "any country with the political will and a competent scientific base can produce" toxins or infectious agents.[16]

Although only three or four nations were thought to have offensive biological weapons programs when the Biological Weapons Convention (BWC) entered into force in 1975, the intelligence community currently assesses that perhaps a dozen states maintain offensive programs and warns that "credible biological warfare capabilities are becoming more advanced," a trend that may enhance the prospect of biological weapons use in the years ahead.[17] The lasting demand for biological weapons, the relative ease of concealing any offensive effort, the growing availability of weapons-related technologies and expertise, and an ongoing revolution in biotechnology that could significantly alter the threat environment all suggest that determined states—as well as particular subnational actors, especially those supported by states—face few real constraints in establishing, developing, or improving offensive programs with a national decision to do so.

Although some might argue that the threats presented by the greater availability of WMD materials can be addressed by inspections, they will not likely be effective or satisfactory long-term solutions. Even after a series of post–Gulf War "full, final, and complete disclosures" by the Iraqi government and despite more than seven years of intrusive inspections, the United Nations Special Commission (UNSCOM) was ultimately unable to account for critical elements of the Iraqi biological weapons program. Its self-described "select and incomplete" history of the program contained key gaps, including "considerable uncertainty" regarding weaponization; "consistently understated" agent production; an "incomplete" declaration of equipment and raw material imports; "omitted" planning references; "thoroughly planned" research and development, despite Iraqi claims that they were "unplanned"; and, finally, an absence of Iraqi evidence "concerning the termination of its offensive program."[18]

In light of UNSCOM's past experience, there is little reason to believe that its successor—the United Nations Monitoring, Verification, and Inspection Commission (UNMOVIC)—will fare any better with a truncated time line and fewer dedicated personnel and other supporting resources. Meanwhile, the Iraqi government has had years to improve its deception and denial practices based on several years of experience with UNSCOM—sanitizing key sites, migrating program elements to nontraditional locations (e.g., mobile or civilian facilities), and continuing clandestine program-related activities.

## U.S. Intelligence Won't Cut It

The states of most egregious proliferation concern and the terror cells probably most willing to strike U.S. equities are what the intelligence community would reference as hard targets. Their restrictive nature, closed processes, and highly stratified leadership structures make timely and accurate threat assessment a difficult prospect.

With respect to the spread of WMD-related technologies, the intelligence community's intrinsic assessment challenges are rooted in at least four principal causes:

- improved deception and denial efforts by would-be proliferants;

- increasing access to dual-use technologies that effectively mask proliferants' intentions;

- the availability of expertise from which proliferants can advance WMD and missile programs; and

- an accelerating pace of technological progress as information and advanced technologies become increasingly available worldwide.[19]

As a result, there are clear reasons to believe that the United States and, by extension, allied nations and the international community as a whole will find it increasingly difficult to track the development of WMD and missile capabilities by key states and within the shadowy networks of subnational actors. Combined with these alarming trends, the research, development, and acquisition community has also warned that improved defenses will lag behind adversarial advances in offensive chemical- and biological-weapon capabilities.[20]

At the same time, getting a handle on adversary capabilities is likely to be considerably easier than obtaining accurate data on their plans and intentions. Although some indicators of an actor's intentions can be revealed through technical means (e.g., movement of forces, unique signatures for particular types of facilities), uncovering planning documents, developing informed and current perspectives on WMD-related issues, or learning the intentions of key-program or senior leaders is a daunting task that will ultimately be only as credible as the human intelligence upon which such judgments are predicated. This is an acute challenge in combating the distinct threats posed by both terrorism and proliferation and the new, greater threat they pose in conjunction. Improving intelligence collection and analysis is critical to a more effective warning capability that hopefully will help prevent specific attacks against the U.S. homeland, allies, and interests abroad. Still, even if U.S. intelligence does improve its net performance, strategic and tactical warning of both WMD proliferation and terrorism are clearly prone to failure.

## CHANCES ARE, ONCE THEY'VE GOT THEM, THEY'LL USE THEM

For this reason, and because the consequences of particular WMD attacks may be severe, White House officials have argued that the United States must plan as if such weapons will be used. Indeed, not only does the continuing proliferation of WMD capabilities appear inevitable, the potential for adversarial use of WMD against U.S. forces, U.S. friends and allies, or the U.S. homeland is increasingly likely. This reality is hardly news to the Defense Department, which as early as 1997 concluded that the use of chemical and biological weapons would be a "likely condition" of future warfare.[21] In an extended battlefield, however—one that transcends traditionally defined overseas areas of operation, joins civilian with military targets, and relocates the forward edge of the battle area to rear-area targets including the U.S. homeland—this is no longer a judgment for the military alone.

The national security strategy's call for proactive counterproliferation stems directly from the premise that the security landscape has undergone a profound transformation. In this new era, key regional states and terror organizations "are determined to acquire weapons of mass destruction, along with other advanced military technology, to be used as threats or offensively to achieve the aggressive designs of these regimes." As a result, there is a "greater likelihood" that rogue states and terrorists "will use weapons of mass destruction against us."[22] For the U.S. homeland, this judgment differs fundamentally from previously widespread conceptions of the threat. The first Bush and Clinton administrations clearly recognized U.S. vulnerabilities to WMD and other asymmetric attack modes and sought to develop and implement particular defensive measures as well as operational capabilities, but it took the hijacked commercial airliners of September 11 to effect more sweeping change. At the time of the Gulf War, WMD were generally viewed as a last resort to be used principally in overseas theaters and in wartime. Now, however, the possibility of their employment in peacetime, against population centers or on the U.S. homeland, cannot be discounted.

## Advancing U.S. National Security

Critics of the shift toward counterproliferation and preemption often promote enhancing existing multilateral nonproliferation agreements while diminishing reliance on the more proactive approach.[23] But it is unclear what a substantially improved nonproliferation regime would look like or whether, in fact, such a regime would ultimately be capable of preventing further proliferation of WMD or weapons-related technologies or expertise, let alone rolling back existing capabilities in key states of proliferation concern. Nor is it necessarily plausible that an inherently reactive, diplomacy-oriented, or multilateral approach would diminish the possibility of a rogue state or terror cell attacking or threatening U.S. interests more than a proactive, military-operational, or unilateral approach. Pandora's box has been cracked open: mass-destructive capabilities continue to spread; there are plausible reasons to believe U.S. adversaries may elect to employ them; U.S. vulnerabilities from the front lines to the homeland remain acute; and warning is failure prone.

To advance U.S. national security in an era when nuclear, biological, and chemical weapons serve to strengthen traditionally weak actors, existing counterproliferation policies, programs, and plans systematically built since the Gulf War must be significantly but carefully extended. To meet the current security threat presented by the proliferation-terrorism nexus, policy officials must address at least four core challenges.

## CONFRONTING STRATEGIC ACTORS

Potential requirements for preemptive or preventive action are not new to U.S. policy debates. The last time U.S. officials contemplated preventive war, however, was almost a decade ago on the Korean peninsula, when Pyongyang threatened to withdraw from the NPT and intelligence assessments indicated that North Korea had produced fissile material sufficient for at least one and possibly two nuclear devices.[24] Policymakers ultimately pursued diplomacy over military action to prevent the North from succeeding in its nuclear quest. Nevertheless, eight years later, the measure negotiated has proven a temporary fix as the issue has reappeared with new revelations of a continued nuclear weapons development program.[25]

In determining how best to respond to either Iraq or the North Korean nuclear issue, it is possible that a diplomatic approach, whether cooperative or coercive, will again carry the day. It is also possible that policy officials, in concert with regional allies, will ultimately opt to explore available military options further. In both cases, it is likely that some mixture of diplomatic, economic, and military options will be brought to bear. Yet, it is unlikely that a one-size-fits-all approach will—or should—be developed and applied equally in these or other cases because regional political-military contexts, operational environments, and available options will vary. Certainly, discussion of options for preventive war, preemption, or other responses to Iraq, North Korea, and other tough proliferation cases will continue for as long as terrorism and WMD proliferation jeopardize U.S. security interests.

At the same time, policy officials will have to continue to balance contending foreign policy priorities. Rediscovering an old truth, single-issue policies tend over time to be difficult to pursue in the face of the more complex mosaic of a state's aggregate foreign policy. For example, in the proliferation context there is a clear tension between potential legal requirements to impose sanctions against such strategic allies as Pakistan for their WMD or missile development (and export) activities, on one hand, and identified strategic requirements and tactical imperatives to bolster a key regional ally, on the other.[26] Similarly, with states such as Yemen, policy officials will have to find the appropriate balance between objectives that sometimes appear to conflict. Although Yemeni antiterrorism cooperation appears generally positive, counterproliferation cooperation is evidently weak—as that state's importation of ballistic missile technology from North Korea would suggest.[27]

Nor are these difficult policy trade-offs limited to decisionmakers in the United States: to avoid military action in Iraq, it appears that the United Nations must demonstrate its ability to implement the relevant Security Council resolutions satisfactorily and that the Iraqi government must unambiguously comply. Similar questions regarding the North Korean nuclear weapons development program confront both the International Atomic Energy Agency and key regional allies. The effectiveness of the strategies pursued by international organizations in these cases will go a long way toward determining their continued relevance—or lack thereof—in managing today's capabilities-proliferated world. Clearly, it is critical to develop more effective options to confront states that do not abide by nonproliferation norms and to counter subnational actors with mass-destructive intent.

## SURPRISE, SURPRISE, SURPRISE

Although tactical warning of a specific attack timing, mode, location, or even perpetrator is difficult to come by, the intelligence community has provided credible strategic warning of the attempted development and probable intent to employ WMD against U.S. interests by a range of potential actors at the state and subnational levels. Because adversaries have improved their ability to deceive U.S. threat assessments, the United States must prepare to protect against surprise developments and attacks by expanding its intelligence and law enforcement capabilities and bolstering operations and technologies that seek both to prevent the use of WMD and, if they are used, to defend the homeland against such attacks.

Historically, proliferation surprise has resulted primarily from mistaken estimates of the nature or maturity of specific national indigenous programs, but the potential for strategic surprise also exists if, for example, actors acquire unforeseen capabilities covertly from external sources. At the same time, the states of greatest proliferation concern are also among the hardest intelligence targets, often with closed or restrictive political processes that can make obtaining sensitive information difficult. Crucial information may be unavailable, fragmentary, or misleading, or may change quickly; U.S. security policy, therefore, must hedge its bets by seeking to develop effective capabilities to defend against and mitigate undetected attacks. Employing diplomatic and active operational measures to dissuade adversaries from employing and, where possible, even developing WMD- and missile-delivery vehicles is now and should remain a principal task of national efforts to combat proliferation.

Preparing for and mitigating the effects of surprise, however, also means maintaining a robust counterproliferation science and technology base capable of hedging against emerging—and to some degree unpredictable—threat developments. Similarly, to prove resilient against potential WMD surprise on the battlefield, U.S. military forces must prepare for a range of unforeseen operating conditions and regional circumstances, not just those rigidly validated by intelligence. This capabilities-based approach is central to the Defense Department's 2001 *Quadrennial Defense Review*: an effort to "anticipate the capabilities that an adversary might employ to coerce its neighbors, deter the United States from acting in defense of its allies and friends, or directly attack the United States or its deployed forces."[28]

## Focus on Offense As Well As Defense

The United States cannot afford to model future military engagements against WMD-armed regional adversaries after the 1998 and 1999 air-only campaigns against Iraq and Serbia, respectively, or even after the post–September 11 operation in Afghanistan, where the substantial use of special operations forces and precision-guided munitions proved sufficient to defeat battlefield opponents. Indeed, more than a decade ago, the Gulf War demonstrated that an adversary equipped with significant WMD capabilities has the potential to alter the equation fundamentally.

In that conflict, even conventionally armed ballistic missiles arguably had an impact, both strategically, by altering the political dynamics of a coalition, and operationally, by diverting military assets from their assigned wartime missions. Serious deficiencies in the U.S. and coalition ability to locate and target WMD and mobile targets were exposed. Coalition forces expended considerable resources in a largely unsuccessful effort to find and destroy Iraqi mobile missiles, while allied planners significantly underestimated the number, location, and type of Iraqi WMD assets. This left numerous important sites, and a substantial portion of Iraq's WMD capabilities, untouched and undiscovered until postwar UN inspections.[29] Even when nuclear-, chemical-, or biological-weapon sites were detected, their targeting carried with it the potential for collateral release of toxic materials.

Post-Gulf War counterproliferation programs have attempted to come to terms with these vexing challenges. For several years, the Defense Department has undertaken research and development activities to develop strike capabilities that can achieve operational objectives, including the destruction of an adversary's assets located in hardened and/or buried targets with attention to minimizing collateral effects. Developing nonnuclear capabilities that rapidly allow U.S. forces to identify, target, and destroy both fixed and mobile targets is critical to effective counterproliferation planning; some have suggested that development of low-yield nuclear weapons may further enhance U.S. capabilities to hold at risk hardened or deeply buried targets. As the U.S. ability to credibly target such facilities improves, some of the leverage adversaries may have gained by possessing WMD will begin to erode. Although the 1990s witnessed evident progress on this technical front, policy concerns over the potential for collateral effects remained critical seven years after the Gulf War, when the risk of inadvertently releasing chemical or biological materials led the United States and the United Kingdom to proscribe certain targets during Operation Desert Fox.[30] In future military engagements against WMD-armed regional adversaries, policy officials will again have to weigh the prospect of collateral release against the imperative to ensure adversarial nonuse of such weapons.

Finally, the new National Security Strategy specifically calls for adapting "the concept of imminent threat to the capabilities and objectives of today's adversaries," which rely on "acts of terror and, potentially, the use of weapons of mass destruction."[31] In this strategic calculus, effectively defending U.S. national security against certain threats emanating from hostile WMD-armed nations and terrorist organizations calls for the United States, together with committed international partners, to act offensively today to preclude the development and delivery of graver threats down the line. The administration persuasively argues that, under particular strategic or operational circumstances, the best defense against proliferants and terrorists is a good offense. Yet, translating this strategic guidance into credible operational capabilities and plans will present a clear challenge to technicians and operators alike. This challenge is no less acute for the intelligence community, which will have to improve its ability to provide high-fidelity actionable intelligence, or for the policy community, which will need to develop appropriate criteria and standards for the preemptive use of force.

## IMPROVING DETERRENT AND DEFENSIVE CAPABILITIES

Still, a good offense is insufficient to meet the threats emerging from the proliferation-terror nexus. Rather, it is just one of a long continuum of needed responses—from cooperative and coercive efforts to prevent or roll back WMD acquisition; to measures to defend against WMD if they are obtained or developed; to capabilities and plans designed to mitigate their effects should WMD be used.

Traditional nonproliferation measures including export controls, sanctions, and nonproliferation accords have long been considered the first line of defense against WMD and missile proliferation. More recently, substantial emphasis has been placed on cooperative threat reduction programs with key former Soviet states. Nonproliferation and cooperative threat reduction clearly remain essential parts of the national security strategy. The current national security strategy calls for the continuation of such activities but seeks to bolster them with emphasis on greater—and a different kind of—deterrence and defense. The move toward a national counterproliferation strategy presupposes that, although nonproliferation remains a laudible objective, the United States must come to terms with already proliferated capabilities in the hands of unfriendly or irresponsible actors.

The United States should move, and is moving, beyond traditional deterrent conceptions of retaliatory punishment to implement deterrence by denial—the ability to defeat, defend against, and operate in the context of WMD and, if needed, overcome the effects of WMD use. Although the United States seeks to preserve its ability to deter by threatening overwhelming destruction (whether through nuclear or nonnuclear means) as during the Cold War, the national security strategy is grounded in the conclusion that yesterday's strategies are insufficient for today's threats.

In this context, the June 2002 U.S. withdrawal from the 1972 Anti-Ballistic Missile Treaty and commensurate efforts to field capable missile defense systems more rapidly are part of a new and necessary approach to deterrence. Further, missile defense is just one manifestation of improved denial capabilities; for instance, anthrax and smallpox vaccinations for forces deployed to high-threat areas have also resumed. Nor have defensive measures been limited to the U.S. military. Following the September 11 and subsequent anthrax-by-mail attacks, the administration, together with key members of Congress, moved to improve homeland security. This has translated into activities designed to improve national responses to bioterrorism significantly, for example, in part by increasing the budget to almost $6 billion for fiscal year 2003 alone.[32] Although homeland security and force-protection measures have improved over the past few years, much more remains to be done.

Only a cogent and well-implemented response across the spectrum—preventive, offensive, defensive, mitigative, and restorative capabilities—can enhance U.S. security in this new era. The key challenge for the years ahead will be to sustain the momentum, build on the interest of senior leaders on both ends of Pennsylvania Avenue, allocate scarce resources judiciously, and continue developing improved capabilities throughout this layered strategy to combat the security challenges inherent in the WMD proliferation-terrorism nexus.

## The Proliferation Endgame

U.S. and international success in this fundamentally transformed security landscape is likely to be measured more by an actor's ability to cope effectively with the persistent threat posed by potential adversaries in a post-proliferated world than its ability to defeat these adversaries unambiguously or even to roll back extant capabilities. This means that smart policy planning is every bit as crucial as improved counterproliferation or counterterrorism operational capabilities.

This new environment yields a number of key questions, including:

- How will the international community respond to the next significant use of nuclear, biological, or chemical weapons? The answer will be precedent setting. When Iran and Iraq exchanged chemical weapons-fire in the 1980s, the international community was virtually silent. To prevent further use, key states and international organizations will have to take appropriate punitive measures or risk an eradicated norm of nonuse in the years ahead.

- How relevant are prominent international organizations in combating WMD proliferation? Clearly, the Iraqi and North Korean challenges to UN affiliates are clear test cases and will provide important data points about the continued viability of concerted multilateral responses to proliferation. If the ultimate penalty for noncompliance with international accords and underlying norms is a round of ineffectively applied or quickly lifted sanctions, why should states not continue to acquire, develop, and export WMD? For many national governments, security competition, rather than trust in unenforce-

able and unverifiable international restraint mechanisms, may become the preferred alternative.

• Finally, can the United States, along with its friends and allies, effectively reevaluate policy responses to intractable regional proliferants
and determine what additional or modified options are needed? These
should include solutions that neither reward nor ignore those that
seek WMD capabilities but, rather, seek to fundamentally alter the
existing perceived incentives for potential adversaries to develop or
employ unconventional capabilities.

The reality is that the world has moved completely beyond the time of
just five nuclear (and few chemical and biological) weapons states. The
United States must similarly move beyond traditional nonproliferation
approaches toward a comprehensive counterproliferation strategy. Such
a strategy requires the United States to pursue ambitious diplomatic
offensives against recalcitrant proliferants, to improve deterrent and
defensive capabilities, and to develop appropriate consequence management and homeland security plans, tools, and organizational structures. It requires the United States to prepare for plausible situations
where nonproliferation fails (or has already failed) and WMD capabilities spread, where deterrent measures prove insufficient and WMD use
occurs, and where protective and mitigative measures diminish the
consequences of such an attack. There is no greater strategic imperative for the United States and its friends and allies—indeed, for the international community as a whole—than to pursue a multipronged
approach to preclude the development of future threats and to protect
against those threats that very much exist today.

## Notes

1. Office of the Secretary of Defense, *Proliferation: Threat and Response* (Washington, D.C.: Department of Defense, January 2001), p. 78.
2. On the origins and evolution of counterproliferation, see Jason D. Ellis and

Geoffrey D. Kiefer, *Combating Proliferation: Strategic Intelligence and National Policy* (forthcoming, 2003), chap. 1; Harald Müller and Mitchell Reiss, "Counterproliferation: Putting New Wine in Old Bottles," *The Washington Quarterly* 18, no. 2 (spring 1996): 145–149; Thomas G. Mahnken, "A Critical Appraisal of the Defense Counterproliferation Initiative," *National Security Studies Quarterly* 5, no. 3 (summer 1999): 91–102.

3. Gilles Andréani, "The Disarray of U.S. Non-Proliferation Policy," *Survival* 41, no. 4 (winter 1999–2000): 43. See also Brad Roberts, "Proliferation and Non-proliferation in the 1990s: Looking for the Right Lessons," *Nonproliferation Review* 6, no. 4 (fall 1999): 70–82.

4. *A National Security Strategy for a Global Age* (Washington, D.C.: U.S. Government Printing Office, December 2000), pp. 2–3.

5. Ibid., pp. 16–18.

6. *The National Security Strategy of the United States of America* (Washington, D.C.: U.S. Government Printing Office, September 2002), p. 14 (hereinafter *National Security Strategy*). See also *National Strategy to Combat Weapons of Mass Destruction* (Washington, D.C.: U.S. Government Printing Office, December 2002).

7. *National Security Strategy*, pp. 13–15.

8. Robert S. Litwak, "The New Calculus of Pre-emption," *Survival* 44, no. 4 (winter 2002–2003): 54–60; Jason D. Ellis, "The Gravest Danger: Proliferation, Terrorism, and the Bush Doctrine," *Monitor* 9, no. 1 (winter 2003).

9. Les Aspin, address to National Academy of Sciences on the Defense Counterproliferation Initiative, Washington, D.C., December 7, 1993.

10. Office of the Secretary of Defense, *Report of the Quadrennial Defense Review* (Washington, D.C.: Department of Defense, May 1997), p. 4 (emphasis in original). See also Paul R. S. Gebhard, "Not by Diplomacy or Defense Alone: The Role of Regional Security Strategies in U.S. Proliferation Policy," *The Washington Quarterly* 18, no. 1 (winter 1995): 167–179.

11. Center for Counterproliferation Research, *The Counterproliferation Imperative: Meeting Tomorrow's Challenges* (Washington, D.C.: National Defense University, November 2001), pp. 2, 4–6.

12. George Tenet, testimony before the Senate Select Committee on Intelligence, February 6, 2002, p. 3.

13. National Intelligence Council, "Foreign Missile Developments and the Ballistic Missile Threat 2015," unclassified summary, Washington, D.C., December 2001.

14. U.S. Government Printing Office, *The Biological & Chemical Warfare Threat*, rev. ed. (Washington, D.C.: 1999), p. 32; Office of the Secretary of Defense, *Proliferation: Threat and Response*, p. 4.

15. John A. Lauder, "Unclassified Statement for the Record by Special Assistant to the Director of Central Intelligence for Nonproliferation John A. Lauder to the Commission to Assess the Organization of the Federal Government to Combat the Proliferation of Weapons of Mass Destruction," April 29, 1999, pp. 1, 3 (hereinafter Lauder statement).

16. Office of the Secretary of Defense, *Proliferation: Threat and Response*, p. 4.

17. Lauder statement, pp. 1, 3; U.S. Government Printing Office, *The Worldwide Biological Warfare Weapons Threat* (Washington, D.C.: 2001), p. 1.

18. United Nations Special Commission, *Report to the Security Council on the Status of Disarmament and Monitoring*, S/1999/94, January 29, 1999, app. III.

19. George J. Tenet, testimony before the Senate Foreign Relations Committee, March 21, 2000. See also Director of Central Intelligence, "Unclassified Report to Congress on the Acquisition of Technology Related to Weapons of Mass Destruction and Advanced Conventional Munitions, 1 July Through 31 December 2001," Washington, D.C., January 2003.

20. Center for Counterproliferation Research, *The Counterproliferation Imperative*, p. 27.

21. *Report of the Quadrennial Defense Review*, p. 13. See also John F. Reichart, "Adversary Use of WMD: A Neglected Challenge," *Strategic Forum* 187 (December 2001); Peter R. Lavoy, Scott D. Sagan, and James J. Wirtz, eds., *Planning the Unthinkable: How New Powers Will Use Nuclear, Biological, and Chemical Weapons* (Ithaca, N.Y.: Cornell University Press, 2000).

22. *National Security Strategy*, pp. 13–14. See also Office of Homeland Security, *National Strategy for Homeland Security* (Washington, D.C.: White House, July 2002), pp. vii, ix, 9.

23. See, for example, G. John Ikenberry, "America's Imperial Ambition," *Foreign Affairs* 81, no. 5 (September/October 2002): 56–60.

24. Stephen Engelberg and Michael R. Gordon, "Intelligence Study Says North Korea Has Nuclear Bomb," *New York Times*, December 26, 1993, p. A1.

25. David E. Sanger, "In North Korea and Pakistan, Deep Roots of Nuclear Barter," *New York Times*, November 24, 2002.

26. See Ellis and Kiefer, *Combating Proliferation*, chap. 2. See also Joseph Cirincione with Jon B. Wolfsthal and Miriam Rajkumar, *Deadly Arsenals: Tracking Weapons of Mass Destruction* (Washington, D.C.: Carnegie Endowment for International Peace, 2002), pp. 207–220.

27. Thom Shanker with Terence Neilan, "Yemen Protests Seizure of North Korean Ship; Says Scuds Were Bound for Its Army," *New York Times*, December 11, 2002; Thomas E. Ricks and Peter Slevin, "Intercepted Missile Shipment Released to Yemen," *Washington Post*, December 11, 2002.

28. Office of the Secretary of Defense, *Report of the Quadrennial Defense Review* (Washington, D.C.: Department of Defense, September 30, 2001), p. 14.

29. Center for Counterproliferation Research, *The Counterproliferation Imperative*, pp. 28–31. See also *Gulf War Air Power Survey, Volume I, Part I: Planning and Command and Control* (Washington, D.C.: U.S. Government Printing Office, 1993); Department of Defense, *Final Report to Congress on the Conduct of the Persian Gulf War Pursuant to Title V of the Persian Gulf Conflict Supplemental Authorization and Personnel Benefits Act of 1991, Public Law 102-25* (Washington, D.C.: U.S. Government Printing Office, April 1992).

30. See Ellis and Kiefer, *Combating Proliferation*, chap. 7.

31. *National Security Strategy*, p. 15.

32. See Center for Counterproliferation Research, *Anthrax in America: A Chronology and Analysis of the Fall 2001 Attacks* (Washington, D.C.: National Defense University, November 2002), pp. 1–13. See also George W. Bush, *Securing the Homeland, Strengthening the Nation* (Washington, D.C.: White House, February 2002); *Public Health Security and Bioterrorism Preparedness Act of 2002, Public Law 188, 107th Cong., 2d sess.*

**Gu Guoliang**

# Redefine Cooperative Security, Not Preemption

Asymmetric warfare launched by terrorist groups is correctly defined in the 2002 U.S. National Security Strategy (NSS) as "today's most urgent threat" to the United States. Strategists define asymmetric warfare as conflict deviating from established norms in which a potential opponent—a state, a transnational group (such as an international terrorist organization or a drug cartel), or various other types of players—seeks to counter the superior capabilities of a superpower or regional power with unconventional, asymmetric means.[1] Unfortunately, President George W. Bush's strategy of preemption is not the solution to the problem; in practice, it won't work and, in principle, it breaks all existing rules. Rather, preemption only diminishes the role of diplomatic cooperation and nonproliferation regimes, weakening their effectiveness against terrorism and the proliferation of weapons of mass destruction (WMD).

## It Won't Work

Preemption is not a new strategy. What is new is Bush's emphasis on this strategy since September 11 and its emergence as the nameplate for U.S. national security strategy. In a speech to the Veterans of For-

Gu Guoliang is a deputy director and research fellow at the Institute of American Studies, Chinese Academy of Social Sciences, in Beijing.

Copyright © 2003 by The Center for Strategic and International Studies and the Massachusetts Institute of Technology
*The Washington Quarterly* • 26:2 pp. 135–145.

eign Wars in Nashville on August 26, 2002, Vice President Dick Cheney cited Israel's June 7, 1981, attacks on Iraq's Osirak nuclear facility near Baghdad as an example of the ability of preemptive strikes to set back Saddam Hussein's nuclear ambitions.[2] The strategy of preemption, however, is a risky option that can backfire. Politically, a government needs a legal basis and moral grounds to support preemptive attacks; technically, it needs reliable intelligence about the rival nation's capabilities and intent as well as assurances that attacks on the targets will be accurate. Otherwise, the consequence of violating other countries' sovereignty and hurting innocent people will be significant. Beyond these practical concerns, other historical examples show that the strategy of preemption has empirically proven ineffective at preventing or deterring either WMD use or even WMD-capability acquisition in the first place.

## CAN'T PREVENT WMD USE

In 1994 the Clinton administration threatened to launch preemptive strikes against North Korea but refrained because it feared serious consequences. In mid-June 1994, the Senate passed a resolution urging President Bill Clinton to take action to prepare U.S. troops "to deter and, if necessary, repel an attack from North Korea."[3] Secretary of Defense William Perry asked Gen. John M. Shalikashvili to prepare a contingency plan for a preemptive strike against North Korea's nuclear facilities to be included in Operation Plan 5027—a U.S. plan for defeating a North Korean attack.[4] Both Pentagon officials feared, however, that such an attack would incite the North Koreans to launch a military attack on South Korea; even though North Korea would surely lose any subsequent war, war between the North and the South would kill hundreds of thousands, perhaps millions, before it was over. According to Perry, the two sides were on the brink of a war that might involve WMD. Nevertheless, through the mediation of former president Jimmy Carter, the North Korean and U.S. governments began to negotiate and finally signed the Agreed Framework in Geneva on October 21, 1994, a pact that "drew the region back from the brink of conflict."[5]

## CAN'T PREVENT WMD PROLIFERATION

The strategy of preemption also cannot prevent the so-called rogue states from acquiring WMD in the first place. Although Bush rhetorically dubbed Iraq, Iran, and North Korea as the "axis of evil," in practice the administration has taken different approaches in dealing with each of these countries. While planning to launch preemptive strikes against Iraq, the United States is not planning any risky attacks against North Korea or Iran, although the U.S. government suspects and has even provided evidence that North Korea and Iran are developing WMD.

At a November 2002 briefing at the Foreign Press Center in Washington, D.C., James Kelly, U.S. assistant secretary of state for East Asian and Pacific affairs, told reporters that Bush had "made clear that we have no intention or plans to attack or invade North Korea."[6] One U.S. official told me during his recent trip to Beijing that the United States fears the possibility of North Korea's heavy artillery attacks against South Korea more than it fears North Korea's use of WMD because the potential of artillery attacks is more realistic and serious.[7] In the case of Iran, the Bush administration does not seem to have come up with an established policy to deal with that government's development of a WMD capability.

Although preemption may be the theoretical basis for U.S. attacks against Iraq, the goal of potential U.S. preemptive attacks against Iraq is unclear. Is the objective to eliminate Iraq's WMD or to change the country's regime? The Bush administration has changed statements about its goal several times. On one hand, the White House recognizes that it should use force only as a last resort. The NSS states clearly that "[t]he United States will not use force in all cases to preempt emerging threats, nor should nations use preemption as a pretext for aggression."[8] On the other hand, the Bush administration is preparing for a war against Iraq, with or without the mandate of the United Nations, that may not, once and for all, prohibit Iraq from developing WMD in the future.

Moreover, preemption is not the answer to the war on terror precisely because it cannot eliminate all nonstate terrorists. Neither the superior military power of the United States nor its preemptive strikes can deter terrorist groups from launching suicide attacks. Former U.S. secretary of defense William Cohen once warned that "American military superiority actually increases the threat of nuclear, biological, and chemical attack against us by creating incentives for adversaries to challenge us asymmetrically."[9] Preemption cannot keep terrorist groups from using trucks, container ships, civilian airliners, private planes, and subway cars to attack the United States anywhere they choose. With the military operation in Afghanistan at an end and Osama bin Laden and other Al Qaeda leaders still at large, how can the strategy of preemption help the United States to wipe out terrorist groups in the near future?

## It Breaks All the Rules

Preemption is not only ineffective in deterring or preempting terrorists or states attempting to acquire or use WMD; it also undermines existing strategies to combat WMD cooperatively. A national security strategy of preemption poses a serious challenge to the existing tenets of international law and to the framework of the UN—the single institution founded with the objective of collectively maintaining world peace. Article 2.4 of the UN Charter states, "All Members shall refrain in their international relations from the threat or use of force against the territorial integrity or political independence of any state." Under international law, the United States is entitled to attack Iraq only as an act of self-defense unless otherwise authorized by the Security Council. According to the definition of self-defense proposed by U.S. secretary of state Daniel Webster in 1837 and universally accepted ever since: "There must be a necessity of self-defense, instant, overwhelming, leaving no choice of means, and no moment for deliberation."[10] Thus far, although Iraq has not fully complied with UN resolutions, no imminent military threat to the United States has been detected. Therefore, the United States cannot legitimately attack Iraq.

Furthermore, Article 33 of the UN Charter clearly stipulates that international disputes should be handled through peaceful means. Not only is the very definition of what justifies a preemptive strike at stake but also who has the right to make that judgement. Even European nations—longtime U.S. allies—consider preemption "as a sign of a permanent break by the United States from the international system ... [and as] the assertion of supremacy unburdened by international laws or institutions."[11] No country is entitled to deprive the UN of its right to judge whether or not a war is justified. The international community as a whole, therefore, cannot accept preemption as the national security strategy of one single nation. Otherwise, any single nation may become the judge and jury of international law.

## CATALYZING A CHAIN REACTION

Adopting a preemptive strategy sets a bad example for other governments and could have a seriously negative global impact. If the U.S. example were to be followed, Israel could launch preemptive attacks against Palestine or other Arab countries, and India and Pakistan could launch preemptive strikes against each other. By acting on its goal of eliminating the supposed threat of Iraqi WMD, therefore, the United States would increase the potential for more military conflicts, making the world even more insecure and unstable.

Moreover, if the United States were to use missiles or tactical nuclear weapons to strike deep underground bunkers or bioweapon facilities in its preemptive attacks, on what moral grounds could the U.S. government justify prohibiting other nations from acquiring or using WMD? Such action would only demonstrate the power afforded by WMD and, therefore, further inspire others to acquire them. An old Chinese adage says, "Do not unto others as you would not have them do unto you."

## FROM MUTUALLY TO UNILATERALLY ASSURED DESTRUCTION

Traditional arms-control theory aims to avoid and decrease the danger of preemptive attacks and war between major powers through negotiations and arms regulation. But this notion should also apply to relations between major powers and small powers. Bush's new emphasis on preemption does not abandon deterrence but instead attempts to change its nature. His administration has simply replaced mutually assured destruction with unilaterally assured destruction.

In his May 1 speech at the National Defense University, Bush made it clear that "Cold War deterrence is no longer enough. ... Deterrence can no longer be based solely on the threat of nuclear retaliation."[12] The Bush administration has shifted the target of deterrence from Russia to rogue states and nonstate terrorist groups, stating that "today's most urgent threat stems not from thousands of ballistic missiles, in Soviet hands, but from a small number of missiles in the hands of these states, states for whom terror and blackmail are a way of life."[13] Thus, the Bush administration has extended the implications of deterrence strategy from deterring others from using WMD to attack the United States to deterring others from acquiring WMD in the first place.

Finally, preemption reflects the Bush administration's penchant for unilateralism. Bush has made it clear that the United States "will not hesitate to act alone, if necessary, to exercise our right of self-defense by acting preemptively against such terrorists."[14] Since Bush assumed the presidency, his administration has taken a number of unilateral steps to remove the United States from international arms-control and nonproliferation regimes. Bush announced the formal U.S. withdrawal from the Anti-Ballistic Missile (ABM) Treaty on December 13, 2001, stating, "I have concluded that the ABM Treaty hinders our government's ability to develop ways to protect our people from future terrorist or rogue-state missile attacks."[15] The Bush administration has shelved the ratification of the Comprehensive Test Ban Treaty (CTBT), and the U.S. Department of Defense's 2002 Nuclear Posture Review stated that "[t]he DOD and [Department of Energy] will reassess the need to resume nuclear testing and will make recommendations to the president."[16] The administration has also refused to comply with the proto-col of the Biological Weapons Convention (BWC). These unilateral steps taken by the U.S. government not only weaken some of the arms control and nonproliferation regimes it has worked to help establish but also blatantly contradict its own goal of stemming WMD proliferation.

## A Better Alternative: Getting Everyone on Board the Same Plan

International terrorism and WMD proliferation are global problems; only the global community as a whole can effectively act to resolve them. Achieving that solution is only possible by redefining cooperative security and bolstering the existing international arms-control re-gime—not writing it off.

### REDEFINE COOPERATIVE SECURITY

At the outset, it is essential to address the root causes of WMD prolif-eration, meaning that nations' incentives to acquire, distribute, and use WMD must be eliminated. That Brazil, South Africa, and other nations have voluntarily forfeited their nuclear capabilities proves that, if a na-tion feels it has no need for nuclear capability and it is secure with the security guarantees provided by the international system, then WMD proliferation can be contained. The 2002 U.S. NSS rightly acknowl-edges the need to address the causal factors by noting the importance of "diminishing the underlying conditions that spawn terrorism."[17] But effectively diminishing those conditions requires redefining cooperative security—to feature mutual trust, mutual benefits, equality, and coop-eration—so that it yields greater benefits for all nations.

To help establish and maintain a stable international order in which people of all nations can live free from the kinds of poverty, disparity, discrimination, and resentment that so often yields terrorist activity and the pursuit of WMD proliferation, a credible guarantee of security should be provided to those countries that have given up their aspira-tions to acquire WMD. Specifically, the nuclear-weapon states should give unconditional security assurance to the non–nuclear-weapon states. The existing positive and negative security assurances, as expressed in the P-5 declarations, are not enough.[18] The Conference on Disarmament, the international community's single multilateral disarmament negotiating forum, should negotiate an internationally legally binding instrument that will assure non–nuclear-weapon states protection against the use or threat of use of nuclear weapons.

Meanwhile, nations that have already developed nuclear capabilities should continue the process of nuclear disarmament and make a commitment not to resume nuclear testing (or use), thus maintaining the credible bargain made with nonnuclear states under the Nuclear Non-Proliferation Treaty (NPT). Treaties declaring nuclear weapon–free zones, such as the Antarctica Treaty, the Treaty for the Prohibition of Nuclear Weapons in Latin America and the Caribbean (Treaty of Tlatelolco), the South Pacific Nuclear-Free Zone Treaty of Rarotonga, the Southeast Asian Nuclear-Weapon-Free-Zone Treaty (Bangkok Treaty), the Central Asia Nuclear-Weapon-Free Zone Treaty and the African Nuclear-Weapon-Free-Zone Treaty (Pelindaba Treaty), should be fully implemented.

As the world's only superpower, the United States plays the leading role in maintaining world peace and order and has the capability to solve numerous global issues, including WMD proliferation. In the case of North Korea, for example, if the United States were willing to sign a mutual nonaggression and security agreement and give North Korea a credible guarantee of security and survival, North Korea would be ready to give up its nuclear and missile programs.[19] It is doubtful whether the United States can achieve its narrow goal of solving the issue of North Korea's nuclear and missile program without addressing the broader issue of a general improvement in political relations between the two countries. What North Korea wants is not just economic aid or commercial bargains but concrete political and security guarantees, which the Bush administration is not ready to offer. Only through peaceful negotiation; the cooperation of the United States, South Korea, China, Russia, Japan, and other countries; and a return to a low-tension political atmosphere in Korea as seen in the late 1990s can the issue of North Korea's nuclear and missile programs be effectively addressed.

## BUILD ON—DON'T WRITE OFF—NONPROLIFERATION AGREEMENTS

Currently, most countries—including Iraq, North Korea, and Iran—have acceded to the NPT, the BWC, the Chemical Weapons Convention (CWC), and other arms control and nonproliferation treaties. The existing international nonproliferation regime has been effective and should be enhanced, not weakened, in light of today's threats. Although today's headlines are driven by the absence of inspectors in Iraq since 1998, significant positive steps had been taken after the UN Security Council's adoption of Resolution 687 on April 3, 1991, demanding that Iraq eliminate unconditionally its WMD under international supervision. After visits by more than 400 UN inspections over seven years, according to a UN assessment in 1998, "the bulk of Iraq's proscribed weapons programs has been eliminated" by the inspections regime.[20]

The first half of the 1990s clearly witnessed significant achievements in the field of arms control and nonproliferation: the CWC was concluded in November 1992, the NPT was indefinitely extended in May 1995 at the UN's NPT Review Conference, and the CTBT was concluded in September 1996. But when the Republican-dominated U.S. Congress refused to ratify the CTBT in October 1999 and accelerated the pace of the development of a ballistic-missile defense program in January 1999, all momentum was brought to a halt.

Since the Bush administration entered office, its apparent belief that arms control and nonproliferation regimes inhibit U.S. power has further contributed to the failure of global nonproliferation efforts. Military buildup, a missile defense program, and preemption have become the key components of the Bush administration's national security strategy. U.S. military buildup and the ambitious U.S. ballistic missile program have negatively impacted the global strategic balance as well as international arms control by causing other countries to lose faith in the international nonproliferation regime. Now, the U.S. turn toward preemption may incite other countries to aspire to acquire or modernize WMD.

The international community cannot afford to lose confidence in international nonproliferation regimes, treaties, and agreements because of recent failures to enforce these regimes. The facts show that UN-led efforts toward nonproliferation have delivered results—if not solved the problem entirely; it is, after all, under a UN mandate that weapons inspectors are leading inspections in Iraq. The United States should take the lead in setting a good example in supporting these efforts and enforcing and abiding by international arms-control and nonproliferation treaties and not use them as the justification for preemptive strikes.

Furthermore, national governments cannot choose to adhere to the NPT but neglect nuclear disarmament and the CTBT regimes. The NPT requires that nuclear states also fulfill their obligations toward disarmament. Article VI of the NPT stipulates that "[e]ach of the Parties to the Treaty undertakes to pursue negotiations in good faith on effective measures relating to cessation of the nuclear arms race at an early date and to nuclear disarmament, and on a treaty on general and complete disarmament under strict and effective international control."[21] The fact that the Bush administration continues to delay ratification of the CTBT and plans to develop tactical nuclear weapons only provides greater reason for currently nonnuclear states to seek WMD.

Under the framework and guidance of the UN, the existing international nonproliferation regime, including the NPT, BWC, CWC, and CTBT, should be enforced with full compliance. The export control system and verification regime should also be enhanced. Existing institutions such as the Nuclear Suppliers Group, the Australia Group, and the Missile Technology Control Regime have played positive roles in preventing WMD proliferation. Nevertheless, their roles are limited by their limited membership. Universal participation in nonproliferation regimes is essential so that those countries that violate the norms of the regime can be punished effectively.

WMD proliferation is a global problem and one of the greatest dangers that all nations will face in the twenty-first century. Therefore, it is not a problem that the United States can solve on its own, especially with threats of preemptive attacks. Rather, international cooperation, particularly among the five permanent members of the Security Council, is essential for dealing effectively with this issue.

Cooperative measures designed to prevent nuclear materials, including plutonium, highly enriched uranium, and nuclear technology, from falling into the hands of terrorists have produced positive results. The Nunn-Lugar Cooperative Threat Reduction program has made significant progress in dismantling WMD and WMD materials in the Commonwealth of Independent States countries since the disintegration of the Soviet Union. International cooperation in freezing the assets of terrorist groups and in sharing intelligence have contributed to the success of the international campaign against terrorism. A universally accepted nonproliferation regime would also prove more effective against nonstate actors. With all countries—not just a few—committed to nonproliferation treaties and regimes, nonstate actors would lose their bases for political, financial, and logistical support. Without the base and backing of a state, nonstate terrorist organizations will find it very difficult to get the materials or technologies needed to develop weapons of mass destruction.

## Conclusion

Preemption reflects the Bush administration's perception of a changed threat facing the United States and is an extension of the U.S. government's unilateral foreign policy; this strategy proceeds entirely from the security interests of the United States. It implies that, with the end of the Cold War, because "the United States possesses unprecedented—and unequaled—strength and influence in the world,"[22] the U.S. government is now entitled to do whatever it sees fit in pursuit of its own national interests. The United States seeks to establish a new international order, guided by U.S. interests and values. But the world is diverse, composed of countries with distinct systems, religions, and cultures. The United States should instead work with other powers to address this threat, heightened in everyone's eyes after the tragic attacks on September 11, cooperatively.

## Notes

1. David I. Grange, "Asymmetric Warfare: Old Method, New Concerns," *National Strategy Forum Review* (winter 2000).
2. Ray McGovern, "The Origin of Bush's Preemptive Attack Strategy," *Hill,* September 18, 2002.
3. Amendment to S. 2201 (FAA Authorization Act), *Congressional Record,* vol. 140, pt. 9, June 16, 1994, pp. 13278–13292 (offered by Senator Robert Dole [R-Kans.] and others).
4. Ashton B. Carter and William J. Perry, *Preventive Defense* (Washington, D.C.: Brookings Institution Press, 1999), p. 128.
5. Ibid., p. 132.
6. U.S. Department of State, Office of International Information Programs, "Kelly Says No Final Decision on Status of N. Korea Agreed Framework," *Washington File,* November 20, 2002.
7. Unnamed U.S. official, interview with author, Beijing, November 25, 2002.
8. *The National Security Strategy of the United States of America,* September 2002, p. 15 (hereinafter *National Security Strategy*).
9. Center for Defense Information, "Military Domination or Constructive Leadership?" *Defense Monitor* 27, no. 3 (1998): 8.
10. John Bassett Moore, *A Digest of International Law* vol. II (1906), p. 412 (letter from Secretary of State Daniel Webster to Lord Ashburton, dated August 6, 1842).
11. Tomas Valasek, "The U.S. National Security Strategy: A View from Europe," Center for Defense Information, www.cdi.org (accessed October 9, 2002).
12. President George W. Bush, speech at the National Defense University, Washington, D.C., May 1, 2001, www.whitehouse.gov.
13. Ibid.
14. Todd Haskins, *Preemptive Doctrine,* www.mypoliticaltake.com/article09-20-02preemptive.htm (accessed January 11, 2003).
15. The White House, December 13, 2001 (Bush's remarks).
16. U.S. Department of Defense, *Nuclear Posture Review,* January 8, 2002, p. 55.
17. *National Security Strategy.*
18. United Nations Security Council Resolution 984, April 11, 1995, www.nti.org.

19. Leon V. Sigal, "North Korea Is No Iraq: Pyongyang's Negotiating Strategy," *Policy Forum Online*, December 23, 2002, http://nautilus.org/fora/security/0227A_siga.html (accessed January 11, 2003).

20. Daryl G. Kimball, "Prevention, Not Preemption," *Arms Control Today* 32, no. 8 (October 2002): 2.

21. Jozef Goldblat, *Arms Control: A Guide to Negotiations and Agreements* (Oslo: International Peace Research Institute, 1994), p. 343.

22. *National Security Strategy*, p. 6.

# Part II

---

# Regime Change

## Pascal Bonifac e

# What Justifies Regime Change?

What accounts for the widespread opposition to the U.S.-led military campaign for regime change in Iraq in an international system increasingly intolerable of certain internal behavior? Has anti-American sentiment given rise to opposition to U.S. efforts? No. To come to such a conclusion would be to confuse cause and effect. Rather, even in today's globalized world where boundaries are no longer barriers, sovereignty remains sacred in international relations. Even in cases where regime change might be justified—and international consensus on this exists—war is acceptable only when waged in legitimate self-defense or as the collective decision of the United Nations Security Council.

## A Regime's Wrongs Do Not Make Military Action Right

Saddam Hussein had few, if any, supporters on earth. Everyone was well aware of his credentials as one of the world's most brutal dictators. The Iraqi people lived under a regime of political terror, where anyone who dared to oppose Saddam or to present a view that differed from his was imprisoned or killed under odious conditions, with their family likely to be punished as well. Saddam launched his country into two major wars,

Pascal Boniface is director of the Institute for International and Strategic Relations (IRIS) in Paris.

Copyright © 2003 by The Center for Strategic and International Studies and the Massachusetts Institute of Technology
The Washington Quarterly • 26:3 pp. 61–71.

against Iran in 1980–1988 and against Kuwait and the international community in 1990–1991, both of which ended disastrously for Iraq.

Unlike some other dictators who have admittedly contributed to the development of their countries—whatever reservations one might have about their political behavior—Saddam led the most promising country in the Middle East—the only state that has benefited from three main assets: oil, water, and an educated population—to economic and social failure. He successfully transformed a rich, promising, and advanced Arab country into a devastated one. A comparison of Iraq's economic, political, diplomatic, and social situation in 1979, when Saddam came to power, and the situation today illustrates a striking, total waste of resources. Saddam was one of the fiercest proliferators of weapons of mass destruction (WMD) and defied international law by using chemical weapons against both Iranian soldiers and Iraq's own Kurdish population. Saddam's behavior not only harmed Iraq but also contributed significantly to destabilization in the Middle East, particularly with his designs to create a greater Arab nation under his rule.

For the sake of Iraq as well as for world stability, who wouldn't have liked to see someone else in charge in Baghdad? The idea to wage war to topple Saddam nevertheless invoked significant opposition worldwide. Global rejection of the war was, of course, multifaceted. The United States initially presented the war as justified by a cause other than Saddam's oppressive regime: the disarmament of Iraq—a goal that could have been efficiently pursued by diplomatic means and international inspections. Only a few outspoken advisers in the Bush administration stated that the real goal of the war was to get rid of Saddam and give Iraq's people a chance to live under better conditions. President George W. Bush and British prime minister Tony Blair claimed this goal as their official position only after the war plan had been decided. Although disarmament could have been perceived to be possible through diplomatic means, regime change—to liberate the Iraqi people from an oppressive dictator and a stifling economic and social structure—was a more efficient way to sell the war to a reluctant international audience.

This approach did not succeed in winning support for war in Iraq, even though the world has become increasingly committed to the idea of humanitarian intervention. How can that contradiction be explained? Among the countries that opposed this war in Iraq, a vast majority supported the military operation in Kosovo in 1999, and nearly all of them backed both the Persian Gulf War in 1990–1991 and the war in Afghanistan after September 11, 2001.

Most world leaders and the international public thought that a war to topple Saddam was a cure worse than the disease. The fear that that the Iraqi population would suffer was significant, but other outcomes were feared even more: the destabilization of the Middle East, the radicalization of the Arab and Muslim worlds, an increase in antagonism between the Western and Muslim worlds, the growth of terrorism, and the weakening of the UN. These fears are not speculative but grounded in the lessons of history.

## Balancing Bad Regimes against Imperial Hegemons

In September 1933—the year Adolf Hitler came to power—the League of Nations granted an audience to a Jewish German from Silesia named Bernheim, who had protested against the Nazis' barbaric behavior toward their own fellow countrymen. The German delegate to the league—none other than Hitler's minister for information and propaganda, Joseph Göbbels—responded, "We are a sovereign state. What this man has told you is none of your business. We do whatever we want with our Socialists, our pacifists, our Jews. We need not submit to the control of either mankind or the League of Nations."

Had the Nazi regime been removed from power at that time, humanity would have been spared the Holocaust and World War II. In reaction to that war and its accompanying atrocities, international society came to the conclusion that such a regime must never again impose its rule on a people. In response to the Nazi atrocities, the UN Charter included the notion of self-determination as a major principle of international law. Self-determination was balanced against one of the charter's other major tenets: noninterference in the internal affairs of another country, based on national sovereignty. Noninterference was seen as a way to protect weak states against intervention from strong states. Self-determination was perceived as a way to ensure progress in international order but, at the same time, recognize that humanity needs a "*droit de regard*," or right to examine, the relationship between the state and the individual. In this way, self-determination could prevent the excesses of sovereignty that might otherwise allow a government to hide from international reaction behind a shield of noninterference while oppressing its own people. For this reason, the UN General Assembly, with the exception of Communist and Muslim states, adopted the Universal Declaration of Human Rights in December 1948. Andrei Vichinskii, Stalin's representative to the conference, stated at the time, "We refuse this text, which brings interference in internal affairs."

Historically, interference (*ingérence* in French) has had two conflicting effects: it has been seen either as a progressive principle that prevents dictators from freely abusing their own populations or as a repressive tool used by big powers to impose their rule on other nations. During decolonization and its aftermath (the 1950s–1970s), self-determination may initially have helped liberate newly independent states, but noninterference was one of the most important principles protecting these new states from the imperial threat of great powers. The nonaligned movement—comprised mostly of Third World countries, such as India and Algeria, that refused to align with either East or West—was created in Belgrade in 1961 for precisely this purpose. The 1974 adoption of General Assembly Resolution 3314 (XXIX) on aggression, which states that "aggression is the use of armed force by a state" against the sovereignty, territorial integrity, or political independence of another state, has been considered a significant victory for international democracy and a way to protect the weak from the strong—a victory against imperialism or neo-imperialism. This declaration was preceded by Resolution 2625 (XXV), adopted in 1970, declaring "the inadmissibility of intervention in internal affairs" and the "protection of independence and sovereignty"—statements that were warmly welcomed by developing countries.

This history helps explain the current distinction between Western and non-Western perceptions of interference: whether or not a state sees intervention as progressive or regressive largely depends on the position a particular state is in. The Western world sees foreign intervention as proof of generosity and a concern to help others; other countries consider interference as a way for the Western world to challenge another country's independence. Interference is hardly a two-way street—no African country tries to send troops to Northern Ireland or to Corsica to restore order.

How can the global community necessarily forbid dictators to act with impunity and prevent national boundaries from becoming a dictator's way to avoid human rights regulations without recalling fears of past hegemonic or imperial order? Finding and agreeing upon the answer to this question may be the linchpin to preserving international law and order today.

## Principles to Consider for Regime Change

What conditions obligate the international community to enforce a policy of regime change or at least make it preferable to other options, especially the status quo? Does toppling a regime, followed by temporary instability, lead to a better and more stable world? Events of the last 15 years have raised at least four scenarios where regime change has been considered.

### DICTATORSHIP

In the case of a regime change to end a dictatorship, several issues need to be contemplated. Democracy is no longer just a Western value but a universal one, having spread to Latin America, Asia, and Africa. Yet, should the international community topple all dictators, and realistically, can it?

Unfortunately, such a goal is unattainable because, even with the spread of democracy throughout the world, one cannot assume that promoting democracy is a primary concern of the majority of states. Of course, an example could be set, but there are no guarantees that ousting one dictator would be sufficient to make others realize that they have no alternative but to establish democratic governments. A decision could thus be made to concentrate on the most repressive or the bloodiest regime and then hope that such efforts have a ripple effect.

How can the international community make that choice? Who decides what regime is at the top of the list? Who decides the agenda, the general motion, or the speed of the measures taken to topple such a dictator? Should the Security Council make such decisions? If so, how would the members' right to veto be bypassed? Should cases meriting regime change be determined by nongovernmental organizations concerned with humanitarian issues? If so, which organizations should make the decision, and what is their democratic legitimacy? Perhaps the General Assembly—as the representative body of all world governments—should decide, but this course risks mutual protection among dictatorships.

Should each major regional power decide within its own sphere of influence? This alternative gives legitimacy to regional imperialism but not to international democracy. In fact, this model was dominant during the Cold War: Moscow accepted de facto U.S. intervention in the Western world (primarily in Latin America), and Washington accepted de facto Soviet intervention in countries that were members of the Warsaw Pact.

Should the United States act on behalf of the rest of the world or according to its own national interest? How can the rest of the world make sure that Washington distinguishes between U.S. interests and the general interest of the global community? The past—and present—do not speak in favor of U.S. credibility in this regard. The problem is not the sincerity of U.S. leaders. The problem lies in the fact that it is not always possible—for the most sincere leaders, it is often even more difficult—to distinguish what is a matter of national interest from what is a matter of general interest.

## WMD PROLIFERATION

Is WMD proliferation a valid reason to topple a regime? The international community agrees that WMD proliferation is a significant threat to international security. Although some may argue that the current legal division between five nuclear weapons states and all other non–nuclear weapons states, for example, creates a double standard, this inequality has been widely accepted in the interest of international security, even by nonnuclear states. The Nuclear Non-Proliferation Treaty (NPT) is probably the most widely subscribed international pact, with 187 signatories and only four major countries—India, Pakistan, Israel, and Cuba—not participating.

A 1992 Security Council summit was held after a statement officially declared that proliferation was a major threat to international security and, according to the UN Charter, granted the Security Council the right and the duty to deal with proliferation. Even with the authority to deal with this particular threat clearly assigned, however, what action to take is not so clear. What is the real objective: nonproliferation or respect for the NPT? If the former, then the international community would have the right to demand that Israel, India, and Pakistan disarm. Few political leaders would ask for this step, and few strategic experts would argue that it is at all realistic that these states would comply. To ascertain that a state-party to the NPT is violating its legal obligations and deserves to be punished is an entirely separate matter from punishing a non-NPT state-party for pursuing nuclear capabilities. Then, what is the scope and severity of violations that could lead to unseating a regime? What if a country simply threatened to withdraw from the treaty, as North Korea has, ending its obligations and the legal basis for regime change? Who then leads the effort in unseating them?

If a single nation led the campaign, it would always be suspected of pursuing national interests, not enforcing universal values. The United States thinks of itself as the official repository of universal values and the epitome of democracy and that it has never been a colonialist power. In the past, the United States has been accused of isolationism more than of interventionism; thus, trying to take care of others and to offer the country's incomparable powers as a service to the world is a sign of generosity, not imperialism, in American eyes. Europeans, on the other hand, and probably many developing countries would suspect that the choices being made are not as altruistic but rather part of the pursuit of national interest.

Almost any security threat, including WMD proliferation, faces a problem if it is proposed as the basis for regime change by the international community: whom does that state or that behavior threaten? For example, a clear definition of the rogue states has never been given. Does it matter if a problem state is democratic? Cuba is certainly not a democracy, but are conditions all that much better in Saudi Arabia or Uzbekistan, the new U.S. ally in the fight against terrorism? What about Cuba's attempts to export revolution? Exporting Wahhabism seems a far greater threat to world stability. When it comes to WMD proliferation, is Syria, Libya, or even Iran really more dangerous than Pakistan? The reality is that whether a country is perceived as a threat or a rogue state or a member of the "axis of evil" is more closely linked to whether countries are perceived to be friendly toward the United States than it is to a state's actual behavior or the actual threat it poses to international order.

## GENOCIDE

A third potential justification for regime change could be genocide. Had the international community reacted promptly in 1994 in Rwanda, one of the darkest moments of history could have been avoided. The same applies to Cambodia's Khmer Rouge, who killed at least a million Cambodians while in power from 1975 to 1979.

If any regime were to commit mass murder, there would be a large consensus that the regime should be terminated, even without a formal UN resolution. Acting without UN authorization, however, requires that a clear case be made. The regime's responsibility for the crimes must be clearly defined, and the only goal of military intervention in an emergency that would be allowed without UN preapproval would have to be limited to preventing continued murders. Subsequently, the international community would have to be in charge of the country in order to establish a new regime for international acceptance and to give legitimacy to the unilateral intervention. After the end of the Cold War, however, it is difficult to imagine a scenario in which the Security Council would not unanimously agree to topple a regime clearly guilty of committing genocide. As no state would risk vetoing a resolution to this effect, the greater theoretical risk lies in a delay before intervention, not a veto preventing it.

Still, the international community has not acted in the past—and cannot be expected to act—uniformly toward regimes guilty of genocide. In the case of the Khmer Rouge, the regime kept Cambodia's seat in the UN with the support of the Western world, based on the sole argument that the regime had been toppled by Vietnam, an ally of the Soviet Union and a Communist country. Even today, those regimes deemed more strategically important will be treated differently than those more peripheral to international affairs.

The international community did not react to the events that took place in Kosovo in the same manner that it did to events in Chechnya. In both cases, largely Muslim ethnic populations on peripheral territories desired to secede from the central territories occupied by Orthodox Slavs. The Slavs' refusal to accede to Muslim demands for independence resulted in an armed struggle, which resulted from political repression. In both instances, the international community decided not to recognize the ethnic population's right to secession. Kosovo did not contest the sovereignty of Yugoslavia, nor did Chechnya contest that of Russia. In the case of Kosovo, the international community considered the repression excessive and invoked an urgent humanitarian situation to legitimize the use of armed force. The war in Kosovo did not have a clearly and publicly defined goal, even if it did succeed in overthrowing Slobodan Milosevic's regime; the intervention simply put an end to a policy of ethnic cleansing. In the case of Chechnya, however, the international community has not claimed that Russia's use of military force justified the use of external force to overthrow the regime in Moscow.

Should one thus conclude that political repression was weaker in Chechnya and resulted in a lesser loss of human life? This conclusion would be wrong; the number of deaths in Chechnya has already well exceeded that in Kosovo. What made the difference was not Yugoslavia's or Russia's degree of culpability but rather their influence in the international arena. In Yugoslavia's case, its guilt as a result of committing atrocities against the population of Kosovo is certainly unquestionable; however, it is not inconceivable to think that Yugoslavia's relative place in the international system influenced the international decision to resort to force against Belgrade. If Yugoslavia had had nuclear weapons or a permanent seat on the Security Council, the war in Kosovo never would have taken place. Quite simply, politics matter.

Some might argue that the international community (or the UN) should establish a rule explicitly justifying regime change both to deter such atrocities from being committed in the first place and to bind the international community to respond, even against the strongest states, if such a rule is broken. Merely declaring such a rule, however, would not make it enforceable. Realistically, the international community would more likely deny that such atrocities had been committed by the stronger states, jeopardizing the credibility of not just the declared rule but of the international community more broadly. Not passing such an unenforceable rule in the first place would be better than pretending that it were possible to enforce.

## State-Sponsored or -Condoned Terrorism

A state's support for or practice of terrorism could also conceivably merit regime change. Assessing terrorism, however, must be approached cautiously. Throughout history, the definition of terrorism has varied according to political positions. For example, in occupied France during World War II, the Nazis considered those who used force to resist them terrorists; the French who fought the Nazis considered themselves the resistance. History portrays them as the latter.

Because those considered terrorists are unlikely to consider themselves as such, terrorism can be defined accurately not by its political objectives—to liberate a territory or to change a regime—but by the means employed. Terrorism typically puts civilian populations at great risk in an arbitrary and brutal manner. If a government should knowingly practice, support, or condone terrorist activity, it can therefore be considered just as great a threat to the international community as the non–government-related movement behind it. In this case, the legitimacy of that government to rule this state could be justifiably questioned. Similarly, in the case of a failed state, where a government is too weak to control its state territory effectively and thus gives terrorist groups—whether voluntarily or not—the possibility of sanctuary, it should be legitimate for the international community to intervene to restore order.

Who could lawfully challenge those regimes? According to Article 51 of the UN Charter, if a government directly or indirectly attacks another country, the latter is, from then on, in a state of legitimate defense and thus able to use force against the offending party. The United States employed its right to self-defense against the Taliban in Afghanistan, a regime that was deemed guilty of refusing to deliver Osama bin Laden, the accused mastermind behind the attacks on the World Trade Center and the Pentagon, to U.S. authorities. The international community unanimously approved the U.S. plan of action and supported regime change in Afghanistan. The overthrow of the Taliban regime was not attributed to its unacceptable and totalitarian nature but to its unquestionable ties to a terrorist organization that had attacked the United States.

The example of the Taliban was simple, however, because the United States was retaliating in self-defense, the September 11 attacks were clearly terrorism, and the international community unanimously authorized the U.S. actions. In the future, consensus may be more elusive if questions arise about whether a certain government or terrorist organizations operating with its support (or on its territory) were actually terrorists, if ties between governments and those organizations are unclear, or if calls to change a regime precede a terrorist attack in the first place.

## Who Acts, Not Why, Is the Devilish Detail

In light of these examples, regime change with multilateral approval of the use of force is not impossible and can be envisioned under certain circumstances. It is not so much that the various motives are problematic; instead, it is a question of who determines them and who decides on the course of action and the method of operation.

European countries clearly prefer a collective and multilateral assessment of such situations. The United States is rhetorically in agreement with this analysis but believes that there can be exceptions it must pursue in its own interest—a notion embodied in the famous formula "multilateral if we can, unilateral if we must." The United States considers this approach mere pragmatism. In Europe, this formula is deemed ambiguous, if not hypocritical, and is largely interpreted as that the United States will accept the multilateral route if other countries are in accord with its point of view but will act unilaterally in cases when agreement is lacking. This formula is reminiscent of the Soviet Union's concept of détente: "What's mine is mine, what's yours is negotiable."

A policy of changing the regimes of other states unilaterally, pursued by any state in its own national interests, obviously gives the state affecting the regime change greater freedom to act. It does not obligate that state to convince other powers of its arguments, even though international assent is more legitimate and leaves less room for suspicion. The danger of unilateral action is precisely the risk of imperial hegemony that the principle of noninterference was established and enshrined in the UN Charter to prevent. During the Cold War, skepticism about the UN's ability to act in such matters was clearly justified as a Security Council resolution could be blocked if a superpower's client was accused of a violation. This is no longer the case. Ideological divisions no longer exist, even when national interests are involved. (In fact, Israel is the only country for which protection by a permanent Security Council member is frequently and regularly used.) Thus, a collective decision is not out of reach for the UN, and a member that abstains from voting no longer prevents a decision from being made. Even beyond the UN, such approval can be given on a regional level by organizations such as the Organization for Security and Cooperation in Europe, NATO (though only for an affair concerning its members), the African Union, and the Organization of American States.

The debate on regime change, or intervention in pursuit of regime change, is far from closed. Unforeseeable cases will arise where regime change is justified. In other instances, general rules to change regimes and preserve international order may be foreseeable and reduce the risk of imperial hegemony. To design any such guidelines, though, several significant questions currently remain unanswered:

- How can protecting sovereignty be reconciled with the need to act against massive and flagrant violations of human rights, such as those committed in Rwanda and Srebenica?

- How can universal norms that might justify regime change, if violated, be defended if they are not defined universally?

- How can the international community establish rules applicable to both strong and weak states to stop terror from spreading freely under the protection of noninterference in national borders?

- Who could legitimately judge these norms and make incontestable decisions toward their eventual enforcement?

Although skeptics may doubt the international community's ability to agree upon solutions to these critical questions of international order, the nations of the world are already finding answers. In May 2002, the Security Council officially discussed the need for humanitarian intervention when civil populations are placed under grave threat. A report submitted to the Security Council at that meeting attempts to define "the threshold of just cause" that legitimizes international military intervention: "the considerable loss of human life, potential or actual, whether or not there may be the intention of genocide, attributable to the deliberate action of the state, its negligence, its inability to take action or its internal shortcomings"; or "an ethnic cleansing on a grand scale, potential or actual, be it perpetuated by murder, forced expulsion, terrorism or rape."

Regime change must be a last resort, undertaken after all other possibilities of prevention and diplomatic procedures have failed to resolve the problem. Military action to change regimes must be implemented with a minimum of force and have a reasonable chance of attaining its goals. Any proposed efforts to change regimes that do not receive general, if not unanimous, approval from the international community are unlikely to be sustainable in the long run.

Although it will take time to reach answers to these questions, those answers are vital to reduce the fear of imperial hegemony that exists beyond U.S. borders, where others are not as confident in the altruistic motives of Washington. Under certain circumstances, just reasons exist to preserve international order through multilateral action to accomplish regime change, but impatience and inconvenience are not sufficient reasons to weaken that international order through unilateral action.

Catherine Lotrionte

# When to Target Leaders

Targeting regime leaders has resurfaced as a moral, legal, and practical debate worthy of serious consideration. Before ousting Saddam Hussein, U.S. officials argued that the Iraqi regime must be dismantled to prevent the use of weapons of mass destruction (WMD) and ensure the safety of the United States and its allies. As an instrument of foreign policy to combat WMD and act in self-defense, killing regime leaders not only might be fair game, but also might be the best alternative under certain circumstances. In examining the advantages and disadvantages of targeting regime leaders, what criteria should policymakers consider when determining whether to take such action?

## Lessons from History

Ethical concerns have historically tended to bar killing heads of state as a policy option. In the United States, both for practical reasons and on moral grounds, killing foreign leaders as an instrument of foreign policy has been condemned; the United States is the only state that has en-

Catherine Lotrionte is an adjunct professor in the School of Foreign Service and the Security Studies Program and a senior fellow in the Institute for International Law and Politics at Georgetown University. She previously served as an assistant general counsel at the Central Intelligence Agency.

Copyright © 2003 by The Center for Strategic and International Studies and the Massachusetts Institute of Technology
The Washington Quarterly • 26:3 pp. 73–86.

acted a clear declaratory policy renouncing assassination, through executive order. Furthermore, U.S. officials have publicly denied that targeting foreign leaders would be part of any U.S. foreign policy objective. In 1990, for example, Air Force Chief of Staff Gen. Michael Dugan stated that, if war were to erupt between the United States and Iraq, U.S. military planes would probably target Saddam, his family, and his mistress. When then-Secretary of Defense Richard Cheney learned of the general's statement, he immediately fired Dugan.[1] In 1991, responding to questions about whether the U.S. military had targeted Saddam, President George H. W. Bush stated, "We're not in the business of targeting Saddam Hussein."[2]

Much public attention was given to the issue of killing foreign leaders in the mid-1970s, when Congress investigated alleged Central Intelligence Agency (CIA) improprieties in conducting intelligence activities, including plots to assassinate state leaders. The most comprehensive investigation was conducted by the Church Committee, whose results were published in a report entitled "Alleged Assassination Plots Involving Foreign Leaders."[3] The Church Committee opposed the use of assassinations because it "violates moral precepts fundamental to our way of life … [and] traditional American notions of fair play."[4]

The Church Committee specifically questioned the CIA's role in the deaths or attempted killings of five world leaders: Cuba's Fidel Castro; the Congo's Patrice Lumumba; the Dominican Republic's Rafael Trujillo; South Vietnam's Ngo Dinh Diem; and Rene Schneider, commander in chief of the Chilean Army, who opposed a military coup against Salvador Allende. Each of these leaders other than Castro was killed in connection with a coup. The Church Committee concluded that:

- U.S. government officials initiated plots to assassinate Castro and Lumumba, apparently believing such activities were lawful and authorized;

- U.S. officials encouraged or knew about the coup plots that resulted in the deaths of Trujillo, Diem, and Schneider;

- no foreign leaders were killed as a result of assassination plots initiated by U.S. officials;

- the plots occurred in the atmosphere of the Cold War, perceived to be of crisis proportions; and

- assassinations should not be characterized as a legitimate method of foreign policy because the act of assassination is "incompatible with American principle, international order, and morality."[5]

The public outcry stemming from these investigations led President Gerald Ford to issue Executive Order 11905, which stated that "[n]o employee of the United States Government shall engage in, or conspire to engage in political assassination."[6] Both President Jimmy Carter and President Ronald Reagan issued subsequent executive orders banning government-sanctioned assassination.[7]

In light of recent U.S. foreign policy actions overseas in places such as Kosovo and Somalia and those taken during the Persian Gulf War and in response to terrorist attacks against the United States, public debate has increased about the prohibition against targeting leaders such as Slobodan Milosevic and Saddam. An increasing number of calls have emerged from Congress and various commentators to rescind any legal ban on the use of assassinations as a foreign policy tool with an executive order or otherwise.[8] The most recent of these congressional initiatives was the Terrorist Elimination Act of 2001, a bill proposed by Representative Bob Barr (R-Ga.) that asserted that the prohibition of assassination "limit[ed] the swift, sure and precise action needed by the United States to protect our national security."[9] Furthermore, the U.S. public's views on the use of assassination reveal that Americans may be more receptive to killing leaders than they were in the 1970s.[10] A poll taken during the Persian Gulf War revealed that 65 percent of the U.S. public favored "covert assassination of Hussein to end the war quickly."[11]

Some analysts have highlighted the "ethical disconnect" between prohibiting killing a tyrannical ruler while allowing the casualties of a bombing campaign to claim the lives of thousands of civilians and soldiers.[12] Others, such as George Washington University law professor Jonathan Turley, have added the practical objection that the assassination ban encourages an alternative policy of using military strikes, which not only target and kill those leaders anyway but also claim innocent lives in collateral damage. Collectively, these commentators argue that when considering the alternatives—full-scale war, massive casualties, and devastating diplomatic and economic sanctions—killing the regime leader appears comparatively humane.

## When Is Killing Leaders Not Assassination?

One of the primary challenges of analyzing the legality of killing regime leaders is reaching a clear definition of the term "assassination." According to Black's Law Dictionary, assassination is an "act of deliberately killing someone, especially a public figure, usually for hire or for political reasons."[13] In addition, the 1980 Oxford Companion to Law states that assassination is "the murder of a person by lying in wait for him and then killing him, particularly the murder of prominent people from political motives, e.g., the assassination of President Kennedy."[14] Based on these definitions, a case can be made that killing regime leaders in self-defense to ensure international security is not an assassination as it is not for political beliefs.

As for U.S. laws that define assassination as a foreign policy tool, there are none. Furthermore, in the U.S. Constitution, specifically those provisions enumerating the president's foreign affairs powers, there is no mention of assassination. A usable body of law that governs assassination can be compiled, however, from U.S. domestic laws related to intelligence activities and international legal conventions related to the conduct of armed conflict.

### U.S. DOMESTIC LAW

Nowhere in the executive orders of Ford establishing—nor those under Carter or Reagan that continued—the ban on assassination is there a definition for the term. Although this omission may possibly have been a mere oversight in drafting, it was more likely an intentional effort to grant the president flexibility in interpreting the applicability of this order. The congressional hearings that led Ford to sign the first intelligence executive order can, however, shed light on its intent.

Based on these hearings, the presidential orders against assassination were intended to prohibit the killing of foreign political leaders as long as the United States was not engaged in armed conflict with the countries of those leaders.[15] Nothing in the language of any of these executive orders indicates that their intent was to replace any aspect of the legal framework of the law of armed conflict with something more restrictive. In fact, the ban in the executive orders meant to control the activities of the intelligence community during a time of peace, not the military or the intelligence community during times of armed conflict.

Among the Church Committee investigations into the five cases in the 1950s and 1960s, two—Castro and Lumumba—involved plots to kill political leaders as ends in themselves, in the absence of any broader political-military effort to overthrow a regime. The remaining plots against Diem, Trujillo, and Schneider were incidental to coups. In making its recommendations, the Church Committee made a distinction between the "targeted assassinations instigated by the United States" in the absence of any military conflict and "support for dissidents seeking to overthrow local governments."[16] The committee recommended that "targeted assassination" be prohibited, but it did not recommend any restrictions on U.S. support for coups, whether supported by the military or otherwise, even though the committee recognized that "the death of a foreign leader is a risk foreseeable in any coup attempt."[17] Indeed, the Reagan administration interpreted Executive Order 12333 specifically to "exempt[] death incidental to a military action"[18] from any executive order banning assassination.

In its final report, the Church Committee endorsed Ford's order, which banned government-sanctioned assassinations.[19] A Senate anti-assassination bill was pending at the time Ford issued his executive order. Ford did not endorse the Senate bill when he issued the order, although he agreed to support "legislation making it a crime to assassinate or attempt to conspire to assassinate a foreign official in peacetime."[20] In the 1970s and early 1980s, a number of legislative proposals that would create a flat ban against assassinations were introduced.[21] None of the proposals were ever successfully enacted into law. Numerous commentators writing during the Church Committee investigations have offered explanations for Congress's failure to legislate such a ban, including the apparent lack of public support,[22] Congress's unwillingness to fight with the intelligence community,[23] and difficulties involved in acquiring sufficient information from the intelligence community.[24] Ultimately, the reason why Congress has not legislated a ban against assassinations is probably the ambiguity that exists over the meaning of the term "assassination" itself.

Today, both scholars and policymakers alike have argued that changes in the contemporary security environment seriously undermine the continued peacetime applicability of any legal prohibition against killing regime leaders. One scholar of international relations, Ward Thomas, attributes the weakening of the "international norm against assassination" to two specific structural changes in the post–World War II international system.[25] The first is the increasing prevalence of unconventional violence, including guerrilla warfare and terrorism.[26] The second is the destructive and brutal nature of modern warfare, including but not limited to the advent of nuclear weapons and WMD. Indeed, the high level of concern in U.S. security considerations regarding asymmetric threats such as WMD use is unmistakable. The increasing challenges to state sovereignty, particularly from nations that threaten the peace with WMD; the very nature of the international political order; and its inability to contain such threatening actors may require policymakers to reexamine preexisting policies concerning foreign leaders.

Under any circumstances, the prohibition of peacetime killings of specifically targeted leaders was never intended to apply to all cases in which a leader's life may be lost. When the United States is engaged in armed hostilities with another country, it acts in accordance with the laws of war as developed under international law.

## INTERNATIONAL LAW: *JUS IN BELLO*

The principles derived from international law dealing with the use of force can be used to develop the pertinent criteria to consider when deciding whether to kill regime leaders during armed conflict. Under international law, two elements deal with the use of force: *jus ad bello*—the rules related to when a state can use force—and *jus in bello*—the rules related to how a state must conduct hostilities when engaged in the use of force. These international rules that guide states in their conduct against other states are based on both the practice and behavior of states, as well as the rules codified in international conventions or agreements between states.

To guide conduct during war, states, including the United States, abide by the principles of the laws of war as codified in the 1907 Hague Convention on the Laws and Customs of War and the 1949 Geneva Conventions.[27] When the United States is engaged in a state of armed hostilities, whether as a result of congressional declaration or presidential initiative,[28] the killing of enemy combatants is considered a legitimate act. Such enemy combatants may include regime leaders. Although no international law, including the Hague and Geneva Conventions, bans "assassinations" per se, the laws of war do recognize that there are limits to the means combatants may use to injure the enemy. These prohibitions would apply to any legitimate targets, including regime leaders.

According to Article 23(b) of the regulations annexed to the Hague Convention, "It is especially forbidden to kill or wound treacherously individuals belonging to the hostile nation or army."[29] Treacherous behavior would include deceit, such as a breach of confidence or a perfidious act or attack on an individual who justifiably believed that he had nothing to fear from the attacker. For example, the convention prohibits fighting under false pretenses that would include flying the enemy's flag or wearing the enemy's uniform to lure him to his death. The Hague Convention also forbids the use of weapons that would cause "unnecessary suffering" to the enemy, such as projectiles filled with glass, dum-dum bullets, or lances with barbed heads.[30] Also, according to the 1977 Protocols Additional to the Geneva Convention, Article 51 prohibits "indiscriminate attacks," defined in part as attacks where incidental injury to civilians or incidental damage to civilian objects would be "excessive in relation to the concrete and direct military advantage anticipated."[31]

There is precedent in U.S. military history of targeting regime leaders or aiming at targets that put leaders at risk during conflict. In 1986, U.S. Air Force and Navy planes bombed Libya after a Libyan terrorist attack against a nightclub frequented by U.S. soldiers in Berlin; Mu'ammar Qadhafi's tent was one of the targets. During Operation Desert Storm in 1991, the U.S. military bombed Saddam's official residences and command bunkers. Under international law, both of these actions were legitimate acts of self-defense against an ongoing threat; for purposes of the law, it is irrelevant whether an individual, including a regime leader, was a target. Under international law, if the United States had known that these attacks were going to occur before they actually had, it could have acted in self-defense preemptively, thus preventing the attack; killing the regime leader as part of this act of self-defense also would have been legitimate under international law, provided that the action was not carried out under any of the means of killing prohibited by the laws of war.

According to international law and U.S. domestic law, the president of the United States, in executing his constitutional authorities as commander in chief of the U.S armed forces, may legally order the killing of a regime leader as part of an armed conflict as long as it is not a "treacherous" killing, an indiscriminate killing, or cause "unnecessary pain and suffering." As commander in chief, the president alone is directly responsible for the use of force by the armed forces, and he alone must determine the appropriate, most effective means by which to bring the conflict to a conclusion. If the president were to determine that the most effective way to bring the armed conflict to a successful conclusion—minimizing the loss of life while accomplishing the objective of the conflict—is to eliminate the enemy state's leader, he has the legal authority to do so.

## Policy Merits to Targeting a Regime Leader

To evaluate the complex moral and practical, as well as legal, considerations involved in any policy of regime change by killing leaders, a close
analysis of the consequences of such an action is necessary. Depending
on the specific circumstances, the particular costs and benefits involved
should be weighed in making a final decision. Some of the advantages
and disadvantages may be different or nonexistent, and other factors
may emerge. Nevertheless, considering, in advance, some of the general
advantages and disadvantages of killing regime leaders can help security planners formulate criteria for evaluating specific cases.

• *Preclude greater atrocities.*

Can killing a regime's leader be morally justified? If a leader's death
would prevent the murder, torture, serious injury, or continued suffering of many innocent people, then killing that leader is clearly the best
option, at least according to some. Alternatively, large-scale use of
force or devastating economic sanctions might be employed, but such
actions are likely also to harm the same individuals who have already
suffered at the hands of the dictator. If international legal principles
based on moral considerations allow states to use deadly force in self-
defense, the same principles should provide for the use of deadly force
in defense of others. If an Adolf Hitler or a Milosevic had been assassi-
nated, millions of lives would have been saved from genocide. When
other policy alternatives are found to be ineffective, international law
grants states the right to take action, including removing a leader by
deadly force.

• *Minimize military and civilian casualties.*

Killing a regime leader and any other leaders in control of the regime
takes a far smaller toll on both sides' militaries than conventional war
would. Considering the dramatic differences in the numbers of deaths
likely to result from the two types of warfare—warfare against a state
and warfare against a leader—some, such as Ralph Peter, have criti-

cized any notion of ethical restrictions on killing a leader: "While it was acceptable to bomb those divisions of hapless conscripts, it was unthinkable to announce and carry out a threat to kill Saddam Hussein, although he bore overwhelming guilt for the entire war and its atrocities. ... Where is the ethical logic in this?"[32]

Moreover, killing a leader would prevent fewer innocent victims from becoming the collateral damage of an armed conflict. Even with precision-guided weapons, any type of armed conflict will inevitably cause the deaths of innocent victims. Although these victims may not have been direct targets in the conflict, that will matter little other than to provide legal protection to war fighters. Modern warfare is destructive, and the consequences of such wars may reverberate for far longer then the armed conflict itself. A world in which nuclear weapons are no longer the anomaly and WMD are readily available to both state and nonstate actors willing to use them must be especially wary of large-scale war.

For those such as Michael Walzer, a contemporary scholar on principles of just war, the military codes—principles of norms that control behavior in armed conflict—must "first be morally plausible" and "must correspond to our sense of what is right."[33] Only then can such principles, codes, or norms constrain behavior in conflict. Where, exactly, is the sense—or moral plausibility—in prohibiting the killing of one individual while allowing for the deaths of thousands of innocent people?

- *Disrupt the regime's brutal activities.*

Strategically removing a tyrannical regime leader may impair followers' ability to operate and carry out any command and control decisions. If the leader is a charismatic individual who cannot be replaced easily, his loss is likely to cause confusion and disarray. Particularly in the case of authoritarian regimes, where a single individual is often in power for many years, eliminating that leader is apt to lead to a lack of direction at the top level. Indeed, if a number of potential successors emerge, their vying for control may further exacerbate the disorder. If there is doubt about who perpetrated the killing, speculation may arise about an inside traitor and cause further deterioration among the leadership. The cumulative result of the confusion and disruption may lead to the interruption of operational direction, which, even if temporary, may give enough time to complete a regime change.

Depending on the status of the individuals immediately surrounding the regime leader who have command and control authority, removing those individuals by force may become necessary as well. At a minimum, a plan ought to be in place for dealing with those individuals until some stability has been reached. If these individuals resist with deadly force, however, nothing would prevent the armed forces from defending themselves and responding with deadly force.

- *Avoid complications of taking high-profile prisoners.*

If a regime leader is eliminated, he will not be in jail nor will he stand trial. The elimination of the leader avoids the potential for acts of reprisal or retribution against the state that holds the leader prisoner. It also prevents the leader from becoming a talisman for his followers or from seeking sovereign immunity for any illegal actions taken while he was head of state. Furthermore, if the leader remains at large or in criminal custody, he may still be able to communicate and to direct and control certain operations.

- *Prevent WMD use.*

Once a dictatorial regime leader and his command and control apparatus are eliminated, security forces and armed forces may take action to eliminate WMD that the regime may have acquired. By killing such regime leaders, the threat from these weapons is eliminated once and for all. Further, by using the element of surprise inherent in killing a regime leader, the leader will likely have little or no time to issue orders and coordinate the use of any of these weapons, thus preventing the unnecessary suffering those weapons could have inflicted on civilians and military personnel. By preventing the devastating harm that would befall victims of WMD use and minimizing the feelings of bitterness that would have ensued, the removal of the regime's leader may also bring the two sides closer to a lasting settlement with less of a chance that hostilities will reignite.

## Policy Arguments against Killing Leaders

Few observers would deny that some of these advantages are quite attractive, but national security planners also must consider the disadvantages to be weighed against them.

- *Moral questions.* Times may have changed, but in 1976, the Church Committee concluded that assassination "violates moral precepts fundamental to our way of life ... traditional American notions of fair play" and is not an acceptable foreign policy tool.[34] Irrespective of legal considerations and notwithstanding any policy considerations that support killing foreign leaders, consensus in the international community has historically held that it is an inappropriate means of conducting foreign policy. As far back as 1598, scholars such as Alberico Gentili condemned it on moral grounds, calling it a "shameful" and "wicked" practice and arguing that objectives of war should be achieved by valorous means.[35] Even in light of some recent congressional support to rescind Executive Order 12333's ban on assassination, a significant outcry might arise in Congress nonetheless if the president were formally to authorize killing a leader, whether at a time of war or peace.

- *Possible loss of U.S. domestic and international legitimacy.* If a presidentially approved policy to kill a regime leader were publicly disclosed, it might fracture any international support the president had garnered for the military conflict. For most of the international community, such a public approval of a morally questionable action would not be acceptable. Even if these nations privately supported the president's actions, it would be unlikely that they would be able to show their support of such an action publicly. Any perceived loss of legitimacy and any damage to the president's reputation could also have further long-term political implications, both domestically and internationally.

- *Retaliation.* A state that engages in plots to kill leaders also faces some short-term consequences that would be harmful to the interests of its leaders and to the interests of the state itself. For one, killing an enemy leader will inevitably arouse hostile feelings among the successors or followers of the regime leader against the perpetrators. Acknowledgement or disclosure of a state's involvement to the world would likely incite revenge against the individuals who authorized the targeting, creating a dangerous situation for any president. In a political system that is open to the public and where presidents frequently travel the globe, leaders are particularly vulnerable to such retaliatory assassination attempts.

  One way to minimize this danger would be to pursue assassination through covert means—never acknowledging any authorization of, or involvement in, an assassination—rather than as part of an overt military campaign. That nations find yielding to or accepting the terms of a secret, rather than public, threat much easier is well established. It is one thing for a president secretly to condone or authorize an activity that some states may question, whether for legal, political, or moral reasons. It is another thing for a president to broadcast the activity to the world, forcing states to respond, potentially causing a rift in otherwise positive relationships with those opposing such a U.S. action and potentially resulting in the withdrawal of support for the armed conflict.

- *International or regional instability.* Losing a leader may diminish a state's safety and security and may cause regional instability and unpredictability. To minimize this risk, any plan to kill a regime leader would have to exist within a broader strategy that contained options such as working in a cooperative fashion with any successors, legitimate followers of the former regime leader, and neighboring states in the region. Here the United Nations could play a useful role, helping to provide humanitarian aid and establishing legitimate domestic institutions that would accompany any regime change, with or without the loss of the former leader's life, although the level of international and UN support may well depend on the hidden identity of those responsible for killing the former leader. Particularly if the UN Security Council did not authorize the use of force in the first place, UN member states would be less likely to condone any intentional killing of a regime leader and may limit the support in building stability in the area.

- *Chances for success.* Targeting a regime leader and killing him may not be that easy. In fact, the United States does not have a good record of success in this area, particularly during times of peace. According to the Church Committee investigations, the United States made numerous attempts to kill Castro but failed repeatedly. Spy planes, bombers, and tanks can be quite effective in destroying an enemy's infrastructure. The targeted killing of a single or a few individuals, however, is much more difficult. With conventional weapons, it is rather easy to kill a lot of people but difficult to kill just one moving target. The ability to locate, track, and target an individual will depend on accurate and timely information. During a time of armed conflict, this task may not be easy to accomplish.

## When to Target Leaders

In the international community, states have always reserved the right to use force to maintain world order and safeguard their own defense. When containment fails, diplomacy is ineffective, and a full-scale war is too costly, killing a regime leader is an option a state should seriously consider. In a world in which states will amass WMD, unlawfully invade their neighbors, and threaten other's national and international security, national security experts and policymakers may need to reexamine their choices, including killing regime leaders, as a means of ensuring security.

If the international system were more adept at preventing threats to the peace of other nations or if the system were more effective at deterring or punishing such actions, a discussion about the legality, morality, and utility of killing regime leaders would not be necessary. In the absence of an effective collective security system, and in a world with increasingly dangerous weapons in the hands of actors willing to use them, killing regime leaders, however regrettable, may be an appropriate policy option.

When deliberating over some of the complex consequences of such a policy, policymakers may want to consider satisfying the following criteria:

- *The target.* The killing itself should be limited to the greatest extent possible to the persons within the regime that are responsible for the threats.

- A *level of certainty.* Accurate and reliable intelligence information that provides a high level of certainty of the identity of the individuals responsible for the threats should be accessible.

- A *likelihood of success.* It should be likely that the attempt to eliminate the leader will be successful and that the elimination of the leader will remedy the problem and do less harm to civilian populations then another option would.

- A *last resort.* There should be no other feasible, reasonable, less extreme way of stopping the regime leader's actions.

- A *proportionate action.* The killing of the regime leader should be proportionate to the threat posed by that leader, and the consequences of killing the regime leader should be less destructive than the use of conventional warfare to resolve the threat.

- A *discriminate action.* Targeting the responsible individuals should be likely to avoid the deaths of innocent victims.

It could be exceptionally difficult to determine these criteria, particularly in the fog of war, and decisions may be founded on erroneous information or assumptions. The only alternative to making these difficult determinations, however, would be a general renunciation of the killing of regime leaders as part of lawful armed conflict or a general reliance on more aggressive uses of force, such as full-scale war. This alternative, under a general ban on killing regime leaders, could ultimately result in thousands of innocent victims and the physical devastation of war—a far costlier means of ensuring international security.

## Notes

1.  George J. Church, "Saddam in the Cross Hairs," *Time*, October 8, 1990, p. 29.

2.  Eric L. Chase, "Should We Kill Saddam?" *Newsweek*, February 18, 1991, p. 16.

3.  John Prados, *Presidents' Secret Wars: CIA and Pentagon Covert Operations Since World War II* (Chicago: Ivan R. Dee, Inc., 1986). See also Select Senate Committee to Study Governmental Operations with Respect to Intelligence Activities, *Alleged Assassination Plots Involving Foreign Leaders*, S. Rep. No. 94-465 (Washington, D.C.: U.S. Government Printing Office, 1975), p. 1 (hereinafter Church Committee report).

4.  Church Committee Report, pp. 257, 259.

5.  Ibid.

6.  Ibid., p. 101; Executive Order No. 11,905, 5(g), 3 C.F.R. 90 (1976).

7.  Executive Order No. 12,036, 3 C.F.R. 112 (1978); Executive Order 12,333, 3 C.F.R. 200 (1981).

8.  See Paul Richter, "Congress Ponders Whether the U.S. Should Ease Ban on Assassinations," *Los Angeles Times*, September 18, 1998, p. A6; George Stephanopoloulos, "Why We Should Kill Saddam," *Newsweek*, December 1, 1997, p. 34; Newman and Bruce Bueno de Mesquita, "Repeal Order 12,333, Legalize 007," *New York Times*, January 26, 1989, p. A23.

9.  107th Cong., 1st sess., H.R. 19.

10. Brian Jenkins, "Assassination: Should We Stay the Good Guys?" *Los Angeles Times*, November 16, 1986, p. A2; Allan C. Miller, "Americans Favor Killing Saddam Hussein," *Los Angeles Times*, June 29, 1993, p. A6.

11. Miller, "Americans Favor Killing Saddam Hussein."

12. Ralph Peters, "A Revolution in Military Ethics?" *Parameters: The Journal of the Army War College* 26, no. 2 (summer 1996): 104.

13. *Black's Law Dictionary*, 7th ed. (1999), p. 104.

14. David M. Walker, *Oxford Companion to Law* (1980), p. 84.

15. Church Committee report, p. 1; app. A; 1118(e)(2), p. 289.

16. Ibid., p. 258.

17. Ibid., pp. 256–258.

18. See Daniel Schorr, "Stop Winking at the Ban," *Christian Science Monitor*, September 20, 2001, pp.1–2.

19. *Foreign and Military Intelligence: Final Report of the Select Committee to Study Governmental Operations With Respect to Intelligence Activities*, 94th Cong., 2d sess., 1976, S. Rept. 755, p. 448 n. 29.

20. "Special Message to the Congress Proposing Legislation to Reform the United States Foreign Intelligence Community," vol. I (public papers of Gerald R. Ford, February 18, 1976), p. 362 at 2.

21. See 94th Cong., 2d sess., H.R. 15542, sec. 9(1) (criminalizing assassination, introduced by Representative Robert N. McClory [R-Ill.]); 95th Cong., 2d sess., S. 2525 (banning assassination, introduced by 20 senators); 96th Cong., 2d sess., H.R. 6588, sec. 131; 96th Cong., 2d sess., S. 2284, sec. 131.

22. Nicholas M. Horrock, "The Meaning of Congressional Intelligence Inquiries," *New York Times*, April 30, 1976, p. A20.

23. Leslie Gelb, "Spy Inquiries Begun Amid Public Outrage, End in Indifference," *New York Times*, May 12, 1976, p. A20.

24. Ibid.

25. Ward Thomas, *Ethics of Destruction* (Ithaca: Cornell University Press, 2001), pp. 80–83.

26. For scholars analyzing terrorism and the implications for assassinations, see Jami Melissa Jackson, "Legality of Assassination of Independent Terrorist Leaders: An Examination of National and International Implications," *North Carolina Journal of International Law and Commercial Regulation* 24 (1999): 669; Daniel B. Pickard, "Legalizing Assassination: Terrorism, the Central Intelligence Agency and International Law," *Georgia Journal of International and Comparative Law* 30 (2001): 1.

27. *The Hague Convention on the Laws and Customs of War on Land, with Annex of Regulations*, October 18, 1907, 36 Stat. 2277, T.S. No. 539, 1 Bevans 631, Annex, art. 23, e (hereinafter Hague Convention).

28. U.S. Air Force, "International Law: The Conduct of Armed Conflict and Air Operations," AFP 110-31, November 19, 1976.

29. Hague Convention, arts. 22 and 23(b).

30. Hague Convention, art. 23e.

31. *The 1977 Protocols Additional to the Geneva Conventions*, December 12, 1977,

16 I.L.M. 1391, DA Pam 27-1-1, art. 51. Although the United States is not a signatory to Protocol I, it recognizes Article 51 as well as other articles of Protocol I as legally binding customary international law.

32. Peters, "A Revolution in Military Ethics?" p. 104.

33. See Michael Walzer, *Just and Unjust Wars*, rev. ed. (New York: Basic Books, 1991), p. 133.

34. Church Committee report, p. 257.

35. Alberico Gentili, *De Jure Beli Libri Tres* (1612), reprinted in *The Classics of International Law*, trans. John C. Rolfe (Oxford: Clarendon Press, 1933), p. 166.

David B. Rivkin Jr. and Darin R. Bartram

# Military Occupation: Legally Ensuring a Lasting Peace

The military occupation model, under which victorious belligerents occupy the territory of a defeated country and administer it for a period of time before turning power over to a successor government, is a viable and legal instrument of statecraft. It will remain so as long as war continues to be an accepted norm of international conduct. Indeed, rather than making military occupation illegal, international law prescribes the conditions under which military occupation should occur and regulates the way in which such an occupation should be carried out. Certain circumstances on the ground might lead policymakers not to adopt or pursue a lengthy military occupation or even a relatively short one, but policy imperatives always drive this choice; it is not a matter of law. Working within the parameters of a legal military occupation, an occupying power(s) can institute needed structural economic and democratic reforms to ensure a lasting peace with its adversary and restore international stability.

Significantly, the law of military occupation is an integral part of the law of armed conflict and is based on several multilateral conventions as well as centuries-old customary international law norms. Together

David B. Rivkin Jr. and Darin R. Bartram are partners in the Washington, D.C., office of Baker & Hostetler LLP. Mr. Rivkin served in the Department of Justice and in the White House during the Reagan and George H. W. Bush administrations. Both frequently write and comment on international law issues.

Copyright © 2003 by The Center for Strategic and International Studies and the Massachusetts Institute of Technology
*The Washington Quarterly* • 26:3 pp. 87–103.

with the rules governing when and how military force can be used, the rights and obligations of a belligerent occupier are carefully balanced to help inculcate a more responsible attitude toward the use of force. The decision to go to war should not be taken lightly, at least in part because being a victor and administering the territory of a defeated enemy triggers an awesome set of responsibilities.

Often-invoked arguments that modern international law bars military occupation are either misinformed about historical precedent and doctrine or, more likely, are being employed to oppose a war for other reasons. This was clearly the case during the prelude to war in Iraq as many U.S. allies and most U.S. adversaries made a concerted effort to limit U.S. freedom to use force, arguing that, without the United Nations Security Council's explicit blessing, international law bars the United States from resorting to force unilaterally or even multilaterally. A similar set of legalistic arguments, setting forth unrealistic expectations about the legal rules applicable in combat, such as the permissible extent of collateral damage and the obligation to commence humanitarian relief operations promptly, was employed by war opponents while the combat operations in Iraq unfolded. Now, having effected the regime change in Iraq, the United States and its coalition partners face yet another specious set of legal arguments, threatening to impede or even vitiate entirely their legal rights to administer Iraq as belligerent occupiers.

The current case of Iraq and the rights and obligations of the United States and coalition forces as occupying powers following the defeat of Saddam Hussein's regime illustrates the broader issues associated with military occupation as a means of accomplishing regime change. Even today, however, this is not the only relevant case. Postconflict reconstruction and nation building is still underway in Afghanistan, and the concepts undoubtedly come into play when considering Israel's status as an occupying power in Gaza and the West Bank. In light of the new threat of weapons of mass destruction (WMD) and the increased need to take preemptive action against rogue states threatening to use them, the rights and obligations of an occupying power are likely to be at issue more now and in the future than they have been for half a century.

## Weighing the Options

Although the regime change in Iraq has been effected by coalition forces, many issues relating to how post-Saddam Iraq will be governed remain unresolved, including the precise roles to be played by the United States and its coalition partners and other countries, as well as the European Union and the UN. The only model that is not under consideration in Iraq is the notion that, once the U.S.-led coalition deposed Saddam's regime, everybody would simply go home. All serious stakeholders have come to realize that, if Iraq is to be prevented from posing a future threat to regional and international security, the United States, other coalition members, and international organizations will have to play a long-term role in rebuilding and restructuring that country. The administration's oft-articulated goals of fostering democracy in Iraq and facilitating other democratic transitions in the Arab world also require a sustained engagement on the ground.

The realization that a difficult set of issues surrounding Iraq's political and economic transformation will have to be addressed by the coalition countries has prompted significant debate both within the administration and in broader circles. In the last several months, some administration officials have proposed instituting a military occupation government much like those that emerged in Germany and Japan after World War II. Other arguments call for a prompt transition of authority to a successor administration, à la Afghanistan, with the government most likely composed of a coalition of Iraqi dissidents, religious and civic leaders, and possibly some junior civil servants and local and regional government officials who are not too closely aligned with Sadd_us clique. Another argument, advanced by most U.S. allies and n˪e of nongovernmental organizations (NGOs), favors postwar go⸳ Iraq driven by the Security Council.

The military occupation model provides the U˫⸱ coalition partners with the greatest flexibility.nim changes to Iraq's political and economic s⸱ UN's track record in rebuilding war-torr

⸱s and its
⸳nt durable
⸳contrast, the
⸱impressive; its

123

legal right to govern postwar Iraq is uncertain; and the ability of an Iraqi successor administration to be constructed quickly and to run the vast bureaucracy of the government is low.

## The Policy Debate

Legal issues aside, the policy merits of the occupation option have not drawn widespread acclamation. Most U.S. European allies, for example, have expressed a strong preference for a UN-led, post-Saddam Iraq. Not surprisingly, virtually all Iraqi dissidents also oppose military occupation, particularly the Kurds, who for many years have been enjoying de facto independence. To be clear, there is no apparent international opposition (with the possible exception of France and Russia) to a relatively short—measured in months—U.S. and British military occupation. Most realize that some form of military rule will be needed to tackle such urgent tasks as completing the eradication of Iraq's WMD; ending all military opposition from the remnants of the old regime, including suppressing any large-scale guerrilla activities; and launching needed humanitarian relief and reconstruction operations. There is also consensus that any protracted U.S. and British military occupation would be both undesirable and unnecessary. Thus, the debate about military occupation really focuses on the pros and cons of any type of midterm occupation, lasting from 10 months up to 2–3 years.

In the United States, many in the media and in Congress, despite their oft-expressed desire to build democracy in post-Saddam Iraq, have been quite skeptical about the benefits to the long-term development of Iraq that could be set in motion by a military occupation. Support this option has not been universal even within the administration. are on to debate among political appointees, some army officers 60,00 ed that the military occupation duties might tie up 45,000– or as m oops (the low-end estimate by the Joint Chiefs of Staff) the army ,000 U.S. troops (the high-end estimate furnished by the bulk of taff, Gen. Eric Shinseki), with the army providing ver. The army's fear is that major resource commitments will constrain the ability of the United States to operate elsewhere in the world and that an Iraq occupation-related mission will be tough, unglamorous, and potentially career threatening for senior army officers.

The major reason for opposition within the United States, however, is the belief that a military occupation government led by U.S. forces would greatly inflame Arab and Muslim hostility. These arguments are not unreasonable, but ultimately, they appear wanting. It would be difficult for even the most biased Arab media to condemn a well-run military government, in which the United States shared responsibility with other countries and rapidly improved Iraq's economic and civil affairs, particularly if Iraqi people were demonstrably managing local affairs and the arrangement was helping to promote good relations among the various ethnic groups in Iraq.

Moreover, the military occupation model offers two immediate diplomatic benefits for the United States. First, it could help the United States build and maintain a broader post-Saddam coalition because joining such a coalition would be a legal prerequisite to participation in the occupation government, as was the case in post–World War II Germany. This factor was particularly influential in shaping the thinking of several key Arab leaders about the war in Iraq. Once they realized that the U.S. military campaign against Saddam was inevitable, their interest in having a meaningful role in postwar Iraq became an important policy driver. Shortly before the bombing began, Saudi Arabia's ambassador to the United States, Prince Bandar bin Sultan, was quoted as saying that, "once we join the club [the anti-Saddam coalition], then we can negotiate what Iraq will be like after the war. But, without being a part of the club, then we have no role in the day after."[1]

In addition, even though the intense French opposition—a position backed by Russia and China—to the use of U.S. military power in Iraq prevented the Bush administration from getting the Security Council to pass yet another use-of-force authorizing resolution, the military occupation model may well offer some important UN-related diplomatic benefits in the future. Specifically, the administration may find it easier to procure a new Security Council resolution confirming U.S. occupation rights and obligations in Iraq if support for such a resolution becomes the benchmark for involvement in postwar Iraq.

Obtaining the UN imprimatur for a military occupation of Iraq is likely to be a difficult process with an uncertain outcome. Precisely because they realize the diplomatic, economic, and political leverage that comes with militarily occupying a territory, the French have already indicated that they would veto any Security Council resolution that would confirm the U.S. and British belligerent occupation rights in postwar Iraq. It remains to be seen whether France's diplomatic obstructionism after the war will prove as successful as its prewar efforts.

Unfortunately, the prospects for a broad accord between the United States and all of its traditional allies are not promising because the efforts of France, Belgium, and a few other members of "old" Europe have permutated beyond just occupation-related matters in an effort to limit U.S. freedom to use force. In addition to such *jus ad bellum* doctrinal musings, efforts have been made to constrain the way in which the United States can use force legitimately once the fighting starts. Such *jus in bello* doctrinal innovations deal with matters such as the extent of permissible collateral damage, targeting individual commanders as distinct from attacking enemy troops en masse, engaging dual-use targets (e.g., bridges and power stations), and a host of other combat-related issues. The overall underlying goal is to complicate U.S. efforts to practice its customary and successful way of war, which emphasizes speed and massive yet discriminate use of firepower.

Not satisfied with advancing a set of policy arguments concerning the combination of the *jus ad bellum* and *jus in bello* issues, parallel efforts have been undertaken to assert, also allegedly as a matter of law, that a military occupation model or any efforts to change the political make-up of the defeated country in the aftermath of war are proscribed. Shortly after the war against Iraq began, France and Russia demonstrated their intent to make the U.S.-led military occupation of Iraq as burdensome as possible, with the Russian envoy to the UN asserting—contrary to the entire set of international law bearing on occupying powers' rights and obligations—that occupying belligerents must "make reparations for the damages caused in the conflict."

Here again, policy arguments masquerade as law. If one were to assume the illegality of effecting a regime change in Iraq, this would vitiate all reasons for commencing the war. Having been presented with decades of repression and aggressive conduct by Saddam's regime and his defiance of various Security Council resolutions for years, the notion that all coalition forces could have done would be to disarm his regime and then withdraw is absurd on its face. Indeed, all of the doctrinal innovations related to the laws of armed conflict, even if followed in their somewhat milder version, would greatly complicate U.S. recourse to force, both against Iraq and in other conflict scenarios for the foreseeable future. In their most extreme version, these doctrinal innovations would permanently leash the U.S. use of force.

In any event, the military occupation model is both legal and useful and, although not a panacea, makes it easier for the United States to handle the daunting political, economic, and security challenges it faces in post-Saddam Iraq. As the problems encountered in Afghanistan demonstrate, once power is transferred to a successor regime, the U.S. government's ability to influence the new regime's policies and push it to make difficult policy choices becomes quite constrained. For example, despite otherwise exemplary cooperation with the United States, President Hamid Karzai has been quite reluctant to move against his country's recalcitrant regional warlords.

Meanwhile, the Security Council–driven governance model is certain to be plagued by numerous disagreements among council members, pitting the United States and Great Britain against France, Russia, and China. There is already ample evidence that disputes among the permanent Security Council members are alive and well and likely to be just as contentious in the postwar period as were the prewar debates about authorizing the use of force. Moreover, the track record of UN-controlled postconflict operations demonstrates a very low level of basic managerial competence. More than four years into the UN tenure in Kosovo, electric service in Pristina has yet to be fully restored.[2] On the other hand, having U.S. and coalition forces retain the levers of power, while delegating responsibilities for local and regional governance to the indigenous Iraqi leaders and Iraqi dissidents, would avoid the problems (such as inexperience with running a large-scale bureaucracy to meet the needs of the entire Iraqi population) associated with other options and enable the United States to pursue an ambitious set of economic and political reforms.

There is also no reason to believe that military occupation will demand a great deal of U.S. and British human resources. Just as the United States can wage war by drawing on both high-quality U.S. troops and indigenous military forces (as was the case in Afghanistan), it certainly can augment its occupation forces with Iraqi military and civilian personnel. This situation is similar to post–World War II Germany and Japan, where U.S. occupation authorities were able to utilize the services of thousands of German and Japanese nationals who functioned as interpreters, advisers, police officers, mayors, and civil servants.

Nor does the occupation model require U.S. and British authorities to be responsible, even during the early stages, for all aspects of Iraq's governance. Indeed, it is both feasible and desirable to transfer the control of at least some national-level ministries to Iraqi officials very quickly. Furthermore, depending on the progress made, Iraqi officials can also assume many local and regional government functions. Using this approach, the military occupation authorities would retain control over areas dealing only with security, key political issues, and economic matters. This entire arrangement and the pace of the eventual transition would be very flexible and responsive to the developments on the ground in any similar situation.

## Lessons from Germany and Japan

Immediate benefits aside, the military occupation paradigm—appropriately revised to accommodate some trends in post–World War II international law and the unique circumstances of Iraq—arguably offers the best opportunity for the United States to effect sorely needed long-term positive political and economic changes in both Iraq and the Persian Gulf region. The lessons of the German and the Japanese occupations are quite instructive for U.S. involvement in postwar Iraq; both were tremendous successes at transforming aggressors with war-ravaged economies into productive, free societies, and both defied contemporary skeptics.

Clearly, there are differences between Iraq in 2003 and Japan and Germany in 1945. On one hand, Iraq presents the difficulties of factionalism. On the other hand, Germany and Japan had devastated economies after their defeat, while Iraq—given the precise targeting employed by coalition forces—has much of its infrastructure and economy intact. Thus, although Iraq is indeed a new and different case, these differences are both positive and negative, and the overall level of success of a military occupation in Iraq might well be, on balance, very similar to that achieved in Japan and Germany.

In the case of Germany, the Allied powers, having accepted Germany's unconditional surrender, became the country's effective rulers for several years. Supreme Allied Commander Gen. Dwight D. Eisenhower was vested with vast rights and obligations in his role on the Allied Control Council: "You are, by virtue of your position, clothed with supreme legislative, executive, and judicial authority in the areas occupied by forces under your command. This authority will be broadly construed and includes authority to take all measures deemed by you necessary, appropriate or desirable in relation to military exigencies and the objectives of a firm military government."[3] Although the victorious Allies legally would have been justified in legislating as the sovereign government of Germany, they·chose not to do so; instead, they proffered a package of reforms that were enacted by the German government once it was vested with appropriate legislative powers. The primary goal of the occupation was:

> [to] prevent Germany from ever again becoming a threat to the peace of the world. Essential steps in the accomplishment of this objective are the elimination of Nazism and militarism in all their forms, the immediate apprehension of war criminals for punishment, the indus-

trial disarmament and demilitarization of Germany, with continuing control over Germany's capacity to make war, and the preparation for an eventual reconstruction of German political life on a democratic basis.[4]

The military government, which was directed to demilitarize Germany, engaged in a broad denazification program. This policy was applied statewide, with the exception of the Soviet-controlled zone, which slipped behind the Iron Curtain. As a result of the Allies' efforts, the entire political, legal, and educational system of West Germany was reformed. Allied-run military commissions arrested and prosecuted hundreds of war criminals. The military occupation was basically over by 1949, and Germany promptly rejoined the family of democratic nations, becoming a full-fledged member of NATO and a key player in the new postwar Europe.

In the case of Japan, its postwar government retained sovereign power, at least formally. In the 1945 Instrument of Surrender, however, Japan conceded a number of key prerogatives to the Allied powers, including the right to punish war criminals. (Unlike the case of Germany, the United States was the only foreign power to govern Japan. The Far East Commission, comprising the 11 Allied powers, failed to be an effective organization because of Cold War–related tensions among the members.) Given the daunting task of running Japan through military occupation, however, the United States decided to act largely through the existing Japanese government structures. Emperor Hirohito retained his title, although his role became symbolic rather than substantive. Accordingly, Japan agreed to "comply with all requirements which may be imposed by the Supreme Commander for the Allied Powers, or by agencies of the Japanese Government at his direction."[5]

Over the course of his six-year rule of occupied Japan, Gen. Douglas MacArthur rewrote the country's laws, including its constitution; revised school textbooks; and attempted to break the grip of the monopolistic *zaibatsu* on the Japanese economy. Through the newly formed Japanese legislature, the Diet, MacArthur implemented the Deconcentration Law in 1947, which made great strides toward weakening the centralized control of industries. MacArthur enacted major land reforms and expanded civil rights, particularly for women. Articles 13 and 19 of Japan's new constitution provided a progressive statement on human rights in its prohibition of discrimination on the basis of race, sex, social status, creed, or family origin. When the general had accomplished the many reforms, the United States and Japan signed a formal peace treaty—the Treaty of San Francisco—in September 1951. After the treaty took effect on April 28, 1952, Japan again assumed full sovereignty. The military occupation of Japan enabled the United States to implement reforms to ensure a lasting peace with Japan—reforms designed not to gain an economic advantage from victory but to improve the political and economic landscape of that country.

## The Legal Debate

Centuries-old norms of customary international law, which permitted occupying powers to wield the totality of sovereign powers that had formerly been vested in the defeated governments, guided the victorious Allies' rule of Germany and Japan. Since then, to note but one key change, the UN Charter has come into force, with Article 2.4 indicating that "[a]ll members shall refrain in their international relations from the threat or use of force against the territorial integrity or political independence of any state." Construed literally, this admonition would bar any efforts, for example, to effect a regime change in a foreign country. Indeed, many opponents of intervention in Iraq—whether for the purpose of effecting an immediate regime change or to institute an interim military government—rely on this article blindly, without considering its context within the UN Charter in particular or within the whole of international law.

The literal reading of Article 2 also can be plausibly supported by Article 107 of the charter, which specifically exempts from the charter's reach any actions taken against the former Axis powers. The implication here is that the Allied occupation of Germany and Japan might have departed from the charter's strictures but that the charter's prescriptions only looked forward. This interpretation of Article 2, however, even when buttressed by Article 107, would vitiate the entire venerable law of military occupation. It would also run counter to Article 51, which indicates that "nothing in the present charter shall impair the inherent right of individual or collective self-defense." Indeed, the literal reading of Article 2 would prevent victims of even repeated aggression from doing anything more than liberating their own territory and would certainly bar such victims or their allies from taking the war to the aggressor.

Given the entire experience of World War II, which provided the formative basis for the UN system, this interpretation of the UN Charter is most implausible. The more reasonable interpretation of Article 2 is that it prohibits states, even when exercising the right of self-defense, from dismembering or absorbing an enemy state, but it does not bar or impair the right to engage in a military occupation to change the regime of that state.

The 1949 Geneva Convention Relative to the Protection of Civilian Persons in Time of War supports this contextual interpretation of Article 2. A literal reading of Article 2 would have ruled out any form of belligerent occupation, thus rendering the 1949 Geneva Convention, which defines precisely how a belligerent occupation is to occur, entirely superfluous. Far from banning occupation altogether, the convention provides a whole array of prescriptions that require the occupying state to ensure the provision of food and access to civilians by relief agencies as well as a number of proscriptions, which prohibit forcible deportations, detention without trial, and destruction of property. The agreement has been signed by 189 countries, including the United States and Iraq. Significantly, the 1949 convention came into force after the UN Charter was ratified.

Under the convention's terms, the United States has wide latitude to implement a number of positive reforms during the course of its occupation. Both the Geneva Convention and customary international law allow the United States and its coalition partners to carry out activities designed to eliminate all military and guerrilla opposition, ensure the safety of coalition troops and personnel, secure WMD stockpiles, carry out whatever other disarmament tasks they consider appropriate, and maintain law and order.

An occupying coalition force is not just permitted, but is obligated, to establish the orderly governance of Iraq. For this reason, the United States and other coalition countries arguably cannot delegate the responsibility for the postwar governance of Iraq to the UN or any other entity. The belligerent occupying powers have the ultimate responsibility and obligation to administer the country whose government they have just displaced, at least until a new national government vested with all attributes of sovereignty has been created. Although they can enlist the support of other countries, international organizations, and NGOs, the ultimate responsibility must remain with the belligerent occupying powers. In this regard, Article 43 of the Hague Conventions of 1907 imposes an affirmative obligation to administer a country following conquest and directly addresses the transfer of power, providing as follows: "The authority of the legitimate power having in fact passed into the hands of the occupant, the latter shall take all measures in his power to restore, and ensure, as far as possible, public order and safety, while respecting, unless absolutely prevented, the laws in force in the country."[6]

Meanwhile, the *U.S. Army Field Manual*—a single document containing the Hague Regulations, Geneva conventions, and other documents relating to customary international law, compiled by the U.S. Department of the Army in 1956—depicts this obligation as follows:

> Being an incident of war, military occupation confers upon the invading force the means of exercising control for the period of occupation. It does not transfer the sovereignty to the occupant, but simply the authority or power to exercise some of the rights of sovereignty. The exercise of these rights results from the established power of the occupant and from the necessity of maintaining law and order, indispensable both to the inhabitants and to the occupying force.[7]

Under Article 55 of the 1949 Geneva Convention, the United States has a duty to provide food and medical supplies to the Iraqi population and, in cooperation with national and local authorities, to provide for their hygiene and public health, including maintaining the medical and hospital establishment. The convention also requires that the free exercise of religion in Iraq be permitted,[8] and that the occupying power undertake relief measures[9] and facilitate the proper workings of education systems for children.[10]

Thus, international law not only permits the military occupation of a defeated country in the form of the Hague Regulations and the Geneva conventions but also carefully and comprehensively orchestrates that occupation. To be sure, the documents do not set out the length of occupation but this matter clearly will very much depend on the ability and willingness of the next Iraqi administration to assume responsibility for running the country. The United States has stated its commitment to providing interim governance, which will be subject to the terms of the Geneva conventions, the Hague Regulations, and other terms contained in the *U.S. Army Field Manual.*

## Utilizing Indigenous Infrastructure and Resources

Although military occupation laws oblige the occupying powers to ensure the public welfare of the civilian population, they would not need to carry that burden alone. The Geneva Convention's Article 51 allows the coalition forces to require that Iraqi workers carry out many or most of the government services, provided the services are primarily for the benefit of Iraqi civilians. In fact, given the sheer magnitude of this task, in a country of 22 million people, it would be impossible to deliver necessary services and keep the peace without the assistance of existing Iraqi institutions. These workers must be paid, of course, and their efforts must be directed only at the needs of the civilian population, but these limitations would not deter the use of Iraqi citizens.

The United States and coalition forces will have to sort out the various claims of those who hold private contract interests in the Iraqi economy, particularly in the oil industry. Article 43 of the Hague Regulations gives the occupying power the authority to establish courts. Undoubtedly, many foreign companies will claim an interest in redeveloping the petroleum industry; at the same time, the viability and long-term value of those claims even under Saddam's authoritarian regime were in some doubt.

Whether the occupying powers are obliged to recognize those claims in a post-Saddam Iraq should be determined by a tribunal established specifically for this purpose. Although such a tribunal can certainly be staffed by the coalition countries' personnel, given the political sensitivity of invalidating or even just reforming the various one-sided contracts that foreign companies signed with Saddam's pariah regime, it might be preferable to have Iraqi officials handle this task, with this particular function being one of those transferred quickly by the coalition occupation authorities to an Iraqi transition government.

To handle pre–military occupation legal issues that might come into play, particularly to ensure that all the senior officials of Saddam's regime are punished for war crimes and other offenses, the United States can and should rely on Iraqi courts to the maximum extent possible. This approach would underscore the U.S. commitment to and preference for national legal institutions as the best forum for handling the prosecution of international law offenses.[11] Using Iraqi courts for this purpose would also help mute the inevitable criticism in the Arab world if Iraqi officials were prosecuted directly by the United States. At the same time, to provide an appropriate fallback if Iraqi officials prove unwilling or unable to carry out their duties, the United States should consider obtaining the same rights to prosecute war criminals that the Japanese government ceded to General MacArthur. Under the 1949 Geneva Convention Articles 64 and 66, the occupying powers would retain broad penal and law enforcement authority, subjecting Iraq's population to laws that are necessary to maintain an orderly government and guarantee the security of the occupation troops.

In any case, existing international law fully empowers the U.S. military to prosecute, through its courts martial and military commissions, those Iraqi officials who have committed war crimes and other offenses against the laws of war, including unlawful combatancy against U.S.

troops from the period beginning with the Persian Gulf War in 1991 to the present.

The management of postwar Iraq is a daunting task, to say the least, but it need not be a significant economic drain on the U.S. economy. Under the 1907 Hague Regulations, occupying powers are lawfully entitled to take control of Iraq's sovereign assets and use them for all appropriate government purposes. The *U.S. Army Field Manual* notes that the costs to the occupied state's economy should not be more than it could reasonably be expected to bear.[12] Article 53 of the Hague Regulations states that an occupying army can "only take possession of cash, funds, and realizable securities which are strictly the property of the State, depots of arms, means of transport, stores and supplies, and, generally, all movable property belonging to the State which may be used for military operations." In the case of Iraq, these resources are substantial.

Unspent Iraqi oil-for-food funds, currently held in various UN escrow accounts pursuant to Security Council resolutions (principally 661 [1990], 986 [1995], 1284 [1999], and 1409 [2002]), are clearly an Iraqi national asset that can be used for reconstruction. Indeed, the occupying powers would even be entitled to recoup all the costs associated with governing Iraq during the occupation. At the same time, the United States cannot use the occupation of Iraq as a profit-making operation because the concepts of private war, with the attending looting and pillaging, were rejected as long ago as the nineteenth century.[13]

Article 55 of the Hague Regulations supports the right of the occupying state to use the natural resources of the enemy state. The resources can be subject to normal use in the administration of a country but not depleted:

> The occupying State shall be regarded only as administrator and usufructuary of public buildings, real estate, forests, and agricultural estates belonging to the hostile State, and situated in the occupied country. It must safeguard the capital of these properties, and administer them in accordance with the rules of usufruct.[14]

Building on this, Article 55 of the 1949 Geneva Convention permits the occupying power to requisition foodstuffs, articles, and medical supplies needed for use by the occupation forces and administrative personnel, provided that the needs of the civilian population have been taken into account. If not for the current restrictions on the sale of Iraqi oil, however, the country's economy could bear a significant portion, if not the entire portion, of that country's reconstruction and rebuilding costs. Indeed, the U.S. Department of Energy estimates that Iraq possesses 112 billion barrels of oil and can produce about 2 million barrels per day,[15] but this production could increase by about 50 percent if current production hurdles were overcome. Concerning the UN sanctions-related resolutions, one can argue that those resolutions were predicated upon and could only be implemented within the context of a Saddam-led regime or a similar Iraqi government running that country. Under this approach, the regime change effected by the coalition forces has effectively vitiated these resolutions and, although a new Security Council resolution confirming this fact would be helpful politically, it is not legally required.

There is a significant distinction between the use of natural resources to meet the occupying state's needs arising from the occupation and the acquisition to satisfy general military or civilian needs. This matter has a well-established litigation history, with the Singapore Oil Stock Case being the lead example.[16] During World War II, the Japanese occupation authorities seized oil stocks from Dutch owners. Upon Japan's defeat, the Dutch owners sued to recover their property, arguing that the title to the property never passed to Japan because the original Japanese confiscation was illegal. The War Damage Commission, convened to hear claims following the war, upheld the Dutch claims. It noted that, although stocks were indeed immovable property that could be taken by the Japanese, it was a violation of international law for Japan to have used oil for the "purpose of supplying the naval, military, and civilian needs of Japan," rather than using it for occupation costs.[17]

Another exercise of occupation authority to produce oil was vigorously contested when the Israelis, having taken control of the Sinai Desert during the Six-Day War, began drilling for oil. This oil was used both for occupation costs and for general revenue. The U.S. Department of State took the position that Israel could properly draw from already producing wells but could not engage in new exploration.[18] Israel took the position that the 1907 Hague Regulations only prohibited the wanton waste or destruction of an asset.[19] The resulting general consensus on the issue was that the use of existing wells to finance the costs of occupation is acceptable, but not to generate general revenue. With regard to Iraq, it appears that existing oil fields would provide enough oil for the foreseeable future, and therefore, the more difficult issue of whether an occupying state can engage in new exploration does not need to be answered.[20]

With the regime change in Iraq now complete, the United States faces a number of legal, diplomatic, and military imperatives, all of which would require it to create an effective interim governance structure. During the period of occupation, the U.S.-led coalition government would have the opportunity to address and propose ways to resolve the difficult set of governance, cultural, and religious issues related to the Kurds, Shi'ites, and Sunnis, as well as establish the proper balance between the national and local governing structures. The military government could also implement needed economic reforms, including measures to minimize corruption to ensure that Iraqi oil revenues directly benefit the country's people. A rapid improvement in the quality of life of the Iraqi population would be key to achieving long-term stability and acceptance of the reforms.

The occupation government must be able to cope with continuing security-related missions, such as the completion of Iraq's disarmament and possible combat against elements of the Iraqi military or paramilitary units that may continue to engage in intermittent resistance, as well as constructing new economic and political institutions capable of governing the country in the years to come. The ideal model is a military occupation regime, led by the United States and all the other countries that have joined the anti-Saddam coalition. The precise level of involvement would depend on the level of support provided by those countries and their interest in participating in the occupation regime. To the maximum extent possible, the postwar occupation forces should rely on existing Iraqi institutions and, when appropriate, should allow transition to self-government for well-pacified and well-reformed portions of Iraq. The legal and policy experiences amassed during the German and Japanese occupation, and the strictures of the 1907 Hague Regulations and the 1949 Geneva Convention, provide excellent context for a legal and efficient belligerent governance of Iraq. In turn, lessons to be drawn from the Iraqi post-Saddam governance experience will be instructive for future uses of a belligerent occupation model.

## Winning the Peace Is the Issue

Upon examination of an entire range of criticisms and policy arguments used in the ongoing debate about military occupation to govern postwar Iraq, it is difficult not to conclude that the real dispute is not about military occupation itself. Rather, it comes down to the more fundamental issues relating to the endgame in Iraq and, thus, the real debate is about the ends, not the means. To the extent that the means matter, it is undeniable that a military occupation model would allow the United States and its coalition partners maximum leverage and flexibility for dealing with difficult and potentially dangerous postwar challenges in Iraq.

There is also little doubt that, at the end of the day, the assessment of the U.S. role will be based largely if not exclusively on the political, economic, and security environment the coalition will be able to establish in post-Saddam Iraq. How the United States was able to achieve these results is not likely to be of much significance, provided, of course, that the United States acts lawfully.

Because military occupation remains fully compliant with the relevant norms of international law, the United States would be acting lawfully if it chooses to use this model for governing Iraq. Arguments to the contrary have no legal merit and are advanced by countries and organizations that have decided to use pseudolegalistic assertions to oppose and constrain the exercise of U.S. military power both in Iraq and elsewhere. The global community should pay these naysayers no heed.

## Notes

1. Antony Shadid, "War's Aftermath Now Arabs' Focus," *Washington Post*, February 21, 2003, p. A1.

2. For an excellent discussion of Kosovo's reconstruction problems and the UN's role, see Stephen Schwartz, "U.N. Go Home," *Weekly Standard*, April 14, 2003, pp. 28–34.

3. See "Directive to Commander-in-Chief of United States Forces of Occupation Regarding the Military Government of Germany," April 1945, www.usembassy.de/usa/etexts/ga3-450426.pdf (accessed April 17, 2003).

4. Ibid.

5. First Instrument of Surrender, September 2, 1945, www.taiwandocuments.org/surrender01.htm (accessed April 17, 2003).

6. Convention IV, Article 43, Respecting the Laws of Customs of War on Land, U.S.T.S. 539, October 18, 1907.

7. *U.S. Army Field Manual* (1956), 27–10, para. 358.

8. Geneva Convention, art. 55.

9. Ibid., art. 60.

10. Ibid., art. 50.

11. See Lee Casey and David Rivkin, "The National Justice," *Washington Times*, March 26, 2003, p. A23.

12. *U.S. Army Field Manual*, 27–10, art. 364.

13. The Lieber Code of 1863 was assembled by Francis Lieber at Abraham Lincoln's instruction as a code of conduct for Union troops during the Civil War.

14. Hague Regulations, art. 55.

15. Energy Information Administration, U.S. Department of Energy, "Iraq," in *EIA Country Analysis Briefs* (February 2003), www.eia.doe.gov/emeu/cabs/iraq.html (accessed April 10, 2003).

16. *N.V. de Batafsche Petroleum Maatschappij and others v. The War Damage Commission*, Singapore Court of Appeal, *American Journal of International Law* 51 (1956): 802.

17. Ibid., p. 803.

18. *Department of State Memorandum of Law on Israel's Right to Develop New Oil Fields in Sinai and Gulf of Suez*, 16 I.L.M. 733 (1977).

19. *Ministry of Foreign Affairs Memorandum of Law on the Right to Develop New Fields in Sinai and the Gulf of Suez*, 17 I.L.M. 432 (1978).

20. See Dobie Langenkamp, "What Happens to the Oil: International Law and the Occupation of Iraq," January 17, 2003, www.energy.uh.edu/documents/behind_the_gas_pump/DobieLangenkamp.pdf (accessed April 17, 2003).

**Barry Rubin**

# Lessons from Iran

The paradoxes of foreign-initiated regime change can be better understood by analyzing the U.S. role in overthrowing Iranian prime minister Muhammad Mossadegh, who took power in 1951, and in ensuring the shah's rule after the countercoup in August 1953. By reviewing the longer-term significance of foreign involvement in regime change in Iran in 1953, without necessarily dwelling in this analysis on the details of the original events, applicable lessons may be derived for the situation in the contemporary Middle East. Without a doubt, U.S. involvement in Iran in 1953 is the most important previous instance of U.S. action to bring about regime change in the region.

## Was Iran in 1953 Really Regime Change?

Before the events in Iran involving the United States, two other countries tried to change the Iranian regime. British intervention forced the abdication of the shah's father in 1941 and brought Muhammad Reza

Barry Rubin is director of the Global Research in International Affairs (GLORIA) Center in Herziliya, Israel, and editor of the *Middle East Review of International Affairs*. His recent books include *The Tragedy of the Middle East* and *Anti-American Terrorism and the Middle East*. His biography of Yasir Arafat was published by Oxford University Press in July 2003.

Copyright © 2003 by The Center for Strategic and International Studies and the Massachusetts Institute of Technology
*The Washington Quarterly* • 26:3 pp. 105–115.

Shah Pahlavi to the throne in the first place. At that time, London acted to remove pro-German aspirants to power from Tehran as part of a great-power struggle—World War II in this case—just as motivations in 1953 aimed to prevent the rise of a group suspected of pro-Soviet sympathies during the great-power struggle of the Cold War.

Then, in 1946 the United States, to counteract the Soviet Union's attempt at regime change, exerted major pressure on that nation after Moscow, which had temporarily occupied northern Iran during World War II, installed two pro-Soviet puppet republics in the Kurdish and Azeri regions of Iran. The United States forced Moscow to keep its earlier commitment to pull out of Iran within six months of the end of World War II, leading to the quick collapse of these regimes and the consolidation of the shah's power.

The events of 1953, although fascinating in greater detail, can easily be condensed for these purposes.[1] In the early 1950s, Mossadegh—a populist nationalist of great personal eccentricity—nationalized the British-controlled oil company in Iran and allied himself with the Tudeh (Communist) Party, among others, to compete with the shah for power. Subsequent British pressure on other countries not to buy oil produced by the nationalized company seriously harmed Iran's economy. Fearing for his regime, the shah and some of his loyalists—along with the British—requested U.S. help in 1952 to bring down Mossadegh.

President Harry Truman refused to assist the shah, but when President Dwight Eisenhower took office in January 1953, the new administration agreed to cooperate with the British in a covert operation in Iran. A few Central Intelligence Agency operatives in Tehran gave money to key Iranians to organize pro-shah demonstrations. Initially, the shah, who feared that his own days on the throne were numbered, moved to leave the country. Mossadegh's regime quickly crumbled, however, and the shah regained full power.

Although this event was nominally a coup against the incumbent Mossadegh government, it ultimately resulted in the maintenance of the Pahlavi regime. Thus, U.S. efforts in Iran could be interpreted as regime preservation as easily as regime change. Yet, because the 1953 events apparently changed the course of Iranian history—ending the leading role of the prime minister and the independent power of Iran's parliament and setting the foundation for a government characterized by the shah's direct rule—one can reasonably term the coup as an example of regime change.

Beyond the facts themselves, there is no simple or definitive interpretation of these events because, in a real sense, what happened cannot be counterfactually compared to what would have happened if the event had never taken place. Without external intervention, would the shah or Mossadegh have won his battle? Or, as those who advocated the coup feared, would a third party—Communist forces—have come to power and turned toward the Soviet Union, thus changing the history of the Cold War and perhaps that of the Middle East in general? Did U.S. action crush an otherwise promising seedling of Iranian democracy, led by Mossadegh? To what extent can later events be traced to 1953 as opposed to other or far broader factors influencing Iran's development?

This author, at least, does not believe that it is possible to say whether the 1953 coup was good or necessary or whether it was a terribly damaging mistake based on serious misperceptions. Even with the benefit of hindsight 50 years after the event, accurately assessing its advisability (or necessity) and value (or costs) is difficult. For example, although the Tudeh Party was small, it was organizationally strong compared with other political forces in Iranian life and was concentrated in key sectors. That potency, coupled with the Soviet occupation of northern Iran as late as 1946, certainly contributed to the U.S. fear that Mossadegh—whom no one considered a Communist himself—might pave the way for a pro-Soviet regime in Iran through his alliance with the Tudeh—an action thus constituting a major turning point in the Cold War. In other Arab states, leftist nationalist regimes, such as that of Gamal Abdel Nasser in Egypt, soon became major Soviet allies even though the United States had been initially friendly toward Nasser after his coup.

In hindsight, it seems reasonable to conclude that Mossadegh's personal ineptness, economic difficulties, and political problems would have led to his downfall within a matter of months even without U.S.

involvement. His regime was not universally popular, and the shah had a strong political base of his own, including backing from the Iranian army. Nevertheless, the Islamic clergy, including key figures who later became role models for Ayatollah Ruhollah Khomeini, sought U.S. intervention at the time because it also feared a Communist takeover.

Even if Mossadegh were to lose power in any case, would the shah have survived over time without U.S. involvement? Perhaps one key feature is the personal weakness of the shah himself. Despite the myth that he was a powerful leader, he was an indecisive and insecure man, although also one who usually ignored foreign advice. In 1978, when the United States did not intervene or offer strong support either publicly or behind the scenes for the shah's repressive measures to put down the Iranian revolution, the shah's own relative inaction ensured the revolution's success.

## Did the 1953 Regime Change Cause the 1979 Revolution?

Critiquing the perception of the role that the 1953 countercoup has played in Iranian history is a much simpler challenge. The accepted narrative goes something like this: The United States intervened against a popular nationalist leader and helped install the shah's repressive regime. Supposedly resenting both the shah and the behavior of the U.S. government, the 1979 Iranian revolution naturally targeted the United States. To put it bluntly, 1953 made 1979 inevitable, and 1979 was revenge for 1953.

Yet, such an assessment ignores too many factors, including:

• *The U.S. image in Iranian politics.* In Iran, as in the Arab world, decrying the United States and crying for U.S. help often went hand in hand. Thus, a sharp break with the United States was necessary not because Iranians had come to hate the United States so much already but because Khomeini feared that seeking U.S. help might moderate the revolution or split the Iranian people into factions. Certainly, the precedent of the 1953 regime change provided a model for this expectation, but its relevance should not be overstated when examining what shaped the thinking of Khomeini's followers a quarter century later.

- *The U.S. role in the 1970s.* Largely as the result of both the shah's own demands and a U.S. effort to use the shah to police the Persian Gulf, the U.S. position in Iran expanded significantly in the 1970s. When the shah nationalized the Iranian oil company in 1973—thus completing 20 years later what was Mossadegh's main objective—the United States did not complain in any way. Aside from the direct presence of U.S. advisers and the shah's substantial expenditures on weapons, Khomeini's key complaint was that modernization in Iran in the 1970s was actually Westernizing the country, thus threatening both its religion and its traditional ways.

- *Iranian history and political culture.* Historically, Iranians—unlike Afghans, for example—have bent to foreign conquerors, trying to win foreign support for their own programs and ambitions rather than fight the foreign powers. Khomeini promoted anti-Americanism and blamed the United States for the shah's regime largely to break what he saw as a servile tradition by ensuring that this dependence on foreign support did not happen again.

- *Khomeini's political agenda and talent.* Khomeini's rise to leadership of the revolution was not a matter of historical inevitability rooted in 1953. Khomeini was no ally of Mossadegh; he had no sympathy for Mossadegh and ruthlessly suppressed his political heirs, who would have been quite ready for a rapprochement with the United States in 1979. To discredit the shah, Khomeini falsely portrayed him as a puppet of foreign powers, a tactic that allowed Khomeini to unite Iranians around himself and discredit any opponents as traitors to both Iran and Islam. Khomeini and his ideology gained political power for reasons having little to do with earlier events and far more to do with his determination, charisma, and refusal to compromise as well as the factionalism and disorganization of alternative movements.

- *The new regime's radical nature.* If the revolution had not been radical Islamist in nature, Iran's new leaders probably would have accurately assessed the fact that the United States did not try to save the shah in 1978 and both wanted and needed good relations with the new regime. Similarly, Iran's leaders likely would have decided that they would greatly benefit from good relations with the United States and that such relations would guarantee the irreversibility of their takeover. The ultimate barrier to good relations between Iran's new leaders and the United States was the radical nature of the new regime and its own ambitions for fomenting revolution elsewhere.

Given all these complex developments, can the 1953 regime change in Iran be considered a successful U.S. policy? The answer, of course, depends on one's definition of success. The aftermath of these events—though again, the shah's regime may or may not have been reinstalled without external assistance—was a stable, pro-American government in Iran that significantly contributed to the containment of Soviet and radical influence for a quarter century. For the Iranian people, the shah's regime, although repressive, did nationalize Iran's oil production and promote its economic development. If Iran had been unstable, pro-Soviet, or allied with radical Arab regimes, the Middle East would have become an even more unstable and violent region.

Of course, the situation changed dramatically in 1979, but assuming that the Iranian revolution in 1979 was a result of U.S. actions in 1953 is too simplistic. If a longer-term, peaceful, and more moderate transition in Iran would have occurred without foreign intervention, then the 1953 coup was counterproductive. Assuming that one event was inevitable 25 years after another, however, ignores too many variables. The greater the length of time between one event and another, the harder it is to draw direct causal links between them.

## Fifty Years Later, Can Lessons Be Drawn?

What, if anything, does the U.S. experience in Iran in 1953 teach us about the U.S. policy to change Iraq's regime today? Obviously, the case of Iraq is distinct from that of Iran in significant ways:

- The Iraq case is completely overt and widely debated by the United States and most other countries around the world.

- The consequence of inaction is much more certain—Saddam Hussein would have stayed in power—although the degree of the threat he would have posed is hotly disputed.

- The stated goal of regime change in Iraq is to achieve a government that is more, rather than less, representative.

- A regime change in Iraq required a full-scale war with direct U.S. involvement instead of a handful of U.S. agents operating behind the scenes with a small bankroll.

Apart from these numerous differences is one obvious parallel: both regime change efforts were initiated by partnerships between the United States and Great Britain, although the initiating Anglo-American partner has changed. What lessons the United States might have learned from its experience in Iran in 1953 and thereafter hardly appears to be on the mind of either the advocates or the opponents of U.S. policy toward Iraq but are, in fact, worth considering.

Opponents of current U.S. policy toward Iraq are using a backlash argument, maintaining that U.S. involvement in overthrowing a foreign regime will inevitably lead to a patriotic reaction in that country, which would breed radicalization and widespread opposition to the United States. On the other hand, the problem may not lie in the U.S. role in initially changing the old regime but rather in a long-standing U.S. presence, which could be seen as overbearing at some future point after the new regime has been perceived as failed or unsatisfactory.

Anti-Americanism is often originated by Middle Eastern regimes, even while those regimes enjoy good relations or receive aid from the

United States, as a demagogic way of strengthening their own popular support. For example, before and during the 2003 war against Iraq, other regimes organized popular demonstrations against U.S. policy. Regime-controlled media, schools, mosques, and statements by leaders are often the main sources of taught anti-Americanism.

Ideological anti-Americanism is based on the assumptions of radical Pan-Arabists, Islamists, and leftists that U.S. power is the main problem in the region. Political culture—belief in conspiracy theories and feelings of weakness that attribute all influence to foreigners—certainly contributes to such thinking. Opportunistic anti-Americanism also appeals to opposition groups. Claiming that the country is ruled by foreigners—thus delegitimizing the rulers in Arab, Muslim, and patriotic terms—is a way of trying to mobilize everyone's support.

In Iran in the 1970s, anti-Americanism developed in these two contexts. Whatever the influence of Westernization, modernization, memories of 1953, and a real U.S. presence, the importance of anti-Americanism was not inevitable. If, for example, moderates and democrats had seized power in 1979 instead of Khomeini, they probably would have sought good relations with the United States.

Today, those involved in changing the regime in Iraq understandably want to avoid a later anti-American reaction. Helping the Iraqis attain the gift of democracy—and thus avoiding association with a dictatorial, incompetent, unpopular, or unstable regime—is seen as a key way of preventing this dangerous problem from developing.

In suggesting that democratization might be achieved, many try simplistically to apply the German and Japanese postwar models and argue that a military occupation could be the midwife of democracy. Although things might work out this way in Iraq, this analogy has many problems. For example, Germany—or more specifically West Germany—was heir to a long history of democratic political and cultural structures. This is not true of Iraq, despite its parliamentary monarchical system that ended in 1958. In addition, the German regime was not only overthrown; its basic ideas were discredited, which is not so likely in the case of Arab nationalism in Iraq. The German people also ultimately accepted their fundamental cultural identity with the occupiers; the Iraqi people may not. Despite the exigencies of the Cold War, Germany's neighbors were not able to intervene easily to subvert its stability and restore the old order; it is not clear that Iraq's neighbors will be similarly restrained. These are only some of the differences.

Some, though by no means all, of these factors could be raised in Japan's case as well. Clearly, the cultural and ethnic gap between the Japanese and its occupiers was great. Japan, however, was a highly structured society in which the unquestioned leader—the emperor—ordered his people to accept the foreign presence and ensuing reforms. The country's main pillars—from religion to social order and emphasis on discipline—reinforced the changes being made. Again, these factors do not apply to Iraq.

This does not mean that a new, more democratic, and far more successful system cannot be put in place in Iraq. Yet, such an effort looks far easier and more certain to succeed to those who know little about the specificity of the country's history, structure, and people. In the Middle East context, however, Iraq is a relatively promising place to try such an experiment. In comparison with other Arab countries, some of the elements necessary to achieve economic prosperity, such as large oil revenues, and political stability are present.

Today, some aspects of the Iraqi regime change seem to be fairly clear. In the short run, liberation from an especially repressive dictatorship in Iraq is likely to be greeted with joy. The end of sanctions in Iraq, coupled with foreign aid and investment as well as lower military spending and higher oil revenue, is likely to produce major material gains for Iraqis. Hope for a better and more democratic life will inspire many to support U.S. action and thank the United States.

Yet, when the honeymoon comes to an end, tough decisions will need to be made. How will Iraq's government be organized? In what ways will power be distributed among the key ethnic and other groups, and who might be excluded from power altogether? If Iraqis make these choices, disputes are likely to remain internal. Everyone will seek U.S. backing and be glad if they get it. However, each group will be angry if the United States seems to support opposing rivals or policies. This type of situation could already be seen in the quarreling and complaints about U.S. policy seen in the Iraqi opposition even before the war began. The overwhelming temptation among Iraqis would be to turn to patriotism, Arab nationalism, Islam, and group solidarities and against what they consider foreign interference.

This happened in Iran, of course; but such a process took 25 years, and external actions simply reestablished a long-existing stable polity with its traditional ruler. In Iraq, the creation of an entirely new system—and one probably based on a weaker central government—would likely produce a faster reaction; and for those who fail in government or opposition, the temptation to blame the United States for their defeats and disappointments will be enormous.

## What Lessons?

In other words, the lesson that can be learned from the U.S. experience in Iran is that, whatever its role in the initial, relatively brief moment of regime change, the United States should not stay too long or become too deeply involved in the governance of another country.

Regime overthrow through U.S. intervention may be immediately popular and remain so for many years, but at some point in the future, disputes and power struggles are bound to arise which challenge the system that has been created. Factions will privately seek U.S. backing and then publicly denounce the United States if they do not receive it. If one is in control of a country, this paradox cannot be avoided. But if one has a powerful influence from the outside, it is possible to give multiple forces the feeling that you are friendly to them. As was the case in Iran, the problem, of course, is that the United States is not going to back groups like Khomeini and his followers that are basically antagonistic to U.S. interests. Their hostility is inevitable. These possibilities all should offer an important lesson for a post-Saddam strategy in Iraq.

A significant difference between these two cases is the certainty about who would rule Iran after the 1953 regime change. The shah was in place, had legitimacy and his own base of support, and faced no other significant rivals once Mossadegh was overthrown. In the case of Iraq, however, the future governmental organization and composition is not clear, and there are many rivals for power. This situation could produce a more pluralistic and democratic system or one that is conducive to chaos.

Finally, the primary and ultimate lesson thus far learned about regime change is unpredictability, at least in the long run. The 1953 operation initially transpired very smoothly. It was quick and low cost, remained secret, and immediately resulted in a regime that enjoyed a great deal of popularity as well as power. A quarter century later, however, much had changed in Iran in every respect. Both the regime's failures and its successes—to the extent that they transformed the country or raised expectations to that effect—counted against it. The public's principal antagonism was dissatisfaction with the system and its results. Negative reaction to the United States—as important as it did become—was secondary.

One can imagine a purely hypothetical parallel situation. Suppose that the United States helps establish a stable, reasonably popular, and successful regime to replace Saddam and that regime remains well regarded for many years thereafter. In the future—say, 25 years later—that system may be overthrown by a revolution that takes a very different position. Whether fairly or unfairly, that movement would resent U.S. influence and would adopt a hostile attitude toward the United States. Under such circumstances, would a U.S. policy of regime change in Iraq be judged a tremendous success or an enormous failure? The answer would depend in part on what year the assessment was being made.

Two points from the Iran case are especially key for a post-Saddam scenario in Iraq: responsibility and control. By bringing about regime change in Iraq, the United States becomes responsible in the eyes of Iraqis and others in the region for what that government does in the future. The idea of a long, post-Saddam U.S. presence in Iraq is designed to ensure a better functioning, more stable regime. Yet, the United States will also be judged and criticized if it is perceived to control the

Iraqi government like a puppet. This is not just a matter of nationalism but also of natural opportunism and careerism. Every individual, party, or ethnic group that does not get into power or fails to receive the rewards it wants can then attribute—fairly or unfairly—that denial to the United States. This outcome would argue for a shorter-term post-Saddam U.S. presence.

In Iran, the United States was blamed even though the actual intervention of regime change in 1953 was a very brief period. The shah was not a U.S. puppet in the following years; he did as he wished. The opposition, however, was able to persuade much of the population that the United States was the true ruler of Iran—tendentious as such claims were. A large U.S. presence was exploited to convince Iranians of this point.

U.S. responsibility for overthrowing Saddam is an obvious fact and will continue to be so, but a shorter U.S. presence in Iraq would be more beneficial for at least three reasons. First, if a post-Saddam Iraqi government is deemed independent of U.S. control, it will be more credible and successful both at home and in the region. Second, if the United States governs Iraq for a protracted period of time, any complaint about the government, the state of the economy, the fate of individual ambitions, and every detail of governance will be directed against the United States. Third, as an Iraqi government inevitably makes enemies and faces internal conflicts, a smaller U.S. presence would place the United States in a stronger position to pose as an evenhanded arbiter and reduce the credibility of an anti-American focus for anyone with a grievance against the rulers.

Ultimately, any criticism of regime change must also evaluate the costs and benefits of the alternatives as well as those of inaction. This principle is an integral part of the policy debate over Iraq. Nevertheless, as the case of Iran and the regime changes of 1953 and 1979 demonstrate, even when a strategy is implemented—and long after the event—there is still ample room for dispute over whether a regime change was successful, necessary, well implemented, ethical, or beneficial to all parties involved. Indeed, the case of Iran shows that the evaluation of any foreign policy initiative depends greatly on the point in history when judgment is being passed.

## Note

1. See Barry Rubin, *Paved with Good Intentions: The American Experience and Iran* (New York: Viking Press, 1981).

# Part III

---

# North Korea

## Michael O'Hanlon and Mike Mochizuki

# Toward a Grand Bargain with North Korea

The most promising route to resolve the worsening nuclear crisis in Northeast Asia is for Washington, Tokyo, Seoul, and Beijing to pursue a grand bargain with Pyongyang. These governments need to recognize that North Korean economic atrophy, caused largely by North Korea's excessive conventional military force as well as its failed command-economy system, is at the core of the nuclear crisis and that curing the latter can only be done by recognizing the underlying disease. This grand bargain should be big and bold in scope, addressing the underlying problem while providing bigger and better carrots with the actual potential to entice, together with tough demands on North Korea that go well beyond the nuclear issue. In this comprehensive way, policymakers would provide a road map for the vital and ultimate goal of denuclearizing North Korea. Through the stages of implementation, each side would retain leverage over the other as aid would be provided gradually to the Democratic People's Republic of Korea (DPRK) while the DPRK would cut or eliminate its weapons and reform its economy over time, thus reassuring each side that it was not being hoodwinked.

Michael O'Hanlon is a senior fellow at the Brookings Institution in Washington, D.C. Mike Mochizuki is a professor of political science and international affairs at George Washington University. O'Hanlon and Mochizuki are coauthors of *Crisis on the Korean Peninsula: How to Deal with a Nuclear North Korea* (McGraw-Hill, 2003).

Copyright © 2003 by The Center for Strategic and International Studies and the Massachusetts Institute of Technology
*The Washington Quarterly* • 26:4 pp. 7–18.

## The Benefits of Thinking Big

North Korea is likely to find a broad plan tough and demanding. Such a plan would result in major changes in DPRK security policy as well as its economy and even, to some extent, aspects of domestic policy such as human rights. Yet, such broad road maps are often useful. If the parties lay them out clearly and commit to them early in the process—even if implementation occurs over time—they can help countries on both sides focus on the potentially substantial benefits of a fruitful diplomatic process, thus reducing the odds that negotiations get bogged down in pursuit of marginal advantages on specific issues. Specific pledges can also help countries verify each other's commitment to actual results and thus enhance confidence.[1]

### The Failure of Diplomacy Du Jour

U.S. policy toward North Korea in the last decade has been, for the most part, narrow and tactical, focusing on the crisis du jour rather than on a broader game plan. The 1994 Agreed Framework on North Korea's nuclear program required that the DPRK cease activities that could have given it a nuclear arsenal of 50 weapons by the decade's end; in exchange, the United States and other countries promised to provide North Korea with alternative energy sources. This deal was beneficial within its limited scope, but it failed to address the underlying problem or lead U.S. policymakers to pursue a broader vision beyond the specific attempt to buy out the North Korean missile program later in the decade. Such a tactical approach was perhaps inevitable in the early 1990s, when the Clinton administration was focused on domestic issues and was inexperienced in its foreign policy, as Somalia, Haiti, and Bosnia had shown. As a result of these distractions and inexperience, the Clinton administration had a difficult time at the highest levels of government focusing strategically on North Korea and thus failed to develop an integrated approach for dealing with Pyongyang that combined incentives with threats and deterrence.[2]

A tactical, nuclear-specific focus that involved incentives to alter one specific type of behavior could have been defended as a reasonable approach in the early 1990s. Indeed, until stopped by the Clinton administration, Israel had reportedly been pursuing a deal to compensate North Korea for not selling missiles to Iran.[3] If it made strategic sense for a security-conscious country such as Israel to consider buying out North Korea's missile program, why did it not make sense for the United States and its regional allies to buy out North Korea's even more dangerous nuclear program?

In addition, after the dissolution of the Soviet bloc, many U.S. policymakers expected that North Korea would no longer enjoy the aid or favorable trading arrangements that it needed to survive and would soon collapse, thus obviating the need for a long-term solution. Other policymakers may have expected that concluding a deal on nuclear weapons would naturally lead to a quick thaw in relations on the peninsula without any need to articulate a broader vision. In any event, even if some had wished to articulate such a vision, domestic politics in the United States and in South Korea, where hawks discouraged dealing with the Stalinist regime to the north, stood in the way. Moreover, a tactical, crisis-driven approach to dealing with North Korea did produce some temporary successes, the most significant being the Agreed Framework.

Despite its reasonable logic, however, this approach is not as promising today.[4] President George W. Bush has made it clear that he is opposed to new deals with North Korea on the nuclear issue that smack of blackmail. North Korea has now demonstrated its disinterest in an incremental, slow process of improving relations. It would not have developed its underground uranium-enrichment program—a clear and blatant violation of the Agreed Framework, which required North Korean compliance with the Nuclear Non-Proliferation Treaty—were it content with the benefits of such a patient approach.

In addition, the type of limited engagement pursued over the last decade may have inadvertently encouraged the DPRK to develop a counterproductive habit of using its weapons programs to gain money and diplomatic attention. Whether one views this tendency as extortion or as the desperate actions of a failing regime, the outcome has been the same.

## THINKING BIG

Aiming for a big, multifaceted deal might seem counterintuitive when Washington and Pyongyang cannot even sustain a narrow agreement on a specific issue. A recent CSIS report even explicitly argued against making any proposal that included ambitious conventional-arms reductions on the grounds that such broad demands could only be a recipe for stalemate and failure.[5] The 1999 Perry report, drafted by a policy review team led by former secretary of defense William Perry, also took aim at broad proposals, suggesting that they would meet resistance in Pyongyang, which would see any attempt at major reforms as a measure designed to undermine the regime.[6]

The current situation is at an impasse, however; a new idea is needed. The Bush administration's proposal, which demands broad concessions from North Korea, especially on the nuclear weapons front, without offering any concrete incentives in return and which resists bilateral negotiations with Pyongyang, is probably not that new idea. It stands little chance of convincing Pyongyang to change course. Coercion is unlikely to bring about North Korea's collapse or to convince Pyongyang to change its policy quickly enough to prevent a major nuclear crisis in Northeast Asia. Furthermore, this approach elicits little support from key U.S. security partners in the region. South Korea under the Roh government certainly prefers diplomatic engagement over coercion, and although Japan has recently become tougher by stopping North Korean shipping and considering tighter economic sanctions, it still wants to avoid a military crisis that risks war on the Korean peninsula.

Aiming for a larger bargain in which more is offered to North Korea but more is also demanded in return risks little except a bit of money. On the upside, it has the potential to break the current impasse in Northeast Asia, just as broad visions or road maps have guided other recent peace negotiations in the Balkans and the Middle East (with many obvious limitations and setbacks, but some real successes to date as well). The grand bargain approach can benefit both sides. The United States and its allies can reduce the DPRK threat across the board and begin to turn that police state away from a policy of reflexive confrontation and blackmail, while North Korea can gain greater levels of assistance over time and perhaps can begin to reform its economy in the way China did—and as Pyongyang seems to desire, at least occasionally.

Moreover, studies of North Korean negotiating behavior[7] suggest that broader deals may work better than narrow proposals on specific issues. This seemed to be the pattern in the 1993–1994 negotiations leading to the Agreed Framework. Although these talks progressed slowly for a year or so, they produced an accord once the negotiations were broadened beyond the nuclear weapons issue to include energy, economics, security, and diplomatic incentives. Alas, the promises made in this deal were never realized, as all parties (especially the DPRK) put up roadblocks, but the inclusion of these dimensions of the relationship nonetheless helped produce the initial agreement.

In addition to other advantages, a broader approach would also provide the bold initiative that the Roh government suggested that the United States offer to Pyongyang.[8] Without strong cooperation between Seoul and Washington, no plan for dealing with North Korea can work. Indeed, if Pyongyang senses dissension and discord in the U.S.–South Korean alliance, the North Korean government will probably revert to its traditional temptation of trying to split the two allies.

Beyond cooperation with South Korea, a grand bargain proposal can make U.S. policy much more palatable to other key regional players—Japan and China. Collaboration among these four countries in their basic approach to resolving the North Korean problem is essential to prevent Pyongyang from being tempted to play one government off against the others, as it often has done in the past, and to enable these four countries to work together to pursue their common goals.[9] Yet, they will not unite behind a policy that begins with hard-line measures; in particular, South Korea and China will consider taking a tough stance against

Pyongyang only after serious diplomatic steps have clearly been attempted and have failed. Uniting the four players is thus the best way both to improve the prospects for diplomacy and a successful coercive strategy, should that diplomacy fail.

## Making It Work

For the grand bargain to work, both carrots and sticks are needed—incentives as well as resolute deterrence and even threats if need be. Beyond the nuclear issue, such a grand bargain must also address the broader problems on the Korean peninsula—most notably North Korea's oversized military and undersized economy, as well as a horrible human rights record that is repressive even by Communist standards.

### BALANCING CARROTS AND STICKS

A policy that uses carrots and sticks is not necessarily a contradictory one. Although the world should not give Pyongyang substantial aid and other benefits simply to appease a dangerous leader or to solve an immediate security crisis, the United States and its allies can and should be generous if North Korea is prepared to eliminate its nuclear weapons programs, transform the broader security situation on the peninsula, reform its economy, and even begin to change its society. Doing so would not show weakness but rather provide a way to solve—not postpone—an important security problem by changing the fundamental nature of the adversary.

Moreover, depending on the particular circumstances surrounding negotiations, the grand bargain's strategic use of carrots can help retain the threat of a military strike against Yongbyon as a last resort. Although Washington has been unable to convince Seoul of the need for such a threat today, that situation could change. A committed, initial attempt at diplomacy, including the offer of numerous inducements for North Korea, would give the United States a better chance of getting its regional allies to support a military threat as a last resort. By providing more carrots, the U.S. government might thus gain greater support for the possible, subsequent use of a stick.[10]

Any military strike at North Korea's nuclear reactors and plutonium reprocessing facilities at its Yongbyon site north of Pyongyang would be extremely risky in light of the possibility that a larger war would result. Furthermore, a military strike would probably fail to destroy or render unusable many of North Korea's spent fuel rods, meaning that the DPRK might still manufacture one or more weapons even after an attack. (Although some may be concerned about direct radioactive fallout, studies conducted by the Pentagon in the early 1990s concluded that radioactive release would probably be quite limited, unless an operational nuclear reactor with heavily irradiated fuel was struck.)

Nevertheless, the preemption option would arguably be preferable to an unchecked, large-scale DPRK nuclear program, if someday that was the only alternative. Such a threat was credible when the Clinton administration made it in 1994 because South Korea did not fundamentally object. The Bush administration can probably make it credible again by pursuing better diplomacy and better coordination with Seoul, Tokyo, and Beijing. A military strike is, of course, not likely to destroy either the DPRK's hidden uranium-enrichment program or the bomb or two that North Korea might have already, nor would military action destroy any additional plutonium moved from Yongbyon prior to the attack. Nevertheless, a strike could destroy the DPRK's nuclear reactors at the site, entomb the associated plutonium, and destroy the reprocessing facility—all with limited risk of radioactive fallout, according to former secretary of defense Perry and former assistant secretary Ashton Carter.[11]

North Korea's true hard-liners may fear the Bush administration to such an extent that they argue against giving up their nuclear program at present—which also may have been the case during the Clinton administration.[12] The grand bargain proposal may be able to convince the DPRK to abandon its nuclear programs gradually, however, through a combination of reassurances and inducements.[13] Kim Jong Il has demonstrated sufficient interest in engaging with the outside world as well as in exploring economic reforms—evidenced by the creation of special economic zones, the recent liberalization of prices, and other tentative but real steps to try some of what China and Vietnam have successfully attempted in recent decades. The United States and other countries should seriously test his willingness to go further.

Moreover, Kim Jong Il's position within North Korea now appears strong. He has used purges and promotions to produce a top officer corps loyal to him, and the likelihood that military commanders think that they have a solution of their own to solve North Korea's economic problems is slim. If a proposed package deal were to address the country's core security concerns while providing a real opportunity for recovery and greater international engagement, North Korea may very well take the idea seriously.[14] A grand bargain that allowed North Korea to surrender its nuclear capabilities gradually while allowing it to keep some fraction of its conventional weaponry near the demilitarized zone (DMZ) just might persuade Pyongyang to get on board.

The DPRK might prefer to have both aid and nuclear weapons, but the United States should try to force North Korea to choose between the two.[15] This is in fact the crux of the logic behind the grand bargain approach: that North Korea can be forced to choose and that it can probably be induced to make the right, peaceful choice.

The allies would not let down their military guard at any point during the proposed process nor would a failed experiment cause any other irrevocable harm. Even a failed effort to negotiate a grand bargain would at least temporarily ice the larger, visible part of the DPRK's nuclear program because no negotiations would proceed unless Pyongyang allowed monitoring of its program and froze it as well. Further, because the aid would be provided mostly in kind, not in cash, it would by itself do little to prop up a desperate regime with the hard currency it so desperately craves.

## Going Beyond the Nuclear Issue

By not fixating on just the nuclear program, ironically, a grand bargain is more likely ultimately to denuclearize North Korea and, most importantly, prevent any further development of North Korea's nuclear inventory. The proposed plan would begin by rapidly restoring fuel oil shipments and promising no immediate use of U.S. force if North Korea agreed to freeze its nuclear activities, particularly plutonium production and reprocessing at Yongbyon, while negotiations are under way. These steps would simply ensure that neither party had to negotiate under duress.

As for its main substance, the approach would then seek to strike a deal on nuclear weapons. The proposal would replace North Korea's nuclear facilities at Yongbyon with conventional power sources and include rigorous monitoring of North Korea's nuclear-related sites as well as short-notice challenge inspections at places where outside intelligence suspected nuclear-related activity.

Given North Korea's concerns about the Bush administration's doctrine of preemption and the success of military operations against Iraq, convincing the DPRK to give up all its nuclear capabilities immediately might not be feasible.[16] In fact, it might take several years, perhaps even until the end of the decade, to reach that final goal. The United States could accept any deal, however, that could immediately freeze the DPRK's nuclear activities verifiably and then quickly begin to get fuel rods out of North Korea.

Beyond nuclear issues, both sides would cut the overall number of conventional forces as well as accompany those cuts with a commitment by South Korea, China, Japan, and the United States to help North Korea gradually restructure its economy. Cuts of 50 percent or more in conventional weaponry would reduce the threat that North Korea's artillery and rocket forces currently pose to South Korea, particularly to nearby Seoul. Unlike some proposals, the grand bargain would not entail the North Korean withdrawal of all its conventional capabilities from the DMZ. North Korea almost surely considers its forward-deployed forces necessary to deter South Korea and the United States. Hence, the DPRK cannot realistically be expected to surrender both its weapons of mass destruction (WMD) and its conventional deterrent.

The principal purpose of these conventional reductions actually would be as much economic as military. Offering aid tied to cuts in conventional arms makes more economic sense than buying out nuclear and missile programs. Secretary of Defense Donald Rumsfeld recently convincingly argued that the real solution to North Korea's problems is for the country to move toward a market economy, because that approach has worked for other Communist states in East Asia, notably China and Vietnam.[17] North Korea may actually be planning secretly to make cuts in its conventional forces anyway.[18] A combination of cuts in DPRK forces and economic reforms in the country stands the best chance of producing stabilizing and desirable results.

If Pyongyang agreed to such reductions, North Korea's economy would benefit twice: by a reduction in the size and cost of its military and by obtaining greater technical and economic aid from Japan, South Korea, the United States, and perhaps China (as well as the lifting of U.S. trade sanctions). Specifically, such a deal should reduce North Korea's military expenditures substantially, helping reform the country's economy and increasing the likelihood that aid is used productively. North Korea's conventional military forces comprise one million individuals and are backed up by large reserve forces as well as a large arms industry. This situation suggests that the lion's share of North Korea's defense budget, which represents 20–30 percent of its gross domestic product, is consumed by conventional forces; therefore, reducing them should be a main focus of any reform proposal. External aid can help in that process.

This policy would reduce the core threat that has existed in Korea for half a century, while offering at least some hope that economic reform in the DPRK might begin to succeed. Given this economic logic and rationale, it would only make sense to keep giving aid so long as North Korea continued down the path of economic reform. China could provide technical help, in light of its experiences over the last 25 years in gradually introducing entrepreneurial activity into a Communist economy.

China's experience could also offer reassurance—surely important to North Korean leaders—that it is possible to reform a command economy without losing political power in the process. Even though most Americans would surely prefer to see North Korea's corrupt and ruthless government fall, pursuing a policy that would achieve that outcome does not seem realistic without incurring huge security risks and exacting an enormous humanitarian toll on the North Korean people—nor would China and South Korea likely support it under current circumstances. Moreover, by accepting this grand bargain proposal, North Korea would be agreeing to at least a gradual and soft, or "velvet," form of regime change, even if Kim Jong Il were to retain power throughout the process.

Additional elements of the grand bargain would include North Korean commitments to:

- continue to refrain from terrorism;

- permanently return all kidnapping victims to Japan;

- participate in a human rights dialogue, similar to China in recent years;

- end DPRK counterfeiting and drug smuggling activities;

- sign and implement its obligations under the chemical weapons and biological weapons conventions; and

- stop exports and production of ballistic missiles.

For its part of the grand bargain, the United States would offer numerous benefits beyond economic and energy assistance, none of which would require a change in the U.S. government's fundamental regional policies. The White House would:

- commence diplomatic ties with North Korea;

- end economic sanctions;

- remove North Korea's name from the list of state sponsors of terrorism;

- give a binding promise not to be the first to use WMD;

- provide a nonaggression pledge—a promise not to attack North Korea first with any types of weaponry for any purpose (and perhaps even an active security guarantee if North Korea wished, akin to what the United States provides to its allies); and

- sign a formal peace treaty ending the Korean War.

## Breaking the Stalemate

After a decade of issue-by-issue and initially fruitful negotiations, a broad vision is now needed to resolve the impasse on the Korean peninsula. This idea must address the underlying cause of the problem—North Korea's economic and societal collapse, together with its failed experiment in communism and its *juche* system of self-reliance—as well as the immediate nuclear symptoms of that disease.

Although couched in broad and ambitious terms, the proposed road map could be put into effect gradually. Intrusive nuclear inspections typically take months or longer, reductions in conventional forces take at least a couple of years, and development programs take even longer. Thus, the concept is grand in its intent and scope, but implementation of the policy need not be rushed. In fact, the need for gradual implementation would provide each side with leverage over the other.

The United States and its partners would continue to provide aid and economic support only if North Korea upheld its end of the bargain. Similarly, security guarantees would be contingent on complete compliance with denuclearization demands as well as other elements of the proposal. For its part, North Korea would not have to give up all its nuclear potential until it gained a number of concrete benefits, and the government would not have to keep reducing conventional forces unless outside powers continued to provide assistance.

Although reductions in conventional forces are the linchpin of the grand bargain's success, numerous additional key elements are involved, the most important of which is a broad approach to economic reform in North Korea. There is reason to believe that the economic reform model that worked in China starting about a quarter century ago can work in Korea today, although each case is distinct. If that is the case, a grand bargain could do much more than address an acute nuclear security problem; the approach could begin to transform what has been one of the world's most troubled and dangerous regions for decades.

## Notes

1. Richard N. Haass and Meghan L. O'Sullivan, "Terms of Engagement: Alternatives to Punitive Policies," *Survival* 42, no. 2 (summer 2000): 120–121.

2. Leon V. Sigal, *Disarming Strangers: Nuclear Diplomacy with North Korea* (Princeton, N.J.: Princeton University Press, 1998), pp. 52–65.

3. Ibid., pp. 66–67.

4. See Morton I. Abramowitz and James T. Laney, *Testing North Korea: The Next Stage in U.S. and ROK Policy* (New York: Council on Foreign Relations, 2001), www.cfr.org/pdf/Korea_TaskForce2.pdf (accessed June 19, 2003). For more recent arguments along similar lines, see Brent Scowcroft and Daniel Poneman, "Korea Can't Wait," *Washington Post*, February 16, 2003; Samuel R. Berger and Robert L. Gallucci, "Two Crises, No Back Burner," *Washington Post*, December 31, 2002; William S. Cohen, "Huffing and Puffing Won't Do," *Washington Post*, January 7, 2003; Ashton B. Carter, "Alternatives to Letting North Korea Go Nuclear," testimony before the Senate Committee on Foreign Relations, Washington, D.C., March 6, 2003; Sonni Efron, "Experts Call for N. Korea Dialogue," *Los Angeles Times*, March 7, 2003 (citing testimony by Robert Einhorn); Morton Abramowitz and James Laney, "A Letter from the Independent Task Force on Korea to the Administration," November 26, 2002, www.cfr.org/publication.php?id=5304 (accessed June 18, 2003); "Turning Point in Korea: New Dangers and New Opportunities for the United States," February 2003, www.ciponline.org/asia/taskforce.pdf (accessed June 18, 2003) (report of the Task Force on U.S. Korea policy).

5. CSIS International Security Program Working Group, "Conventional Arms Control on the Korean Peninsula," Washington, D.C., August 2002, www.csis.org/isp/conv_armscontrol.pdf (accessed June 18, 2003). See Alan D. Romberg and Michael D. Swaine, "The North Korea Nuclear Crisis: A Strategy for Negotiation," *Arms Control Today* 33, no. 4 (May 2003): 4–7.

6. William J. Perry, "Review of United States Policy Toward North Korea: Findings and Recommendations," Washington, D.C., October 12, 1999, www.state.gov/www/regions/eap/991012_northkorea_rpt.html (accessed June 18, 2003).

7. Scott Snyder, *Negotiating on the Edge* (Washington, D.C.: U.S. Institute of Peace, 1999), pp. 58–60, 143–153; Sigal, *Disarming Strangers*, pp. 52–65, 78.

8. See "S. Korea Urges U.S. Initiative for North," *Washington Post*, March 29, 2003.

9. See Snyder, *Negotiating on the Edge*, pp. 149–150.

10. Gary Samore, "The Korean Nuclear Crisis," *Survival* 45, no. 1 (spring 2003): 19–22.

11. See Ashton B. Carter and William J. Perry, "Back to the Brink," *Washington Post*, October 20, 2002.

12. See Philip W. Yun, "The Devil We Know in N. Korea May Be Better Than the Ones We Don't," *Los Angeles Times*, May 7, 2003.

13. See Michael Armacost, Daniel I. Okimoto, and Gi-Wook Shin, "Addressing the North Korea Nuclear Challenge," Asia/Pacific Research Center, Institute for International Studies, Stanford University, April 15, 2003, www.asck.org/reports/APARC_Brief_1_2003.pdf (accessed June 18, 2003).

14. See Kongdan Oh and Ralph C. Hassig, *North Korea Through the Looking Glass* (Washington, D.C.: Brookings Institution, 2000), pp. 114–124.

15. For a similar argument, see Joseph S. Nye, "Bush Faces a Tougher Test in N. Korea," *Boston Globe*, May 7, 2003.

16. See Doug Struck, "Citing Iraq, N. Korea Signals Hard Line on Weapons Issues," *Washington Post*, March 30, 2003; James Brooke, "North Korea Watches War and Wonders What's Next," *New York Times*, March 31, 2003.

17. Bill Sammon, "N. Korea 'Solution' a Market Economy," *Washington Times*, May 14, 2003.

18. The North Korean statement of June 9, 2003, that justified its nuclear weapons programs as a way to compensate for reductions in conventional military forces suggests such an inference. David Sanger, "North Korea Says It Seeks to Develop Nuclear Arms," *New York Times*, June 10, 2003, p. A9.

David Shambaugh

# China and the Korean Peninsula: Playing for the Long Term

The unfolding international crisis concerning North Korea's nuclear weapons program has focused global attention on China's relations with its rogue neighbor. President George W. Bush and other world leaders have personally sought the Chinese government's influence and pressure on Pyongyang, only to be given the nebulous reassurance that China seeks a nonnuclear Korean peninsula and that the problem must be solved peacefully. China's position is indeed central to resolving the crisis, but governments and analysts alike seem vexed to understand China's assessment of the situation, opaque positions, and apparent unwillingness to use its presumed leverage in tandem with others.[1]

Understanding China's calculus requires, at the outset, recognition that North Korea has been a long-standing headache for China. This is not the first time since the Chinese Communists came to power in 1949 that they find themselves in a difficult international quandary over the behavior of their erstwhile comrades in North Korea. Ever since Kim Il-sung's forces invaded the South in 1950, China has repeatedly found its own national security interests affected and compromised by the pro-

David Shambaugh is a professor of political science and international affairs and director of the China Policy Program at the Elliott School of International Affairs, George Washington University; a nonresident senior fellow in the Foreign Policy Studies Program at the Brookings Institution; and a 2002–2003 fellow at the Woodrow Wilson International Center for Scholars in Washington, D.C.

Copyright © 2003 by The Center for Strategic and International Studies and the Massachusetts Institute of Technology
*The Washington Quarterly* • 26:2 pp. 43–56.

vocative and confrontational policies pursued by the Kim dynasty and Pyongyang regime.

It is true that the Chinese Communist Party (CCP) and its North Korean counterpart have had long-standing ties and that the late Kim Il-sung was educated in China and was once a member of the CCP. It is also true that the two countries once had a formal alliance and mutually described their relationship as one of "lips and teeth." And it is true that China probably has better relations with the Democratic People's Republic of Korea (DPRK) than any other country on Earth. Despite these facts, however, the relationship between Beijing and Pyongyang has been severely strained for many years, particularly since Kim Jung-il succeeded his father in 1995. Thus, from Beijing's perspective, the current crisis over North Korea's withdrawal from the 1994 Agreed Framework and the Nuclear Non-Proliferation Treaty, as well as the DPRK's resumption of its nuclear weapons program, is only the latest chapter in a half-century of North Korean brinksmanship brought on by domestic desperation and disregard for its neighbors' interests and preferences.

Beijing considers the latest crisis an extremely serious situation, but permanently short-circuiting Pyongyang's nuclear ambitions is only a piece of a larger and more complicated puzzle for China. Despite China's strong and long-stated policy in favor of a nonnuclear Korean peninsula (both North and South), halting North Korea's nuclear program is not the ultimate end that China hopes to achieve. China's calculations, interests, and goals are more long term and more complicated. The United States and other involved nations must understand these perspectives and complexities if they are to effectively attain China's cooperation.

## China's Endgame

China's policy calculus toward the DPRK—both in general and in the current crisis—involves a hierarchy of several interrelated interests:

1. DPRK regime survival;

2. DPRK regime reform;

3. maintaining and developing more comprehensively robust relations between China and South Korea;

4. establishing China's dominant external influence over the Korean peninsula (North and South);

5. integrating North and South, through economic and social means, leading to political unification over time; and

6. unprovocative and responsible North Korean behavior on security issues ranging from its nuclear weapons program to proliferation of other weapons of mass destruction (WMD) and their means of delivery to the deployments of DPRK conventional forces.

It is important to recognize that this hierarchy does not mean that China accepts the status quo on the peninsula. Although some analysts, particularly in the West, assume that China prefers the status quo to regime change, this is not in fact the case. China may favor the status quo over regime collapse, but China's preferred future for the DPRK is regime reform. China does not believe that the current situation on the peninsula or in the DPRK is stable or conducive either to regional stability or China's own national security, economic growth, or other national interests. For Beijing, enhancing stability is critical.

Consequently, China advocates a comprehensive policy package that would help set North Korea on the path to real reforms that involve the DPRK intensively with all its neighbors in Northeast Asia as well as the United States. For China, the issue is not simply whether the DPRK develops a nuclear weapons capacity or whether it will have a soft or hard landing from its current catastrophic state; the question is whether North Korea can embark on a sustained and comprehensive path of reform à la China. This is Beijing's positive vision for North Korea. (A less positive vision involves more incremental reform.) Understanding this long-term vision or goal is central to understanding the elements of China's strategy and tactics, or Beijing's "hierarchy of calculus."

## Regime Survival

Most fundamentally, Beijing seeks to avoid the implosion or collapse of the DPRK regime and nation-state. Preventing collapse is Beijing's bottom line because collapse would have enormous tangible human and economic consequences for China, not to mention the intangible political impact of another failed Communist state. DPRK regime collapse could also potentially harm China's security.

China's aim to sustain the DPRK regime in no way suggests that Beijing likes the regime in Pyongyang. Quite to the contrary, Chinese officials and North Korea analysts in Beijing and Shanghai sometimes speak with disdain, despair, and heightened frustration when discussing the DPRK and China's relations with it. These critics deplore the sycophantic cult of personality surrounding the Kim dynasty, the Stalinist security state, the command economy, the poverty of the populace, the use of scarce resources for military purposes, the mass mobilization techniques of the regime, the autarkic paranoia about the world beyond its borders, and so forth. China's Korea analysts draw explicit parallels to Maoist China (particularly during the Great Leap Forward) and argue that North Korea's only viable option to avoid national suicide is to follow China's reformist example. They also recall anecdotal accounts of North Korean condescension toward visiting Chinese officials and confrontations with them.

As part of its regime survival strategy, Beijing believes that it must deal with the DPRK government and extends it aid in the form of foodstuffs and energy supplies to alleviate public suffering in North Korea. The exact amounts of this aid are not known, but estimates are in the range of 1 million tons of wheat and rice and 500,000 tons of heavy-fuel oil per annum since 1994. This estimate accounts for 70–90 percent of North Korea's fuel imports (and nearly 100 percent since the cutoff of U.S. heavy-fuel oil in December 2002) and about one-third of the DPRK's total food imports. Trade between the two countries, while minimal (amounting to $740 million in 2001 and approximately one-quarter of the DPRK's entire foreign trade), does supply needed consumer durables, energy supplies, and transport infrastructure. For a nation with negative economic growth, a paltry per capita income of $714, stagnant industrial production, an agricultural wasteland, and teetering on the verge of famine, China's aid and trade has been keeping the North Korean economy from total ruin and human calamity.

High-level Chinese visits to Pyongyang are infrequent, although visits by DPRK officials to China are on the rise. Military exchanges occur between People's Liberation Army (PLA) officers from the Shenyang Military Region and their North Korean counterparts across the border and occasionally between military personnel at higher levels. Such meetings usually note the "friendship cemented in blood" between the two countries, but the sheer propagandistic pabulum that accompanies such visits and the relative paucity of such exchanges are indications of the formality and frostiness of the ties between the two governments.[2]

Another irritating issue in the relationship has been cross-border migration, which has received international attention over the past year as North Korean migrants have made brazen attempts to enter diplomatic compounds in China to seek diplomatic asylum in South Korea or other countries. The refugee influx into China peaked in 2000 at approximately 200,000 by one estimate but has fallen to 100,000 or fewer since the Chinese government began a crackdown and forced repatriation in 2001.[3]

The vast majority of migrants seeks work in the cross-border area, while a smaller minority has filtered south in search of work in Beijing and other large cities or attempted to emigrate to South Korea through diplomatic compounds. The approximately 130 migrants who have infiltrated embassies and consulates in Beijing and Shenyang have embarrassed the Chinese government internationally (particularly in the few instances when the Chinese People's Armed Police violated international law by entering some compounds to apprehend the intruders). Yet, before the 2001 crackdown, China had a hand in facilitating the cross-border migration, probably because Beijing recognized that it was a kind of social safety valve for the Pyongyang regime and because the Chinese government chose to ignore the smuggling rings and bribery which operated openly in the border region.

The majority of migrants (particularly those of ethnic Korean-Chinese origin) work in Chinese factories in the adjacent Jilin and Liaoning provinces, where they are paid a fraction of the wages paid to Chinese laborers (which are not high to begin with), thus increasing the profit margin of the Chinese enterprise. Many female migrants have also been sold into prostitution or to Chinese husbands. The provincial Chinese governments in Jilin and Liaoning also put many refugees into small resettlement camps, soup kitchens, and other half-way-house accommodations before they could be employed, resettled, or repatriated.

Prior to March 2001, when the crackdown began, those migrants who were apprehended were returned to North Korea, but most (even multiple offenders) were simply subjected to a 30-day reeducation program rather than harsh treatment. Since then, however, there is substantial evidence of a stricter Chinese policy aimed at apprehending and returning the migrants to North Korea, who often "meet execution, prison, torture, and detention in labor camps."[4] Chinese motivation for the crackdown appears threefold. First, the break-ins to diplomatic compounds proved to be an international embarrassment to China and forced the Chinese government to increase security around embassies and compounds substantially—a financial cost absorbed by the Chinese government. Second, China recalled the precedent set by Hungary opening its borders to East German migrants in 1989, who then entered West Germany and helped trigger the downfall of the Communist regime. China feared a similar mass exodus and result in North Korea. Third, the DPRK government was demanding the return of the refugees—something Beijing could not ignore.

On balance, China has been a critical actor in keeping the North Korean regime afloat and the North Korean population from a full-fledged and catastrophic famine. The Chinese government calculates that it is in its national interests to do so—both because a regime implosion would put a far heavier burden on China and because doing so is a half-step toward China's preferred strategy: real reform in North Korea.

## REGIME REFORM

Since the early 1990s, Beijing has probably been the strongest external advocate of extensive economic and social reform to North Korea's autarkic *juche* policy. China calculates that, if managed carefully, reforms do not necessarily bring about the collapse of Communist regimes, as was the case in the USSR and Eastern Europe, but can strengthen the ruling party's base of support.

Kim Jong-il may be listening. He has visited China at least three times since May 2000 and may have made other secret visits. He has been shown the Zhongguancun computer district in Beijing, the skyscrapers and shopping centers of Shanghai, and export industries in Shenzhen. He has also received extensive briefings from Chinese officials and economists and has reportedly demonstrated a relatively sophisticated knowledge of various matters and asked astute questions.

Further exchanges to explore reforms have taken place at lower levels between the CCP's International Liaison Department (ILD) and its counterpart in the Korean Workers Party. (The ILD's annual almanac lists exchanges of between one and two dozen delegations annually in recent years.) Of course, the most noteworthy sign of Pyongyang's move down the Chinese reform path was the establishment of the Sinuiju Special Administrative Region near the Chinese border and the appointment of China's wealthiest businessman, Yang Bin, as the "governor" of the region. Before Yang Bin could take up his appointment, however, Chinese security officials arrested him on charges of tax fraud and other unspecified economic crimes.[5]

While advocating economic and social (and implicitly political) reform, China realizes that reform in North Korea is a gamble—one that could easily exacerbate many of North Korea's dilemmas. Nevertheless, Beijing believes that pursuing reform is the best option and one in which China would play a significant economic role.

## RELATIONS WITH SOUTH KOREA

The third element of China's policy calculus is deepening already robust ties with South Korea—both in their own right today as well as in anticipation of eventual unification of the two Koreas. Over the past decade, the relationship between China and the Republic of Korea (ROK) has completely transformed; it is now one of the strongest in the East Asian region. A kind of "China fever" has swept across South Korea, or at least the business community.

In 2001, China became South Korea's largest trading partner, surpassing the United States; South Korea is China's third-largest trade partner. Two-way trade in 2001 was approximately $40 billion and probably grew by 30 percent in 2002. The ROK is now the fifth-largest foreign investor in China, investing $830 million in 2001 and a projected $1 billion in 2002, and more than 8,000 South Korean companies now operate in China and employ hundreds of thousands of Chinese workers (particularly in the rust belt in the northeastern part of the country, where the Chinese government is trying to restructure and retool traditional heavy industries).[6] South Korean firms are also very active in developing China's border region adjacent to North Korea. A dense network of transport links connecting the ROK with northeastern China and the Shandong peninsula facilitates the movement of goods, capital, and people.

In 2000, approximately one million South Koreans visited China and more than 60,000 were long-term residents in China (including 13,000 students).[7] In 2001, almost 450,000 Chinese visited South Korea.[8] Diplomatically, a series of presidential, ministerial, and subministerial visits take place annually, with the two governments having proclaimed a "comprehensive, cooperative partnership" in 2000. Military exchanges between central-level officers, individual services, and region-level commands are also quite extensive; and in 2001 the two navies exchanged their first official port calls.

This relationship has become extremely important to Beijing as well as to Seoul, and the People's Republic of China (PRC) is not about to sacrifice it to placate Pyongyang in any way. (Needless to say, the PRC-ROK relationship now dwarfs PRC-DPRK relations.) Indeed, China's robust relations with South Korea act as a form of leverage with North Korea.

China's strategy for building ties with the South is born not only of economic motives but also of strategic calculations. Since the rapprochement more than a decade ago, Beijing has realized that it would have little leverage in shaping the eventual outcome of the divided Korean peninsula if it did not enjoy strong ties with South Korea. Such ties would also serve to offset any potential threat from the U.S.-ROK alliance and from U.S. forces on the peninsula. A close relationship would also serve to undercut or offset Japanese attempts to gain a stronger foothold on the peninsula. Beijing's strategy has been a net success, but both sides have reaped the benefits.

Beijing and Seoul consult with and support each other about strategy toward the DPRK. Both governments favor engagement with the North, a reformist North Korea, and eventual peaceful unification. The PRC and the ROK both oppose a punitive approach based on sanctions, and neither seems to endorse the Bush administration's policy of tailored containment. Both governments strongly oppose Pyongyang's WMD development, withdrawal from the Agreed Framework and the International Atomic Energy Agency (IAEA) safeguards program, and otherwise belligerent behavior. When ROK president Kim Dae-jung paid a state visit to Beijing in November 2002 to commemorate the tenth anniversary of the establishment of diplomatic relations, both sides reiterated the desire to maintain the Agreed Framework and to keep the peninsula free of nuclear weapons and other WMD.[9]

In sum, China's entire approach to South Korea over the past decade has been motivated by four main factors: as a hedge against regime collapse in the North and/or potential unification of North and South Korea; as an astute economic investment; as a key component of its proactive peripheral diplomacy; and as a strategic ploy to gain long-term influence over the Korean peninsula.

## DOMINANT EXTERNAL INFLUENCE

Although never publicly articulated, China tends to view the Korean peninsula as its natural sphere of influence—much as the United States views Latin America and Russia views Central Asia (and previously viewed the Baltic states and eastern Europe). Over the long term, geography will determine a great deal of the balance of power in Northeast Asia. China's proximity and growing interdependence will become, China hopes, the determining factor in the strategic orientation of both Korean states. This does not necessarily mean that China is looking to establish a new form of tributary vassal state (such as the one it maintained for several centuries), nor will it necessarily evolve into an asymmetrical patron-client relationship. The relationship will be deferential, however, and will likely mean that China will become more important to the Koreas than Japan, Russia, or the United States. At least, that is China's strategic calculus.

The outlines of this reconfigured relationship between China and the Koreas are already evident in the manner in which Seoul and Beijing now deal with each other. Not only is the relationship fully institutionalized, but both governments defer to each other's preferences (which are nearly identical when it comes to policy and strategy toward North Korea). Furthermore, China has been able to exploit South Korea's antipathy toward Japan to its advantage.

Any consideration of a dominant Chinese influence on the Korean peninsula must include the role of the United States and the presence of U.S. forces. How will China react to the alliance between the United States and the ROK and to U.S. military forces stationed on the peninsula following (presumptive) unification? Personal discussions with civilian analysts, Foreign Ministry officials, and military officers in China suggest that China's strong preference is that U.S. military involvement would no longer be an issue following unification and that the alliance would be naturally dissolved and troops withdrawn.

The logic underlying this option is China's view that alliances require declared adversaries as a rationale for their existence; thus, because an adversarial relationship between North and South Korea would no longer exist (and indeed the two Koreas would by definition no longer exist), there would be no continuing reason for the alliance and presence of U.S. troops. An unarticulated but crucial element of this line of thinking is that the China-Korea relationship would, by this time, be fully normalized, cooperative, and one of good neighbors. Hence, a rationale for the presence of U.S. troops and an alliance based on a possible perceived threat from China would not be realistic, and Beijing would question Seoul's sincerity should South Korea seek the continuation of the U.S. alliance and troop presence. Such reasoning already resonates in South Korea, where U.S. suggestions of a "China threat" ring hollow. South Korean scholar Jae Ho Chung has succinctly summarized the position in which Seoul would find itself: "China's growing influence over the Korean peninsula is real. The bottom line for Seoul is not to antagonize China; in this regard, South Korea being sucked into a U.S.-China conflict over Taiwan or elsewhere must be avoided."[10]

If this is an accurate analysis of Beijing's vision of how the issue would play out, it is helpful to consider a series of variations by Chinese officials, analysts, and PLA officers that have been articulated over the past two years. The official position, of course—as reiterated by China's ambassador to the ROK on the occasion of the tenth anniversary of ties—is that China opposes the stationing of foreign troops abroad (although Ambassador Li Bin did not go so far as to denounce the generic existence of alliances per se).[11] Some PLA officers have privately voiced the view that under no circumstances could China tolerate the continuation of U.S. forces on its border. Other PLA officers, however, have offered the opinion in personal interviews that, as long as the forces were stationed below the thirty-eighth parallel and not "aimed against China," then China (and presumably the PLA) could live with them. Another position frequently heard from Chinese Foreign Ministry officials is that whether to maintain the U.S. alliance and the presence of U.S. troops is a sovereign decision to be made by a newly unified Korea and that, as long as the situation did not threaten any other nation, the decision is one to be worked out between the Korean and U.S. governments.

The common denominator of all these views, of course, is the configuration and orientation of the troop deployments and the nature of the alliance after unification, but the broader issue is the state of Sino-

U.S. relations at that time. If relations between the United States and China are troubled or antagonistic, with prominent persons in the United States arguing that there is a China threat, then China would undoubtedly judge the presence of U.S. forces in Korea as a U.S. measure oriented against China and as front-line forces for intervention in Taiwan. If the United States and a unified Korea were to renegotiate the terms of the alliance and status of forces following unification, it is highly likely that China would seek some kind of assurance from Seoul that such forces could not be deployed in any U.S. conflict with China, especially in the instance of a flare-up in the Taiwan Strait.

## PHASED INTEGRATION

Concomitant with China's aversion to the DPRK's sudden implosion is its opposition to a hasty integration of North and South Korea. Chinese analysts estimate that rapid unification would inevitably be both unmanageable and disruptive, making the burdens of German unification pale in comparison. A substantial part of the human, financial, energy, and environmental costs would ultimately fall on China.

Beijing prefers to pursue a gradual, phased integration (*tonghe*), which will eventually lead to formal unification (*tongyi*). A German *Ostpolitik* model (or in the case of the ROK, a *Nordpolitik* model) is deemed the best way to proceed. This would involve a phased program of gradually increasing family, cultural, social, professional, and sports exchanges; direct transport links including rail links across the demilitarized zone (DMZ); commercial interchange, investment, and aid; intergovernmental exchanges; and a series of military confidence-building measures (CBMs) on both sides of the DMZ (one interesting model for these might be the CBMs that China and the Central Asian republics negotiated in the mid-1990s through the Shanghai Cooperation Organization). Once in place over several years, these various interactive measures would build the trust and confidence the two sides need to move toward discussions about formal political unification.

## A MORE RESPONSIBLE NORTH KOREA

The last of China's goals is somehow to persuade Pyongyang to halt its roguish behavior when it comes to weapons proliferation as well as its WMD development. North Korea's conventional military deployments are also a concern, but they are secondary to issues of nuclear proliferation and WMD development. To this end, China advocates a complete return to the Agreed Framework.

Although containing North Korea's nuclear program is a high Chinese priority, it is not by any means the first issue on Beijing's agenda. China sees these issues as part and parcel of the broader set of policy goals outlined above. There certainly exists exigency at present, and it must be addressed, but China's longer-term vision for North Korea goes well beyond WMD issues.

## China's Role in Resolving the Current Crisis

Beijing's basic approach to the current crisis is to seek a package deal, concluded multilaterally, which trades North Korea's abandonment of WMD for a clear road map that will:

- set North Korea on the path to real reform,

- initiate a phased integration of North and South Korea, and

- help normalize relations between the United States and the DPRK.

Chances range from very doubtful to nil that Beijing will go along with Washington's new strategy of tailored containment or participate in a collective, sanctions-based punitive policy toward Pyongyang. This is simply not the way China prefers to deal with the problem. Ever since the 1994 crisis, China has been very clear that it firmly believes that a strategy of coercion and isolation not only will be counterproductive to gaining Pyongyang's cooperation but also is likely to prompt the North Korean regime to take desperate and potentially catastrophic actions.

The obsessive and singular focus on the issue of a nuclear buildup misses the broader environment that China wishes to foster on the Korean peninsula. At a minimum, from China's perspective—as clearly articulated by Chinese president Jiang Zemin and Russian president Vladimir Putin at their December 2002 summit meeting—the nuclear issue must be linked to "normalization" of U.S. relations with the DPRK.[12] (In this context, at least, "normalization" does not necessarily imply diplomatic recognition; rather, it implies the kind of Liaison Office arrangement that the United States and China had between 1972 and 1979.) Beijing's bottom line is that there must be a package deal linked to a range of initiatives to help alleviate North Korea's chronic economic and social crises and to bring the DPRK into the international community.

Moreover, despite the strains in relations between Beijing and Pyongyang, China is simply not going to allow North Korea to implode. The Chinese government will do whatever it can to alleviate human suffering and to keep the North Korean regime on life support. If worst came to worst, however, and the regime did peacefully collapse, Beijing believes that it holds a very strong hand in exercising its influence over a unified Korea.

China's current close relations with Russia also strengthen Beijing's influence. The solidarity on the North Korea issue that Jiang and Putin demonstrated at their December 2002 Beijing summit has sent a strong signal that the two governments do not wish to pursue a coercive and confrontational policy toward Pyongyang in an effort to resolve the current nuclear crisis. Even though the call to return to the Agreed Framework is probably unrealistic, the two leaders clearly signaled a preference for a multilateral and comprehensive solution to the nuclear problem.

## China's Influence on Current U.S. Policy

Although some U.S. China analysts believe that the current crisis offers China a real opportunity to prove its credentials as a responsible power by siding with the Bush administration's tough approach to North Korea, it's actually the other way around. China seems to have the well-reasoned position based on a long-term perspective and road map for the Korean peninsula. Most importantly, China's position coincides with that of the other major powers and involved parties (South Korea, Russia, Japan, and the European Union). It is the United States that has struggled to find its footing on policy toward North Korea since the Bush administration took office in January 2001. The issue is not so much that Beijing should exercise its presumed influence or leverage over Pyongyang, as China does not have a great deal of influence in the first place and, in any event, does not choose to exercise it in an overtly coercive manner. China has constructively offered to host direct U.S.-DPRK talks in which Beijing could play an important facilitating role.

The Bush administration is still trying to satisfy its own conflicting impulses. On one hand, it is inclined to play hardball with the hard-line North Korean regime; on the other hand, the administration recognizes that only a multilateral and comprehensive approach will solve the problem. Only time will tell whether the Bush administration's dual approach will work or whether the United States will have to join China, Russia, South Korea, Japan, the EU, and other actors in recognizing that only a comprehensive solution that starts by acknowledging that a reforming and outwardly engaged DPRK is the ultimate solution to the problem.

Washington is not seeing the forest for the trees if it continues to believe that the issue of Pyongyang's nuclear weapons program is the primary or only issue that needs to be resolved. It is also mistaken to believe that an explicit security guarantee to Pyongyang will be a sufficient trade-off. If the Bush administration continues with this myopic approach, it not only will fail to resolve the crisis but also will cause deep fissures with key allies and major powers. The United States will then potentially have the worst of all possible worlds: a nuclear-capable North Korea and severely strained relations with key nations that the United States needs on a range of other critical issues. Washington would be well advised to recognize this linkage sooner rather than later.

To be sure, Beijing has a variety of good reasons to work with the United States to halt Pyongyang's withdrawal from the Agreed Framework—not the least of which is that the existence of a nuclear North Korea is likely to prompt South Korea, Japan, and possibly Taiwan to follow suit. This development would change the entire balance of power in Northeast Asia—and not to China's advantage. Thus, China finds common cause with Washington, Seoul, Moscow, Tokyo, and Brussels to seek a permanent halt to North Korea's nuclear weapons program. Such cooperation will be most successful, however, if all key parties work with a common vision of a North Korea on the road to reform.

## Notes

1. See John Tkacik, "China's Korea Conundrum," *Asian Wall Street Journal*, December 2, 2002; Jasper Becker, "China's Influence Is Limited," *International Herald Tribune*, January 10, 2003; Philip Pan, "China Treads Carefully around North Korea," *Washington Post*, January 10, 2003.

2. See "Fu Quanyou Meets with DPRK People's Army Goodwill Mission," Xinhua News Service, October 11, 2002.

3. See John Pomfret, "China Cracks Down on N. Korean Refugees," *Washington Post*, January 22, 2003.

4. Ibid.

5. "Don't Get Too Capitalist Comrade," *Economist*, October 12, 2002.

6. James Brooke, "China 'Looming Large' in South Korea as Biggest Player, Replacing the U.S.," *New York Times*, January 3, 2003.

7. Jae Ho Chung, "South Korea between Eagle and Dragon: Perceptual Ambivalence and Strategic Dilemmas," *Asian Survey* 41, no. 5 (September–October 2001): 781.

8. Brooke, "China 'Looming Large' in South Korea."

9. "China Committed to Peninsular Peace: Jiang," *People's Daily* (internet edition), November 21, 2002, http://english.peopledaily.com.cn/200211/20.

10. Jae Ho Chung, "South Korea between Eagle and Dragon," p. 795.

11. Kim Ji-ho, "China's Envoy to ROK: U.S. Troops Must Not Pose Threat to Neighbors," *Korea Herald*, August 21, 2002, in FBIS/East Asia, August 21, 2002.

12. "Jiang Joins Putin in Leaning on Pyongyang," *International Herald Tribune*, December 3, 2002.

Derek J. Mitchell

# A Blueprint for U.S. Policy toward a Unified Korea

Unification of the Korean peninsula will occur on its own timetable. U.S. decisionmakers cannot wait for Korean unification, however, to develop strategies to address its aftermath and to ensure that U.S. security interests are protected in that environment. The creation of a new Korean nation-state, most likely through the demise of the Democratic People's Republic of Korea (DPRK) and the ascension of the Republic of Korea (ROK), will generate more variables and uncertainties than any other contingency in East Asian affairs. Failure to anticipate how this catalytic event might affect U.S. interests and to develop and implement forward-looking policies for a postunification security environment threatens both U.S. and regional security in the long term.

## The View from Washington

This article assumes that the outcome of unification will be primarily on South Korean terms and defines unification as the creation of a unified polity rather than unified societies or economic structures. The cir-

Derek J. Mitchell is a senior fellow in the International Security Program at CSIS. The author wishes to thank the CSIS working group participants from the United States, South Korea, Japan, China, and Russia whose contributions are reflected throughout this piece.

cumstances under which unification may occur—peaceful integration, the gradual or sudden collapse of the DPRK, or war—is an important if unpredictable variable in any policy-planning assessment of Korea's future. Nonetheless, however unification occurs, a number of fundamental U.S. strategic interests in postunification Korea, and postunification East Asia more broadly, will remain substantially similar to what they are today.

Regional stability may become even more critical in the tenuous period of uncertainty and turmoil likely to characterize Korea's transition. Having fought three major wars in East Asia during the twentieth century, including one on the Korean peninsula that resulted in a substantial loss of American lives and resources, the United States understands well the importance of helping to maintain stability, prevent the emergence of regional rivalries, and promote the peaceful resolution of differences within and among regional nations. Nearly a half-million U.S. citizens live, work, and study in the Asia-Pacific region. More than one-third of total U.S. trade is conducted with the region, with millions of U.S. jobs depending on its continued growth and development. Sustained regional economic growth through the promotion of market economies and open sea-lanes—essential to the free flow of resources and trade into and within the region—will remain just as much a core U.S. national security interest following unification as it is now.

Long-term U.S. active engagement in East Asia—whether political, diplomatic, economic, or military—has traditionally managed to promote a peaceful security environment by providing a buffer against tensions. To continue to safeguard its regional interests, even after change on the Korean peninsula, U.S. security strategy should preserve U.S. treaty alliances as the cornerstone of peace and stability in East Asia. It is unlikely that a multilateral institution akin to NATO will be possible in Asia for the foreseeable future. The U.S. alliance structure and regional military presence will remain the most viable guarantor of regional security in its absence. At the same time, Korean unification will not minimize the profound U.S. interest in strengthening U.S. engagement with other nonallied nations in the region, particularly China, Indonesia, Singapore, Malaysia, and Vietnam. Multilateral dialogues to promote a common approach to regional affairs and to sustain broad regional support for the alliance structure will also be increasingly necessary and appropriate.

To give form to this ongoing commitment to regional security and to mitigate potential military rivalries, the United States will have to maintain a robust and credible military presence in the region. This presence will have to be altered to address the new domestic environment in Korea as well as the changed security environment in the region. The maintenance of a ready, balanced, and forward-deployed U.S. force would fulfill important U.S. interests in regional deterrence and burden sharing and would demonstrate political commitment that a fully remote posture off the peninsula would preclude. Ideally, a unified Korea would maintain a capable, conventional, national military, prepared and trained to work with the United States not only to defend the Korean homeland but also to promote regional stability.

Finally, on the Korean peninsula itself, the United States will have a substantial interest in a stable, liberal-democratic, free-market-oriented nation, free of weapons of mass destruction (WMD) and allied with the United States. Stability will require strong Korean political and civil control over the entire territory, with functioning institutions operating under the rule of law with general popular support.

## Postunification Korean Interests

Although U.S. national interests will obviously play the most important role in determining U.S. postunification policy toward the Korean peninsula, the interests and perspectives of Korea itself will clearly set parameters for U.S. policymakers. The full integration of the two Koreas will be extraordinarily challenging for many years following formal unification, but even in such an uncertain environment, certain national interests of a postunification Korea may be anticipated.

The predominant domestic goal of a unified Korea likely will be to establish a stable, democratic government based on an open-market economy, akin to the ROK today. The temptation may exist for the South to impose a more restrictive, perhaps occupation-style control over the North or to curb full participation in unified Korean affairs during at least the transitional period. The challenge for the new government will be to balance what it views as internal security needs with an overall commitment to sustain democratic progress through the gradual development of transparent institutions, civil liberties, electoral processes, and the rule of law in the North.

A unified Korea also will continue to have vital interests in preserving stability and peace in the Asia-Pacific region to promote its economic and political goals. At present, South Korea conducts more than two-thirds of its trade within the region. The amount of current ROK trade through Asian sea-lanes accounts for more than 40 percent of its total trade, and about two-thirds of its energy supplies flow through the South China Sea. Unification will not substantially change these trends. The absence of a stable regional security environment, however, would inhibit Korea's ability to enjoy sustained economic progress or, worse, might challenge its ability to garner sufficient resources for reconstruction.

One of the first acts of a unified Korean state will be to reassess its long-term security strategy and orientation carefully. The Korean military will likely move toward a defense-oriented, crisis-management strategy and away from a war-fighting posture. Korea will be preoccupied for some time with internal instability as South Korean authorities focus on decommissioning the DPRK military and integrating its personnel productively into popular Korean society. The ROK military will need to safeguard and account for residual DPRK military equipment and material, particularly any weapons of mass destruction and the delivery systems or laboratories associated with them.

A unified Korea would be expected to have no interest in WMD development or deployment as such an act would likely spur a regional arms race and create tensions with the international community, especially the United States, over nonproliferation. This calculation will ultimately depend on the state of the regional security environment at the time of unification, including the status of Korea's alliance with the

United States as well as its confidence in the U.S. nuclear umbrella, Korea's relationship with Russia and China, and whether or not Japan develops nuclear weapons.

Arguably, Korea's interest will continue to lie in the retention of its alliance with the United States following unification. Despite some frictions, the alliance has served to help preserve Korea's essential freedom of action and to facilitate its historic political and economic development over many decades. Maintaining an alliance with the United States will also help preserve the U.S.-led, alliance-based security structure in East Asia that has served as a stabilizing force in the region, hedged against the rise of an aggressive regional power, and protected Korea from becoming the political if not military battleground upon which the major Asian powers have historically sought regional advantage. Indeed, a unified Korea will need the stability and reassurance engendered by its alliance with the United States more than ever during the many years of transition following unification, particularly under collapse or war scenarios.

A unified Korea also will arguably have a substantial interest in accepting a U.S. military presence on the peninsula following unification. This presence would serve as a key component of continued alliance relations and the overall U.S. regional military presence to preserve stability throughout East Asia. Korea's continued hosting of U.S. forces would sustain the special relationship between the governments and armed forces of both sides, facilitate their coordination of regional strategy, and continue to serve as a deterrent to others seeking advantage on the peninsula.

Korea, however, will likely seek greater independence in its overall relationship with the United States. Unification may bring about a resurgence of Korean nationalism and self-confidence commensurate with its growing national strength and increased international prestige. As a result, the new Korea will likely seek a more equal bilateral relationship.

A united Korea will likely aim to avoid acting in any way that might give the impression that it is siding strategically with either the United States or China against the other. Korea's future development will depend greatly on good relations with and between its traditional ally and its sizable neighbor. Korea's substantial economic and security interests in the United States and China ensure that antagonizing either side would only be detrimental to Korean progress. Perhaps above all else, the United States can expect Korea to seek to retain maximum flexibility in its foreign policy and to avoid the appearance of being tied too closely with the policies or attitudes of either side in any U.S.-Chinese rivalry, including over Taiwan.

Finally, how unification is achieved, including the nature and degree of international involvement in the unification process, will shape the outlook of Korea toward its external environment and the context in which Korea ultimately will make its strategic choices. For instance, should North Korea collapse, the need for U.S. engagement and external security guarantees is likely to be greater than if unification comes through peaceful integration over time. Should the United States fight alongside the South in a war against the North, the fresh strategic and personal bonds created would likely tie the two sides closely together for many years thereafter. Alternatively, should unification occur under conditions in which Koreans view the United States as hindering rather than helping the process, resentment could build between the United States and the Korean people, poisoning postunification relations regardless of objective calculations of mutual national interests.

## Regional Views

Korea has long served as a strategic battleground for regional powers who desire to safeguard their security by providing a buffer zone against the aggression of others. Because Korea is a traditional pathway into China, Japan, and the Russian Far East, each surrounding actor perceives the strategic importance of the Korean landmass. China, Japan, and Russia can each point to moments in history in which their territory was threatened by vulnerabilities from the Korean periphery. That history will continue to inform their future strategic perspectives.

Residual tensions among the major East Asian powers due to history, overlapping territorial claims, border disputes, and continued mistrust and uncertainty over the future trajectory of major powers—particularly China and Japan—will remain critical challenges for regional security. Even without the DPRK threat on the Korean peninsula after unification, in the absence of effective institutions to address conflicting interests and safeguard common security, such residual challenges mean that regional balance of power considerations will remain central to regional peace and stability.

Yet, the major powers in Northeast Asia—China, Japan, and Russia—share a common interest in a politically and socially stable, economically vibrant, capitalist Korea following unification, free of weapons of mass destruction. Each of these nations has based its future development on a commitment to free trade and investment flows and will support the emergence of a unified Korea that conforms to such capitalist norms. Each prizes the free flow of shipping in the region and recognizes the essential links between its own economic health and that of its neighbors; Korea's economic development is included in this calculation.

In regional affairs, common interests in trade, stability, and the free flow of shipping reflect unified perspectives on fundamental issues. Each nation fears the potential flood of refugees as well as other social and monetary costs of reconstruction that may result from a difficult political, economic, and social transition on the peninsula. Most of these powers have committed themselves to liberal democracy and open societies as the most effective method of maintaining internal stability and external relations and will likewise support the emergence of liberal democracy and an open society in Korea—perhaps akin to the democratic tradition established by South Korea. Moreover, no East Asian power wants to see WMD proliferation on the peninsula, recognizing how such a development would destabilize regional strategic calculations and spur potential for an unproductive arms race.

East Asian perspectives on the future relationship between a unified Korea and the United States, however, will differ from state to state. Japan will likely seek to preserve the U.S.-ROK alliance and the U.S.

military presence in Korea to guarantee that the unified state will be neither hostile to it nor allied with unfriendly countries. Japan would also welcome a unified Korea that may share the burden of its regional security partnership with the United States. China and Russia, on the other hand, seek a unified Korea more independent of the United States. China, in particular, will strive to exert significant influence over political and security developments in the new Korean state to help shape an immediate neighbor that is not too closely allied with the United States or Japan.

At a minimum, China and perhaps Russia will question the purpose and intent behind a continued U.S.-Korean alliance and U.S. military presence on the peninsula and suspect that the continuation of both over the long term will allow the United States to assert its power and pursue its interests in the region at their expense. The loss of its DPRK buffer is bound to leave China feeling exposed on its northeast flank and to create strategic uncertainties that a U.S. troop presence will exacerbate. Beijing also hopes that the establishment of a newly unified Korea outside the U.S. alliance system would weaken Washington's overall influence in the Asia-Pacific region, constrain U.S. freedom of action (particularly with respect to Taiwan), and reduce the potential of encirclement. More so than China, Russia's take on the U.S.-Korean alliance and U.S. military presence on the peninsula will ultimately depend on the state of its bilateral relations with Washington, as well as Moscow's relations with Beijing, at the time of unification, which cannot be anticipated with certainty today.

## Roadblocks Ahead

Considering U.S. policy toward a unified Korea not only requires assessing future U.S. interests, but also anticipating what potential obstacles to the achievement of U.S. regional interests could arise. First, financial burdens inherent in the process of unification will likely constrain Korea's ability and possibly its inclination to support the U.S. troop presence and alliance obligations. Regardless of the method of unification, the financial and social cost of Korean unification on South Korean society will be enormous. In this environment, host-nation support for maintaining U.S. forces on the peninsula will be highly controversial, if not politically difficult to sustain. Similarly, the unified Korean military will focus on internal challenges such as civil defense and civil reconstruction, constricting for some time its ability to work with the United States on regional operations.

In addition, growing anti-American sentiment within Korea's body politic may serve as one of the greatest dangers to U.S. interests on the peninsula following unification. Public opinion polls and anecdotal evidence in South Korea today reveal that, despite residual good will toward the United States for its commitment to Korean security and admiration for U.S. culture, resentment toward the United States within Korean society is growing. The nature, depth, and sustainability of this sentiment over time is not clear, but leaders in the United States and Korea should not lightly dismiss the potential for this sentiment to become an impediment to future bilateral relations. Resurgent nationalism resulting from unification could direct greater attention to perceived grievances and humiliations inflicted on Korea in recent history and exacerbate anti-American attitudes.

Growth in the scope and intensity of anti-Japanese sentiment following unification is an obvious corollary and may also complicate future coordination of U.S. alliance policies. Likewise, potential growth in popular attraction to China for ethnic and cultural reasons, of which there is evidence today, may further develop, complicating Korean relations with Beijing's likely future rivals.

Furthermore, the United States should be keenly aware of how effects of Korean unification on the U.S. strategic position on the peninsula will have concurrent, ripple effects on the U.S. position in Japan and in the region as a whole. Japan and Korea both closely watch U.S. alliance relations with the other and seek as much parity in their arrangements as possible. Concessions or alterations in host-nation support, the Status of Forces Agreement, and troop presence in Korea are likely to be used as ammunition for critics or reformers of the U.S. presence in Japan, potentially leading to a destructive spiral throughout Asia. A sustainable burden-sharing arrangement will be critical to preventing this contingency and will require close consultation between Japan and Korea.

A final wildcard is the continued commitment of the U.S. populace, including Congress, to sustaining its role as security guarantor in East Asia and to expending the economic, political, and military resources necessary to maintain its presence. Currently, no evidence exists that the United States will attenuate its commitments to East Asia in the future, following Korean unification or otherwise. Given the nature of democracy, however, U.S. domestic politics or public opinion could complicate U.S. international policy. The state of the region, the world, and the U.S. domestic environment at the time of unification is impossible to predict. Variables include developments in the war on terrorism; the U.S. fiscal situation; U.S. relations with other regional states; and the political, military, and financial support of regional allies and friends to help meet U.S. interests. Nonetheless, given the tremendous interest the United States will retain in the peace and stability of East Asia following unification, as indicated above, the U.S. regional security strategy of alliances, military presence, and sustained diplomatic engagement will likely endure regardless of such potential complications.

## Pillars for Postunification Strategy

To best meet U.S., Korean, and regional interests following Korean unification, as outlined above, the United States should construct a U.S. policy toward a unified Korea based on the following approach.

- *Reaffirm U.S. commitment to the terms of the 1954 U.S.-ROK Mutual Defense Treaty and expand its scope to encompass a postunification alliance focused on maintaining regional peace and stability.*

Broadening the U.S.-Korean alliance to encompass regional rather than merely peninsular security will require that the United States remain comprehensively engaged in the political, diplomatic, economic, and military affairs of the entire region. Reaffirming the U.S.-Korean alliance will reassure the region that the U.S. commitment to its alliance-based regional security strategy will continue and will promote investment in U.S. power as a regional security guarantor. The alliance must become a more equal partnership, involving regular, close consultation on regional security matters in coordination with other U.S. regional allies. Both sides should be transparent about the purpose and nature of the alliance, which should serve as an overall hedge against regional instability. The alliance should guard against being defined or perceived as being directed against any particular third country.

- *Maintain a military presence on the peninsula as a symbol and guarantor of continued U.S. security commitments to the peninsula and the region.*

The United States should be flexible about the structure of its presence on the peninsula but firm about maintaining some form of presence after unification. During a difficult transition, a continued U.S. presence on the peninsula will allow a unified Korea to focus on the challenges of domestic development, including the long process of reconciliation, rather than on its external security. The United States should consult closely with Korean authorities concerning an appropriate structure according to regional security needs and domestic Korean sensitivities.

Given the absence of a North Korean threat, U.S. capabilities should evolve from a heavy, dug-in force focused on peninsular security to a light, mobile, expeditionary presence that can deploy quickly and effectively elsewhere in the region. After unification, the United Nations (UN) Command should dissolve. The Combined Forces Command should also be disbanded in favor of a parallel command structure under which independent U.S. and Korean forces may cooperate and coordinate activities, akin to the arrangement under which U.S. and Japanese armed forces operate. Independent parallel forces provide both sides with maximum flexibility and plausible deniability should either side deploy for operations the other may find undesirable, either for political or military reasons. Nonetheless, both sides should immediately establish guidelines for future cooperation to allow for joint training and operations, which should prove relatively smooth given their long experience as a combined force. U.S. forces on the peninsula, meanwhile, should be fully integrated into the operations of other U.S. defense assets in the region.

The United States should be prepared to consider a combination of basing and access arrangements to sustain its presence and enable U.S. and Korean forces to continue close personal contact and joint/combined training. The United States should seek to maintain pre-positioned equipment to facilitate regional operations and training. Such training should be oriented toward both fighting and peacetime regional operations such as search and rescue, antipiracy patrols, counterterrorism, sea-lane security, humanitarian assistance, disaster relief, and peacekeeping/peace enforcement. The two sides should enact any reductions in numbers or changes in arrangements for U.S. military personnel on Korean soil (e.g., Status of Forces Agreement and host-nation support) in close cooperation with Japan. This consultation would ensure an appropriate balance and mix of U.S. capabilities in the region and help to alleviate potential domestic pressures on U.S. forces in Japan induced by changes on the peninsula.

- *Maintain its nuclear umbrella over a unified Korea (and Japan) to solidify the U.S.-Korean security alliance and prevent a regional arms race.*

The U.S. nuclear umbrella over South Korea and Japan during the past 50 years has been an essential element of the bilateral security alliance and has been effective in maintaining ROK security. The U.S. commitment has enabled the ROK to renounce the development, stockpiling, or deployment of nuclear weapons and has prevented emergence of a regional arms race. Encouraging a unified Korea to renounce WMD because of the U.S. retention of its nuclear umbrella will serve this end and further solidify the basis of a postunification security alliance.

- *Encourage a unified Korea to join an integrated, regional missile defense network to protect allied assets as an essential element of the postunification alliance.*

Over time, missile defense will become an increasingly important element of U.S. defense doctrine and posture and conceptions of international security. The United States has committed itself to developing and deploying such defense capability in East Asia to protect its allies, friends, and forward-deployed personnel from future missile attack by rogue nations or others with hostile intent. As a key regional ally, Korea should be encouraged to participate in a regional missile defense network to support this goal. At the same time, a unified Korea should be part of a broader regional and international dialogue among responsible nations concerning a strategic doctrine that incorporates missile defense to prevent such deployments from becoming a rationale for a destabilizing regional arms race.

- *Fill gaps in logistics support and other domestic functions for Korea during its transitional period.*

The Korean people must handle the process of unification on the peninsula themselves. Particularly in a war or collapse scenario, however, the challenges to domestic security in the aftermath of unification may be substantial. Despite the high quality of Korean personnel, such turmoil may prove overwhelming for Korean capabilities. The United States will have substantial interests in ensuring that the peninsula is stable and under sufficient police control to prevent the emergence of a haven for transnational crime including terrorism, narcotics trafficking, counterfeiting, and WMD proliferation. The United States should be prepared to organize and provide assistance to Korean civil authorities as requested by the Korean government, perhaps in conjunction with regional or UN forces. Such assistance might take the form of transport, construction, engineering, refugee repatriation, or other public safety initiatives.

- *Provide extensive material support for political and economic reconstruction of a unified Korea, potentially playing a leadership role in any international effort, as appropriate.*

The political, economic, and social challenges of unification will impose enormous financial and social costs on the Korean people. The

United States should lead, through its own efforts and through the UN and international financial institutions, the provision of political and material assistance to promote the development of a stable, prosperous liberal democracy on the peninsula, even as it takes care not to usurp the sovereign rights and responsibilities of the Korean government. U.S. aid agencies should provide resources for official and nongovernmental U.S. organizations to take common U.S. and ROK political values of democracy, free enterprise, civil liberty, and rule of law to the then-former North Korea through education and other services. The agencies should, at the same time, maintain vigilance against retreat from such values in South Korea due to the stresses of managing the unification process. By seeing the task of reconstruction through to the end, the United States would affirm its abiding ties with the Korean people and fulfill a solemn security commitment to a close ally.

- *Prioritize the accounting and responsible control of the former North Korea's nuclear, biochemical, missile, and conventional capabilities, as well as the decommissioning of DPRK forces.*

The DPRK's admission in October 2002 of a clandestine uranium enrichment capability and separate evidence that North Korea has developed and stockpiled chemical and biological (if not nuclear) weapons suggest that the North's military arsenal will remain a potential threat to international security, particularly in the area of nonproliferation, even after unification. An immediate task for the United States and the international community following (if not before) Korean unification, particularly under a collapse or war scenario, would be ensuring that Korea be free of WMD. The United States and Korea must work with the International Atomic Energy Agency and regional nations through existing treaties in this endeavor. To ensure Korea's continued commitment to the abjuration of the development, stockpiling, or deployment of nuclear weapons, the United States should reaffirm its regional nonproliferation strategy, including support for Japan's Three Nonnuclear Principles, because developments in nations such as Japan will affect key political and military calculations of unified Korea.

The United States must also work closely with Korea to ensure that no rogue elements on the peninsula are able to engage in illicit activities involving WMD amidst the turmoil of a postunification environment. In the United States' own interest and as Korea's ally and security guarantor, the decommissioning of DPRK soldiers and their weapons will be an immediate and central U.S. concern following unification.

- *Facilitate the development of minilateral dialogues among Northeast Asian nations following Korean unification to ensure regional confidence in the trajectory of a united Korea.*

The security environment in Northeast Asia following Korean unification will change substantially as Korea may once again assume its traditional status as a strategic buffer for Japan, China, and Russia. Although the United States should remain committed to alliances as the core of its security approach to East Asia, the United States should help establish trilateral, quadrilateral, or other such "minilateral" dialogues to address peninsular and regional security issues.

Such dialogues may serve to promote trust and transparency about the orientation and trajectory of a united Korea and provide strategic reassurance necessary to maintain a stable regional security environment. How the United States handles Asia-Pacific affairs on a regional basis, particularly with Japan and China, may affect Korea's desire to remain closely affiliated with the United States over the long term. Building on cooperation established within the Four Party process among the United States, China, North Korea, and South Korea to establish an official Northeast Asian Security Dialogue process, adding Japan, Russia, and perhaps Mongolia as well as a unified Korea, could serve such a function.

## What Can Be Done Now?

The United States should also consider pursuing the following policy initiatives today to prepare for and shape a positive postunification environment for U.S. interests.

- *Cooperate with Korean leaders to address conditions that promote anti-American sentiment within the Korean body politic to garner public support in Korea for a continued U.S. alliance and military presence following unification.*

The proud and emotional nature of Korean society makes many Korean citizens sensitive to any kind of U.S. interference in intra-Korean affairs. In particular, Koreans often feel humiliated for being treated less than equally in the alliance or being casually disregarded on issues of their own national well-being and sovereignty, including the impact of U.S. military presence. Although some of this sentiment cannot be avoided due to the nature of the relationship and the power imbalance between the two sides, the United States should nonetheless take greater care in its initiatives and rhetoric concerning peninsular affairs to avoid the appearance of arrogance or other perceived affronts to Korean national pride and sovereignty.

U.S. forces in Korea and their political/military leaders should similarly pay substantial attention to any measures that will reduce the footprint of U.S. military personnel based or stationed on the peninsula. These measures could include consolidating and reducing bases where possible, good-neighbor initiatives to promote understanding and good will between base personnel and local communities, and heightened sensitivity to the environmental (including noise) and other hazards that the U.S. military presence poses to local populations. The United States should also consider reforms in the combined military command structure that will provide greater responsibility and authority to Korean leaders.

In the process, the United States should do a better job of promoting a general knowledge of its good works and other alliance benefits as part of an active public diplomacy campaign. For instance, the United States might promote greater exchanges between members of Congress and the ROK National Assembly to develop personal relationships and comprehensive understanding of U.S. policies and perspectives. The United States might provide Seoul greater face by enhancing the stature of its ambassadors to Seoul, along the lines of the elder statesman model the United States follows in Japan. The United States should also ensure that senior foreign policy defense and economic leadership, including the president, travel regularly to Seoul for consultation and to coordinate the most critical role in shaping public perceptions and attitudes toward the bilateral relationship. Perhaps most important, the United States should lean heavily on the Korean leadership itself to promote better understanding of the U.S. role in Korean security and development and aggressively counter misperceptions that fester through the media concerning U.S. policies, presence, and the overall alliance.

- *Continue to strongly support reconciliation between Japanese and Korean societies as a key component of future security in East Asia.*

Historical enmity rooted in Japan's colonial domination of Korea earlier in the century and the inability of Japan to account adequately for the raw emotions that remain in Korean society concerning the period have led to deep divisions and recurring tensions between Japanese and Korean societies. Such lingering resentment prevents full reconciliation between the two sides and threatens any U.S. effort to sustain trilateral coordination in the long term. Today, South Korea and Japan are brought together by a common concern over the DPRK threat. Without this common threat, cooperation may founder in the face of resurgent Korean nationalism, leading to severe bilateral tensions if unchecked.

The United States should elevate positive Japanese-Korean relations to the status of a key strategic concern. Current official and unofficial trilateral dialogues help this process. The United States might promote interaction and exchanges at the legislative level, aimed perhaps at the younger generation, to facilitate personal bonds further. Ultimately, however, the United States cannot and should not seek to mediate such a sensitive divide between these two nations, whose resolution necessarily resides in national good faith efforts by both sides.

- *Consult strategic planners and key policymakers in Japan and Korea to discuss the outlines of a postunification security structure.*

Although Korean unification is unlikely to occur in the near term, the United States and its two Northeast Asian allies must begin the critical process of talking seriously about their respective visions of a postunification security environment in East Asia. Changes in the U.S. relationship with one ally will affect U.S. relations with the other. This dynamic requires that the three nations consult with each other and coordinate their visions to ensure stability and control of the postunification security environment.

Issues the parties should address during such consultations include the structure and nature of the U.S. military presence, the roles and missions of the three forces in safeguarding regional security, and anticipated complications to their respective visions. Either the current Defense Trilateral process (among the U.S., Korean, and Japanese defense ministries) may be used or an entirely new forum may be developed to serve as the vehicle for such talks. These discussions should not, however, occur within the Trilateral Coordination and Oversight Group process, which should remain focused on common approaches to the current North Korean threat. The three sides should eventually engage in consultation and dialogue with other allies and friends who may serve as partners in regional security.

## Anticipate, Don't React

Korean unification will fulfill a commitment to an ally that the United States has expended tremendous national resources to protect and develop for more than fifty years. Yet, with the elimination of the North Korean threat following unification, the United States will find that the original reason for both its presence on the peninsula and its bilateral alliance with Korea will vanish even as challenges to stability in Northeast Asia are likely to increase. No one can predict when unification will occur, but the last 15 years have shown that dramatic international change is often swift and unexpected. On the Korean peninsula, the United States must act today to plan for this contingency to ensure that it can safeguard its interests in the Asia-Pacific region even after the region's strategic environment radically transforms.

**Victor D. Cha**

# Focus on the Future, Not the North

As the Republic of Korea (ROK) gears up for elections in December 2002, the South Korean presidential candidates are invariably arguing over how to deal with the recent revelations that the Democratic People's Republic of Korea (DPRK) has uranium enrichment facilities, the merits of engagement in the face of these revelations, and the future of the U.S.-DPRK Agreed Framework. But as the presidential hopefuls focus on these proximate issues, they are barely discussing the most fundamental and important policy debates the next Korean administration will contemplate before its departure in 2008. A confluence of security and political trends, including the emergence of Korean concerns about the U.S. military presence and the need to prepare for the contingency of Korean unification, argues that changes in the status of U.S. Forces in Korea (USFK) and the direction of the U.S.-ROK alliance are inevitable, if not imminent.[1] Despite all the transient deafening noise over the North's newly declared nuclear ambitions, those in Seoul and Washington who seek a foundation for a long-term U.S.-ROK alliance continue to hone in on three durable tenets:

Victor D. Cha is an associate professor of government and D. S. Song–Korea Foundation Endowed Chair at the Edmund A. Walsh School of Foreign Service at Georgetown University.

Copyright © 2002 by The Center for Strategic and International Studies and the Massachusetts Institute of Technology
*The Washington Quarterly* • 26:1 pp. 91–107.

- an understanding that the alliance's foundation does not depend solely on the nuclear or conventional military threat posed by the DPRK;

- an assessment that the current form of U.S. military presence is in-definitely untenable; and

- a persistence in privileging the long-term alliance rationalities over the temptation to allow the latest DPRK threat to postpone such a discussion.

Even before the June 2000 inter-Korean summit, respected military analysts argued that a reassessment of both the benchmark 100,000-troop presence established by the 1995 Nye report and a concurrent re-evaluation of U.S. force structure on the Korean peninsula were long overdue.[2] Divergent U.S. and ROK policy approaches since that time and mounting civil-military tensions over the USFK have likely intensi-fied these calls. Evidence of these concerns is contained in a September 2000 National Intelligence Council study that warned that a stagnant U.S. attitude about its force presence is certain to risk nationalistic backlash in Korea and Japan.[3] Another study put it more bluntly: "It is imperative to reduce the footprint of U.S. bases in the major cities. Relatively large concentrations of U.S. forces in the middle of metropo-lises are crises just waiting to happen."[4] Thus, as Michael O'Hanlon observes, "it behooves policymakers to begin focusing on this subject without further delay, at least in a preliminary fashion."[5]

In spite of this urgency, surprisingly little discussion of the problem has taken place. None of the presidential candidates in Korea have spo-ken specifically about the issue. Newspaper editorials, many protests by nongovernmental organizations (NGOs) and activists, and general com-plaints about the USFK no doubt provide the undertow for a rising tide of anti-Americanism. Missing beneath all this noise, however, is a deeper substantive discussion between the two sides (and Japan) about the fu-ture of the U.S. military presence in Asia and on the peninsula.

Details, not vision, have driven the dialogue on the USFK in Wash-ington and Seoul. Much of the long-term debate between the two governments on the USFK's future has been a product of process-oriented changes on the ground, such as housing, rather than a mutually agreed strategic outlook for the alliance's future. The three governments should invert this prioritization and begin to construct a viable vision for the future of the U.S. presence in Northeast Asia generally and in Korea specifically.

## Should the USFK Stay or Go Now?

The debate over USFK changes is often cast in terms of the progress of tension reduction on the peninsula. Some doves argue that the main rationale to restructure or withdraw the USFK should be to achieve peace on the peninsula.[6] Although there is an intuitive appeal to this view on the South Korean side, especially if one posits that the ROK military is capable of standing on its own, it is less appealing from the U.S. perspective. At a minimum, such a view assumes that North Korea has implicit veto power over the disposition of U.S. forces in Korea.

At the same time, though, the hawkish argument that contemplating any USFK change must await a stable peace on the peninsula, defined as the elimination of the northern threat, is too inflexible. The more interesting and challenging question is whether one can contemplate incremental change in the USFK presence given continued conventional and nuclear threats from the North. Such a plan of action would maintain traditional deterrence against the North and sustain the U.S. allied defense commitment to Seoul, but it would also allow a new vision for the alliance to be introduced that looks beyond the DPRK. USFK changes should be neither the sacrificial lamb nor the bargaining chip for peace on the peninsula but should be driven by a larger U.S.-ROK joint vision.

Regardless of how one perceives the DPRK threat, it is not difficult to argue that certain aspects of the USFK, as currently constituted, are obsolete. Established in 1957, the USFK was built to deter and if necessary defend against a second North Korean ground invasion. Although U.S. force structure is prepared for this one contingency, ROK forces continue to improve their capability of defending against a replay of June 1950, particularly as DPRK forces simultaneously continue to deteriorate. Given the ROK's increased confidence in its own capabilities, policymakers reportedly made a conscious decision in the 1990s to build national military capabilities beyond the peninsula into a regional force.[7]

Nevertheless, the competency of the ROK military to win an actual war does not reduce the important deterrent role played by the USFK. The U.S. pledge to defend South Korea is of far greater significance than any actual military capability. Given ROK capabilities and the favorable trends regarding the balance of forces on the peninsula, the United States can at any time begin thinking about ways to provide such a credible security commitment with a different force structure.

Beyond these military trends, civil-military tensions over the U.S. footprint in Korea have grown measurably. This friction is not due to a growth of radicalism in Korea but stems from democratization and generational shifts among the middle class that have served to elevate labor, environment, and other quality-of-life issues on the political agenda. NGOs and civic action groups have focused the South Korean public's attention on the negative effects of USFK activities to such an extent that a majority of South Koreans now favor a reduction in U.S. forces.[8] The sunshine policy of engagement and reconciliation with North Korea, established by ROK president Kim Dae-jung when he entered office in 1998, has had the unintended consequence of worsening perceptions of the USFK in the body politic in South Korea.

On one hand, the initial exaggerated claims by proponents that the sunshine policy has removed the threat of war on the peninsula has reduced South Korean public support for a sustained U.S. presence. On the other hand, moments in which Kim's policy fell short of expectations have contributed to a current South Korean search for scapegoats; the USFK is a prime target. Host nations accept the U.S. forward presence around the world because of the military missions and symbols of U.S commitment that presence is perceived to offer. Occasionally, however, a point is reached at which these benefits pale in comparison to the political damage that the presence causes the alliance relationship overall. Although the U.S. forward presence in Korea has not reached this point yet, it is on the horizon. As one military official who had served in Korea and Japan noted, "Korea could go the way of Okinawa if we are not careful."[9]

Beyond these factors specific to the peninsula, larger trends in U.S. security thinking presage an imminent reevaluation of the USFK. The 100,000-person benchmark for the U.S. presence in Asia reported in the 2001 quadrennial defense review is increasingly seen by government and nongovernmental experts as obsolete, although the U.S. government still formally adheres to it.[10] Moreover, the revolution in military affairs anticipates long-range, precision-strike fighting capabilities that could fundamentally change the face of the U.S. forward presence around the world.

## TAIL WAGGING THE DOG

Despite these trends, neither the ROK Ministry of National Defense nor the Pentagon has initiated a serious dialogue. Instead, a buck-passing response to these imperatives has emerged. Seoul responds to complaints from domestic constituencies about the U.S. footprint by demanding that Washington lay out a plan of action. At the same time, the United States wants its ally to volunteer a vision of its own. Each side draws up lists of discussion questions both at security and military consultative meetings, but neither side really wants to take a crack at answering them. Why?

The problem is that the tail is wagging the dog. First, rather than a larger, joint strategic vision of the U.S.-ROK alliance driving changes to the U.S. force presence on the ground, bureaucratic issues related to USFK maintenance are driving the larger vision. For example, measures such as the land readjustment program or Yongsan relocation, designed to reduce the military footprint, get bogged down in planning and implementation because a consensual big picture about what the future force structure should look like does not exist. As a result, the larger vision of the USFK becomes incrementally developed, ad hoc, and subject to transient bureaucratic needs.

Second, the absence of a long-term vision on the Korean side, as one specialist noted, is due in part to a void of substantive and serious thinking on the issue,[11] partially explained by political imperatives created by the sunshine policy. Although an important and unprecedented strategy of engagement undertaken by Kim Dae-jung, the policy has had the unintended consequence of stifling discussion about the future. Those opposed to the policy feel obligated to emphasize the threat posed by the DPRK and therefore do not believe the time is right to contemplate the long term. Those who support the sunshine policy and believe it has reduced tension on the peninsula also do not want to talk about a post-DPRK alliance for fear of upsetting the North and undercutting the sunshine policy.

### REGIONAL STABILITY—WHAT IS IT GOOD FOR?

Any discussion about the USFK's future must start with a broader discussion of U.S. grand strategy in Asia. The U.S.-ROK alliance does not enjoy a resiliency equivalent to U.S. alliances in Europe. As one study noted, NATO could muddle through an entire decade in search of a mission, but the U.S.-ROK alliance cannot afford to allow events to overtake a discussion of the future.[12]

Perhaps the most often-cited rationale for the future of U.S. alliances in Northeast Asia is "regional stability." This justification, however, raises more questions than it answers. Many have defined this phrase with regard to Korea implicitly to mean enabling the alliance to operate in regional contingencies beyond the peninsula. If this definition implies a combat or logistics role for the USFK in a Taiwan Strait contingency, however, then current U.S. basing on the peninsula is still too distant, at 800-plus nautical miles away.[13] The alternative would be to station long-range aircraft, heavy bombers, and hardened fuel assets in Korea (rather than their current location in Guam), all of which would probably be politically unacceptable for the Koreans. Furthermore, if regional stability implies using the USFK for contingencies in Southeast Asia, then this too is unnecessary. A crisis in Indonesia, for example, to which U.S.

forces might respond, would potentially require the use of U.S. air bases as far north as Kadena and Iwo Jima or the Philippines, not Korea.

More useful than using regional stability as a code word for contingencies that imply a quasi-containment of China, Susan Bryant and Gen. (Ret.) John Tilelli, former commander in chief of the UN Command in Korea, define regional missions for the U.S.-ROK alliance more broadly to include nontraditional security activities such as humanitarian intervention, peacekeeping and peacemaking, and counterterrorism operations.[14] In one of the more useful characterizations of the term, some define regional missions in military terms as antipower projection. In other words, the primary operational concept for U.S. forward deployment is to prevent power projection by others beyond the East Asian littoral. The rationale behind this thought is that the projection of power by any others incites indigenous security dilemmas, historical animosities, and arms competitions destabilizing to the region.[15]

Though the latter two definitions of regional stability offer useful guidelines, they lack a specific vision about what strategic landscape best suits the interests of the United States and its Asian allies in the future. What is the goal of the U.S.-ROK alliance beyond peninsular security? If regional stability includes peacekeeping and antipower projection, then how would the U.S.-Korean alliance contribute to these larger missions? Contrary to twentieth-century U.S. attitudes toward Korea, does a rationale for the alliance exist that can be more than ad hoc, reactive, and derivative of larger balance-of-power concerns in Asia?

Answering such questions must begin with a frank assessment of the geostrategic landscape in Northeast Asia after Korean unification—the likely, if not inevitable, fate of the peninsula. This landscape is unfavorable to U.S. interests. For reasons of geography, history, culture, power, economics, and demography, trends in Asia may emerge such that the domestic politics of Korean unification push the U.S. military off the peninsula. The new Korean entity could seek a continental accommodation with China against Japan as resurgent Korean nationalism and new military capabilities combine to incite security dilemmas with its historical enemy. At the same time, a demographically aged Japan could become isolated from the rest of Asia and be perceived as the last remaining U.S. outpost in the region.

Korean unification certainly might generate a range of alternate scenarios, but given current and past geostrategic trends, this estimate of how events might transpire is most probable. What is striking about this scenario is how heavily it weighs against U.S. interests. If the United States has the will to remain an Asia-Pacific power after Korean unification, then it has no interest in being pushed out. Moreover, this situation is not in the region's interests. An older, weaker, and isolated Japan that does not want to be considered the last U.S. military colony in Asia might finally choose greater self-reliance for its security. This decision would provoke balancing reactions in China and Korea that would degrade the region's security as tensions, armaments, and the almost-certain prospect of nuclear proliferation rose.

## THE WAY FORWARD: PREVENTIVE DEFENSE

U.S. strategic planners should not only seek to avoid future war in Northeast Asia but also should contemplate avoiding this sort of future peace.[16] Geostrategic currents in Asia following unification therefore create a preventive-defense rationale for the alliances in Asia. In other words, the United States and its allies should take prudent and premeditated actions to prevent the emergence of potentially dangerous situations, not simply deal with a threat once it has become imminent.[17] The imperative for the United States is to forestall these unfavorable geostrategic currents in Asia that would follow unification. At its core, this long-term necessity compels Washington to promote stronger relations between its two main Asian allies and to consolidate the trilateral U.S.-Japanese-Korean relationship. Such a U.S. strategy has three elements.

First, in the most immediate and pragmatic terms, the DPRK contingency continues to provide a vehicle for building Japanese-Korean security cooperation. Throughout the 1990s, the threat of North Korean implosion or aggression drove the unprecedented security cooperation involving defense minister–level bilateral meetings, search-and-rescue exercises, port calls, noncombatant evacuation operations, and academic military exchanges despite the deep historical mistrust between Seoul and Tokyo. Although previous South Korean presidents vowed during the Cold War never to engage in these security cooperation activities with past colonizer Japan despite the imminent North Korean threat, more recently they have built bilateral confidence and created an entirely new dimension to Seoul-Tokyo relations beyond the political and economic relationship.

A second critical ingredient in the medium-term strategy for consolidation is to infuse the U.S.-Japanese and U.S.-Korean alliances with meaning and identity beyond the Cold War. History shows that the most resilient alliances share common ideals, a basis that runs deeper than the adversarial threats that might have initially brought the alliance into existence. Currently, this process has elevated maintaining regional stability to become the alliance's future purpose, but there is room to go further. Beyond regional stability, a host of extraregional issues, such as liberal democracy, open economic markets, nonproliferation, universal human rights, anti-terrorism, and peacekeeping, among others, define the relationship. Ideally, the U.S.-ROK and U.S.-Japanese alliances will stand *for* something rather than simply against a threat. This common ideational grounding makes the relationships more sustainable, becoming the glue that prevents these alignments from being washed away by regional geostrategic currents.

Third, this U.S. strategy for Korea should hedge, or have a straddle component. Theoretically speaking, the United States should commit to deterring a Korean adversary but should not grant the kind of unconditional commitment that might allow the ROK to feel comfortable free-riding its way through the alliance and doing little on its own to ensure Korean national security. In practical terms, the United States should seek to consolidate the trilateral U.S.-Japanese-ROK axis to reaffirm U.S. continued alliance relationships in the region but should do so without the type of unconditional and asymmetric security guarantee it provided to its allies during the years of Cold War patronage.

This is a lesson of history. The United States has always been the strongest advocate of better Japanese-Korean relations, but ironically, Seoul and Tokyo have responded more favorably to burden-sharing entreaties when Washington has been perceived to be somewhat less interested in underwriting the region's security.[18] The U.S. position in Asia should therefore be recessed enough in this new arrangement to impart responsibilities on the allies to consolidate their own bilateral relationship, but not so recessed that Japan and South Korea choose self-help solutions outside the alliance framework. Specifically, two elements of this strategy would be to reduce the U.S. ground presence greatly but still maintain a minimal forward presence as a tangible symbol of commitment and to reinforce the U.S. political commitment by maintaining the nuclear umbrella.

Any discussion about the USFK's future should begin with antipower projection and counterterrorism as two rationales for regionalizing the U.S.-ROK alliance. To supplement them, the U.S.-ROK (and U.S.-Japanese) alliance(s) should serve a nonproliferation function, dampen security dilemmas, and prevent the rise of regional hegemons, currently and postunification, particularly but not exclusively to mitigate against the contingency where Japan is isolated, the United States is expelled, and tensions are heightened between a unified Korea and her neighbors.

## The Next USFK

To perform these new missions and address its traditional role, the United States should restructure its forces on the peninsula to be:

- *Credible.* In spite of any transformations in the USFK, the resulting force must still represent and preserve the traditional role as a reliable manifestation of the U.S. commitment to the defense and security of Korea.

- *Flexible.* While being large enough to be militarily significant, the U.S. presence should be flexible enough to handle a broad range of tasks ranging from antiterrorism operations to peacekeeping to force-projection dominance in the region.

- *Deployable.* Combined with other U.S. capabilities in the region (especially in Japan), the presence in Korea must be capable of reacting swiftly to regional developments and offer an integrated joint force with the full range of mobility, strike, maneuverability, and sustainability.

- *Unobtrusive.* While being politically equivalent to the old force structure as a symbol of the alliance, the new presence should possess a footprint that the Korean people do not perceive as an obstacle to peace.

With these objectives in mind, the United States should transform USFK ground, air, and naval assets from a heavy, ground-based force to a more mobile, rapid-reaction force. The types of changes needed in Korea will certainly be contingent on the status of other U.S. forces and bases as well as on access arrangements elsewhere in the region, but such a restructured USFK could resemble the force described below.

The United States should restructure the existing ground presence along the lines of Gen. Eric Shinseki's objective force concept, as a mobile, medium-sized force, easily deployable but more lethal and sustainable than existing light infantry.[19] This army force of about one medium-sized deployable brigade (5,000) could react quickly to regional developments, including but not limited to unification of the peninsula, and maintain a strong U.S. presence in the region. These forces might be stationed in the southern portion of the peninsula around the demilitarized zone and outside of Seoul.

Although air assets on the peninsula would vary somewhat, they would likely remain relatively constant compared to the other services. For domestic political reasons in Korea, retaining two main operating air bases at Osan and further south at Kunsan will be difficult. The presence at Osan could be reduced and redeployed in Kunsan or even further south, placing aerial assets as much as 500 miles closer to southern contingencies. Although reductions are likely, the reconfigured force in Korea must be capable of assisting Guam in supporting some assets that might be transferred from U.S. air bases in Japan to aid the reduction of the U.S. footprint there.

Ultimately, between reconfigured U.S. air bases in Korea and the Kadena air base in Japan, the United States would ideally retain air-to-air, air-to-ground, surveillance, refueling, and airlift capabilities for a truly regional role. The current force structure in Korea will support contingencies extending only about as far as the Senkakus, but the addition of longer-range craft, heavy bombers, refueling, and hardened fuel assets might enable range rings to be extended as far as the Taiwan Strait, which conceivably might be problematic for Koreans as previously mentioned. The United States could base most assets in Guam and move them if China misbehaves in the strait. Reconfigured aerial assets on the peninsula, however, would probably not be able to assist with contingencies in the South China Sea, even with aerial refueling.

Of all the services, the navy could host the largest augmentation in the USFK presence on the peninsula, depending upon how widely the force presence would be oriented and how the U.S. presence in Japan and Australia might be concurrently changed. For example, some have advocated reducing the U.S. Marine presence in Okinawa by moving them to Australia, while augmenting the presence in Northeast Asia by homeporting a second aircraft carrier in the region, possibly in Korea, with the crew based in the United States to reduce the infrastructure and base footprint. Unlike restructuring aerial assets, this plan would effectively mean a USFK presence able to assist in contingencies as far south as the South China Sea. Such missions might not be necessary if U.S. forces were positioned in, or gained access to, bases in Southeast Asia. Under any circumstances, a revised force presence in Northeast Asia should include a carrier homeport, U.S. Army and Marine training capability, and an operational air force hub, which would constitute the foundation for any anticipated subregional buildup.[20]

## COMMAND STRUCTURE ISSUES

Integrating assets in Japan and Korea as part of a broader USFK transformation would most likely necessitate revising the regional combatant commands. Some have advocated a joint headquarters for Northeast Asia with a three-star commander reporting to Pacific Command rather than the two existing, separate Korea and Japan commands.[21] Others have advocated a separate Northeast Asia command covering China, Japan, Taiwan, and Korea. This commander would have the equivalent status of the other four existing regional commanders. As these proponents argue, "Northeast Asia hosts five of the six largest militaries in the world and stands out as a subregion too critical to the United States to be subsumed under an umbrella-like regional command including the entire Asian subcontinent, Southeast Asia, and the South Pacific."[22]

To remain consistent with the vision of a more equal alliance, the full transfer of operational command authority over Korean forces should be transferred to the ROK. As far back as the establishment of the USFK during the Eisenhower administration, the traditional rationale for the United States holding operational command authority was not just for enhanced defensive-fighting efficiency but also to keep a leash on unilateral offensive acts by the South Koreans. Little known even to most experts and historians of the alliance, declassified documents show a standing U.S. policy that any unilateral ROK military actions would prompt Washington to take the severest of actions against the ROK, including the immediate cessation of economic and military aid, disassociation of the United Nations Command from support of ROK actions, and even use of U.S. forces to impose martial law.[23] President Dwight Eisenhower even confidentially considered the forcible removal of South Korean leadership and covert support of new leaders.[24]

The U.S. concern about a South Korean preemptive attack has abated considerably over the years, particularly after democratization in 1987, to the point in 1994 when the United States transferred peacetime authority to the ROK. Although military concerns may remain that still dictate a combined command, a future, regionally oriented alliance would do well to distance itself from a command structure that epitomized the asymmetrical nature of the alliance during the Cold War. Instead, a joint-planning headquarters with two independent militaries led by the ROK joint chiefs of staff and the USFK, operating under a set of mutually agreed defense guidelines, would be the blueprint. Admittedly, from a U.S. military perspective this development would mean a less integrated and potentially more difficult alliance to manage with the Koreans than in the past. It could mean tedious negotiations and contractual wrangling over definitions of regional contingencies, much along the lines of the U.S.-Japanese alliance. To do otherwise, however, would violate the unobtrusive precondition for an acceptable USFK outlined above.

## PLACES, NOT BASES?

A potential alternative to basing the USFK in Korea permanently would be for Seoul and Washington to negotiate an access arrangement while redeploying these facilities and troops elsewhere. The United States has negotiated such agreements in Southeast Asia, and the question may become a salient one from the Korean perspective. Access arrangements, however, would not be an optimal alternative. Although they might meet the unobtrusive prerequisite for the alliance's future, they would not meet other key conditions, primarily, providing a credible U.S. security commitment to Korea.

First, access arrangements are not consistent with the broader vision of the U.S.-Korean alliance going beyond a transitory bilateral defense arrangement to becoming a permanent relationship based on similar political values and economic ideologies. The United States will seek a variety of access arrangements and military understandings networked throughout the region, but at the center of these varied relationships, a set of core alliances involving Korea, Japan, and Australia should remain. These core partnerships are based on common views about constitutional democracy, market economies, civil liberties, nonproliferation, and counterterrorism that are not necessarily shared throughout the entire region. They are distinguished by their relatively higher level of military ties with the United States, which include hosting some base and troop presence. The model for the future therefore is not "hub and spokes," in which the United States has discrete relationships with other Asian powers and little interaction takes place between them, but a "core and network" model in which the United States' primary stake in the region lies with these core countries.[25]

Second, the core countries have strong reasons themselves to accept bases rather than merely access arrangements with the United

States. Alliances offer allies ways to dampen U.S. tendencies toward unilateralism.[26] In the Korean case, an alliance with two independent militaries would enable Seoul to say "no" to the United States in ways that they could not before. In military terms, this situation might not be ideal, particularly given the history of this alliance, but politically this potential could be the ultimate symbol of a new, more equal, and long-term alliance relationship. Some European allies did not allow the United States to fly over their air space during attacks on Libya in 1986. U.S. allies also did not allow U.S. planes to refuel on their territories while carrying supplies to Israel during the 1973 Mideast war.[27] Under certain circumstances, the ROK might refuse to allow the United States liberties with the bases. Bases, rather than places, actually give Korea more leverage. With a relationship based merely on access arrangements, saying "no" could mean the end of that relationship, as happened with New Zealand. A relationship undergirded by a basing and forward presence, however, is much more difficult to abrogate.

## CREATING ACCEPTABILITY

The first key to making the USFK more acceptable in Korea and throughout the region centers on China. In order to enhance regional stability and mollify geostrategic tensions between China and the United States over Korea, efforts at remaking the U.S.-ROK alliance, the USFK, and trilateral cooperation should be as low profile and transparent to Beijing as possible. Promoting Seoul-Tokyo bilateral security cooperation, for example, should not focus on military assets but on transport platforms for preplanned disaster relief or on joint use of transport craft for out-of-area peacekeeping operations. Transforming the language of Cold War alliances into, for example, permanent unions among U.S.-Asian market democracies would address Beijing's incessant complaints about the anachronistic nature of U.S. alliances in Asia.

Beyond the broader alliance missions, the ground troop presence on the peninsula, which the Chinese have always found disconcerting, would appear less provocative to Beijing after restructuring. China will undoubtedly still oppose any configuration that maintains a U.S. presence in Korea, but a USFK that relies less on pre-positioned heavy equipment and two-division-sized ground force deployments and more on air and naval presence (excluding long-range bombers) to improve regional stability would generate less opposition in Beijing than the alternative.

The second key to improving USFK sustainability is to engage in some public diplomacy to adequately address the perceived negative aspects of the Cold War U.S. force presence. My interviews with USFK personnel have revealed that one of the biggest sources of civil-military tensions remains the asymmetric reporting that highlights negative USFK activities. The Korean media underreports any positive or conciliatory actions taken by the United States to appease complaints about the military footprint. It often omits or ignores information that might contribute to a more balanced public debate on civil-military relations between the USFK and the host nation. An agreement, for example, to move USFK bases to Pyongtaek in recent years failed largely because the South Korean government's commitment to underwrite costs did not materialize. Korean press reporting, however, focused largely on U.S. unwillingness to pay for the move, underemphasizing the South Korean pledge. On economic issues related to the military presence, such as host-nation support or land use, the United States is generally portrayed as a selfish patron, trying to push costs onto Seoul. Missing from the picture is the overall long-term savings that the ROK accrued from the alliance. Indeed, preliminary data shows that the ROK's defense spending as a share of gross domestic product is lower over time than that of other newly industrialized countries and exponentially lower than countries with less of a U.S. forward presence, such as Israel or Saudi Arabia.[28]

Although the press coverage of crimes committed by U.S. servicemen in Korea is massive, what goes missing is the other side of the story. Some crimes by U.S. servicemen are indeed brutal and deserve public attention, but overall a much higher percentage of servicemen in the Korean military than in the USFK commit crimes. In a related vein, the aftermath of the June 2000 inter-Korean summit coincided with several random attacks by inebriated Koreans against U.S. servicemen, one of which was an unprovoked stabbing of a USFK physician shopping alone in Itaewon. Internal USFK precautionary warnings ensued about walking in pairs and avoiding off-base activities in the evening. This episode received no coverage in the South Korean press.

The press and NGO community were, however, galvanized by revelations in the summer of 2000 regarding the illegal disposal of formaldehyde through the wastewater sewage system on the Yongsan compound into the Han River (the main river flowing through central Seoul). Press reports fixated on discrepancies between USFK reports of the amounts disposed and Green Korea United's (Noksaek Yonhap) reports. Although its absence does not excuse the USFK's inappropriate and unwarranted action, completely missing from this controversy was any discussion of environmental damage committed by the South Korean military over the years, which far exceeds USFK actions. The point here is not to deflect blame from the USFK, but to illustrate some very strong biases in public images of the USFK that detract from a rational, balanced public discussion.

The reason for these disparities stems from both press reporting in Korea and the way the two governments have passed the buck between them. In the former case, corporate Korean state manipulation of the press was historically the problem. South Korean governments were infamous for utilizing public media channels to distort messages and stir anti-American sentiment when convenient to deflect blame from an angry public or to gain leverage in bilateral negotiations with its ally.[29] The problem today is different. Overt government intervention has decreased somewhat, but what has emerged is a culture of newspaper editorial offices as well and a generation of Korean journalists that contribute to a bias toward reporting negatively on the U.S. presence. Young, ambitious, and overzealous reporters operate with a cowboy mentality trying to seize the story and give it the most sensationalist slant. Often, the intrusive U.S. military footprint provides a ready target. Editors gain no points, let alone respect from their peers and subordinates, for choosing stories that might report positively on the U.S. military. They sell more papers when they report negatively.

In the latter case, USFK spokespeople feel that their public briefings do not get adequate attention from the domestic press. When the USFK makes these complaints to their Korean counterparts, the South Korean government responds that this problem is a U.S., not Korean, one. When the USFK pushes the problem up the chain of command, the Pentagon responds that the military is not in the business of public relations. The legacy of the USFK today will be a critical image that will determine the future acceptability of a transformed USFK tomorrow and the attendant level of residual anti-Americanism.

## Ad Hoc No More

No matter how successful a U.S. public diplomacy campaign might be in Korea, it is now time to begin to restructure the U.S. forward presence and reconceptualize the U.S.-ROK alliance. The rationale is not that there is no longer a threat from the North—as the recent revelations about its secret nuclear weapons program have shown—nor that improved ROK military capabilities have rendered the USFK expendable. A confluence of trends argue that the U.S.-ROK alliance is slowly but steadily approaching a moment of change likely to occur in the next South Korean administration. The DPRK continues to pose threats, but their conventional fighting capabilities have declined. Meanwhile, Korean civil society increasingly calls for a change in the U.S. footprint in Korea as anti-U.S. sentiments slowly spread among media, political, and business circles in a post–Korean War generation. None of these trends is overwhelmingly compelling on their own, but together they constitute a critical mass that could induce a crisis if left unaddressed. It is time to stop thinking about the alliance in ad hoc terms and start creating the vision for the future.

## Notes

1. The U.S. Forces Korea (USFK) is defined as the U.S.-only subunified command on the Korean peninsula of the U.S. Pacific Command. This group can be broadly construed as consisting of three components: the United Nations

Command, the Combined Forces Command, and the 37,000-strong military presence and attendant base structure.

2. Ralph Cossa, "The Role of U.S. Forces in a Unified Korea," *International Journal of Korean Studies* 5, no. 2 (fall/winter 2001): 118.

3. Richard Halloran, "Ground Forces in Japan, S. Korea under Review," *Washington Times*, September 29, 2000, p. A1.

4. Jiyul Kim, "Continuity and Transformation in Northeast Asia," *Korean Journal of Defense Analyses* 13, no. 1 (autumn 2001): 259.

5. Michael O'Hanlon, "U.S. Military Force Structure after Korean Reunification," *Korean Journal of Defense Analyses* 13, no. 1 (autumn 2001): 215.

6. Selig S. Harrison, "Time to Leave Korea?" *Foreign Affairs* 80, no. 2 (March/April 2001): 62–78.

7. Michael McDevitt, in *Korea's Future and the Great Powers*, eds. Nicholas Eberstadt and Richard J. Ellings (Seattle: University of Washington Press, 2001), note 6. See also Victor Cha, "Strategic Culture and the Military Modernization of South Korea," *Armed Forces & Society* 28, no. 1 (fall 2001): 99–128.

8. See Larry Niksch, "Korea: U.S.–South Korean Relations—Issues for Congress," *CRS Issue Brief for Congress*, March 5, 2002, p. 10; Balbina Hwang, "New SOFA Agreement Strengthens U.S.-Korea Alliance," *Korea Herald*, January 19, 2001; Scott Snyder, "Anti-Americanism and the Future of USFK," *Korea Times*, August 10, 2000.

9. U.S. official, conversation with author, Seoul, September 12, 2002.

10. Halloran, "Ground Forces in Japan, S. Korea under Review"; Cossa, "The Role of U.S. Forces in a Unified Korea."

11. Chung Min Lee, "Future of ROK-U.S. Security Relations and Command Structure" (paper presented at "Practical Steps from War to Peace on the Korean Peninsula," Sejong and Asia Foundation, September 20–23, 2000).

12. Michael Finnegan, "The Future of the U.S.-ROK Alliance: Challenges and Opportunities" (unpublished manuscript).

13. Zalmay Khalilzad et al., *The United States and Asia: Toward a New U.S. Strategy and Force Posture* (Arlington, Va.: RAND, 2001), pp. 67–68.

14. Gen. John H. Tilelli (Ret.) and Maj. Susan Bryant, *Keeping the Calm: Northeast Asian Regional Security,* (Arlington, Va.: Association of the United States Army, 2002), pp. 39–40, http://www.ausa.org/RAMPnew/tilellibryantpaper.pdf (accessed October 10, 2002).

15. Michael A. McDevitt and James A. Kelly, "In Search of Stability: Designing for a Better Peace in East Asia," in *U.S.-Korea-Japan Relations: Building toward a Virtual Alliance*, ed. Ralph Cossa (Washington, D.C.: CSIS, 1999). See also McDevitt in *Korea's Future and the Great Powers*, p. 286.

16. Nicholas Eberstadt and Richard J. Ellings, "Assessing Interests and Objectives of Major Actors in the Korean Drama," in *Korea's Future and the Great Powers*, eds. Nicholas Eberstadt and Richard J. Ellings (Seattle: University of Washington Press, 2001), p. 323.

17. Ashton B. Carter and William J. Perry, *Preventive Defense: A New Security Strategy for America* (Washington, D.C.: Brookings Institution Press, 1999), p. 14.

18. For the full argument, see Victor Cha, *Alignment despite Antagonism: The United States–Korea–Japan Security Triangle* (Stanford, Calif.: Stanford University Press, 1999).

19. Gen. Eric Shinseki, "The Army Transformation: A Historic Opportunity," *Army Magazine* (October 2000).

20. For further details, see Michael E. O'Hanlon, "Restructuring U.S. Forces and Bases in Japan," in *Toward a True Alliance: Restructuring U.S.-Japan Security Relations*, ed. Mike M. Mochizuki (Washington, D.C.: Brookings Institution Press, 1997), pp. 168–173.

21. McDevitt and Kelly, "In Search of Stability."

22. Tilelli and Bryant, *Northeast Asian Regional Security*, p. 41.

23. "Statement of U.S. Policy toward Korea," NSC 5817 (August 11, 1958), in *FRUS, 1958–1960*, vol. XVIII, doc. 237, p. 485.

24. See NSC 170/1, Annex A. See also "U.S. Objectives and Courses of Action in Korea," NSC 170/1 (November 20, 1953), in *FRUS 1952–1954*, pp. 1620–1624; "Memorandum from the Acting Executive Secretary of the National Security Council (Gleason) to the Secretary of State, February 18, 1955," in *FRUS, 1955–1957*, vol. XXII, doc. 21, pp. 37–38.

25. See Dennis C. Blair and John T. Hanley Jr., "From Wheels to Webs: Reconstructing Asia-Pacific Security Arrangements," *The Washington Quarterly* 24, no. 1 (winter 2001): 7–18.

26. See John Ikenberry, "Getting Hegemony Right," *National Interest* 63 (spring 2001): 17–24. See also Yoichi Funabashi, "Tokyo's Temperance," *The Washington Quarterly* 23, no. 3 (summer 2000): 135–144.

27. O'Hanlon, "U.S. Military Force Structure after Korean Reunification."

28. Taejoon Han, "An Economic Assessment of USFK" (paper presented at the "U.S. Troops in Korea" seminar, Pacific Forum and Ilmin Institute, Honolulu, August 8, 2002), p. 4.

29. See Jae-Kyoung Lee, "Anti-Americanism in South Korea: The Media and the Politics of Signification" (Ph.D. dissertation, Dept. of Mass Communications, University of Iowa, 1993).

# Part IV

## Iran

**Gary Sick**

# Confronting Terrorism

Charges of terrorist activities have plagued Iran from the earliest days of the Islamic revolution to the present. More than any other factor, they have interfered with Iran's ability to establish a responsible foreign policy image. Yet, terrorism is murky and highly ambiguous. As penalties for terrorism escalate, terrorists try to mask their identities; determining who planned and executed an act of terror is extremely difficult, and it is often virtually impossible to establish with any certainty the policy motives behind such acts. Iran is a particularly complex case.

Iran has a split personality. Some parts of its government—the presidency, the Majlis (parliament), and the functional ministries—though far from a fully functioning democracy, are held accountable for their policies and actions through public review and frequent elections. A second set of government institutions, including the Supreme Leader (*velayat-e faqih*), oversight committees such as the Guardian Council and the Expediency Council, and the security services, are dominated by a conservative clergy who are officially above reproach, essentially accountable only to themselves. These institutions have veto power over government policies and command a shadowy but potent network of influence and protection that grew out of the revolution, permeating

Gary Sick is director of the Middle East Institute at Columbia University.

Copyright © 2003 by The Center for Strategic and International Studies and the Massachusetts Institute of Technology
*The Washington Quarterly* • 26:4 pp. 83–98.

Iran's national security structure and economy. The tension between these two unevenly balanced power centers affects Iranian policy at all levels so that, at times, Iran appears to be pursuing different or even contradictory objectives.

Since at least the mid-1990s, the main objectives of the elected government have been to attract foreign political and economic support. Especially since President Muhammad Khatami's election in 1997, Iran has played a significant and constructive role at the United Nations, normalized its relations with its neighbors in the Persian Gulf region, and moved much closer toward mutually respectful relations with the European Union. At the same time, some unaccountable elements of Iran's power structure have seemed unwilling to accept this normalization process and have clung to a very different agenda of destabilization, revolutionary vengeance, and violent intimidation, including terrorist acts. The two sets of policies, often directly contradictory, reflect the struggle that lies at the very heart of the Iranian revolutionary experience.

The triumph of the Iranian revolution in February 1979 kindled a burst of radical actions by Iran that deserve to be called terrorism.[1] These include kidnappings sanctioned and sponsored by the government itself, such as the taking of American hostages in the first years of the revolution, and reputed Iranian support for and suspected direct involvement in Hizballah operations in Lebanon, including the bombings of U.S. installations and hostage-taking throughout the 1980s. During the Iran-Iraq War, Iran pursued a strategy of maritime terror, using unmarked gunboats and floating mines to attack noncombatant shipping. Numerous assassinations of enemies abroad in the late 1980s and 1990s were widely and persuasively attributed to Iranian official sponsorship, and Iran was accused of sponsoring operations by other militant organizations, such as the Argentinean bombings of 1992 and 1994 and the 1996 Khobar Towers bombing, attributed to Hizballah organizations in Lebanon and Saudi Arabia. Iran is currently suspected of supporting terrorist acts against Israel through its support of radical Palestinian factions.

Given the ambiguities of the public record, if not the intelligence data on which it is based, Iran's actual behavior may be better, worse, or substantially different from the brief survey presented here. We may never have all the facts about many of the terrorist incidents of which Iran is accused. Assuming, however, that the following discussion of Iran's record on terrorism and the main driving forces of that record are at least roughly accurate, certain conclusions can be drawn about Iranian policy on terrorism, the direction in which it is headed today, and possible U.S. responses. Iran undoubtedly behaves differently today than it did nearly a quarter century ago. Iran's postrevolutionary policies of hostage-taking and rebellion promotion among its neighbors have been abandoned, as have its wartime shipping attacks and targeted assassinations of enemies. Today, Iran's promotion of violence seems to be increasingly focused on support for radical anti-Israeli groups in Palestine. This shift calls for a different and more creative set of responses on the part of the United States.

## Iran's Historical Motivations for Terrorism

### EXPORTING THE REVOLUTION

The capture of the U.S. embassy in Tehran in 1979 by a band of students and the imprisonment of a large group of U.S. diplomats and private citizens for 444 days with the explicit acquiescence of the Iranian government set the tone for Iran's relations with the United States and many other countries. The United States and much of the world regarded this act as the quintessential example of state-supported terrorism. It traumatized the U.S. public and darkened the lens through which the United States would view the Islamic Republic of Iran and all of its policies and actions during the decades that followed.

In the years immediately after the revolution, Iranian militants—with or without the official support of the government—attempted to export the revolution by stirring up radical Islamist discontent in Bahrain, Saudi Arabia, and other Gulf states. A botched attempt by

Iranian supporters to assassinate senior Iraqi officials, including Tariq Aziz, in April 1980 was one of the catalysts that persuaded Saddam Hussein to invade Iran in September of that year.

Iran's ambassador to Syria in the early 1980s, Ali Akbar Mohtashemi, provided financing and support for the creation of Hizballah ("Party of God"), the Lebanese political party and resistance movement.[2] Hizballah is widely believed to have been associated with the bombings of the U.S. Marines barracks and the U.S. embassy in Lebanon in 1983, although its leadership denies the charge, as well as the killing and hostage-taking of Americans and others throughout the 1980s. Its success in conducting a guerrilla war in southern Lebanon against Israel, ultimately leading to Israel's departure in 2000, won widespread admiration in the Islamic world and made Hizballah a source of inspiration and training for militant organizations throughout the Middle East, many of which adopted the same name. Iran takes pride in its continued support for Hizballah as a national resistance organization but denies having operational control over decisionmaking. In recent years, Iran has openly called on Hizballah to display "prudence and self-restraint" to prevent Israel from finding a pretext to attack Lebanon again.[3]

## ENEMIES OF THE STATE

Just before he died in 1989, Ayatollah Ruhollah Khomeini, the father of the Iranian revolution, issued his famous *fatwa* against Salman Rushdie. Khomeini regarded Rushdie's depiction of the prophet Muhammad and other Islamic subjects in *The Satanic Verses* as blasphemous, and the *fatwa* in effect incited the general Muslim community to murder Rushdie. It also seemed to signal the beginning of an assassination campaign against individuals associated with Rushdie's book as well as other "enemies of the revolution." The rash of killings that followed included Kurdish leader Abdol Rahman Qasemlu in Vienna in 1989, former Iranian prime minister and opposition leader Shapour Bakhtiar in Paris in 1991, four Iranian Kurds in Berlin in 1992, and several leaders of the opposition Mujahideen-e Khalq movement. In addition, two bombings in Argentina—the Israeli embassy in March 1992 and a Jewish community center in July 1994—were attributed to the Lebanese Hizballah organization, allegedly with Iranian assistance.

To be sure, Iran may often be falsely accused. Many of these crimes were never solved, and the degree of Iranian official responsibility may be overstated. For its part, Iran flatly and unequivocally denied any role in these incidents. A German court that formally investigated the 1992 Berlin murders, however, implicated the highest levels of the Iranian government and indicted the minister of intelligence, Ali Fallahian, for his role. An Argentinean court officially concluded in 2003 that officials in the Iranian embassy provided unspecified support to Hizballah for the 1994 bombing of the Jewish Community Center.

Iran's past reputation for supporting terrorism, the incendiary rhetoric of its ultraconservative clerical leaders, and its almost total lack of transparency concerning issues of national security have created an environment in which it is easy to believe the worst. In fact, Iran's behavior since the revolution has allowed its opponents to accuse it of almost anything and to find a receptive audience for their claims. Iran's vigorous denial in all of the aforementioned cases ultimately undermined its credibility because the formula never varied, even when the evidence was quite incriminating, and there was never any visible effort by Iran to investigate the circumstances or to punish any of the individuals who might have been involved.

## MARITIME TERRORISM

During the Iran-Iraq War (1980–1988), Iranian gunboats—usually small speedboats with hand-held grenade launchers and other weapons—attacked commercial shipping in the Gulf. Iran also seeded the waters of the shipping lanes with floating mines. These tactics were usually regarded as acts of war, and they have not figured into the terrorism charges against Iran. The case can be made, however, that they represented a form of maritime terrorism.

That Iran used these strikes to retaliate against Iraqi air attacks against its own shipping is obvious. Iran could not retaliate in kind because all Iraqi ports were closed and there were no Iraqi ships in the Gulf. Instead, Iran sent unmarked speedboats to fire at commercial ships en route to Arab ports on the unspoken but entirely valid assumption that countries such as Kuwait and Saudi Arabia were serving as a supply channel for Iraq.

Although Iran never formally acknowledged that its military forces were behind these attacks, Iran undoubtedly organized and sponsored them. They were not truly acts of war because they were conducted by nonuniformed personnel against unarmed civilians of noncombatant states; they more closely resembled drive-by shootings or the mining of a busy thoroughfare. These attacks, which threatened the region's shipping lanes, eventually led to direct military clashes between the United States and Iran in the Gulf.[4] They are significant here because they indicated Iran's willingness to use unconventional, even terrorist, methods to pursue a political and military strategy, even if that meant confronting the United States.

### RAFSANJANI AND THE AL-KHOBAR BOMBINGS

Khomeini's death was perhaps an even greater challenge for Iran than war with Iraq. This event brought a new generation of revolutionaries to the top leadership positions and produced substantial changes in the constitution, even though it did not seriously threaten the regime or cause any dramatic shift in policy. Iran's competing foreign policies, however, were dramatically visible during the presidency of Ali Akbar Hashemi Rafsanjani (1989–1997). Rafsanjani's systematic efforts to build constructive political as well as commercial ties with the West were sabotaged repeatedly by a policy that appeared to be driven by revolutionary vengeance and executed by shadowy forces. Tehran never publicly identified the perpetrators or publicly held them accountable, presumably because they enjoyed the protection of individuals at or near the top of the conservative power structure.

A major terrorist event during the last few years of the Rafsanjani presidency was the June 1996 bombing of the U.S. military barracks at Al-Khobar in the eastern province of Saudi Arabia that killed 19 U.S. servicemen and wounded 372. Five years later, the Bush administration issued an indictment that identified Saudi Hizballah as responsible for carrying out the attack and asserted that Iran had "inspired, supported, and directed" Hizballah organizations in Saudi Arabia, Lebanon, Kuwait, and Bahrain since the early 1980s.[5] The indictment specifically identified Iranian contact and exchange of information with various Saudi Hizballah groups during 1993 and 1994, but it contained no evidence of Iranian contact with any of the Saudi perpetrators during the year prior to the Al-Khobar operation and no evidence of Iranian involvement in the operation itself.[6] When the June 2001 indictment was issued, Attorney General John Ashcroft indicated quite clearly that it contained only those charges that the administration believed would stand up in court.[7]

The Al-Khobar case is crucially important to understanding Iran's use or nonuse of terror, at least historically. If, as the Bush administration's indictment asserts, the Al-Khobar incident shows that Iranian intelligence services maintained active contacts with radical Islamist elements opposed to the United States, that should not come as a great surprise. If, however, the Iranian government deliberately orchestrated an attack on U.S. installations and personnel as a means, for example, of driving Americans out of the Gulf region, that would be evidence of a significant shift in Iranian policy toward the United States and Saudi Arabia. Only the year before, Iran had offered a major offshore development contract to a U.S. company as a signal of interest in improved relations and was engaged in a major strategic effort to develop closer relations with Saudi Arabia.

It is impossible to conclude on the basis of the Bush administration's indictment that the Al-Khobar attack constituted a major shift in Iran's willingness to use terror against Saudi Arabia and the United States . As former U.S. national security adviser under the Clinton administration Sandy Berger described the Al-Khobar investigation: "We know it was done by the Saudi Hizballah. We know that they were trained in Iran by Iranians. We know there was Iranian involvement. What has yet to be established is how substantial the Iranian involvement was."[8]

## KHATAMI AND THE NEW IRANIAN DIPLOMACY

With Khatami's landslide election in 1997, Iran's official foreign policy focused more intently on integrating Iran into the international community and on presenting a visage of Iran quite different from the scowling fanaticism of the earliest days of the revolution. Khatami's determination to change Iran's image became clear in January 1998, early in his first term, when he used the occasion of a CNN interview with correspondent Christiane Amanpour to deliver a message to the people of the United States. In carefully prepared remarks, he addressed all the outstanding issues between the United States and Iran, including terrorism:

> We believe in the holy Quran that says: slaying of one innocent person is tantamount to the slaying of all humanity. How could such a religion, and those who claim to be its followers, get involved in the assassination of innocent individuals and the slaughter of innocent human beings? We categorically reject all these allegations. ... Terrorism should be condemned in all its forms and manifestations; assassins must be condemned. Terrorism is useless anyway and we condemn it categorically. ... At the same time, supporting peoples who fight for the liberation of their land is not, in my opinion, supporting terrorism. It is, in fact, supporting those who are engaged in combating state terrorism.[9]

When further asked, "Regardless of the motive, do you believe that killing innocent women and children is terrorism, as for instance what happens on the streets of Israel?" Khatami replied, "It is definitely so. Any form of killing of innocent men and women who are not involved in confrontations is terrorism; it must be condemned, and we, in our term, condemn every form of it in the world."

This statement was and remains the most complete and authoritative to date regarding Iran's formal government policy on terrorism.

Khatami's subsequent handling of the "serial murders" of Iranian intellectuals lent some credibility to his statement. At least four intellectuals were brutally murdered in quick succession in November and December 1998 in what may have been an effort to destabilize the Khatami government. Khatami conducted an investigation, and his government arrested a group of ultraconservative officials, headed by Deputy Director Saeed Emami, in the Ministry of Intelligence. These men were hired originally by Ali Fallahian, the former minister of intelligence, and their arrest was widely seen as a public rebuke to the conservatives as well as a rare case of transparency in the security services. Before the case came up for trial, however, Emami reportedly killed himself in prison by ingesting a toxic powder normally used for hair removal.

When Khatami first took office, he had wanted to remove Emami and his associates from the Intelligence Ministry but had not succeeded in overcoming conservative objections. After Emami's arrest, Khatami was able to replace many of Fallahian's people in the ministry and to install an intelligence minister of his choosing. The unprecedented revelations of rogue operations in the security services, including widespread allegations that Emami was killed to prevent him from implicating other ultraconservative figures at the very highest levels of the clerical leadership, created a public sensation and seemed to indicate that unauthorized terrorist operations might become subject to internal and perhaps even public scrutiny and control. Such a hope was unduly optimistic as no further examples have followed, but Emami's arrest and death did confirm widespread suspicions that pockets of extremists inside and outside the revolutionary structure were operating without the review or approval of the elected government.

## SEPTEMBER 11 AND THE IRANIAN RESPONSE

After the September 11 attacks, in sharp contrast to much of the Arab world's scarcely concealed glee that the United States had gotten a taste of its own medicine, Iran responded with official statements of condolences and unofficial candlelight vigils in support of the American people. Although Iran officially opposed the subsequent U.S. attack on Afghanistan, it made no effort to interfere and even cooperated quietly on issues such as humanitarian relief, search and rescue, and other practical matters. After the Taliban government was deposed, Iran participated positively and creatively in the Bonn talks to establish a new interim government in Afghanistan, drawing rare praise from U.S. officials.[10] At the Tokyo donors conference in January 2002, Iran pledged a total of $560 million for the reconstruction of Afghanistan—the largest donation of any developing country. Speculation emerged among pundits that this would be the beginning of a new U.S.-Iranian relationship. Then, in his 2002 State of the Union address, President George W. Bush identified Iran as the third member of an "axis of evil," along with Iraq and North Korea, stating that terrorism was a major concern:

> Iran aggressively pursues these weapons [of mass destruction] and exports terror, while an unelected few repress the Iranian people's hope for freedom. ... They could provide these arms to terrorists, giving them the means to match their hatred. ... The United States of America will not permit the world's most dangerous regimes to threaten us with the world's most destructive weapons.[11]

Why did the Bush administration go from praising to excoriating Iran in only six weeks? One likely reason was the Israeli intercept and capture in January 2002 of the *Karine-A*, a ship secretly purchased by the Palestinian Authority (PA) that was allegedly carrying some 50 tons of weapons and explosives from Iran's Kish Island to Palestine. Israel arrested the ship's captain, Omar Akawi, who later spoke to the press from his prison cell and identified himself as a member of Arafat's Fatah movement and a lieutenant colonel in the PA's naval police.[12] The Palestinians and Iranians denounced the event as an Israeli setup intended to influence U.S. policy. If so, it worked perfectly. A senior administration official told *The New York Times* that the incident "was a sign to the president that the Iranians weren't serious."[13]

## Ties with Al Qaeda?

The United States also began asserting publicly that members of Al Qaeda were taking refuge in Iran across the border from western Afghanistan. Zalmay Khalilzad, the administration's special envoy to Afghanistan, put the U.S. case succinctly: "Hard-line, unaccountable elements of the Iranian regime facilitated the movement of Al Qaeda terrorists escaping from Afghanistan."[14] The government in Tehran initially denied that any Al Qaeda partisans were in Iran. The very lengthy border between Iran and Afghanistan and Iran and Pakistan is riddled with drug smuggling routes and is far from secure, however, and after some weeks, Iran announced that it had located Taliban and Al Qaeda supporters within its borders and that they were being returned to their countries of origin. Over the following year, the Iranian government detained and extradited more than 500 fugitives, largely volunteers from various Muslim countries who had gone to Afghanistan to join the jihad against the West.

Why would members of the Iranian security services look the other way or perhaps even facilitate the passage of these fugitives? No doubt money was the primary reason. Besides money, however, some hard-line elements may have also seen an opportunity to recruit agents or to incorporate some militant Afghan cadres into their own operations. One can only speculate, though, because neither Washington nor Tehran disclosed the identity of these individuals nor suggested their possible motives.

Some reports, usually ascribed to anonymous intelligence sources, have mentioned a connection between Al Qaeda and some elements in Iran, possibly via Hizballah.[15] Those allegations strained credulity, however, given Iran's vigorous opposition to the Taliban government in Afghanistan and its Al Qaeda supporters. Al Qaeda is a Sunni Muslim group that espouses the views of the most extreme proponents of the Salafi (often called Wahhabi) school of Islamic thought, which regards Shi'ism, the religion practiced most in Iran and by Hizballah in Lebanon, as heretical. One can imagine some low-level tactical contact between the two groups, particularly in view of their shared opposition to the Western presence in the Gulf region. Claims of an alliance, however, lack evidence and logic.

The issue of potential Iranian ties with Al Qaeda took on much greater significance in May 2003 when three suicide car bombs exploded almost simultaneously in Riyadh, Saudi Arabia. Thirty-five people, including nine bombers, died in the explosions, which targeted housing compounds for Americans and other Westerners living and working in the Saudi kingdom. The attack was carried out by a group of Saudi militants, who had previously been identified by Saudi security forces and were on the run, operating under Al Qaeda's direction. Many of the perpetrators were arrested in the following weeks, but the United States released unconfirmed intelligence reports that Iran was sheltering some senior Al Qaeda operatives who may have been involved in planning the attack. Iran denied involvement, then announced that it had several Al Qaeda members in custody, reportedly including some very senior individuals.

The United States responded quite sharply, calling the action taken by the Iranian government insufficient and suspending the potentially significant informal talks that had begun to take place on a regular basis between U.S. and Iranian officials. These talks had been warily resumed in Geneva, technically under the aegis of an informal UN committee created to deal with Afghanistan after the Afghan and the Iraq wars had underscored the mutual interests of the United States and Iran on a number of practical issues, such as preparing for refugee movements and search and rescue missions as well as maintaining stability after war had ended. The discussions were reportedly businesslike and many observers saw them as a precursor to a possible improvement in U.S.-Iranian relations, despite the two countries' many differences and the sour taste left by the axis of evil speech. As had happened in the past, U.S. charges of Iranian association with terrorist activities brought potentially constructive contacts to a halt.

## Has Khatami Ended Support for Terrorism?

Iran has clearly changed its policies substantially over time. The hostage-taking and regional destabilization campaigns of the early days of the Iranian revolution that were so immensely costly to Iran's image and that continue to plague its international relations have vanished. As Khatami delicately put it in his CNN interview, there is no longer any need for such "unconventional methods."[16] Assassinating enemies of the Islamic Republic in Europe ended in 1994. Later killings outside Europe focused primarily on members of the Mujahideen-e Khalq, but those have also largely ceased in recent years and may have been rendered pointless by U.S. occupation of Mujahideen-e Khalq camps in Iraq and severe crackdowns on the organization in France and elsewhere.

As far as we can tell, Iranian direct involvement in terrorist activities in the past—kidnappings, maritime attacks, assassinations—seems to have given way in recent years almost entirely to proxy support for non-Iranian organizations. If so, this may be attributable simply to the realization that these actions were doing immense harm to Iran's broader national objectives and that their cost far outweighed whatever perceived benefits may have been gained. Iran may have taken a very long time to reach what might appear a fairly obvious conclusion, but it suggests at a minimum a capacity to modify its policies in the face of persistent pressure and experience.

The most substantial changes in Iran's apparent policies and behavior have come with Khatami's election. Although Khatami has been largely unsuccessful in his attempt to move the ruling clerical elite toward his vision of greater political liberty, civil society, and rule of law, he has changed the political discourse in Iran. His housecleaning of the Intelligence Ministry—one of the few genuine achievements to come out of his many confrontations with the conservative power structure—may have significantly curtailed Iran's earlier tendency toward interventionism and feckless adventurism.

At the same time, Iran undoubtedly continues to consort with and provide support to organizations that are committed to the destruction of Israel. The list begins with Lebanese Hizballah and extends to include Hamas, the Palestinian Islamic Jihad, and the Popular Front for the Liberation of Palestine-General Command. Virtually all elements of the Iranian leadership do not deny this association; they actually take pride in it. Members of these and other militant organizations are brought to Iran repeatedly for various conferences and meetings; their leaders meet openly with Iran's top leaders, including Khatami and his foreign minister; other Iranian officials meet with them on trips to Lebanon and Syria; and Iran provides material support. Iran regards this as legitimate activity in support of resistance movements fighting against illegal occupation of their land. Although Khatami, as indicated earlier, asserts that bombings of innocent people are prohibited in Islam and are opposed by Iran, many other Iranians, including very senior clerics and officials, maintain that such acts are legitimate and may well be prepared to countenance or encourage violence.

The United States and much of the West regard these organizations as terrorists. Iran's more tolerant view, however, is not that different from popular Islamic opinion (and some official opinion, whether public or private). Iran envisions itself as the true world leader of political Islam, and fierce opposition to Israeli occupation is a touchstone of that core belief. Despite its own strong views, Iran has stated repeatedly that it would accept any settlement that is satisfactory to the Palestinians and that it will not try to impose its views by force. Judging from the fiery anti-Israeli rhetoric of many Iranian leaders and their failure to criticize or condemn even the most extreme actions or claims of its friends in the Palestinian-Israeli arena, including repeated suicide bombings by organizations such as Hamas and Islamic Jihad, Israel and the West have every reason to be skeptical of those assurances.

The alleged sheltering in Iran of Al Qaeda members and other fugitives, such as the Al-Ansar group in Iraq, is a different problem that is less obvious than it may appear. Even without porous borders and isolated, lawless regions, the apprehension of Al Qaeda operatives is not a simple matter, as evident elsewhere. Osama bin Laden and some of his contingent reportedly move back and forth across the Afghan-Pakistani border almost at will, despite the best efforts of both the United States and the Pakistani government to locate and intercept them. The United States itself has repeatedly discovered cells of Al Qaeda operatives within its own borders, including some members who had recently arrived and were reportedly conducting training operations not far from the nation's capital. Washington is quick to assume the worst with Iran, especially in light of Iran's lack of transparency concerning issues of intelligence and national security. Nevertheless, after massive misjudgments of intelligence concerning Iraq, the United States might be well advised to regard its present intelligence reports on Iran with a bit more caution.

## Policy Options

The United States faces two severe problems in dealing with Iran and terrorism. The first is the difficulty of dealing with the legacy of the past. Terrorist acts in which Iran may have had direct or indirect involvement have seriously harmed many U.S. citizens (and others). The U.S. Congress has attempted to address this by passing legislation permitting victims to bring cases to U.S. courts, with awards granted on the basis of uncontested evidence because Iran refuses to appear. The awards are supposed to be paid from Iranian assets, but that would set a precedent that could harm U.S. interests around the world; so, large awards are paid to these plaintiffs from the U.S. Treasury on the presumption that eventually they will be recovered from Iran. The Bush administration fiercely opposes efforts to prosecute U.S. officials or military personnel for possible violations of international law in the courts of other countries or at the International Criminal Court. Yet, U.S. courts are now routinely prosecuting Iranians and others for alleged support of terrorist actions by Hizballah and other militant organizations, mocking judicial due process. The past must be dealt with, but the present remedy will only complicate future efforts to settle past grievances.

The more immediate problem for the United States and the international community is how to deal with Iran's proxy support for pro-Palestinian groups that oppose Israel and the peace process and who resort to terrorist attacks against civilian targets. At least since Khatami's election seven years ago, this proxy support has been the focus of virtually all accusations about Iran's role as a state sponsor of terrorism.

Resolving the Israeli-Palestinian dispute would, among other benefits, remove the *raison d'être* of these violent factions and eliminate Iran's rationale for providing political and financial support. Iranian involvement is, of course, not the primary concern of those involved in the peace process. Nevertheless, as the heat of the intifada increased, with resultant devastating pictures on regional television, so too did Iran's rhetoric and its presumed material support to the extremist opposition. Iran insists that its support of the "forces of national liberation" is not terrorism, but its fervor rises and falls with the intensity of the Israeli-Palestinian conflict. Because of its distance from the conflict, Iran can adopt an irresponsible rhetorical stance that is "more Palestinian than the Palestinians" if only because it sounds appropriately revolutionary in speeches and distracts from the many domestic failures of the Iranian leadership. This is not a factional issue in Iranian politics; reformers and conservatives tend to sound very much alike. Pressure tactics and sanctions have been totally ineffective in changing Iran's behavior on this issue in the past, and there is no reason to believe that the future will be any different. Among the side benefits of progress in the peace process almost surely would be a cooling of Iranian rhetoric, a reduction in Iranian temptation to meddle in Palestine, and a corresponding improvement in U.S.-Iranian relations.

The most complex element of Iran's involvement in terrorist activities is the fact that Iran has two different ruling structures. As Khalilzad has noted, Iran's worst behavior often originates with "hard-line, unaccountable elements of the Iranian regime." How can the United States deal with that reality of Iranian politics? The short answer is regime change. The longer and more thoughtful answer is regime change that grows out of Iranian domestic needs and demands, not imposed by an external power.

One of the few unquestioned positive achievements of the 1979 revolution was its lesson to the Iranian people that they were in charge of their own destiny, rather than blaming every political development on foreign hands. Losing that would be a huge setback. Iran has been in a century-long struggle for freedom that started with the Constitutional

Revolution of the early twentieth century. It has not been an easy or linear process, and the outcome is far from certain. Any attempt to short-circuit the process by sticking a U.S. finger in the Iranian pie, however, is a formula for disaster. Success in prompting a revolt would bring a crushing response from the conservative forces that would at least temporarily halt the democratization movement. Even if U.S. calls for revolution went unheeded, they might taint those seeking change as lackeys of a foreign power.

During nearly a quarter century of Islamic revolutionary rule, Iran has changed and continues to change. This is as true of the country's involvement in terrorist activities as it is in any other aspect of its political life. Iran's early ventures into hostage-taking, bombings, and subversion gave way to terror at sea during the long war with Iraq and then to a vicious vendetta of assassination against its perceived political enemies. Increasingly, Iran has shifted its focus to financing, training, and supporting proxy organizations whose actions provided some measure of deniability for Iran but could not overcome suspicion of Iranian involvement, if not actual control. Over the past seven years, the focus of this proxy relationship has been on the Israeli-Palestinian conflict.

Throughout much of this history, there has been a gap between Iran's declaratory policy and the actions of malevolent forces embedded in Iran's security services. Khatami has been successful in weeding out some of these individuals, but the job is far from complete. The magnitude of the problem that remains may be reflected in alleged Iranian support for arms shipments to Palestine and providing refuge to Al Qaeda fugitives. Iran's denial of involvement is insufficient. For the sake of its credibility, Iran must demonstrate a genuine determination to investigate such charges and to remedy any abuses. Its extradition of hundreds of Al Qaeda fighters was a step in the right direction, but Iran needs to clean its house of all known terrorists, including Lebanese and Palestinian figures with long histories of involvement in bombings and assassinations.

Confronting the hard-line elements that distort its foreign and domestic policies goes far beyond allegations of international terrorism.

That struggle lies at the heart of Iran's political identity and will determine the course of its future. The United States and the international community can keep the spotlight on Iran's abuses and press hard for change. If the pressure for change is applied fairly and if Washington acknowledges Iran's accomplishments as well as its failures, the world will be assured of staunch allies within Iran. Change is a slow and often uncertain process, but it is something that can be done only by Iran itself.

## Notes

1. There is no generally accepted definition of terrorism. For a discussion of the definitional problems, see A. William Samii, "Tehran, Washington, and Terror: No Agreement to Differ," *Middle East Review of International Affairs* 6, no. 3 (September 2002), http://meria.idc.ac.il/journal/2002/issue3/jv6n3a5.html (accessed July 23, 2003).

2. For details on this episode, see Robin Wright, "A Reporter at Large: Teheran Summer," *New Yorker*, September 5, 1988, pp. 32–72.

3. See Daniel Sobelman, "Hizbollah Two Years after the Withdrawal: A Compromise between Ideology, Interests, and Exigencies," *Strategic Assessment* 5, no. 2 (August 2002).

4. See Gary Sick, "Slouching Toward Settlement: The Internationalization of the Iran-Iraq War, 1987–88," in *Neither East Nor West: Iran, the Soviet Union, and the United States*, eds. Nikki Keddie and Mark Gasiorowski (New Haven: Yale University Press, 1990), pp. 219–246.

5. The indictment is located at www.usdoj.gov:80/opa/pr/2001/June/khobarindictment.wpd (accessed July 23, 2003).

6. For a thorough review of the charges and countercharges, see Elsa Walsh, "Annals of Politics: Louis Freeh's Last Case," *New Yorker*, May 14, 2001, p. 68.

7. See statement by Ashcroft released by the Department of Justice on June 21, 2001.

8. Walsh, "Annals of Politics."

9. "Transcript of Interview with Iranian president Mohammad Khatami," CNN.com, January 7, 1998, www.cnn.com/WORLD/9801/07/iran/interview.html (accessed July 23, 2003) (hereinafter Khatami interview).

10. Richard Haas, the U.S. special coordinator for Afghanistan, complimented Iran's "constructive role" in talks on the future of Afghanistan and providing the Afghan people with humanitarian aid. Agence France Press, December 6, 2001.

11. George W. Bush, State of the Union address, Washington, D.C., January 29, 2002, www.whitehouse.gov/news/releases/2002/01/20020129-11.html (accessed July 23, 2003).

12. For a detailed review of reportage on the incident from an Israeli perspective, see "Operation Noah's Ark," Ha'aretz.com, www.haaretzdaily.com/hasen/pages/ShArt.jhtml?itemNo=114367&contrassID=3&subContrassID=0&sbSubContrassID=0 (accessed July 23, 2003).

13. David E. Sanger, "Bush Aides Say Tough Tone Put Foes on Notice," *New York Times*, January 31, 2002.

14. Zalmay Khalilzad, speech to the American-Iranian Council, Washington, D.C., March 13, 2002.

15. For a detailed examination of the facts and allegations concerning Iranian terrorist activities for the first year after the September 11 attacks, see Samii, "Tehran, Washington, and Terror."

16. Khatami interview.

**Shahram Chubin and Robert S. Litwak**

# Debating Iran's Nuclear Aspirations

$T$he International Atomic Energy Agency's (IAEA) June 2003 report on Iran's nuclear program has stripped the Islamic Republic of the agency's seal of approval and elevated international concern about Tehran's nuclear intentions. Heightened suspicion that Iran's civilian nuclear energy infrastructure masks a clandestine weapons program has galvanized international cooperation among the United States, the European Union, and Russia and is likely to result in increased external pressure on Iran to remain in compliance with its Nuclear Non-Proliferation Treaty (NPT) commitments. This international pressure will aim, at a minimum, to ensure Iran's adherence to the enhanced safeguards system contained in the IAEA's Additional Protocol (the so-called 93+2), intended to increase the transparency of a state's nuclear program; yet, the regime in Tehran has resisted or placed conditions on its adherence to this measure. To justify its position at home, the regime has again played the political trump card of Iranian nationalism and has cast its defiance as principled resistance to a discriminatory effort inspired by the United States to deny advanced technology to Iran.

Because the exact status of Iran's nuclear program is unknown, the time available to attempt to resolve this thorny issue diplomatically is uncertain

Shahram Chubin is director of research at the Geneva Centre for Security Studies in Switzerland. Robert S. Litwak is director of the Division of International Studies at the Woodrow Wilson International Center for Scholars in Washington, D.C.

*The Washington Quarterly* • 26:4 pp. 99–114.

as well. External pressure is undoubtedly a necessary element of such a strategy, but it is unlikely to be sufficient in the long term even if it is successful in buying some time in the short term. A complementary effort is needed to influence nuclear politics within Iran by generating a real debate among the Iranian public. This type of political transparency would end Iranian radical hard-liners' monopoly on information and debunk the putative energy rationale for the nuclear program. Moreover, informed discussion would help Iranians distinguish between the development of nuclear technology and that of nuclear weapons, that is, between programs that are legal and accompanied by assurances and inspections and those that are used to cover up illicit activities. Such a debate could similarly subject to hard scrutiny the important strategic motivations for a weapons option, which remain either unstated or mentioned obliquely because the regime denies violating its NPT obligations in the first place.

Formidable political impediments exist, but in the quasi-democracy of contemporary Iran, the nuclear issue could become contested turf—a process that could potentially lead to a positive long-term change in the country's strategic culture and thus help curtail nuclear proliferation in Iran. Government hard-liners have long determined the security policies of the Islamic Republic. The particular experience of Iran—revolution, war, sanctions, and estrangement from international society—has created a shared sense of embattlement in a hostile environment, leaving little scope for debate. In addition, foreign and security policies historically have not been at the forefront of the reformists' concerns. This situation has changed in recent years; as the costs of the hard-liners' choices in security policy have mounted, affecting Iran's development prospects, so have public scrutiny of such security policies as well as the inclination to question their rationale.

The particular character of the Iranian proliferation challenge and the country's dynamic domestic politics present an opportunity for the United States and its allies to pursue a comprehensive strategy that promotes the transformation of Iran's internal debate in tandem with external efforts to induce or compel Iranian compliance with nonproliferation norms.

## Iran's Proliferation Challenge

The IAEA's June 2003 revelations confirmed earlier reports and cited Iran for violations of its safeguard obligations because of its past failures to disclose the importation of nuclear material and the construction of a heavy-water production plant and facilities for uranium enrichment, processing, and storage. The IAEA did not go so far as to say that Iran had violated the NPT, a step that would have immediately led to the referral of the matter to the United Nations Security Council. Rather, the IAEA framed the issue more narrowly as a failure of transparency, prompting calls from the EU and Russia for Iran to accede to the Additional Protocol. The revelations about Iran's expanded nuclear capabilities, however, also heightened concerns about its intentions. In Washington, the IAEA report was received as further confirmation of a persistent, decade-long pattern of Iranian material procurements that clearly points to a clandestine weapons program. The document indicates how far along the path toward developing nuclear weapons a state can go while remaining technically in compliance with the NPT's Article IV, which permits access to atomic energy technology. Iran's advances in acquiring fissile material for weapons production also raised concerns that the country was approaching a threshold of indigenous capability that would soon make it invulnerable to even a complete embargo. Moreover, some have questioned whether the increased transparency required by the Additional Protocol can be effective in dealing with a determined cheater, which the Bush administration believes Iran to be.

The IAEA report was published in the aftermath of the war on Iraq, or at least after the completion of "major combat operations." But the war on Iraq was a unique case, not a counterproliferation policy that can be generalized. Formulating effective strategies to prevent or roll back weapons of mass destruction (WMD) acquisition must begin by recognizing that states neither undertake such programs lightly nor reverse course on a whim. Concern for a country's own national security has been paramount among the motivations attributed to states that have decided to acquire nuclear weapons.

For the Bush administration, which maintains its intention to pursue nonproliferation strategies tailored to the particular circumstances of each case, Iran presents conditions that warrant a different policy from those applied to the other two members of the "axis of evil." The United States views, with reason, outlaw states that indulge in or sponsor terrorism, regional aggression or intimidation, domestic repression, and anti-Western postures as countries that pose the greatest threat if they acquire WMD capabilities. Iran, however, is not a pariah state under UN sanction like Saddam Hussein's Iraq, nor is Iran a hermit-like failed state like North Korea. Iran's nuclear program is far less developed than that of North Korea but more advanced than that of Iraq prior to the 2003 war (although Saddam was closer to acquiring nuclear weapons prior to the 1991 Persian Gulf War than he was before the latest conflict). The latest IAEA report indicates a significant expansion of Iran's nuclear infrastructure, but it is doubtful that Iran possesses all the elements needed for a complete weapons program. Unlike North Korea, which may have reprocessed nuclear material for up to two weapons and is poised to acquire more, Iran is estimated to be two or three years away from having a bomb, according to the Israeli government's worst-case scenario.[1]

## Debating Iran's Nuclear Needs

Perhaps the most important feature distinguishing Iran from the other axis of evil states is its quasi-democracy. In Saddam's Iraq, where insulting the president (liberally interpreted) was punishable by death, politics simply did not exist. In North Korea, Kim Il Sung and his son, Kim Jong Il, have created a dynastic political system and cult of personality that even Saddam must have envied. By contrast, Iran has a vibrant, restive, and skeptical public, which is increasingly given to criticism, debate, and scrutiny of a regime that has squandered its political legitimacy.

With a recent public opinion poll indicating that 70 percent of Iranians seek normalization of relations with the United States and engagement with the global community, Iran is in a different league from

North Korea and Iraq.[2] Public opinion in Iran supports an active international role for the country that allows it to be taken seriously and does not undermine its neighboring states' legitimate search for security. In short, unlike North Korea and Iraq, Iran's dynamic domestic politics present an avenue for influencing the country's decisionmaking about its nuclear program. The gap between the hard-line conservatives in Iran and the rest of society has widened and is evident in almost every issue facing the country. On foreign and security policies, this gap is manifested in the difference between those with an ideological approach toward international relations and those who emphasize national interest, which leads to disparate assessments of Iran's defense needs and of the degree to which the country should be engaged in cooperative or common security with its neighbors and the international community at large. This distinction will only become more acute as international pressure is brought to bear on Iran for its nuclear (and missile) programs.

Some Western observers, in an effort to remain impartial, have sympathized with Iran's quest for nuclear weapons, allegedly because the country is located in a rough, nuclearized neighborhood (with Israel and Pakistan) and because proximate U.S. military power, now extended into Iraq and Afghanistan, poses a threat to the country's security. Some of these same observers also argue that Iran's aspirations to develop nuclear weapons are not peculiar to this regime, given the shah's decision in the 1970s to construct the Bushehr nuclear reactor. Viewed through this political prism, Persian nationalism is said to be the nuclear program's principal impulse. Yet, both of these propositions are oversimplified and unhelpful.

With the demise of Saddam's regime in neighboring Iraq, an Iranian nuclear weapons program has lost any compelling strategic rationale. Iran has used Israel as an all-purpose bogey to criticize the United States for picking on select regimes that possess WMD, to ingratiate itself with the Arab states by supporting the Palestinians, and to argue that the threat posed by Israel justifies Iran's own missile program. No one in Tehran or elsewhere has suggested that Iran seeks to confront Israel militarily or that Iran would be willing to enter into conflict with Israel on behalf of the Palestinians. Indeed, this is precisely the reason that Iran has preferred to use support for proxy groups (such as Hamas or Islamic Jihad) to demonstrate its support of the Palestinians. Israel has served as a diversion and a pretext in that Tehran uses its support for the Palestinians to deflect its neighbors' concerns about Iran's own WMD programs. At the same time, Iran's support for the Palestinians is the Islamic Republic's cynical attempt to gain leverage against the West.

Moreover, Iran's quest for nuclear weapons, combined with its record of not recognizing Israel, supporting attacks against it, and seeking to derail any peace process that might be in motion, adds to the concerns about Iran as a proliferator. An Iran that changed its policy toward Israel, especially its policy of supporting terrorist attacks, would still be of concern as a proliferator, but less so. In theory, Iran might seek to trade a change in its Middle East policies for somewhat more leeway on its nuclear aspirations. In reality, however, such a distinction does not appear likely. Iran seems to have linked the two so publicly that a reversal of its policy toward Israel would have to provoke an examination of why Iran needs nuclear weapons at all.

Iran's invocation of its proximity to Pakistan as a rationale for developing nuclear weapons appears to be even less realistic. Iran and Pakistan have no major bilateral disputes; the principal tensions arise from Pakistan's failure to manage its domestic sectarian rivalries, which has resulted in occasional violence between Pakistan's Sunni and Shi'a communities. Pakistan is necessarily preoccupied with its problems with India, largely over Kashmir, leaving it little energy or inclination for other confrontations. Iran has now established good relations with India, which provides Tehran with further insurance. The only conceivable rivalry that might arise between Iran and Pakistan would result from Iran's very decision to acquire nuclear weapons, thus making the rivalry a self-fulfilling prophecy. In that event, Pakistan might be tempted to assist Saudi Arabia down the same path. In sum, it is difficult to find a plausible strategic rationale for Iran to seek nuclear weapons.[3]

The currently changing nature of public opinion in Iran on the Palestinian issue provides an example of what can happen when an issue becomes the subject of debate. Until about two years ago, the conservatives in Iran had preempted a debate on policy by monopolizing the definition of the issue and hence its implementation. Iranian policy toward the Middle East peace process was based on the proposition that Iranians felt sympathy for the Palestinian cause, and the hard-liners were allowed to define how this sympathy would be expressed. In recent months, however, the floodgates of the debate have widened as Iranians, especially members of parliament, have begun to question the hard-liners' carte blanche on this issue. Although generally agreeing on support for the Palestinians, Iranians increasingly question the form this support should take, asking, for example, why support for the Palestinian cause entails support for groups using violence. Why does it undermine support for the Palestinians' own elected representatives?[4] How does the adoption of radical positions help the people in the region? Can Iran not help diplomatically? Does a militant, rejectionist approach advance Iran's national interests? What price is Iran willing to pay for such policies?

With the reformers and general public now raising such questions, Iran's conservatives have lost control over the issue and are now on the defensive. Even if those authorities not elected by the public but appointed to positions by Supreme Leader Ayatollah Ali Hoseini Khamenei still pursue this policy, it will have a short shelf life when Iranians recognize the cynicism with which the people have been manipulated. Hard-liners will find it increasingly difficult to justify their policies and their retention of power by referring to a hostile, predatory external environment and to burnish their revolutionary credentials by adopting extreme positions, such as nonrecognition of Israel, which goes beyond those of many Arab states.

Could the precedent set by debate over supporting the Palestinians, in which issues are aired and policies come under public scrutiny, breaking the hard-liners' monopolistic grip on policy, apply to Iran's nuclear program? Until now, there has been no nuclear debate on the pluses and minuses of a weapons program for obvious reasons: the government has renounced the right to develop nuclear weapons as a signatory to the NPT, and there is little knowledge about the program in Iran for it has been conceived and developed clandestinely, insulated from public knowledge as much as possible. Compounded with the dearth of public knowledge about nuclear weapons, their history, and capabilities, this secrecy has ensured that whatever limited public debate has occurred to date has been notably ill informed and inexpert.[5]

The issue of Iran's right to nuclear technology has often fronted as a code for its right to nuclear weapons. The energy rationale for Iran— the ostensible argument for Iran's nuclear program—has itself never been subjected to a rigorous debate. As noted, Iranian authorities have not had to do much to argue its merits; they need only point to U.S. attempts to issue blanket prohibitions denying Iran access to any nuclear technology to make the domestic case that the program therefore must be worthwhile. In arguing that the nuclear energy program seeks to make Iran a modern state with access to advanced technology, the regime strikes a sensitive chord.

With pressure now exerted on Iran to clarify its program, however, some Iranians have begun to refer to the necessity to balance the country's needs with its responsibilities to the international community. President Muhammad Khatami stated, "We have the right to use this knowledge and you [the IAEA, international community] have the right to be assured that it would be channeled in the right way."[6] A member of the Majlis National Security and Foreign Policy Committee observed that, "[i]f we do not sign the additional protocol, it will give the impression that Iran is moving towards the non-peaceful use of nuclear energy. Thus we must remove all doubts by talking to, and negotiating with, other countries and signing this protocol."[7]

International pressure on Iran has already led to a certain amount of public questioning of Iran's program and its rationale. For example, in June 2003 the newspaper *Mardom Salari* raised the possibility that the nuclear energy program might be serving as a cover for a nuclear weapons program and as "a kind of deterrence ... [whose] sell by date expired" a decade ago. Another source, the pro-reform newspaper *Hambastegi* argued in a June 2003 issue that, if indeed Iran's intentions were peaceful, accepting the Additional Protocol should not pose a problem.[8]

The important point is that international pressure is forcing the regime to confront choices about its hidden weapons program. Does it continue to argue the energy rationale? In that case, how can it rationalize certain purchases and activities, such as the uranium-enrichment plant? Should the regime avoid signing the Additional Protocol? Does it sign and hope to continue its illegal weapons program undiscovered? International pressure is also forcing the regime to confront a more restless Majlis and press, seeking clearer answers about the program.

As argued above, analysts have often inferred the unstated case for Iran's nuclear weapons development to be the rough regional neighborhood—the possession of nuclear weapons by Pakistan; Israel; Russia; and the new Middle East actor, the United States. Yet, Iran has no historic enemies; existential threats; or giant, hostile neighbors requiring it to compensate for a military imbalance with a nuclear program. A realistic assessment of Iran's security interests does not stretch to include confronting Israel on behalf of extremist Palestinians, a minority within their own land.

The implicit rationale for the nuclear weapons program lies in the worldview of the hard-liners, who see the program as the ultimate guarantor of Iran's influence and security and, not incidentally, their own political power. Meanwhile, by arguing that all nuclear technology, peaceful and military, is necessary for Iran's development, the hard-liners have been able (with considerable help from Washington) to confuse the issue, at least within Iran. If encouraged actually to examine the motivations for pursuing a nuclear weapons program, Iranians would likely realize that it makes little strategic sense.

Clearly, a public debate on the merits of developing a nuclear weapons capability could be problematic within Iran. First, as mentioned, the level of public expertise is low; confusion, emotion, and generality tend to predominate when these issues surface. Second, a debate about a decision theoretically already decided, that is, Iran's renunciation of the right to nuclear weapons by its accession to the NPT, might not send a good signal to the outside world. Third, in the current, charged climate of U.S. saber rattling, such a debate might encourage extremists to argue more persuasively the merits of an asymmetrical strategy to deter the United States.

Discussion in Iran on the country's acquisition of nuclear weapons thus far has tended to focus on Iran's right to acquire the technology needed to develop an independent nuclear energy program, even though weapons-related implications clearly follow. U.S. efforts to impede the flow of requisite technology have been cast by the hard-liners as an attempt to keep Iran backward and dependent. Washington's policy has been depicted as animated by hostility toward an independent Iran. The principle of independence, of course, was one of the touchstones of the Iranian revolution, and few Iranians of whatever political persuasion—nationalists, secularists, or advocates of a strict religious government—would dissent from its importance. The long and painful history of foreign intervention in Iran (of Russia and Great Britain in Persia and, more recently, of U.S. influence in Iran) makes the issue of independence a critical point for Iranians.

At the same time, the regime has cultivated the sense of victimization, grievance, and embattlement that Shi'ite culture finds so congenial to give the government a free hand in defining Iran's defense and security needs. Iran's leadership has attempted to use the Iran-Iraq War to assert Iran's need to prepare for technical surprises and to foster the public mentality of preparedness and vigilance. The regime has sought to capitalize on the early experience of the revolution when Iran was caught friendless and militarily unprepared when Iraq launched a war in September 1980. These attempts to inculcate a mentality of circling the wagons and to appeal to national security at the slightest excuse, however, have begun to wear a little thin. In recent years, Iranians have increasingly seen this tactic for what it is: an excuse to retain power, to monopolize decisionmaking, and to cover an opaque style of leadership.

The same tension is evident in the nuclear policy area. Regime references to Iran's right to nuclear technology have become shorthand for its right to acquire nuclear weapons. Yet, the rationale for an energy program, let alone the rationale for a weapons program, has not been addressed. Thus, the question of whether Iran's determination to pursue an ambitious nuclear program for power generation is based on sound economic or energy foundations has not been subjected to scrutiny. The energy rationale frequently is cited as a response to Iran's population growth and increased domestic energy consumption or to the decline in oil production (or the need to conserve oil domestically so that it can be sold to generate foreign exchange revenues). In the past 11 years, fuel consumption in Iran has doubled, leading to current plans to establish nuclear power plants that will generate 7,000 megawatts of electricity by the year 2020. Tehran aims to become self-sufficient when it comes to providing fuel for these plants.

At present, no public debate exists to examine the assumptions on which the nuclear energy program is based or honestly analyze its costs and benefits vis-à-vis other forms of power generation. Observers have frequently noted that Iran annually vents off as much energy in natural gas as any nuclear power program would generate. A candid nuclear energy assessment would have to look at the life-cycle costs of imported reactors; dependence on foreign suppliers; plant costs; spent fuel disposition; facilities maintenance; operations staff training; the environmental aspects of eventual decommissioning; and the risks involved, including accidents, threats to plant safety, and earthquakes. To inform the public debate, such an evaluation would need to consider the costs of the nuclear energy program relative to other approaches to fulfilling Iran's energy needs.

Debating Iran's nuclear energy program on strictly economic grounds would take the issue out of the grasp of a small group of regime hardliners who have basically made policy in secret, framing the issue thus far as one of Iran's sovereign right to advanced technology being thwarted by a hostile United States. Informing the public and allowing Iranians, including members of parliament, to reach their own judgment on the merits of pursuing a nuclear program for power generation purposes would mark a significant shift. The regime's current appeal to instinctive Iranian support for national independence and equality allows the nuclear program to escape the kind of cool scrutiny now being applied to the issue of Palestine.

Because Iranians across the political spectrum support Iran's rights to acquire the most modern forms of technology necessary for the country's development and to be treated the same as other states are treated on this issue, they have been and remain susceptible to the clerics' critique of the United States' selective concern about nonproliferation norms. This sentiment, however, by no means equates with support for a policy of acquiring nuclear weapons. As the quotes above suggest, Iranians would support a responsible policy that can balance and reconcile their treaty obligations (in letter as well as in spirit) with their own country's needs. This approach entails balancing the right to appropriate technology for power generation and other peaceful applications with the need to reassure the international community of Iran's benign intentions.

## How Can the United States Shape the Debate?

Unlike the current crisis with North Korea, where the danger of nuclear weapons breakout is imminent and the prospects for rolling back the program appear bleak, the international community still has time to address Iran's proliferation challenge. The Bush administration has already ruled out a low-key policy that denies the existence of a crisis. At the same time, the White House has evidently given up on Khatami as an agent of political change and simply cannot wait for the regime to collapse.

Following the release of the June 2003 IAEA report, in what White House officials characterized as "a carefully worded escalation" that went beyond previous expressions of "concern," President George W. Bush baldly asserted that the United States "will not tolerate the construction of a nuclear weapon" in Iran.[9] This formulation, albeit somewhat ambiguous about the meaning of "construction," elevated the issue of Iran's nuclear capabilities and helped ratchet up international pressure from the EU and Russia, who were also furious with Iranian cheating and therefore needed little prodding. The IAEA report both diplomatically iso-

lated the regime in Tehran and placed the political onus on Iran to ensure the transparency of its program and its nuclear intentions.

While rejecting inaction, U.S. administration officials repeat the
policy mantra that all options are on the table. Yet, U.S. deliberations
on Iran are shaped by a persisting tension in policy between the twin
objectives of near-term change in behavior and eventual regime change.
Administration statements accentuating regime change undercut Iran's
incentives to change behavior. For U.S. policymakers, the issue of Iran's
nuclear program remains embedded in the broader one of the future
evolution of that country. After the war in Iraq, some U.S. administration officials depicted that action as a cautionary example for those regimes that refuse to abandon their WMD programs, while others worried
that the war might lead these leaders to conclude precisely the opposite, that only a nuclear weapon could deter the United States.[10]

The U.S. administration basically has two policy options for addressing Iran's nuclear program: military preemption or negotiation. In response to the September 11 attacks, preemption against rogue states
and terrorist groups has been elevated to official U.S. doctrine. The
National Security Strategy document, issued by the White House in
September 2002, characterizes preemption as "a matter of common
sense."[11] The historical record, however, reveals force to be far from
the definitive instrument of nonproliferation policy that some allege or
wish it to be. Indeed, a policy of preemption is as problematic as its
nonmilitary alternatives, and its ability to produce the desired outcomes has proven uncertain.

The successful 1981 Israeli strike to destroy Iraq's Osirak nuclear reactor before it became operational was not a paradigm but rather a rare
instance in which all the conditions for success were present: specific
and highly accurate intelligence and a negligible risk of collateral damage and retaliation.[12] Given Iran's multiple and redundant facilities,
the intelligence and military requirements for preventive action are formidable. Beyond those practical issues, the political consequences of a
military strike on Iran could be highly adverse; an attack might well
trigger an anti-U.S. backlash that would be bound to undermine pros-

pects for near-term political change and eventual rapprochement between the United States and Iran.[13]

For the time being, U.S. officials have declared force to be an instrument of last resort, and they have shown a willingness to allow time for diplomacy to achieve a satisfactory resolution of the nuclear impasse with Iran. Some have proposed that the United States should engage the current regime in a grand bargain in which U.S. security reassurances, that is, a pledge of nonaggression and noninterference, and an end to economic sanctions would be exchanged for major, verifiable shifts in Iranian behavior related to WMD and terrorism.[14] To induce such a road map, the United States would also threaten tangible penalties, such as the imposition of multilateral sanctions if Iran did not fully comply with its IAEA obligations under the NPT. In light of the U.S. experience with North Korean cheating under the terms of the 1994 Agreed Framework, the Bush administration has resisted and expressed extreme skepticism about the efficacy of such agreements with odious regimes.

Bush would certainly have a freer hand than his predecessor had; the Clinton administration's limited engagement with North Korea triggered charges of appeasement from critics from the far Right. Yet, some would still see any incentives granted to Iran, even if reciprocated, as an instance of the United States' succumbing to nuclear blackmail. Although a senior official has declared that the administration does not have a cookie-cutter policy toward rogue states, some question whether the White House has a cookie-cutter mind-set that would effectively preclude security assurances to an axis of evil regime.[15] Such an offer could be seen as sacrificing the moral standards of U.S. society and politically bolstering Iran's unelected leaders at the expense of the reformists.

On the Iranian side, former president Ali Akbar Hashemi Rafsanjani has hinted at receptivity to an agreement that would ensure the survival of Iran's regime, while the head of the IAEA, Muhammad ElBaradei, has suggested that Iranian hard-liners and reformists are now waging a power struggle over the issue of the IAEA's access to Iran's nuclear facilities.[16] Whether the regime would believe U.S. assurances of Iran's security is, of course, open to question. By waging war against Saddam's

Iraq, the United States dealt with Iran's proximate security threat and created a possible opportunity to open a strategic dialogue between the United States and Iran. Still, the combination of axis of evil rhetoric, the new preemption doctrine, and the administration's assertion that the war in Iraq demonstrates the U.S. ability take out a regime without inflicting unacceptable collateral damage to the civilian population may have priced U.S. security assurances to Iran out of the market.

For the time being, despite discussions of a grand bargain outside government, diplomacy is confined to the more limited focus on the IAEA's effort to bring Iran into compliance with its nuclear safeguards obligations. Such external pressure, which may include the imposition of penalties if Tehran does not come around, is necessary but not sufficient. An internal process, in which the Iranians themselves debate and scrutinize the nuclear program in all its dimensions, is the essential complement to any outside effort.

The United States should lead the attempt to energize such a debate in Iran by providing the data and encouraging forums required for such discussions, which, after all, are largely technical and specialized. The better informed the debate, the greater the chances of a healthy skepticism about the panacea promised by those pushing the nuclear program. U.S. policy choices are delicate, as Washington cannot appear to dictate terms or to bully, nor should it interfere in an internal debate. Rather, it needs to help foster that debate. To this end, the United States must first make clear why there are concerns about Iran's program, noting the precise components that are unarguably weapons related. Second, the United States should consider the alternatives to nuclear energy for Iran given the energy rationale for the program. Third, the United States should consider what technologies it would be prepared to provide, sell, or finance as substitutes. Finally, the United States should encourage nongovernmental organization (NGO) experts to discuss and analyze the economics of Iran's energy programs to improve the debate within Iran. This could include track II meetings of experts and contacts among specialized NGOs. At the very least, the debate in Iran would expose those in the regime who are reluctant to allow tighter inspections or more transparency in the program.

In addition to taking pride in their independence, most Iranians value their engagement with the world and their country's reputation; even the regime's domestic critics rankled at the Bush administration's inclusion of Iran in the axis of evil along with Saddam's Iraq and Kim Jong Il's North Korea. Iranians on the whole do not see any inherent contradiction between fulfilling their international responsibilities and assuring their national independence. They do not seek to threaten their neighbors or alienate the wider world. That the Group of Seven, the EU, the IAEA, and possibly Russia are lining up behind the current pressure on Tehran makes the question of the opportunity costs of the nuclear program even more salient.

By working to encourage public debate on the logic underlying Iran's pursuit of nuclear energy, the United States would in effect be helping Iranians to wrench the issue out of the grasp of the hard-liners, who have shielded the program from public scrutiny and shrouded it in secrecy. This effort would thus help to demythologize the benefits of nuclear technology, making it more difficult for elements of the regime to use the program as a cover for acquiring nuclear weapons. In addition, such a debate would create the basis for a sensible agreement that could meet both Iran's reasonable domestic energy needs and the international community's concerns.

An informed and democratized debate within Iran about the pros and cons of a nuclear weapons program would expose its major costs, including the strong negative reaction of neighboring states and the international community, as well as the weakening of Iran's conventional forces through the diversion of the country's financial resources. An open internal debate would also publicly demonstrate the significant toll of the regime's policies, and subsequent international sanctions, on ordinary Iranians' living standards and expectations.

Debate would allow for similar distinctions between Iran's legitimate security needs and nuclear weapons that are illegitimate, as well as between the regime's responsibilities to uphold its treaty obligations and

Iran's sovereign right as an independent state to determine ways to assure its own security. A changed security environment—where a dangerous Iraq has been neutralized and anarchy there and in Afghanistan has abated—gives rise to a renewed possibility of a dialogue on arms control in the region. Such a dialogue would involve both Israel and the Persian Gulf states and would be based on the 1991 Arms Control and Regional Security model, which was the first effort to bring key states together for multilateral talks.

For an internal Iranian debate to bear fruit, however, the United States will need to give the impression that it will accept Iranian compliance and not pocket concessions from Tehran as a prelude to making further demands. Some Iranians currently believe that, even if they accept the Additional Protocol, more demands will be forthcoming and that such concessions will open the door for the United States to seek regime change. Whatever the desirability of such a change, hard-nosed U.S. attitudes will not bring it to fruition. It is more realistic to pressure for legitimate ends, combined with the prospect of much better relations if and when the regime does change its policies as well as its politics. Washington will be challenged to pursue a subtle approach that supports democratic movements in Iran and feeds their impulse to install an accountable government that is under the scrutiny of the public and represented by elected officials.

What if such debate ensues, Iran's nuclear program continues, and suspicions of the weapons program are not allayed? Is it possible that a democratic debate could not lead to a less pliable Iran bent on nuclear weapons? How then does the international community sanction and target a more visibly democratic regime? This consideration is important because it reflects an awareness that there are no guarantees. At worst, however, a more democratic and accountable Iranian government would be a more desirable interlocutor than the current regime is; at best, a debate would put the nuclear weapons issue in perspective, exposing the hollowness of the argument that nuclear weapons bring its owners international prestige or status (as if the example of North Korea were not enough) and advertising the degree to which nuclear weapons would complicate Iran's security without meeting any of its reasonable security needs.

After all, the only conceivable justification for Iran's acquisition of nuclear weapons might be that they are needed as a deterrent against the United States. Yet, it is in fact only Iran's quest for nuclear weapons that makes a U.S. attack on Iran at all likely. A responsible Iran that abided by its NPT commitment to forgo nuclear weapons would be an internationally engaged Iran with better developmental prospects and that is more militarily secure and more secure in its status and role.

Iranians can come to the right conclusion about the country's nuclear program for themselves if the issues are framed in terms of realistic advantages and disadvantages for their country and their individual livelihoods rather than wrapped up in the myth that a nuclearized Iran is tantamount to an independent, secure, and progressing Iran. Impartial and sustained encouragement from nations that assert themselves as friends of Iran rather than define it as their foe can help bring this needed debate to the surface as there exists no necessary or inevitable contradiction between Iran's security needs and nuclear nonproliferation.

Ultimately, the best nonproliferation decision is one that is made indigenously; based on Iranians' own assessment of their country's national interests, such a decision would prove durable and legitimate. Such a decision can be encouraged by the international community, and perhaps especially the EU, which is less shy about offering inducements for good behavior. Iran should be able to see the benefits and rights accorded to states that act responsibly as international good citizens. The United States and its allies should thus encourage this wide-ranging internal debate in tandem with external efforts to induce or compel Iran to comply with nonproliferation norms.

## Notes

1. Michael Dobbs, "U.S. Using U.N. to Thwart Iran's Nuclear Program," *Washington Post*, June 23, 2003, p. A12.

2. An Ayandeh Research Institute poll taken September 2002 reported 75 percent of Tehran residents favored negotiations. The pollsters were subsequently jailed. See *RFE/RL Iran Report* 5, no. 36, October 7, 2002, www.rferl.org/iran-report/2002/10/36-071002.html (accessed July 24, 2003).

3. See Shahram Chubin, "Whither Iran? Reform, Domestic Politics and National Security," *Adelphi Paper* no. 342 (London: Oxford University Press, 2002); Shahram Chubin, "Iran's Strategic Environment and Nuclear Weapons," in *Iran's Nuclear Weapons Options: Issues and Analysis*, ed. Geoffrey Kemp (Washington, D.C.: Nixon Center, 2001), chap. 2.

4. For background on how the issue of policy on Palestine became subject to debate, see Chubin, "Whither Iran?" For examples of the debate and reformists' view, see the comments of Mohsen Mirdamadi (head of the National Security and Foreign Policy Committee of the Majlis) on the *Aftab-e Yazd* website, May 9, 2002, in *BBC Summary of World Broadcasts*, online edition (BBC online), May 13, 2002; *Nowrooz*, April 10, 2002, in BBC online, April 12, 2002 (editorial); *Bonyan*, April 4, 2002, in BBC online, April 7, 2002 (editorial).

5. See Farideh Fahri, "To Have or Not to Have" in *Iran's Nuclear Weapons Options: Issues and Analysis*, ed. Geoffrey Kemp (Washington, D.C.: Nixon Center, 2001), chap. 3, www.ceip.org/files/projects/npp/pdf/nixoniranwmd.pdf (accessed July 24, 2003).

6. BBC online, July 10, 2003.

7. BBC online, July 13, 2003.

8. Both references can be found in BBC online, June 30, 2003.

9. David E. Sanger, "Bush Warns Iran on Building Nuclear Arms," *New York Times*, June 19, 2003, p. A1.

10. David E. Sanger, "Viewing the War as a Lesson to the World," *New York Times*, April 6, 2003.

11. *National Security Strategy of the United States of America*, September 2002, www.whitehouse.gov/nsc/nss.html (accessed July 24, 2003).

12. Robert S. Litwak, "The New Calculus of Pre-emption," *Survival* 44, no. 4 (winter 2002–2003): 53–80.

13. Michael Eisenstadt, "Iranian Nuclear Weapons, Part I: The Challenges of U.S. Preventive Action," *Policywatch*, no. 760 (Washington, D.C.: Washington Institute for Near East Policy, May 27, 2003).

14. See Geoffrey Kemp, "How to Stop the Iranian Bomb," *National Interest*, no. 72 (spring 2003), pp. 48–58. Kemp characterizes this approach as "constructive containment."

15. For background on the "rogue state" concept and policy, see Robert S. Litwak, *Rogue States and U.S. Foreign Policy: Containment after the Cold War* (Washington, D.C.: Johns Hopkins University Press/Woodrow Wilson Center Press, 2000).

16. Najmeh Bozorgmehr and Guy Dinmore, "Anti-Government Demonstrations: Gunfire Heard During Clashes on Streets of Tehran," *Financial Times*, June 14, 2003, p. 13; Roula Khalaf, "IAEA Chief: Insecurity Drives WMD Proliferation," *Financial Times*, June 23, 2003, p. 8. See "Iran sous pression," *Le Monde* (Paris), June 19, 2003, p. 18 (editorial).

## Ali M. Ansari

# Continuous Regime Change from Within

Iran has been and remains the benefactor of a systematic failure of key Western policymakers to understand it. Determined to get to the root of the problem, these policymakers have tended to simplify an otherwise complex polity and reduced irritating intricacies to apparent irrelevancy. One example is the conclusion drawn by many U.S. policymakers following the debacle of the Iran-contra affair that moderate Iranian politicians simply did not exist. Far from the monolithic, totalitarian police state described by some commentators, Iran's politics reflect an intensely complex, highly plural, dynamic characteristic of a state in transition that incorporates the contradictions and instabilities inherent in such a process. Democratizing moderates confront authoritarian conservatives; a secularizing, intensely nationalistic society sits uneasily next to the sanctimonious piety of the hard-line establishment. To the casual observer, contemporary Iran often seems, and may best be described as, curiously surreal.

Far from an oriental stasis, the political upheaval of 1979 in Iran was a thoroughly modern revolution that unleashed social forces whose potential for change is now driving a process of organic democratization. This

Ali M. Ansari is a lecturer on the political history of the Middle East at the Institute of Middle Eastern and Islamic Studies at the University of Durham. He is the author of *Iran, Islam, and Democracy: The Politics of Managing Change* (Royal Institute of International Affairs, 2000).

*The Washington Quarterly* • 26:4 pp. 53–67.

process enjoys a profound historical pedigree, ably sustained by an intellectual renaissance and driven in part by economic necessity. It is a gradual, long-term, dialectical process punctuated and defined by periods of heightened activity that is laying the foundation for a fundamental shift in Iranian political culture through a synthesis of Western and Iranian/Islamic ideas. This marriage, by which Western ideas are authenticated and legitimized for an Iranian constituency, ensures both the complexity and the dynamism of the process. Only if the United States understands the structure of politics in the Islamic Republic and grapples with the complexity of this continuing historical process will it be able to respond constructively to the perennial challenge that is modern Iran.

## The Roots of Iranian Democratization

Iran's contemporary democrats trace their intellectual and spiritual roots to the Constitutional Revolution in 1906 when a coalition of merchants, intellectuals, and clerics, driven by the failures of the Iranian state in the face of European encroachment and influenced by Western ideas, forced the shah at that time to concede to constitutional limitations on his powers and to the establishment of a parliament (Majlis). Although this dramatic achievement established the blueprint for subsequent movements, its narrow social base and irrelevancy to the majority of ordinary Iranians, for whom ideas of constitutional democracy were as yet alien, along with its lack of a cohesive plan for reform ensured that in practical terms the movement steadily collapsed, inaugurating a period of political stagnancy and ultimately autocracy that would last until 1941.

Although this specific political effort failed, the Constitutional Movement's effect on Iran's political culture has been profound; it has proved an enduring point of reference, largely because the participants published copious literary memoirs and musings to keep the movement alive. That the successes and failures of this early-twentieth-century movement are referenced and debated to this day reminds us that history is very much alive in contemporary Iran and still weighs heavily on the actions of contemporary politicians. Contemporary reformers trace their spiritual and intellectual lineage to this event, identifying themselves with a movement that extends beyond the chronological confines of the 1979 Islamic Revolution and contributing to the current political tensions.[1]

This sense of intellectual inheritance is more pronounced when one reviews the next great leap forward in popular political consciousness in Iran—the Oil Nationalization Movement (1951–1953). The growth of education, technology, and the liberalization of political activity following the Allied occupation of Iran (1941–1946) helped develop a new level of political awareness. Industry encouraged the emergence of an urban proletariat whose ideological convictions were buttressed by Soviet propaganda, forcing traditional politicians to turn to the street for support. Popular nationalism would not only deflect the threat of communism but also would facilitate authentic modernization through the nationalization of Iranian assets and the expulsion of foreign interests, most obviously the vast Anglo-Iranian Oil Company. This need to make nationalism truly popular ensured that politics adopted a new vocabulary rich with religious overtones familiar to the masses, whose medium of popular communication remained rich in religious metaphor.

Not surprisingly, the key to this mobilization lay with the masters of religious rhetoric, the clerical classes, or *ulema*, who understood how to communicate with the people. Secular nationalism thus appropriated an Islamic hue in an effort to self-promote. When the nationalist prime minister, Dr. Muhammad Mossadegh, challenged British control over Iranian oil assets, he not only drew on left-wing support, but also depended crucially on the continuing support of Ayatollah Abul Qassem Kashani, the epitome of the religious nationalist. Only when Kashani, along with some other important nationalists, withdrew that support did Mossadegh's government become vulnerable and ultimately succumb to a coup in 1953 that restored royal autocracy to Iran, this time with U.S. tutelage and support.

Central as the 1953 coup was to the demise of the Mossadegh government and the National Front, the real internal political problems that plagued that government have been conveniently disguised by the historically revisionist elevation of the Mossadegh government to mythic status in Iranian political folklore. Indeed, the specter of Mossadegh and a reactionary coup continue to loom large in the Iranian political consciousness today, with the picture of this tragic nationalist politician (arguably the author of his own misfortune) and the symbolism he conveys adorning many a student rally. Emotional content aside, the fact that yet another "democratic" experiment in Iran resulted in dictatorship is not lost on contemporary Iranian politicians, including and perhaps most importantly President Muhammad Khatami himself.

These democratic failures are ascribed to a lack of popular cohesion or unity of purpose and, as far as Khatami is concerned, the problems inherent in seeking extraconstitutional methods to achieve constitutional goals, as well as the difficulties of leading the public once mobilized. At the same time, valuable lessons can be learned from the Mossadegh experience. Properly utilized, mass mobilization is possible and was an effective political tool, and although essentially urban based in a majority rural country and elite driven, the National Front coalition did succeed in evicting the Anglo-Iranian Oil Company and, by extension, the British from Iranian politics. Because the 1953 coup soon returned official power to the shah, the National Front's victory proved incomplete but not insubstantial, especially since their efforts signaled the end of British dominance in the Middle East. Another important lesson for aspiring revolutionaries today was that religion—in this case communicated through Shi'a myths—needed to sanctify Iranian nationalism for it to become a truly political force.

The significant role of religion in Iranian nationalism and political mobilization more generally became even more evident in the aftermath of the shah's return and the repression of the secular National Front and left-wing groups. A renewed and vigorous identification of Shi'ism with Iranian nationalism was defined in opposition to a growing antagonism with the United States that emerged following the 1953 coup, allegedly organized by the CIA, and was then entrenched by widespread revulsion at the apparent reintroduction of the despised "capitulations" by Muhammad Reza Shah Pahlavi in 1964. In exchange for a $200 million loan, the shah granted a U.S. request for extraterritorial rights for all U.S. government personnel (broadly defined) working in Iran. By appearing to have sold his country to the United States, the shah provided the ideal opportunity for a hitherto middle-ranking cleric to establish himself as the leading credible opposition.

## The Battle for Khomeini's Legacy

Ruhollah Khomeini was an unorthodox ayatollah. Criticized by his fellow clerics for having the temerity to indulge in Sufi poetry and teach philosophy, even on occasion Western philosophy, Khomeini's broad appeal, especially among the young, was rooted in his stubborn determination to resist the system, be it clerical juridical dogma or the Pahlavi state. Believing that the *ulema* had every right to participate in politics in its broadest sense (and indeed he could point to the Constitutional Revolution as an example), Khomeini was one of the few mullahs to possess a progressive opinion on the issue of modernization, promoting science and philosophy and attacking those clerics he viewed as reactionary and backward, a reality apparently acknowledged by the U.S. Department of State at the time. Acutely aware of the growing critical literature on development by Iranian writers, Khomeini berated the shah for working with foreigners rather than his own people. Khomeini was therefore a far more complex and nuanced personality than the fundamentalist caricature his opponents later constructed.

When he rose to the podium to criticize the shah vigorously for selling out to the Americans, Khomeini touched a raw nerve among indignant Iranians of all political hues. He was essentially as much a national leader (with a keen understanding of left-wing thought) as he was a religious leader, and his ability to transcend and combine these major strands of Iranian political thought into a particularly potent form of religious nationalism allowed him to become the leader of the dramatic expression of collective will that overthrew the shah. Only by going beyond the popular image can one begin to understand the current bitter contest for Khomeini's intellectual and consequently political legacy.

In 1979, Khomeini found himself leading a revolution that was, and remains, plural in construction and united only in its enmity toward its common foe, the shah and his puppet master, the United States. The revolution was as much if not more defined against the U.S. government as it was against the shah. Nationalists, religious zealots, and the Left all had reason to distrust and in many cases dislike the United States, defined for them by Khomeini as the "Great Satan," or the "great tempter," in an allusion to the temptations offered by rampant materialism (as he understood the United States) and the ruin it could bring to societies.

Using a discourse familiar to most of his constituents, Khomeini had simply but highly effectively conveyed the standard liberal/Marxist critique of capitalism in religious terms. Khomeini proved a political master at synthesizing diverse ideas and authenticating them in religious language suitable for his audience. The most obvious expression of this was the constitution of the "Islamic Republic" (there is no concept of republicanism within the Islamic tradition), but it was also clear in popular slogans where, for example, Khomeini would call on the "oppressed of the world to unite."[2] Khomeini's refrain from expelling Americans from Iran on his triumphal return and his express orders to evict radical Iranian students when they first tried to seize the U.S. embassy in February 1979 demonstrate that "Great Satan" was a term of warning rather than an absolute condemnation.

The students' final seizure of the embassy on November 4, 1979—a definitive moment in the history of the Islamic Republic—had more to do with the growing anarchy within Iran and Khomeini's keen sense of opportunism than with any ingrained antipathy he might have had. Indeed, by November 1979, just ten months after coming to power, Khomeini, for all his vaunted charisma, was rapidly discovering the painful difficulties of governing a society so recently released from the grip of an autocrat. Religious and left-wing factions once united against the shah were vying for positions in the new government, and Khomeini found himself reacting to, as much as dictating, events.

Controversy began to brew over the structure of the new Islamic Republic—a term Khomeini had insisted on, even though his writings on Islamic government made no mention of republicanism.[3] Khomeini was nothing if not pragmatic, and he recognized the need to accommodate a wide range of views, although the constitution that was finally adopted arguably proved a compromise too far. Sitting atop what proved to be a relatively liberal republican constitution with a clear separation of powers and a national focus (Khomeini insisted that all candidates for state positions be born in Iran) was the supreme religious authority of the *velayat-e faqih*, the Guardianship of the Jurist.

The *velayat-e faqih* was a Khomeini innovation, though not without foundation in Shi'a political writings. Its precise remit remained conveniently vague, however, and thus institutionalized ambiguity within the Iranian political system—an ambiguity that Khomeini's actions would define and sustain. Khomeini had no intention of using his position as Guardianship of the Jurist to interfere in the day-to-day affairs of state or even, in spite of his extensive constitutional powers, to be designated "head of state," a position retained by the president. The Supreme Jurist, as has subsequently been confirmed by those who drafted this particular part of the constitution, was meant to guide, not dictate, on broad issues of ethics and Islamic law. Khomeini tended to adopt this style himself, guiding rather than dictating by often establishing committees whenever he faced a problem[4] and by adding yet another layer to government—the Expediency Council—to mediate disputes between the Majlis and the Guardian Council.

The ambiguity institutionalized in the *velayat-e faqih* and the flexibility it incorporated in many ways enabled the force of Khomeini's personality to salvage a constitutional system which was cumbersome and clumsy almost by design. Yet, even Khomeini needed assistance; his decision to back the students who had occupied the U.S. embassy, made after he was notified of what had happened, was a tactical decision intended to satiate the crowd and divert popular attention away from internal disputes. According to many Iranians, including some of the hostage-takers themselves, the seizure of the U.S. embassy was subsequently seen as worse than a crime; it was a mistake. As with the subsequent Iraqi invasion of Iran in 1980, however, it served a purpose: attention was redirected toward an external enemy, and internal disputes were expediently shelved, albeit temporarily. Thus, the Islamic Revolution in Iran headed into its first decade without a satisfactory domestic settlement, driven by a religious nationalism and increasingly defined by its antagonism toward the United States.

## Rafsanjani's Blend of Economics and Religion

With Khomeini's death in 1989, no other leader was able to sustain his ambiguous system. The new president, Ali Akbar Hashemi Rafsanjani, was a successful merchant and a cleric who sought to remold the Islamic Republic in his own image through an alliance with the new Supreme Jurist, the distinctly unqualified Ayatollah Ali Hoseini Khamenei. The new Rafsanjani settlement abolished the post of prime minister and arrogated its powers to the presidency. Yet at the same time, Khamenei's position was buttressed by inserting the much-contested term "absolute" into his constitutional title, controversially implying that he enjoyed absolute authority in scriptural interpretation, which some argued extended into the political sphere.

Structurally, the political system was an alliance between the capital-rich mercantile bourgeoisie and the conservative *ulema*, whose espousal of authoritarian, doctrinaire Islamism provided the ideal opium for the masses. The result was a religious veneer under which the new elite could accumulate capital rampantly through traditional, unaccountable, and opaque means without the fear of being criticized for religious and revolutionary hypocrisy. Rafsanjani sought to govern through a personalized and highly centralized bureaucracy, a process of political normalization which sought to present a maturing and more stable environment but which reminded many Iranians of political structures under the shah.

For all the palpable and likely strengths of a political structure founded largely on an expanding network of commercial vested interests, Rafsanjani's mercantile bourgeois republic was unsuccessful in securing firm and durable social foundations. Above all, this failure was based on a profound misreading by Rafsanjani and his allies of social developments since the 1979 revolution. Most obvious was their inability to recognize the changes wrought in Iranian society by the experience of the 1979 revolution and the war fought with Iraq from 1980 to 1988. Put simply, having successfully overthrown a monarchy just a decade earlier, Iranians were not about to bear witness to the establishment of another autocracy in the form of an imperious presidency with accumulated powers and an absolute Supreme Jurist who, his supporters argued, could overturn any legal ruling. Furthermore, the experience of war had made Iranians more cynical of government. In short, in the 10 years after the shah's demise, Iranians were making the transition from subjects to citizens.

In addition, the environment had changed economically. Having encouraged a high birth rate, the government of the Islamic Republic now found itself with a young and ambitious population open to new ideas and eager for jobs. The new mercantile bourgeoisie found it difficult to provide either, largely because their economic *mentalite* worked against long-term investment. Indeed, when Europe's industrial capitalists met their mercantile counterparts in Iran, they rapidly discovered that they spoke a different language, with the former seeking a transparent environment suitable for long-term investment and the latter talking the language of trade. Moreover, the scourge of wealth disparity, which had significantly helped to bring down the shah, now returned with a vengeance. As the promised economic miracle of the era of reconstruction, as Rafsanjani liked to characterize his administration, failed to materialize, the state increasingly turned to repression administered and justified through a particularly rigorous interpretation of Islamic dogma.

Anxious to deliver on the economic front, Rafsanjani increasingly conceded political ground to his conservative allies at home while reaching out to Western businesses (and by extension their governments) in a bid to secure some form of investment. This strategy failed on both counts, and Rafsanjani the populist discovered that by the mid-1990s his erstwhile allies were promoting an increasingly authoritarian version of Islam, going so far as to debunk the notion of a republic, calling for an Islamic state instead. This increasingly authoritarian trend soon provoked a vigorous intellectual response, which ultimately manifested itself as the Second Khordad Movement, or the Reform Movement.

## Khatami and the Second Khordad Movement

The Reform Movement is the ideological successor to the 1906 Constitutional Movement and the National Front of the early 1950s. Growing in strength during the Rafsanjani administration, it came of age with Khatami's election in 1997. Members include students; journalists; lay and religious intellectuals; and, crucially, members of the government. The movement's chief strategist until he was critically injured in an assassination attempt in 2000, Saeed Hajarian was even a former senior official in the Intelligence Ministry, ostensibly an institutional pillar of the revolutionary establishment.

Its avowed remit is to fulfill the political promise of the Islamic Revolution, the product of more than a century of Iranian political agitation. Originating in the Islamic Left, which had been marginalized during Rafsanjani's presidency, the movement sought "Iran for the Iranians" complete with civil rights, the rule of law, and the establishment of an Islamic democracy. The concept of Islamic democracy was an intellectual synthesis between Western democratic norms and a revitalized, redefined (Iranian) Islam drawing on Islam's philosophical rather than juridical roots. Its model for change derived from the reform process that characterized nineteenth-century Britain, while its model for religious democracy came from the United States as defined by Alexis de Tocqueville, who argued that the secular condition of the American democratic state was held together by the reality of a religious society. "Religious peoples are therefore naturally strong in precisely the spot where democratic peoples are weak: this makes very visible how important it is that men keep their religion when becoming equal."[5]

The intellectual justification for this debt to Western civilization was argued with some success by the lay religious philosopher Abdol Karim Soroush, who argued that Iran was the heir of three cultures: Iranian, Islamic, and Western. This legitimized the appropriation of Western ideas and prepared them for authentification through traditional Iranian/Islamic discourse.

Herein lies the central paradox of the Islamic Republic of Iran: it is both antagonistic toward the West and philosophically intimate with it. Khatami said as much when, following a digression on the Puritans in the United States, he quoted de Tocqueville in his CNN interview:

> In his [de Tocqueville's] view, the significance of this [American] civilization is in the fact that liberty found religion as a cradle for its growth and religion found the protection of liberty as its divine calling. Therefore in America, liberty and faith never clashed, and as we see, even today most Americans are religious people. Therefore the approach to religion, which is the foundation of Anglo-American civilization, relies on the principle that religion and liberty are consistent and compatible.[6]

Even more intriguing was his decision to pay his respects at the tomb of Rousseau. Two other points emerge from these developments: the reformist affinity for the notion of the Protestant ethic[7] and their ease with the concept of secularism. Having been a taboo subject for the first decade of the Islamic Republic under Khomeini, the idea of secularism—distinct from laicism, which was taken to mean irreligiousity—began to take hold among the politically aware public. Invoking the logic of the American Founding Fathers, reformist intellectuals argued that the state could not impose religion but rather that belief is a matter for the individual. Indeed, reformists argued that secularism would enhance religion through the liberation of criticism because "a single examined faith is nobler than a thousand imitated, shaky, and weak beliefs."[8] A society revitalized by such a reinvigorated faith would inevitably produce a religious government. This in essence is the meaning of Islamic democracy in Iran.

Khatami was a product of the Reform Movement and its chosen leader following his nomination by a number of reformist factions, but he did not define it. Acutely aware of the fate of previous democratic experiments, the new reformist administration moved with caution in all areas but one: institutionalizing political consciousness. The reformists recognized that it was the failure to properly connect with the people that led to the collapse of the Constitutional Movement and the fall of Mossadegh, and thus they were determined to develop Iranian political consciousness and socialize the idea of democracy.

Reformists believed that they could hasten the transformation of Iranian social and political culture through an intensive diet of political education, which would in turn change political institutions. They anticipated, somewhat naively, that reluctant conservatives would then bow to the inevitable and compromise by relinquishing some of their power to secure their commercial interests, which could only be enhanced by the existence of a more stable, socially founded, and secure republic operating within a legal framework that protected investment benefiting all. It was a powerful argument, and even the authoritarian Khamenei declared that the era of Islamic Democracy had begun. Significant gains were also made in accountability and transparency, most dramatically in the autumn of 1998 when revelations emerged that rogue elements in the Ministry of Intelligence had conducted a private, lethal vendetta against intellectuals over the past decade. As the government conducted a root-and-branch purge of the Intelligence Ministry, preparations were in hand for the most dramatic electoral triumph—that of the Majlis in 2000.

## The New Reformers after Khatami

Ironically, at the moment of its greatest triumph, the Reform Movement revealed its fundamental weakness: no detailed ideological blueprint for productive action existed, an ailment that had afflicted its predecessors. In short, the movement seemed to have little idea how to proceed, and no concrete plans to realize the attractive slogans that had mobilized the Iranian public in unprecedented numbers. In control of both the executive and the legislature, the reformists were in a position of remarkable strength, and popular expectation was high. Yet at this crucial point, they proved singularly unable to convert their electoral victory. That the conservative establishment would resist was to be expected, yet leading reformist politicians evidently miscalculated the ferocity of the response, especially when conservative economic vested interests came under threat

Arguably, the reformers needlessly provoked a harsher than necessary response when, in the euphoria of the 2000 electoral victory, they decided to target Rafsanjani as the linchpin of the mercantile bourgeois state, with the consequence that obstruction to reform was unusually severe. There were other weaknesses too: an overcautious approach to structural reform; inexperience in the drafting of legislation, causing technical delays; and the depressing reality that some reform politicians were just as seduced by the spoils of power as their conservative opponents.

Khatami's main flaw in approach, aside from his unwillingness to plunge the Islamic Republic into crisis, is his legalism. It is difficult to be legalistic against opponents who have contempt for any practical notion of law, and it is supremely ironic that the citadel of conservative resistance is currently the Judiciary, headed by Ayatollah Mahmoud Hashemi Shahrudi, whose draconian judgments and Iraqi origins have combined to make him the most detested man in Iran today.

Shahrudi has systematically abused the powers of the Judiciary to serve his own interests along with conservative interests in general, amassing his own secret police and a budget larger than that of the presidency. Supporting extremist judges who recklessly dispensed disproportionate judgments on reformist politicians and activists, the Judiciary rapidly has become an embarrassment to Iranians of all hues. On one occasion, the head of the Tehran district announced that all discussion about negotiations with the United States would henceforth be treated as a criminal offense. This proclamation was received with such derision among the Iranian public at large that it was soon rescinded. Indeed, while a succession of long prison sentences combined with political obstructionism succeeded in weakening the credibility of the Reform Movement and its hapless politicians, the continuing judicial repression was judged by some, including some conservatives, to be counterproductive.

As reformists regrouped and reflected on their failures following the harsh repression which succeeded their Majlis victory, clear signs emerged of renewed agitation among key social groups, including the press and crucially the students, with the primary catalyst being the Judiciary's conviction for blasphemy and quick condemnation to death of the war hero and former history professor Hashem Aghajari, following his reported assertion that Muslims did not need to follow their clerics like "monkeys." This single act of grotesque stupidity and injustice succeeded in catalyzing a new, more radicalized Reform Movement among the young, occasionally labeled the "Third Force," with an agenda for political change far in excess of the traditional reformists, who were regarded by the new reformists with hardly disguised disdain. Driven by an intensely nationalist rage, now stripped of religious pretensions, these new reformists are in no mood for compromise.

## Regime Change from Within?

Donald Rumsfeld is a popular man among ordinary people in contemporary Iran. He represents the sort of moral clarity and certainty of purpose that is missing from the seemingly ambiguous morass that is Iranian politics today. In a recent poll conducted in the summer of 2002 by Iranian government agencies, an overwhelming majority of Iranians (approximately 70 percent) were sympathetic to the United States and wanted their government to initiate dialogue with Washington. Moreover, according to the results of one poll reportedly conducted by the Ministry of Intelligence, general public dissatisfaction was so great that some members of the hard-line establishment concluded they could not depend on popular support if the United States attacked.

The Khatami-led Reform Movement seized on this shocking revelation as a warning that a failure to implement a democratic settlement was weakening Iran against external enemies. Conservatives, outraged by these revelations, characteristically lambasted the results as forgeries designed to weaken national morale; the pollsters were accused of being fifth columnists who had sold the country to foreigners and whom, some zealots argued, should therefore be tried for treason.[9] Yet, all sides missed one aspect of the poll: although many Iranians wanted dialogue, a similar number continued to be suspicious of the United States. The results, as one pollster commented, should not be condemned as an act of treason but as a reflection of the real political sophistication of the Iranian public.

The Iranian public is acutely aware of the deficiencies of its political system, of its continuing failures to establish a comprehensive democratic settlement. As even moderate conservatives object to the blatant transgression of revolutionary principles by hard-line members of the elite, the Iranian public is increasingly antagonistic to the state apparatus. The public remains keenly politically aware and can no longer be taken for granted by the revolutionary establishment. Most importantly, it is an intensely nationalistic public with an acute interest in their specifically Iranian identity, which is increasingly defined against the Arabs and Islam.[10] It remains proud of the fundamental principles of freedom and independence that the revolution seemed to herald while condemning and lamenting its excesses and the corruption of those values by an increasingly isolated hard-line conservative elite. It looks forward to the fulfillment of its promise, begun in the Constitutional Movement, whose centenary will encourage reflection on how far the Iranians have come and how much still remains to be done, even if few reformists doubt the end result.

As the United States considers what to do next in Iran, it ought to weigh judiciously the merits and demerits of aggressive intervention in a revolution that has yet to run its course. It should make clear its purpose and communicate that purpose to the Iranian public, making a plain distinction between the Iranian nation and the unelected minority, avoiding any tendency to condescend, and making its criticism specific and its policies surgical. Above all, the United States should align itself with the aspirations of the Iranian people and recognize the reality of the revolution, which has yet to reach fruition and fulfill its promise. The Bush administration should continue with its measured response of support for the democratic aspirations of the Iranian people, coordinating as much as possible with its allies, especially the European Union, so as to internationalize its policy, using language calculated to convey the sincerity of the U.S. government in this respect. Most importantly, the United States should recognize that change will be indigenous and thus not align itself with overseas opposition groups whose understanding of politics on the ground in Iran is limited.

Nobody wants to turn back the clock, and although there is general sympathy for the United States (Iran is one of the few countries that did not have antiwar demonstrations prior to the invasion of Iraq), there remains widespread suspicion of U.S. motives, the U.S. tendency toward short-term–ism, the alleged support for separatist movements, and the belief that the United States will compromise with the conservative authoritarians if U.S. security concerns (and those of her regional allies) are met. The United States must tackle this suspicion head on by developing a coherent and consistent policy which reiterates moral support for human rights and democratization in Iran and by assuring the Iranian people that the United States does not want to see a perpetually weakened and territorially threatened Iran.

Most fundamentally and crucially, the United States must recognize and publicly state that Iran should continue to change from within as it has in the past. At the same time, Washington should resist the temptation to indulge in direct intervention—military, economic, or political—which will only encourage doubt and prevarication by a nationalistic society acutely aware of its historical relationship with the United States and unwilling to be characterized as foreign stooges. In August 1953, the CIA and Great Britain's MI6, driven by Cold War imperatives and encouraged by favorable poll ratings in Iran, orchestrated a coup that overthrew the elected Mossadegh government, restored royal autocracy, and effectively suffocated the fledgling Iranian democratic experiment at birth. Few could have anticipated the enormity of the long-term cost to U.S.-Iranian relations. Upon the coup's fiftieth anniversary this summer, U.S. policymakers need to reflect carefully on the consequences of their actions.

Understanding the consequence of external interference is even more pertinent now, as recent agitation on student campuses and in cities around the country reveals that, far from having been systematically crushed, the reform movement has discovered new vigor. Driven by young, uncompromising idealists and supported by an overwhelmingly young population frustrated by the religious dogma which constrains them daily, there is little indication that the democratic tendency introduced during the Constitutional Revolution in 1906 and methodically nurtured over a century has lost its way. If anything, it is more determined and, unlike its predecessor movements, is sustained and supported by a broad swathe of a politically aware public. For Iran's hard-line establishment, it may be time to consider "[t]hat an army may be resisted, but not an idea whose time has come."[11]

## Notes

1. See Masoud Behnood, "Etemad," 17 Shahrivar 1381, September 8, 2002, p. 5. In this editorial, the author goes even further back to the period of Amir Kabir, who was prime minister from 1848 to 1851.

2. For further details, see Ervand Abrahamian, *Khomeinism* (London: I. B. Tauris, 1993).

3. "Developments in Iran," Tehran Home Service, BBC SWB ME/6043/A/14, February 14, 1979; "Developments in Iran," Tehran Home Service, BBC SWB ME/6044/A/4, February 14, 1979.

4. See Hasan Yusefi Eshkevari, "Law & the Women's Movement" (speech delivered at the Berlin Conference, April 2000), reprinted in *Conference-e Berlin: Khedmat ya Khiyanat?* (The Berlin conference: Service or treason?), ed. M. A. Zakrayi, Tar-e no. 1379, 2000, p. 229.

5. Alexis de Tocqueville, *Democracy in America* (Chicago: University of Chicago Press, 2000), p. 419.

6. BBC SWB ME/3210 MED/2, January 9, 1998.

7. See "John Locke and the Idea of Tolerance," *Tous*, 21 Shahrivar 1377, September 12, 1998, p. 6. This reflected a growing trend among reformist commentators to identify themselves with Protestants (and as pluralist) while the conservatives were characterized as Catholic (and absolute). See *Jame'eh*, 27

Tir 1377, July 18, 1998, p. 6; *Jame'eh*, 29 Tir 1377, July 20, 1998, p. 6 (discussions of the life of Martin Luther).

8. Abdolkarim Soroush, "Tolerance & Governance," in *Reason, Freedom, and Democracy in Islam: Essential Writings of Abdolkarim Soroush*, trans. and eds. Mahmoud Sadri and Ahmad Sadri (Oxford: Oxford University Press, 2000), p. 155.

9. See Ayatollah Jannati, "Voice and Vision of the Islamic Republic of Iran," BBC Mon ME1 MEPol, December 20, 2002 (speech).

10. See Tale H, *Tarikhche-ye maktab-e pan-Iranism* (The history of the ideology of Pan-Iranism), Sarmarqand, 1381, 2002.

11. Victor Hugo, *Histoire d'un crime* (1852).

Mahmood Sariolghalam

# Understanding Iran: Getting Past Stereotypes and Mythology

The deterioration of mutual understanding in U.S.-Iranian relations since the September 11 attacks reflects the disparity between what Iran's current leadership can deliver and the expectations of any U.S. administration. Iran's current leadership makes foreign policy decisions fundamentally on revolutionary idealism, especially on the Palestinian issue, rejecting the two-state solution; pursues a security doctrine based on ambiguity; assists military groups, characterizing them as freedom fighters; and confronts U.S. dominance in the Middle East. In contrast, the United States is determined to institutionalize the two-state solution, regards an unfriendly Iran's security doctrine as opposed to its interests and those of Israel, views Hamas and Islamic Jihad as terrorist groups, and aims to contain Iran's Middle East activities and projection of power.

Since September 11, 2001, the Islamic Republic of Iran has practiced greater caution, toned down its rhetoric, and even been willing to engage in issue-area negotiations with the United States in Geneva. Such stylistic alterations do not reflect shifts in Iran's threat perceptions or in U.S. objectives but do signal calculated adjustments to a new regional

Mahmood Sariolghalam is an associate professor at the School of Economics and Political Science of the Shahid Beheshti (National) University of Iran in Tehran and editor of the English-language journal *Discourse: An Iranian Quarterly*.

Copyright © 2003 by The Center for Strategic and International Studies and the Massachusetts Institute of Technology
*The Washington Quarterly* • 26:4 pp. 69–82.

and international environment. Although Iran and Iranians played no role in the September 11 terrorist attacks, Washington grouped Iran in the "axis of evil." Although Iran played a constructive role in helping the United States bring down the Taliban, many individuals in the Bush administration continued Iran bashing. Furthermore, Tehran was overjoyed to witness Saddam Hussein's fall and stayed out of the way of U.S. operations, only to learn that Washington would speed up efforts for regime change in, and spend more money on, covert operations against Iran. The underlying reality is that no matter what Iran does, unless it alters its attitude toward Israel and the Israeli-Palestinian peace negotiations, no fundamental policy change in Washington will occur.

Objective scrutiny of the contemporary Iranian political system, on the one hand, and its policies, on the other, reveals a relatively stable polity but policies that are subject to change, perhaps in fundamental ways, as a result of the pressures building up inside the country. If Washington were objectively to assess the current Iranian political situation and correctly conclude that the Islamic Republic is here to stay but will steadily evolve, then the United States may not only pursue but also achieve desired policy concessions. If it believes the Islamic Republic is here to stay, then Washington will focus on trying to persuade its leaders to change policies rather than attempt to alter its structure, just as President Richard Nixon accomplished with the Soviet Union and the People's Republic of China during the Cold War.

Moreover, constructive U.S. efforts to develop better relations with this Muslim nation could help Iran's progress as a model of rational, political change in the Middle East as well as improve U.S. relations with the Muslim world at large. To improve bilateral relations, Washington should recognize these realities in Iranian politics and policies as well as the particular roles and value of national sovereignty and Islam in Iran.

## Bilateral Misperceptions

The ongoing bellicose climate of U.S.-Iranian relations dates back to at least the Iranian revolution of 1979 and demonstrates vividly that the fundamental area of contention and tension between the two countries remains: Iran's clerics believe that the United States seeks to remove them from power or at least to isolate Iran globally. Comparatively, U.S. officials believe that Iran is constantly undermining U.S. efforts in the Middle East. Symptoms of this fundamental problem abound. Tehran and Washington continue to define terrorism in drastically different ways. Iran views Hamas and Islamic Jihad as groups attempting to free their land from Israeli occupation. Furthermore, Iran believes that Israelis are not interested in a Palestinian state, that Tel Aviv ultimately seeks a humiliated Palestinian enclave within Israel proper. Conversely, Washington has officially announced U.S. support for a Palestinian independent state and is implementing a road map toward peace with Israeli and Palestinian representatives. In this context, groups that pursue a military solution to the problem, killing innocent people, should be outlawed and characterized as terrorist groups. Perhaps from a neutral stance, one can point out that Iran and the United States have varying perceptions of Israeli intentions in the peace process.

The Iranian government senses that the United States has singled out Iran for its human rights record and system of governance, even though dictatorial regimes run many of Washington's allies in the Middle East, allowing almost no voice for the citizenry in those nations. All recent U.S. administrations have engaged in active diplomacy to deny nuclear technology, allegedly to be used to build nuclear arms, to an unfriendly Iran. Moreover, the United States continues to raise alarms about Iran's defense programs.

With anti-U.S. sentiments so prevalent among Iran's top cleric elites, Washington believes it cannot trust Tehran's nuclear intentions and defense policies. Iran believes that it has natural influence throughout the region, while Washington refers to Iranian influence and actions as "meddling." From the U.S. perspective, Iran's policies and efforts run counter to U.S. interests in the Middle East. Both Iranian nationalism and religious orthodoxy opposes U.S. unilateral policies in the Middle East. That Iran remains the only state in the world that does not recognize the two-state solution to the Israeli-Palestinian conflict leads the

United States to consider Iran's defense capabilities and its anti-Israeli policy as two sides of the same coin.

Iran fails to understand and refuses to accept the fundamental issue that a basic improvement in U.S.-Iranian relations cannot be achieved without Tehran's acknowledgment of the strategic alliance between the United States and Israel; since the 1991 Persian Gulf War, Iran's attempts to separate the issue of Israel from a potential improvement in U.S.-Iranian relations have consistently failed. The Israeli factor is the single most crucial ingredient that must be addressed before any fundamental or incremental resolution of the differences between Tehran and Washington. The unfortunate reality is that the Iranian clerics are not prepared to alter their view of the Palestinian conflict and Washington cannot forgo its strategic attachment to the Israeli component of U.S. interests in the Middle East. In the end, Washington and Tehran are incapable of considering each other's domestic structure and subsequent constraints.

The issue of Israel is part of the political psyche of the current Iranian elites, whose mind-set was shaped in the 1950s and 1960s when they were in their twenties and the developing world was in the midst of anticolonial and anti-imperialist struggles. During the same period, Iranian political activists—both Muslim and non-Muslim—developed a certain opposition to the United States as a consequence of Washington's direct involvement in the removal of Iran's elected prime minister, Dr. Muhammad Mossadegh, and the reinstitution of Muhammad Reza Shah Pahlavi. The Muslim faction of the antishah movement simultaneously became sensitive to, and suspicious of, U.S. support for the establishment of Israel, and Israel soon emerged as a significant supporter of the shah's regime. The roots of the Iranian leadership's current anti-U.S. and anti-Israeli attitudes are thus directly related.

From the perspective of Iran's national interests, however, current trends in Tehran's policy toward the Middle East peace process have an expiration date and may be constructive only for philosophical discourse. The pursuit of justice may be the most predominant feature of Islamic international relations, but even justice cannot be pursued without a powerful foundation in economic productivity and the projection of military capabilities. In Islamic-oriented foreign policy, power differences are not recognized. The Shi'a conception of justice rejects ordering human or national hierarchies based on economic and/or military structures and capabilities. There is certainly a hierarchy; but it is, or should be, an ethical one, according to which people and nations develop themselves spiritually. Furthermore, a nation-state is considered "just" when it does not distinguish itself from others according to its economic power, military and offensive capabilities, and racial distinctiveness.[1]

As the examples of the former Soviet Union and China demonstrate, pressure to put bread on the table and the economic necessities of rebuilding the country will coerce Iran to engage with the West rather than pursue futile confrontation. As leaders who have worked to improve Iran economically in the past, Muhammad Khatami and Akbar Hashemi Rafsanjani each have indicated, albeit ambiguously, that Iran will have to open up to the world and ultimately, as a non-Arab country with no common borders with Israel or direct association with Arab causes, accept the two-state solution to the Palestinian-Israeli conflict.

Because of their existing perspectives, Iranian clerics' anti-U.S. attitudes and Washington's anti-Iranian sentiments fundamentally compel each side to evaluate the other as existential security threats, leaving little room for compromise. Even U.S. offers of engagement and soft language during the Clinton era were viewed with uncertainty; that administration used more carrots but at the same time used larger sticks by enforcing more intensified sanctions. Historically, U.S. legislators' and foreign policy officials' endorsements of covert operations, regime change, and support of the opposition during the Clinton administration and the subsequent Bush administration have led to the Iranian government's paranoia about Iran's security and have delayed efforts to bring about change and develop consensus-building processes between the two countries. U.S. interests in removing the Taliban in Afghanistan and Saddam in Iraq converged with those of Iran, but the broader asymmetry of beliefs and lack of communication caused a steady drumbeat of accusations and impeded cooperation between the two governments. For the Iranian clerics, the underlying issue is the acceptance and recognition of Iran's sovereignty by the United States.

From its birth in 1979 until the present, security has remained an obsession for the Islamic Republic. U.S. threats, economic sanctions, and rhetoric have greatly contributed to Iran's security consciousness in the last two decades. Iran separates issues of disagreement, whereas the United States—with wider domestic, regional, and international power and interests—is driven by the concept of linkage. Tehran's desired relationship with Washington is one that allows economic relations to expand without limitations and simultaneously maintains a calculated political distance. This desire is a consequence of Iranians' fundamental distrust, rooted in the people's historical memory, of U.S. intentions, which Iran perceives as focused on complete subordination of Iran. A mixture of religious and nationalist orientation, based on maintaining sovereignty, continues to overshadow the attitudes of Iranians—both clerics and nonclerics—toward the United States; fear of U.S. domination has shaped much of contemporary Iranian political behavior and thus Iranian history.

Since the crisis in Afghanistan (and even during the Clinton administration), Iran has displayed increments of understanding and cooperation in an effort to encourage the United States to redefine the Islamic Republic, to accept its sovereignty, and to settle the U.S. government's differences with Iran's current structure. Recently, however, the level of confrontation has been elevated to core issues of security, sovereignty, and the structure of conflict between the two sides, demonstrating the lack of U.S. understanding of Iranian politics and resulting in an enduring stalemate.

## Understanding Political Iran

In defining and understanding Iranian politics, Washington tends to focus on the Iranian clerics as the key source of the problem, while it is the concept of sovereignty permeating among Iranians of all strata that is the powerful driving force not to be underestimated. Although recent U.S. policy changes, such as its preemption strategy, threaten the sanctity of sovereignty in international politics, Iran also contributes to the tensions over sovereignty. The fact that Iranians have failed thus far to create accountable institutions that can deliver stability, sovereignty, and growth while keeping potential, foreign hegemonic incursions at bay contributes to Iranian sensitivity on the subject. Regardless of who is to blame, failure to address the deep sensitivity all Iranians attach to their national sovereignty is ill advised.

For Washington to imagine that it can deconstruct and then reconstruct Iran's political system is a strategic miscalculation. Iran is not Iraq, and if the current disarray in post-Saddam Iraqi society is at all alarming, Iranians are far more prepared to defy foreign rule and are passionate about doing so. As Iranians reminded themselves on August 19, 2003, the fiftieth anniversary of the coup that removed the democratically elected Mossadegh from power, Iranian society has changed dramatically. Whereas in 1953 only a few hundred individuals were able to facilitate the process of removing the prime minister, today, with a literacy rate of more than 90 percent, Iranians are far more conscious of the political processes in their country. Even in defiance of the internal squabbles between the reformers and the conservatives and the widespread inefficiencies in the country, Iranians' dismissive reaction to the city council elections in February 2003 was telling: only 11 percent of the voting population turned out.

Moreover, although the regime in Iraq consisted of some 54 individuals at the top level, with no grassroots support and no political intermediaries between the leadership itself and the population at large, Iran is a much more complex and modern system of stratified layers between the top elites and the masses. In Iran, some two million administrators and managers run the machinery of the state. Thousands of individuals work hard to advance Iranian national interests irrespective of what the top elites may wish or direct. In other words, unlike monolithic North Korea or Libya, Iran is a far more differentiated society where the average person enjoys the right to defy the state in very sophisticated layouts. Iran has more than a million schoolteachers, who educate approximately 18 million students throughout the country. Viewed in this light, Iran is perhaps the most politically dynamic society in the developing world.

No consensus exists in Washington on what the problems with Iran are, much less on what approaches would ultimately resolve those problems. For whatever reason, Washington think tanks do not seem to conduct objective analyses of the situation in Iran but inject their wishes and desires. In this context, a number of axioms about Iran exist today that need to be clarified. To be precise, objective and informed analysis would reveal:

• Iran is not, by any measure, in a revolutionary mood.

• The Islamic Republic is conceptually challenged but politically stable.

• Iranians do not recognize any political leadership currently residing outside the country.

• A democratic movement does not exist in Iran.

• Iran has liberalized many of its policies in historic proportions but is far from a democracy.

• The overwhelming majority of the people from of all walks of life is interested in the state's efficiency, not in overthrowing it.

• Although Iranians regard the clerics' method of governance as inefficient and outdated, they view these leaders as part of the country's social and cultural fabric.

• Iran's economy suffers from deep structural problems, and there are no quick solutions that can be adopted by any government in Tehran.

One of the most common misconceptions about Iran is what meaning analysts extrapolate from dissent. Careful observation of Iranian politics shows that almost all Iranians agree that violence should not be used, that incremental change should guide all attempts at reform, and that foreign military intervention would be costly for Iran. Even Iranian-Americans overwhelmingly oppose foreign military intervention as a way to reform Iran's political system.[2] Many individuals and organizations in Washington understandably would like to see the political machinery in Iran collapse, but the realities project different conclusions. Iranian thinking and behavior are ambiguous, and Iranians seem to enjoy demonstrating their ambiguity, feeding this confusion about Iran's true political nature. Because there is a tendency in Iranian political culture to want everything simultaneously, ambiguity allows Iran to make progress incrementally.

Although Iran's polity is not about to change, its policies, particularly its foreign policies and foreign economic relations policies, may expire along with its current top elites. Some of the current ideas will surely continue, particularly Iran's devotion to protecting its national sovereignty, as they are part of the culture that shaped Iran's sociopolitical movements over the last 150 years when confronting foreign rule. The enduring legacy of the Iranian revolution is likely to be that it institutionalized this historical concern to protect Iran's national sovereignty.

Contemporary Iran has a highly stratified society, however, that will change the look of its elite leaders and its foreign policies in an evolutionary manner. Its young population will be the driving force that sets an agenda focused on economic development, cultural diversity, and political openness. The current political stage in Iran requires time to mature; it can be viewed as a transitional period in the country's long and linear historical struggle with despotism and monarchism, one that will peacefully lead to an institutionalized Iran. The Iranians are a dynamic people, who have been at the forefront of change in the Middle East since 1906 when the Constitutional Movement began in the country.

Almost a century ago, Ahmad Kasravi, an Iranian writer, suggested that the Iranian people owe a period of rule to the clerics, who over the last three centuries have been an essential part of Iran's politics, claiming that they could achieve sovereignty and prosperity if they reach power. Political Islam in Iran is a reaction to foreign rule in the country. Islam emphasizes Muslims' sovereignty from foreign rule, providing the Muslim clerics with a basis to confront monarchies with European or

U.S. backing. Any indication that foreigners may find an opportunity to influence the political process in Iran allows political Islam to remain a potent force, capable of social mobilization and political organization. Islam will indefinitely remain a part, but not necessarily the ruling part, of the Iranian culture no matter how the Iranian political system might evolve. Thus, the external promotion of a secular culture in Iran is not a realistic political pursuit at this time and is likely to harm external as well as Iranian interests.

In the end, Iranians cannot avoid settling for a system that will be founded on a combination of Iranian nationalism, Islamic faith, and globalization. This outcome might be a contradiction in terms, but any Eastern culture that desires to coexist in a contemporary global context that is dominated by the West will have to navigate these apparent contradictions and adapt itself to them. Having had the opportunity to travel extensively throughout the region, it is evident to this author that Iran is the most liberal Muslim society. The evolution of Islamic thought on governance within the Iranian political system will have lasting conceptual ramifications throughout the Muslim world in making Islam compatible with globalization. Therefore, it is in the United States' interests to use carrots rather than sticks to accept and gradually influence Islamic thinking into the postindustrialized world.

Rational political change in Iran will have to come from within. Even those who define themselves as secular nationalists in Iran—let alone religious and neoreligious political forces—would feel degraded if outside forces were to come in and rule their country yet again. Both groups would reject such imposition from the outside, even if it required armed conflict. Between those inside Iran who would consider themselves enlightened and those outside the country who care for Iran's progress, there is a vast gap between culture and what is considered relevant and possible. The concerns, political memory, and national agenda of both communities diverge dramatically; those who have lived in Bethesda or Bel Air for two decades or more are far from the reality of today's Iran. To be fair, they are too distant to feel and internalize the nuances that now constitute Iranian political culture.

Reform in Iran will be the outcome of the political forces and dynamics within the country. Yet despite the fact that political competitiveness among various Iranian political orientations in a larger democratic framework is inevitable, no single group across the spectrum of political groupings in today's Iran would qualify as a modern political party with grassroots support and professionalism, which makes democratic change problematic: there can be no democracy without democrats.[3] Although hundreds of individuals in Iran can impress their audiences with their command of the literature on democracy, those same people have little tolerance for accepting differences of opinion, allowing others to advance, and competing fairly with other contestants. Such intolerance is rampant from the educated to the uneducated, from the cleric to the secular, from the rural population to the urban population, and from Iranians in Tehran to Iranian-Americans in West Los Angeles reaching out for change.

Although Iran has liberalized vastly, as a system it remains a collection of political tribes. In the postrevolutionary period, Iran has deteriorated as a nation-state, but it is striving to become one again through a frustrating process. If Iranians as a nation decide to create a democratic society based on original thinking and adequate economic and educational conditions, they first must rid themselves of their "rentier" state, one that is entirely reliant on oil income to sustain itself, and fully globalize. Both developments are far from realistic, however, at least in the near term.

The fact that the so-called conservatives as well as reformists were raised, socialized, and educated under the shah's regime should not be underestimated. Both groups lived under a dictatorial system, were not exposed to the rules of political competition, and indirectly internalized a political culture based on favoritism and patrimonialism. Much of the unconscious workings of political groups across the spectrum was shaped during the dictatorial years of the shah. The great hope for the future of Iran is the huge young population that has a forward-looking and internationalist agenda and is willing to learn from the world as well as contribute to it. Furthermore, Iranian nationalism needs to advance from the current stage of galvanization and drama to a higher stage of rationality and dispassionate calculations of national interest for Iran to become a contributing member of the international community, avoid adventurism, and focus on using all of its human and material assets to enhance its national wealth and thus its national power.

## Policy Necessities in Tehran and Washington

These Iranian realities make it ineffective, injudicious, and imprudent to use military solutions and covert operations to help a talented nation straighten out its historical paradoxes and enter the twenty-first century. Iran has posed no threat to any of its neighbors; Iran's ill-advised policies have, in fact, contributed to the further "Americanization" of the Arab world, the security environment in the Persian Gulf, and the political geography of Central Asia by threatening existing regimes and interfering in their internal affairs. As a consequence, many of these small and mostly vulnerable countries have turned to Washington to secure U.S. protection. Iran's rhetoric against the West, the United States, imperialism, and global justice is merely a demonstration of the psychological needs of its elites, whose rejectionist, anticolonial, and confrontationalist view of the world will not be shared by Iran's youth in the near future.

To tackle the country's level of inefficiency effectively, Iran urgently needs political stability, peace with all of its neighbors, and engagement with major powers. Regardless of the differences between the United States and Iran, Iranians need to enrich their conceptual and analytical process, mature through greater internal and peaceful rational socialization, and develop a sophisticated reference point for their national identity inclusive of all political leanings that have public support.

Iran has accumulated offensive military power over the years; especially since September 11, 2001, however, the Iranian leadership has demonstrated no resolve to wield it because the dominant mood among the rank and file of the country's bureaucracy leans toward focusing on prosperity. Yet, in the postrevolutionary period Iran has been riddled with a pattern of lurching from crisis to crisis, effectively impeding its ability to prosper.

This crisis mentality results from the pursuit of narrowly defined, maximum political sovereignty, ultimately forcing Tehran to resort to the tools of the weak—rhetoric, resentment, and insecurity—while it is interdependence that can achieve maturity and confidence in today's world. Iran's concept of political sovereignty has deep nationalistic and Shi'a roots that will hold for many years to come as Iranians struggle with efforts to balance interaction with the world and enriched confidence-building processes at home over time. Until the floodgates of foreign investment swing open in Iran, such feelings of security and self-confidence in the ability to engage the world will not begin to accumulate. If Iranians do want to be part of the globalization process, it is important for them to come to grips with their sovereignty complex. Reliable rule of law, effective law enforcement, a friendly taxation and regulatory environment, and a transparent government are all conditions that will induce Iran to recapture its historic greatness and assert its regional role.

The top echelons of the conservative and reformist camps in Iran today are not internationalists. Their common revolutionary experience does not include lessons on the interaction of trade, power, and confidence. A stable Iran requires room for everyone: Iranian patriots, nationalists, clerics, and all others, including professional, civil society, and women's groups. As Iran downplays the democracy project, the country needs to focus on the expansion of national wealth, particularly to keep up with the anticipated population growth to 100 million by about 2018.

A psychological examination of the political behavior of the Iranian elites illustrates that they now seek security more than justice. Some of the traditional features of Iran's foreign policy are returning to Iranian foreign behavior. The most important aspect of this change may be Iranian reorientation toward the West. In a sense, the revolutionary period of 1979–1997, during which changing the status quo in the Middle East described Iran's foreign relations, is an aberration. Moreover, Iranian leaders understand that the underlying test of their credibility in the coming years will be delivering economic efficiency rather than pursuing foreign adventurism.

No matter what the political orientation of the next Iranian president (to be elected in May 2005), he or she will be coerced into focusing on economic matters. This reorientation of the national agenda will require buying security in foreign affairs and stabilizing Iran's currently unpredictable and oscillatory foreign relations. As a result, internal issues such as political legitimacy, economic productivity, and stabilization policies are gradually taking precedence over attempts to alter the Middle Eastern status quo.[4] Yet, an analysis of the underlying logic of Iranian behavior makes it apparent that, even without the Islamic Republic at its helm, areas of conceptual and political friction between Tehran and Washington will not wither away completely. Because of its rich culture, historical pride, and sense of confidence, resulting in a national pride among the greatest in the world,[5] Iran, like Russia and China, will always have differences with the United States. Iran's level of conformity with the West in general and the United States in particular will never be like that of Arab or Latin American countries. The logic of geopolitics, oil, and the evolving fabric of Iranian society will, however, ultimately bring the two rivals to agree on a cooperative yet frictional framework.

For Washington, as many Iran analysts have suggested, the United States will gain much more if it begins to court Iran's leadership. Geoffrey Kemp, an American author, urges:

> It is unrealistic to expect Iran to stop its missile program or slow down the modernization of its conventional forces absent a new cooperative regional security environment. ... The future of the U.S. military presence in the Arab world and the size and configuration of Iraq's restructured armed forces will also influence Iranian perceptions. ... Iran will never publicly kowtow to American demands but if approached with respect, Iran's leaders might rethink their agenda in their own national and political interests. If the opportunity for cooperation is missed, the likelihood of an Iranian bomb will increase ... and a confrontation will materialize. This would be good for noth-

ing and for no one. It therefore would be an act of enlightened self-interest for the United States to engage in imaginative diplomacy to prevent it from happening.[6]

In recognizing the fact that the rise of radical Islam in Iran has partly been a response to the antireligious policies of the shah's regime, which the United States fully supported, Washington must also accept that clerics in Iran are not going to alter their course and will continue to make grandiose claims about their reach. At least for the time being, whether in Malaysia, Iran, or Egypt, Muslims have an unconscious sensitivity to maintaining their cultural sovereignty, and a psychological recognition of Muslim political behavior is thus critical for the planning and implementation of U.S. foreign policy.

Part of the inevitable U.S. involvement and interaction in the twenty-first century asserted by Robert Kagan in his recent book, *Of Paradise and Power*, will be toward the Muslim world, which has more than one-fifth of the world's population. In utilizing that power, the United States needs to recognize that Islam will continue to play a determining role in shaping political priorities as well as the cultural outlook of Muslims and thus will develop a realistic policy for engaging the clerical communities in the Muslim world. Demonstrating respect and understanding will prove far more effective than will any other policy instrument.

## Looking to the Future, Patiently

The United States needs to look beyond 2010, when groups that will compete to advance Iran's national interests, economic prosperity, and political openness will manage the Islamic Republic. A corollary can be drawn here with the Chinese Communist Party, which promotes capitalism, globalization, and strategic relations with major powers and today administers the Chinese government. After all, if Immanuel Kant were alive today, he might argue that reason and coherence have a distinct logic east of Turkey and that contradictions on the surface may not be all that relevant if they do not interfere with a country's substance and strategic direction. As the coalition's experience in post-Saddam Iraq clearly shows, the United States must learn to deal more effectively with irregularities and irrationalities in the nations with which it engages.

With little understanding of the local nuances of Iran, the United States cannot develop long-term, strategic thinking or policy. This is precisely the conceptual divide that separates Europe from the United States when it comes to the way the two sides conduct foreign policy. The United States should avoid military solutions to settle its differences with Iran, as military strikes on Iran would delay rapprochement for many years to come. "Occupation" and "foreign occupation" are words that could mobilize Iranians across the political spectrum and resurrect historical memories dating back to the Mossadegh era.

A central idea that can be encapsulated in an aphorism is that Iran is a leader in the process of rational political change in the Middle East. As a reaction to foreign rule, the Iranian revolution caused irreparable damage to Iran's potential economic development but at the same time expedited the clarification of Iranians' sources of identity. Through the Iranian revolution, political Islam surfaced and demonstrated its degree of relevance and viability in the broad mosaic of Iranian sources of identity and political possibilities. From a historical perspective, this was a necessary phase in the evolution of political thinking in Iran. Postrevolutionary generations will be more balanced, focusing on Iran's national interests. The hallmark of the process during the revolutionary period is that Iranians themselves have carried out and internalized this process. While recognizing the historical roots of Iran's current political behavior—that the country's interventionist policies in the 1980s were essentially a natural extension of its revolutionary posturing, while Tehran's behavior in the 1990s and beyond has essentially been based on seeking security and bargaining chips—the United States must also recognize that Iran's geopolitics, energy resources, and even cosmopolitan aspects of its culture will eventually put the country solidly in the Western camp.

Iran's current political oscillations and posturing are largely the pains of its maturation and will result in no conceivable damage to others;

rather, Iranians could prove to be civilizing contributors to evolutionary processes in the Middle East and the Muslim world at large. Given such a framework, a sophisticated and culturally nuanced U.S. approach toward Iran's noncompliant behavior can demonstrate a new, enlightened understanding in Washington with benefits for its relations with the entire Muslim world.

## Notes

1. Mahmood Sariolghalam, "Conceptual Sources of Post-Revolutionary Iranian Behavior toward the Arab World," in *Iran and the Arab World*, eds. Nader Entessar and Hooshang Amirahmadi (New York: St. Martin's Press, 1993), p. 20.

2. See www.niacouncil.org/pressreleases/press097.asp (accessed June 19, 2003).

3. See Ghassan Salame, *Democracy Without Democrats* (London: I. B. Tauris, 1994).

4. Mahmood Sariolghalam, "Iran's Security and the Persian Gulf: An Inside View," in *Il Golfo nel XXI Secolo: Le Nuove Logiche della Conflittualita*, ed. Valeria Fiorani Piacentini (Milan: Il Mulino, 2002), pp. 489–495, 503–507.

5. Minxin Pei, "The Paradoxes of American Nationalism," *Foreign Policy* (May–June 2003): 32.

6. See Geoffrey Kemp, "How to Stop the Iranian Bomb?" *National Interest* (summer 2003).

# Part V

## Iraq after Saddam

**Steven Metz**

# Insurgency and Counterinsurgency in Iraq

$A$n insurgency is born long before the government it seeks to overthrow knows of its existence. Rebels, guerrillas, and terrorists, far from prying eyes, gather in dark buildings, foreign sanctuaries, or—in today's day and age—online. At least initially, survival depends on cloaking intent and strength with ambiguity, deception, and subterfuge. Even after attacks begin in earnest, the intended targets tend to underestimate the problem, believing it to be controllable, unorganized, and isolated rather than a symptom of a deeper pathology.

Understanding the factors leading to such a miscalculation is easy. Gone are the Cold War days when regimes could rely on a superpower patron for increased support against a rebellion. Although the most benevolent and stable government may face isolated violence, an organized insurgency reveals deep flaws in rule or administration. Today, even an unsuccessful insurrection can weaken or undercut a government, hinder economic development and access to global capital, or at least force national leaders to alter key policies. The tendency then is to deny or underestimate the threat, to believe that killing or capturing only a few of the most obvious rebel leaders will

Steven Metz is director of research at the U.S. Army War College's Strategic Studies Institute. The opinions expressed in this essay are strictly the author's own and do not represent the official position of the U.S. Army.

© 2003 by The Center for Strategic and International Studies and the Massachusetts Institute of Technology
*The Washington Quarterly* • 27:1 pp. 25–36.

solve the problem when in fact the problem—the heart of the insurgency—lies deeper.

Like cancers, insurgencies are seldom accorded the seriousness they deserve at precisely the time they are most vulnerable, early in their development. Such is the situation that the United States and coalition forces face in Iraq today. Although U.S. strategists and political leaders may disagree about who is behind the violence in Iraq, the preconditions for a serious and sustained insurgency clearly exist.

The stakes in Iraq are immense. The conflict there will help determine whether the world continues its difficult and uneven movement toward a global system based on open governments and economies or fractures into a new bipolarity. The Arab world is the region most resistant to the U.S. vision of open economies and governments. If it can work there, it can work anywhere. Iraq is the beachhead, the test case, the laboratory.

Given these stakes and the price already paid, the United States must continue to pursue its strategic objective in Iraq but must do so in a way that limits the long-term damage to the United States itself and to the fragile, new Iraqi society. Calls for a speedy U.S. withdrawal will increase as the conflict drags on. Even Ambassador Paul Bremer, head of the Coalition Provisional Authority, has hinted that the United States may leave Iraq by the summer of 2004. Leaving too soon, however, would be disastrous. After all, Osama bin Laden's rise was in part a result of abandoning Afghanistan too soon after foreign occupation in 1979. Departing early would guarantee that strategic objectives are not met and, in all likelihood, force re-intervention to deal with future security problems. Only a carefully designed and cautious counterinsurgency strategy can forestall this.

Accepting the existence of an organized insurgency in Iraq has immense political costs as it requires admitting flaws in preconflict planning and will impede the expansion of the multinational coalition attempting to stabilize Iraq. Although a number of states were willing to volunteer for peacekeeping (at least if the price is right), few are willing to accept the casualties and other long-term costs associated with counterinsurgency. As in Vietnam, the United States is likely to stand nearly alone, with only its closest allies. Even so, history is clear on one point: the sooner that serious problems are acknowledged and a comprehensive counterinsurgency strategy is implemented, the better the chances that the threat can be managed.

## The Emerging Insurgency

An insurgency is born when a governing power fails to address social or regional polarization, sectarianism, endemic corruption, crime, various forms of radicalism, or rising expectations. The margin of error is narrower for an outside occupying power than for an inept or repressive national regime as people tend to find the mistakes or bad behavior by one of their own more tolerable than that of outsiders. Because imperialism was delegitimized in the second half of the twentieth century, minor errors of judgment or practice have provoked armed opposition against rule by outsiders.

By no stretch of the imagination has the U.S. occupation of Iraq been brutal or repressive, but it has had its miscalculations. The first was a serious underestimation of the work needed to secure, stabilize, and reconstruct Iraq after Saddam Hussein's regime had been toppled. Security in Iraq is labor intensive because of the country's long borders and extensive territory, and the coalition did not deploy adequate forces to prevent the infiltration of foreign radicals and criminals. Coalition planners believed that a significant portion of the Iraqi security forces—military and police—would sit out the war in their barracks and then reemerge to form the core of the post-Saddam military and police with new leaders at their fore. None returned, however, leaving a massive security vacuum that the coalition was unprepared to fill. The expectation that international peacekeepers would plug the gaps was also misguided because only a modest number of states proved willing to contribute to what was seen as a U.S.-dominated effort. Coalition planners also underestimated the dilapidated state of Iraqi infrastructure and thus were not able to restore basic services during the first few crucial months following the collapse of Saddam's regime when Iraqis were forming first and lasting impressions.

U.S. strategists also overestimated the ability of Iraqis to govern themselves and underestimated the rapid spread of crime and anomie. This particular shortcoming highlights the tendency to mirror image[1] — to assume that others perceive, understand, and act in the way that Americans do—and a deep misunderstanding of the psychology of totalitarianism. Survival in a totalitarian society is dependent on slavish devotion to those with power and on passivity when neither personal power nor the power of a patron provides protection. Fear is pervasive and paralyzing. Fairness and justice have little meaning, and individuals have difficulty distinguishing truth from propaganda or rumor because the regime controls information. Moving from the psychology of totalitarianism to the psychology of an open society, with its foundation in political initiative, consensus building, and compromise, is a long and torturous journey. Against this backdrop, hopes that a functioning Iraqi civil administration could be constructed quickly proved misguided.

U.S. strategists and political leaders also underestimated how long it would take before resentment of the occupation would spark violence. They assumed that, as long as they provided basic services and evidence of economic and political progress, the Iraqis would tolerate coalition forces. This has not proven true. Even in areas where services have been restored to prewar levels, resentment at outside occupation is escalating to the point of violence. The honeymoon period of universal welcome for coalition forces lasted only a few weeks after the overthrow of Saddam's regime.

In Iraq, U.S. strategists correctly gauged the powerful appeal of liberation but misunderstood how it would be interpreted. For most Iraqis, liberation means removing Saddam's regime and any outside presence. The Arab world has little tolerance for outside occupation, particularly by non-Muslims, and a tradition of violent opposition to occupiers. Long, bloody wars were waged against the French occupation of Morocco and Algeria, the British occupation of Iraq, and the Israeli occupation of the West Bank and southern Lebanon. This tradition, combined with the current appeal of radical *jihad*, is incendiary, yielding recruits driven by ideology and contributions from those unwilling to fight themselves but willing to provide money to hire and equip additional guerrillas. Islamic radicalism will doubtless increasingly provide the motivation, legitimacy, and global network of support for insurgents in Iraq. This mixture is even more volatile than the one that existed in Vietnam, where the insurgency took decades to mount because of the isolation and illiteracy of the peasantry. In today's age of interconnectedness, transparency, and pervasive information technology, the process can be compressed into months or even weeks.

Still, even when the raw material for insurgency—anger, resentment, alienation, frustration, a unifying ideology—exists, other factors must be present. Clearly, the insurgents require access to resources, particularly arms and money. In Iraq, neither is in short supply, at least for the time being. Although coalition forces have seized huge amounts of weapons and explosives, many remain under the control of former regime loyalists, other radicals, or criminals who seized them during the chaotic period between the fall of Saddam's regime and the establishment of control by the coalition. In addition, Iraq's porous borders make importing additional arms easy. Similarly, the Ba'th regime had massive amounts of cash, much of which has also been seized, but enough still remains in insurgents' hands to fuel daily violence.

The final ingredients of insurgency, however, fortunately remain outstanding: no clear leadership, strategy, and ideology have emerged to unite the disparate opponents of the United States and the coalition. At this point, the insurgency's core seems to be remnants of the old regime, particularly members of the special security and intelligence services. Although they are fanatical and well schooled at using violence for maximum psychological impact, their ability to expand their support is constrained. However much the Iraqi people are dissatisfied with the coalition's occupation, very few want a return of the old regime. The remaining Ba'thists can thus build anger and resentment toward the coalition, but they are unable to translate these into active support for their own agenda.

The only way, then, that the Ba'thist core can expand its insurgency is through alliances. Any individual, group, or organization willing to use violence against the occupation is seen as a potential ally. Some of the insurgents appear motivated at least as much by pay as by ideology. With most Iraqis unemployed, the prospect of a significant payment for an assassination is appealing even to those not deeply sympathetic to the Ba'thists. In many ways, one of the trademarks of modern insurgencies from Colombia to Sierra Leone is that cash has proven a much more useful recruitment tool than ideological fervor.

A second expansion of the insurgency comes with the infiltration of foreign Islamic radicals. Ansar al-Islam, an extremist movement with ties to Al Qaeda, seems to be serving as the foundation of this process, linking infiltrators to the Ba'thists. Reportedly, such foreigners were behind the deadly August 2003 bombing of the United Nations compound. At the same time, Iraqi border police have warned that Arab radicals are being smuggled across the Iranian border along with Shi'ite pilgrims. The call is out throughout the global Islamic radical community to turn Iraq into "another Afghanistan." As trained jihadists from around the world stream toward Iraq, the insurgency there is likely to become more professional and proficient.

Finally, now facing a common enemy, the Ba'thist insurgents may be forming common cause with increasingly angry Shi'ite radicals centered around firebrands such as the young and popular cleric Muqtada al-Sadr, son of Grand Ayatollah Muhammad al-Sadr (killed by Saddam's agents) and one of the most adamant opponents of the U.S. occupation of Iraq. Although the objective of Shi'ite radicals—theocracy—is at odds with the more secular perspective of the Ba'thists, they share an interest in ridding Iraq of Americans. Historically, this is not unusual: many successful insurgencies from China in the 1920s and 1930s to Zimbabwe during the war against white minority rule in the 1970s began with what China's Mao Zedong called a "national united front" and only saw a single group emerge to dominate local politics at a later date.

Optimists contend that the diversity of the Iraqi opposition and the absence of a single clear leadership and ideology are proof that the movement does not pose a serious threat. Unifying the various strands of the Iraqi insurgency behind any one strategy or objective, at least in the short term, will certainly be difficult if not impossible. Yet, this same complexity means that quashing the insurgency will be just as difficult or impossible. Actions that prove effective against one part of it might very well inflame another part. For example, an increased and heavy-handed U.S. presence might eradicate the Ba'thist remnants and at the same time inflame Shi'ite radicals and foreign jihadists. The insurgency is like a multiheaded snake, unable to decide on a single course of action but difficult to kill.

The Iraqi insurgency is following another common early pattern as it focuses more on weakening the existing governing regime or occupying power than on offering a clear political alternative. What began a few weeks after the fall of Saddam's regime as sporadic and disorganized attacks against U.S. troops by small arms has now grown into a sophisticated campaign using remotely triggered explosives and complex combinations of weapons as well as shoulder-held antiaircraft missiles. The target list has also expanded. Attacks on U.S. soldiers continue, but new targets include other coalition forces; U.S. civilians; Iraqis working with the coalition, such as policemen or the mayor; and infrastructure such as oil and water pipelines or electrical pylons, the Jordanian embassy, the Imam Ali Mosque in Najaf, and the UN headquarters. The product reflects the old, Russian revolutionary slogan, "the worse, the better." In other words, anything that prevents the coalition from stabilizing Iraq and improving the lives of Iraqis is thought to weaken the coalition, to erode tolerance of the occupation, to provoke greater violence, and eventually to undercut the U.S. public's and the world community's support for the occupation.

## What Makes Iraq Different

As much as the insurgency taking shape in Iraq reflects its historical predecessors, however, it is very much a modern phenomenon. Every U.S. military officer and strategic thinker is familiar with insurgency, but their base of knowledge is a rural "people's war" as developed in

China, refined in Vietnam, and later adapted in Latin America and Africa. It is based on parallel political and military efforts: the former designed to mobilize supporters and provide an alternative government to the existing one, the latter designed to weaken the state through low-intensity and eventually mid-intensity conflict.

On the military side, the insurgents traditionally begin with small terrorist or hit-and-run attacks but eventually build their military strength until they match up to and defeat the government. This pattern will not apply in Iraq. The movement there more clearly reflects the Palestinian strategy for insurgency, which targets an external occupier whose primary weaknesses are a potential lack of will for sustained casualties and sensitivity to public opinion or pressure. The insurgents have no hope of matching the military might of the occupiers, but because the governing force is not indigenous and has the option of simply leaving, the war becomes a contest of wills, with battles fought in the psychological, perceptual, and political realms. Because of the ingrained military weakness of the insurgents in the Palestinian formulation, the insurgents do not seek to control territory and create an alternative government as in the Maoist model but rely instead on internal and international psychological operations fueled by terrorism, riots, guerrilla raids, sabotage, civilian casualties, and uprisings. The intermediate goal is increased tension between the population and the occupiers intended to provoke the occupiers into using force against the civilians, further alienating themselves and building outside political pressure for withdrawal.

Still, the Iraqi insurgency differs from the Palestinian one in one important sense. Because the Palestinians had some degree of international legitimacy, support, and sanctuary, their movement could develop a discernible leadership and hierarchy. The global reach of the United States is likely to preclude any nation, even Iran or Syria, from providing overt sanctuary to Iraqi insurgents, causing the movement to remain more inchoate than the Palestinian insurgency, with Iraqi leadership shadowy and its form a loose amalgamation of diverse groups unified only by a shared dislike of U.S. occupation. For the United States, this news is both good and bad as this form will limit the strength of the insurgency but will also make it headless, without a clear center of gravity, and thus difficult to kill.

Because the Iraqi insurgency remains inchoate, it has not yet shown that it can progress to its next logical steps: to use global information technology, interconnectedness, and émigré communities to develop networks of political support, financing, and recruitment and potentially to launch terrorist operations in the United States. It has not yet solidified linkages with the global Islamic radical movement; global organized crime; or other radical, anti-U.S. movements. It has not developed and may never develop a clear counterideology, instead intentionally choosing to remain vague to be as inclusive as possible. As it exists now, the mounting Iraqi insurgency is explicit about what it stands against—U.S. occupation of Iraq—but not on what it stands for. Yet, those steps may come. The Iraqi insurgency is at a fork in the road. It may move rapidly toward maturation and development, becoming a very dangerous opponent for the United States, or it may be controlled or even quashed. The U.S. response in the next few months to the developments currently underway will determine to a large extent which of these scenarios comes to pass.

## The Keys to Defeating Nascent Insurgency

U.S. strategists have treated the Iraqi insurgency as the death throes of the old regime. Their rationale is that most Iraqis do not support it and thus, if the Ba'thist remnants can be killed or captured, the problem will be solved. Although this analysis is true in part—most Iraqis do not support the insurgency at present—some successful insurgencies, including the Chinese, Algerian, Vietnamese, and American struggles for independence, never had active majority support. A successful insurgency requires only the active support of a small cadre and acquiescence from the rest. Such acquiescence is likely in Iraq. Decades of brutal totalitarianism have taught Iraqis that the best way to survive is to stay out of conflicts between the powerful. Moreover, although few Iraqis want to see the return of the old regime, many also resent the U.S. presence enough to make them unlikely to oppose the insurgents actively.

The insurgency's foundation does not rest on the ambition of former regime loyalists to return an unpopular government to power but rather is based on a broader resentment of foreign occupation by a people promised liberation. Only a comprehensive and coherent counterinsurgency strategy that weaves together the collective resources of the U.S. government can effectively stifle this threat. History suggests some of the keys to success, but U.S. strategists must also understand that the Iraqi insurgency is a new variant of an old problem, both similar to and different from Vietnam and its other predecessors. It is vital to discern the similarities from the differences and use this to build coherent policy. At a minimum, such a strategy would entail the following:

- *Admit the extent of the problem frankly.*

During the early years of U.S. involvement in Vietnam, U.S. strategists tended to focus on killing active insurgents rather than on identifying and rectifying the structural problems that spawned them. The United States is close to replicating this situation in Iraq. Occupation, although vital to attain U.S. objectives, breeds opposition. In an era when national liberation has been deified, even successful control of street crime and revival of the Iraqi economy will not fully obviate the anger and resentment felt by Iraqis toward their U.S. occupiers. Only the full withdrawal of U.S. forces would, but this should not happen until Iraq has undergone several years of tutelage and developed the capacity for self-rule. The persistence of the insurgency in the interim is therefore inevitable.

- *Integrate the strategy within the U.S. bureaucracy and with its coalition partners.*

The United States and its close coalition partners must assure unity of effort across all of the governmental agencies involved. Counterinsurgency is not an exclusively or even predominantly military function but demands the seamless integration of informational, political, social, cultural, law enforcement, economic, military, and intelligence activities. Military strategists consider the successful British counterinsurgency campaign in Malaya that began in the late 1940s the model to replicate.

At every level, from the local to the national, the British military, police, and intelligence services and government agencies concerned with economic development were seamlessly integrated. Military operations were low-key and limited, undertaken with specific, narrow objectives and not used to intimidate insurgents or their potential supporters.

In Malaya, the British also found that carrots—political and economic development—were more important tools of counterinsurgency than sticks. These lessons were applied toward the end of U.S. involvement in Vietnam and had local success, but by then, it was too late to shift the course of the conflict. Yet, it is still early in the Iraqi insurgency. The United States and its coalition partners should follow the pattern of success from Malaya and implement full integration across all governmental agencies, stressing political and economic development.

- *Focus on two key battlespaces: intelligence and Iraqi perception.*

Because the main tactics of Palestinian-style insurgency are to wear down the occupier and alienate the public, reliable and timely intelligence is the lifeblood of counterinsurgency. Every insurgent attack that occurs, even if the attackers lose more lives than the defenders, is a victory for the insurgents because it fuels fear among the public and dissatisfaction with the governing power, both within the beleaguered country and internationally. To the extent that the United States is able to obtain, analyze, and act on information about insurgent attacks in Iraq, it can control the psychological dimension of the conflict. Phrased differently, intelligence specialists are keys to victory in counterinsurgency. Success will require human and technical sources of information as well as effective methods to analyze and share information across agencies and among coalition partners.

The more difficult battlespace may be perception. After decades of totalitarianism, Iraqis are ill equipped to evaluate the credibility of information. As a result, wild, often surreal rumors spread rapidly and are widely believed. An exploding array of domestic Iraqi newspapers and electronic media, Iranian government sources, and other Arabic news media such as Al Jazeera bombard Iraqis with information, much of it unconstrained by objectivity or often truth. This manipulates existing prejudices, fears, and beliefs. Despite great efforts, the United States does not appear to be winning the psychological war in Iraq, at least not yet. It is always difficult to counter misinformation in an environment where people are unprepared to distinguish truth from fiction. The best the United States and its coalition partners can do is to promulgate the truth persistently in a culturally sensitive way, working whenever possible with Iraqis trained in responsible journalism.

- *Break the linkages between Iraqi insurgents and affiliated or allied groups.*

The two most likely allies for the Iraqi insurgents are the global Islamic radical movement, particularly the remnants of Al Qaeda or its offshoots, and global organized crime. Although U.S. strategists have made great efforts to curb the former, less attention has been given to the latter. Iraq is already suffering from a massive growth in organized crime, some built on the remnants of the Ba'th movement, which moved extensively into organized crime during the past decade, and some on Iranian criminal gangs looking to expand their territory. The nascent Iraqi police that the coalition is helping to organize cannot control street crime, much less confront organized crime and insurgents.

As a result, organized crime is burrowing deeper into Iraqi society. Should this continue at such a rapid rate, bringing it under control will take decades. Therefore, a U.S. counterinsurgency strategy should include steps to thwart organized crime now. This specific area is one where an integrated counterinsurgency strategy is vital: law enforcement is as important as military activity and must be an equal partner in planning and distributing resources. If Iraq is left cleared of political radicals but under the control of organized crime, the United States will not have attained its strategic objectives.

- *Design a larger regional and strategic context.*

Solutions to broader national and regional problems are necessary to end the insurgency. Iraq was and is very much part of the Arab and Islamic worlds. Attempts to reconstruct the country politically cannot be fully separated from the larger issues that trouble the Arab world, particularly Palestine, closed political systems, the lack of economic growth, overpopulation, and a general inability to compete in the globalized economy. The notion that a postinsurgency Iraq can serve as a beacon for the region has merit, but more than a vision is necessary.

For the new Iraq to remain stable and prosperous, the region must become stable and prosperous. This is a massive undertaking with at least three very complex components for the United States: solving the Palestinian problem, which appears to require some sort of international intervention; explicitly committing to open government in the region, which will destabilize closed regimes in states such as Saudi Arabia and Egypt at least in the short term and will invariably lead to an increased role for religious parties; and committing to regional economic development that could draw off capital currently flowing to other fragile regions such as South Asia, eastern Europe, or South America. If the United States does not undertake these three steps, a democratic Iraq will remain a beleaguered island in an unstable region.

- *Remind the American public vigorously and continuously of what is at stake in Iraq.*

Like all insurgencies, the one in Iraq will test whose will can be sustained longer, the insurgents' or the counterinsurgents'. If U.S. involvement in Iraq becomes a major point of contention in the 2004 election and the Democrats advocate withdrawal of U.S. troops from Iraq, sustaining American public support for U.S. operations in Iraq could prove very difficult. U.S. politicians who seek to criticize the administration for ongoing operations in Iraq should be challenged to explain their vision of the future of Iraq without a near-term U.S. presence.

## No Easy Way Out

The United States faces an intractable dilemma in Iraq: in effect, it is damned if it does, damned if it doesn't. By staying, the United States will face a protracted insurgency, but by withdrawing before the new

Iraq is able to stand on its own, the ultimate strategic objective—a unified, stable Iraq that does not threaten its neighbors and does not support international terrorism—will not be met. After three decades of totalitarianism, Iraqis will not be ready for several years to run a stable nation on their own. Stability requires an interim period of oversight, occupation, and tutelage. Yet, Iraqis cannot admit this, and so the occupation generates opposition and violence.

A comprehensive and coherent U.S. counterinsurgency strategy is the only feasible solution to confront the strategic dilemma the United States now faces in Iraq. Comprehensive counterinsurgency, focusing on the key nodes for success outlined here, is unlikely to eradicate the violent opposition to the coalition fully but should at least sufficiently weaken the insurgent opposition and ensure that the new Iraqi regime is not born—as the South Vietnamese government was—with a massive internal security threat on its hands.

The idea that open government is a universal model has long served as the essence of U.S. foreign policy strategy. For better or worse, Iraq has been chosen as the place to prove this point. Thus, failure in Iraq would undercut the very foundation of U.S. global strategy. Given these immense stakes, U.S. policymakers are dangerously close to underestimating the nature of the challenge in Iraq. Overoptimistic assumptions about the ease of the transition to stable, open government led to the current situation. It is now time to grapple with the depth and complexity of the opposition. By implementing a comprehensive counterinsurgency strategy now, the United States can forestall the growth of the opposition and hopefully allow a new Iraq to serve as a beacon for change in the region.

## Note

1.   Frank Watanabe, "How to Succeed in the DI: Fifteen Axioms for Intelligence Analysis," *Studies in Intelligence* 1, no. 1 (1997), www.cia.gov/csi/studies/97unclass/axioms.html (accessed October 1, 2003).

Daniel L. Byman and Kenneth M. Pollack

# Democracy in Iraq?

W hat should the government of Iraq after Saddam Hussein look like? The U.S. government has worked feverishly to address the problem—creating working groups and planning cells, formulating options, and discussing ideas with U.S. allies while pundits and analysts in the media, think tanks, and academia have further identified this issue as a vital one to ensure that peace in Iraq and in the region is secured.

Democracy lies at the heart of all of these discussions. President George W. Bush himself declared, "All Iraqis must have a voice in the new government, and all citizens must have their rights protected."[1] As members of a prosperous democratic society, U.S. citizens innately believe that democracy would be good for Iraqis too. The most optimistic have even offered a vision of a future Iraq as a "City on the Hill" for the Arab world that would inspire democracy throughout the Middle East and beyond.[2]

Yet, skeptics abound. Adam Garfinkle, for example, argues that even trying to build democracy in the Arab world would not only fail but also further stoke anti-Americanism in the process.[3] Overall, critics

Daniel L. Byman is an assistant professor in the Security Studies Program at Georgetown University and a nonresident senior fellow at the Saban Center for Middle East Policy at the Brookings Institution in Washington, D.C. Kenneth M. Pollack is director of research at the Saban Center and author of *The Threatening Storm: The Case for Invading Iraq*.

Copyright © 2003 by The Center for Strategic and International Studies and the Massachusetts Institute of Technology
*The Washington Quarterly* • 26:3 pp. 119–136.

raise at least five related objections to creating a democratic Iraq that seem damning at first blush. First, they contend that acceptable alternatives to democracy exist for Iraq that, if hardly ideal, are more feasible and more likely to ensure the stability and cohesiveness of the country. Second, they argue that Iraq is not ready for democracy. Third, they state that Iraqi society is too fragmented for democracy to take hold. Even if Iraq held elections or had other outward institutions of democracy, in practice such a system would yield an illiberal result such as a tyranny of the Shi'a majority. Fourth, they insist that the transition to democracy in Iraq would be too perilous and the resulting government too weak; thus, the institutionalization of democracy, particularly a federal form of it, would fail. Critics often conjure a vision of an Iraq beset by civil strife with rival communities seeking revenge on one another while neighboring armies trample the country. Finally, they assert that the United States is too fickle, and the Iraqis too hostile, to give democracy the time it would need to grow and bear fruit. Overall, primarily for these five reasons, the doubters do not so much question the desirability of democracy in Iraq as they do its feasibility.

Claiming that building democracy in Iraq after the U.S.-led war to depose Saddam would be easy or certain—let alone that doing so might solve all of the problems of the Middle East overnight—would be foolish. Nevertheless, the arguments advanced by skeptics exaggerate the impediments to building democracy and ignore the potential impact that a determined United States could have on this effort. Iraq is hardly ideal soil for growing democracy, but it is not as infertile as other places where democracy has taken root. Iraq's people are literate, and the country's potential wealth is considerable. A properly designed federal system stabilized by U.S. and other intervening powers' military forces could both satisfy Iraq's myriad communities and ensure order and security. Creating democracy in Iraq would require a long-term U.S. commitment, but the United States has made similar commitments to far less strategic parts of the world. Creating a democracy in Iraq would not be quick, easy, or certain, but it should not be impossible either.

## No Other Choice

Perhaps the most compelling reason to invest in building democracy in a post-Saddam Iraq is that the alternatives are far worse. Those who oppose such an effort have offered two alternatives: an oligarchy that incorporates Iraq's leading communities or a new, gentler dictatorship. Although not pleasant, skeptics of democracy argue that the United States must be "realistic" and recognize that only these options would avoid chaos and ensure Iraq's stability. That either of these approaches could offer a stable and desirable alternative to the lengthy process of building democracy from the bottom up, however, is highly doubtful.

### CONSOCIATIONAL OLIGARCHY

One of the most commonly suggested forms for a post-Saddam Iraqi government would be one roughly similar to the new Karzai regime in Afghanistan. A consociational oligarchy would theoretically bring together leading figures from all of Iraq's major ethnic, religious, tribal, geographic, and functional groupings in a kind of national unity government. Such a regime might not be pluralistic in a strict sense; but by including members from all strata of Iraqi society, it would at least represent its key elements, and the various members could be expected to protect the most basic interests of their co-religionists and ethnic kin. Whether or not these groups truly represented the interests and aspirations of the Iraqi people would be largely irrelevant. Advocates of a consociational oligarchy in Iraq maintain that, with the demise of Saddam's regime, tribal chieftains and religious leaders can be expected to emerge as the only forces left in Iraq with some degree of power and would therefore be best able to preserve stability.

A consociational oligarchy would be difficult to establish for the simple reason that Iraq currently lacks potential oligarchs. Before Saddam took power, Iraq had numerous tribal, religious, military, municipal, and merchant leaders of sufficient stature to exercise considerable independent power. "Had" is the key word. Because Saddam ruthlessly eliminated any leaders in the country with the potential to rival himself, strong local leaders are lacking. Those who remain in the armed forces, in the Sunni tribes, and among some of the Shi'ite militias and religious figures are political pygmies, lacking anything resembling the kind of independent power needed to dominate the country. The armed forces, particularly the Republican Guard, had the power to rule the country, but they have been decimated and fragmented by the U.S. military offensive.

Meanwhile, 75 percent of the population is urban, and even those city-dwellers who retain some links to their tribes reportedly do not want to be represented by unsophisticated, rural shaykhs who know nothing about life in Iraq's cities. Nor do these mostly secular Iraqis want to be represented by clerics whose goals might be very different from their own. So, who would represent the urban lower and middle classes that constitute the bulk of Iraq's population? Not the former magistrates of Iraq's cities—these are all appointees of Saddam's regime who owed their positions to their loyalty and service to him. In short, without a democratic process that would allow new leaders to emerge from the greater Iraqi population, the vast majority of Iraqis would be left without a voice.

By failing to include so much of Iraq's populace, attempts at a consociational oligarchy will only foster the potential for instability down the road. Although the current Kurdish leaders could represent their population well because they have led them for years and are widely—though not universally—accepted, they would be the exception. The few members of the Shi'ite clergy who have survived Saddam's purges could represent Shi'ites who favor an Islamic form of government, but they reportedly constitute less than 15 percent of the Shi'ite population in Iraq. Shi'ite shaykhs could represent their small tribal constituencies, just as Sunni shaykhs could represent their followers; but tribal Iraqis—both Sunni and Shi'a—now comprise just a small fraction of the population, probably less than 15 percent. An oligarchic approach thus risks almost immediate chaos by increasing the chances that a form of warlordism would develop in which local leaders might be strong enough to resist any weak central government that would surely emerge with such an approach, as was the case in Afghanistan, but not strong enough to hold the country together.

To the extent that various groups and their warlords did cooperate in a new political structure created by the United States before coalition troops departed, they likely would do so only temporarily to prevent their rivals from gaining control of the central government, to try to gain control of the central government themselves, and to secure as much of the country's resources for themselves as possible. Moreover, this approach would inevitably include the cleansing of other tribal, ethnic, and religious groups as warlords attempted to consolidate control of their territory. Meanwhile, in the Shi'ite south, with no strong central government imposing order, the Shi'a would likely vent their pent-up anger over eight decades of Sunni repression with reprisal killings against Sunnis associated with the past regime. Imagining a consociational oligarchy that fostered stability, let alone good government, in Iraq is difficult.

## A NEW DICTATORSHIP

A far simpler alternative to democracy would be merely to install a new dictator to take Saddam's place. In effect, this would entail the United States acquiescing in the establishment of just one more Arab autocracy that, hopefully, would be no more troubling than that of Hosni Mubarak's Egypt.

In addition to the moral burden of forcing long-suffering Iraqis to again endure dictatorship, this hard-line approach is not practical because the power brokers left standing after Saddam's fall are simply too weak to take or hold power forcibly themselves without constant and heavy-handed U.S. interference. Lacking Saddam's military power, any who try will provoke civil war when they attack but be unable to defeat the military forces of their domestic rivals. To make matters worse, each faction would probably appeal to foreign countries such as Iran or Syria to help defend themselves and gain control over the country.

Because a U.S.-anointed successor to Saddam would find holding power difficult without outside support, the most likely outcome of this approach would be a revolving-door dictatorship in which one weak autocrat is overthrown by the next, who then is himself too weak to hang on. Indeed, the only way that another dictator would have a chance of maintaining power would be to become a new version of Saddam himself—replicating his predecessor's brutal tyranny and even possibly resurrecting the development of weapons of mass destruction, flouting UN resolutions, supporting terrorism, and attacking neighboring countries, none of which would enhance the stability of the region or advance U.S. interests.

At best, a new dictatorship would leave Iraq no better off than other regional autocracies, but this too would be a dangerous result. Under such a dictatorship, Iraq might—as Saudi Arabia and Egypt have—become a breeding ground for anti-U.S. Islamic radicals or might slide into instability, even revolution. Setting post-Saddam Iraq on this path would be folly. Saddling another strategically important Middle Eastern state with all of the same problems as Egypt, Syria, Saudi Arabia, and the others is not an outcome that the United States should seek.

## Difficult but Not Impossible

The second principal criticism leveled by the skeptics of democracy for Iraq is that Iraq is too much of a basket case for it ever to become a democracy. As Middle East expert Chris Sanders argues, "There isn't a society in Iraq to turn into a democracy"[4]—a view shared by a range of experts interviewed by journalist James Fallows. This pessimism contains grains of truth. Building democracy in Iraq will not be easy, straightforward, or guaranteed; others have failed under more propitious circumstances. Moreover, building democracy in Iraq will be a long and laborious process, if it succeeds at all. No particular reason, however, exists to believe that creating a workable democracy in Iraq would be impossible. In this respect, the skeptics have exaggerated the obstacles.

The claim that the historical absence of democracy in Iraq precludes its development today can be easily refuted by the fact that many democracies that have developed within the last 20 years—some with more problems than others—lacked a prior democratic tradition. Any new democracy has to start somewhere. After World War II, many Americans and Europeans believed that Germans were unsuited to democracy because they were culturally bred—if not genetically predisposed—to autocracy, and they pointed to the failure of the Weimar Republic as proof. The same claim was made about several East Asian countries, whose Confucian values supposedly required a consensus and uniformity inimical to democracy. White South Africans similarly argued that their black compatriots were somehow unequipped to participate in the democratic process. The British often said the same about India before independence. Since the fall of the Soviet Union, democracy has broken out across Eastern Europe, and in some cases it has been a relatively quick success (e.g., Poland, Estonia, the Czech Republic, and Hungary) and in other cases a disappointment (e.g., Belarus). In virtually all of these countries, however, and in dozens of others around the world, democracy may remain a work in progress, but it is not hopeless.

## IRAQ'S FOUNDATIONS FOR DEMOCRACY

The various socioeconomic indicators that academics use to assess the probability of democracy succeeding also suggest that Iraq has a reasonably good foundation to make the transition.[5] As Table 1 indicates, in key categories such as per capita income, literacy, male-to-female literacy ratio, and urbanization, Iraq's numbers are comparable to those of many other states that have enjoyed real progress in the transition from autocracy to democracy, such as Bangladesh, Kenya, and Bolivia.

Critics correctly point out that the above statistics are correlates, not causes; simply possessing a certain gross domestic product (GDP) or literacy rate does not automatically lead a country to democracy. Yet, the same uncertainty about what causes democracy also applies to what

## Table I. Socioeconomic Indicators Linked to Democracy: Selected Countries

| Country | Positive Factors | | | | Negative Factors | |
|---|---|---|---|---|---|---|
| | Per Capita GDP (PPP) | Basic Education (Literacy: Percent of population age 15 and higher) | | | Economic Inequality (Gini Index) | Urban Population (Percent of total) |
| | | Total | Male | Female | Male-Female Gap | | |
| Bangladesh | $1,750 | 56 | 63 | 49 | –14 | 33.6 | 22 |
| Bolivia | 2,600 | 83.1 | 90.5 | 76 | –14.5 | 58.9 | 60 |
| East Timor | 500 | 48 | NA | NA | NA | 38 | 24 |
| Egypt | 3,700 | 51.4 | 63.6 | 38.8 | –24.8 | 28.9 | 44 |
| India | 2,500 | 52 | 65.5 | 37.7 | –27.8 | 37.8 | 27 |
| Indonesia | 3,000 | 83.8 | 89.6 | 78 | –11.6 | 31.7 | 36 |
| Iraq | 2,500 | 58 | 70.7 | 45 | –25.7 | NA * | 75 |
| Kenya | 1,000 | 78.1 | 86.3 | 70 | –16.3 | 44.5 | 29 |
| Jordan | 4,200 | 86.6 | 93.4 | 79.4 | –14 | 36.4 | 71 |
| Mongolia | 1,770 | 97.8 | 98 | 97.5 | –0.5 | 33.2 | 61 |
| Nigeria | 840 | 57.1 | 67.3 | 47.3 | –20 | 50.6 | 40 |
| Panama | 5,900 | 90.8 | 91.4 | 90.2 | –1.2 | 48.5 | 55 |
| Peru | 4,800 | 88.3 | 94.5 | 83 | –11.5 | 46.2 | 71 |
| Philippines | 4,000 | 94.6 | 95 | 94.3 | –0.7 | 46.2 | 54 |
| Romania | 6,800 | 97 | 98 | 95 | –3 | 30.5 | 55 |
| Senegal | 1,580 | 39.1 | 51.1 | 28.9 | –22.2 | 41.3 | 44 |
| Turkey | 6,700 | 85 | 94 | 77 | –17 | 41.5 | 69 |

Notes:   NA=not available
         * (High)

Sources: World Bank, "East Timor at a Glance," for East Timor urban population; United Nations InfoNation for urban population of other countries; CIA World Factbook for all other figures.

hinders it. Scholars have some insights into the process, but time and again history has surprised us. Democracy has sprung up in the most unlikely of places: sub-Saharan Africa, Latin America, and South as well as Southeast Asia.

Some noteworthy democratic successes in the Kurdish part of northern Iraq further belie the criticism that Iraq cannot become democratic. Beset by infighting and economic dislocation, among other problems, the Kurds have nonetheless established a reasonably stable form of power sharing. Corruption and tribalism remain problematic, but Iraqi Kurdistan has progressed greatly. At local levels, elections have been free and competitive, the press has considerable freedom, basic civil liberties are secure, and the bureaucracies are responsive to popular concerns and surprisingly accountable. Pluralism—if not full-fledged democracy—is working in Iraqi Kurdistan and working well.

Iraq, in fact, has a number of advantages that would contribute to a successful democracy-building effort; namely, it is perhaps the best endowed of any of the Arab states in terms of both its physical and societal attributes. In addition to its vast oil wealth, Iraq also has tremendous agricultural potential. Prior to the Persian Gulf War, its population was probably the best educated, most secular, and most progressive of all the Arab states. Although it has been devastated economically over the past 12 years, Iraq has many lawyers, doctors, and professors. Together, they could constitute the base of a resurgent Iraqi middle class and thus an important building block of democracy.

Moreover, across the Middle East, popular stirrings indicate the desire for democracy among many people throughout the region. Within the strict parameters of Syrian control, Lebanon once again has a fairly vibrant pluralistic system, while Jordan, Morocco, Kuwait, Qatar, Bahrain, and Yemen have all instituted democratic changes that appear to be building momentum for greater reforms. If poorer, more traditional societies in the Middle East can take steps toward democracy, surely Iraq can take them as well.

## LESSONS FROM OTHER RECENT INTERVENTIONS

A further advantage Iraq would have over other states in a transition to democracy is that U.S. resources would back it up, hopefully along with the assistance of the United Nations and other international organizations. During the last 15 years, numerous efforts to establish democracy after a major international intervention suggest that the same is possible for Iraq. In 1996, after the Dayton peace accords were signed, NATO and the UN created an extensive new program to rebuild Bosnia. Early efforts were disjointed, but the program improved over time. Although Bosnia was hardly a model democracy, by as early as 1998 the U.S. Department of State could brag that Bosnia's GDP had doubled, unemployment was falling, basic services had been restored throughout the country, an independent media was thriving, and public elections had been held for all levels of government.[6]

The Bosnia model was refined and reemployed in Kosovo in 1999 after hostilities ceased, where it worked better because lessons learned in Bosnia were heeded. In particular, the UN Interim Administration Mission in Kosovo planned and coordinated the efforts of international organizations better.[7] The same approach was even more successfully applied in East Timor, where a functional—albeit nascent—democracy is essentially now a reality.

Panama provides another interesting example of U.S. efforts to build democracy. Like Iraq, Panama before 1989 had never experienced anything other than pseudodemocracy in the form of meaningless elections that the ruling junta invalidated whenever it desired. After the U.S. invasion in 1989, the United States instituted Operation Promote Liberty to rebuild Panama economically and politically. Although postinvasion reconstruction in Panama had its fair share of mistakes and inadequacies, Panama today is not doing badly at all. Getting there took roughly 10 years, but it happened.[8]

None of the examples above offers a perfect model for a post-Saddam Iraq. Yet, together they indicate that intervening forces can reduce strife and foster power sharing and that reform movements can blossom in seemingly infertile ground.

## Imagining a Democratic Iraq

Still others who argue against the possibility of democracy in Iraq claim that the nation's unique problems, such as its dangerous neighborhood or explosive communal mix, will pervert elections, freedom of speech, or other democratic building blocks and thus produce illiberal results. Even states with the right foundation can fail if the constitutional system it develops does not match its needs. The failure of the Weimar Republic in Germany, for example, was at least in part the result of a poorly designed democratic system, not the inability of Germans to be democratic. The very features of Iraqi society that make it so difficult to govern and make it unlikely that any system other than a democratic one could ensure stability also demand a democratic system capable of dealing with its serious internal contradictions.

The greatest obstacle to democracy in Iraq is the potential for one group—particularly Iraq's majority Shi'a community—to dominate the country. This problem is not unique to Iraq; it has plagued democracies since their modern inception. As James Madison wrote in 1787:

> Complaints are everywhere heard from our most considerate and virtuous citizens, equally the friends of public and private faith, and of public and personal liberty, that our governments are too unstable, that the public good is disregarded in the conflicts of rival parties, and that measures are too often decided, not according to the rules of justice and the rights of the minor party, but by the superior force of an interested and overbearing majority.[9]

For Madison, the answer was to be found through the cross-cutting identities of U.S. citizens, but Saddam's manipulation of Iraq's ethnic, tribal, and religious divisions have weakened, but not obliterated, such bonds. Thus, the fear is that Iraq's Shi'ite community, which comprises more than 60 percent of the population, might use free elections to transform its current exclusion from power to one of total dominance. Knowing this, Sunni Arabs, and perhaps the Kurds as well, might oppose a majority rule–based system. Thus, the key for an Iraqi democracy will be to fashion a system that addresses the potential problem of a tyranny of the majority.

Envisioning a form of democracy able to cope with Iraq's political problems is, in fact, quite possible. Perhaps surprisingly, a democratic system with some similarities to the U.S. system would appear to best fit the bill. Iraq needs a democratic system that encourages compromise and cooperation among members of otherwise well-defined groupings. Features of Iraqi democracy should include:

- Defining the rights of every individual and limiting trespasses by the central government. In particular, the freedom of language and of religious expression should be expressly noted.

- Declaring that all powers not reserved to the federal government be vested in local governments to constrain the central government further.

- Creating an additional set of checks and balances within the structure of the federal government to limit its powers and particularly to limit the ability of any group to manipulate it to repress other members of Iraqi society.

- Electing a president indirectly, to ensure that different communities have a say in who is chosen. In particular, Iraq should look to other systems (such as Malaysia's) that strive to ensure that candidates are acceptable to multiple constituencies and are not simply imposed on the country by the largest group.

- Employing a system of representation in the legislature that is determined by geography—not pure party affiliation as in many parliamentary systems—to encourage cooperation across ethnic and religious lines.

This last point is an important one in thinking about Iraqi democracy. Although the locations of communities are fairly well correlated to geography (i.e., the Kurds live in the north, the Shi'a in the south, and the Sunnis in the west), there are also important regions of overlap. In Baghdad and in large chunks of central Iraq, Sunni, Shi'a, and Kurds all live together. By insisting on a system of geographically determined representation, Iraqi legislators elected from these mixed districts would have an incentive to find compromise solutions to national problems to try to please their mixed constituencies rather than just one particular community of Iraqis.

Indeed, this points out one of the great risks of a poorly designed parliamentary system—and one of proportional representation in particular—for Iraq. By emphasizing party membership based on communal identity in determining legislative elections, the legislators themselves would have less incentive to try to reach compromises across party lines and much more incentive to follow party ideology slavishly—a system that would tend to push legislators to extremes. Iraqis instead need a system that encourages them to move toward the center and compromise. The U.S. system of geographic representation has become almost infamous for this tendency, so much so that distinguishing among candidates on Election Day is often impossible because they all cling so desperately to the middle ground.

A key difference from a U.S.-style system would be embracing the reality of Iraq's separate and diverse ethnic, tribal, and religious communities—and both working with them and weakening their political influence at the same time. If the electoral system is properly designed, it can also foster moderation, leaving firebrands isolated and out of power. One technique championed by scholar Donald Horowitz is to create political incentives for cross-community cooperation.[10] Malaysia, for example, has successfully overcome tension between Malays, ethnic Chinese, and ethnic Indians using an integrative model that relies on electoral incentives to foster cooperation. Malaysia's system succeeded in part because the country had experienced ethnic violence in the past, which its political leaders then sought to avoid—a possible parallel to Iraq.

## Shepherding the Transition

Because a newborn Iraqi democracy organized on the model sketched above would inevitably begin from a position of weakness, the international community, particularly the United States, must play midwife for democracy to flourish. Even if all goes well, the new government will need years to gain the trust of its people, demonstrate its ability to maintain order and broker compromises, and foster the maturation of democratic institutions. Indeed, the fourth criticism of democracy in Iraq is that even a government designed to ensure that all of Iraq's communities have a voice will not be able to withstand the challenges it will face in its critical early years.

Because Saddam nurtured intercommunal hatred, minor provocations could spiral out of control and spark internecine conflicts in the early months after his fall. As has frequently occurred elsewhere around the world, chauvinistic leaders of all of Iraq's communities might exploit a weak, new government by using their newfound freedoms of speech and assembly to stir up hatred without any penalty. Some groups, particularly the Kurds, might take advantage of a new state's weakness to press for secession. Those who became rich and powerful under the Ba'th regime might use their initial advantages to ensure their continued dominance by ignoring election results. Americans expect losers in elections to leave office gracefully—or at least just to leave. This expectation of a peaceful departure, however, is not universal. Building democratic institutions depends on creating mutual expectations of cooperation and nonaggression both among leaders and the electorate, but developing these expectations requires time and peace to take root.

A weak federal government that was not protected by the United States would also increase the danger of regional strife. Iraq's neighbors have a history of meddling and could take advantage of any weakness to protect their own interests. Turkey may intervene economically, politically, or militarily to ensure that Iraqi Kurds remain weak and do not support Kurdish insurgents within Turkey itself. Ankara already maintains several thousand troops in Iraq to fight its own Kurdish insurgency. Iran may champion its partisans within Iraq's Shi'a community, either by providing them with armed support from Iraqi dissidents residing in Iran or by covertly working with Iraqi Shi'a leaders. Different communities may organize in response to, or in support of, perceived meddling, even when little exists.

These concerns are real, but they are not unmanageable. Critics tend to overlook the success of other international efforts at performing precisely this role in democratic transitions elsewhere around the world.

The UN, the United States, and the coalition of U.S. allies will have to help the new Iraqi government fend off these challenges until it has developed the institutional strength to handle them itself. Minimizing the risks of civil strife, meddling neighbors, and other barriers to successful institutionalization will require the United States to push for and then staunchly back an international effort to address Iraq's political, diplomatic, and security efforts.

Providing security is an essential task for intervening powers. Without internal security, the political process will be badly distorted if not entirely undermined, humanitarian relief becomes impossible, and economic recovery a will o' the wisp. Even in places where the transition to democracy has been rocky, such as Bosnia, a strong international presence has had great success in preserving the peace. The Australian-led effort in East Timor was even more successful—if only because the situation was, in some ways, more challenging—and could provide a good model for a U.S.-led effort in Iraq.

By leading a multinational force of initially at least 100,000 troops with a strong mandate to act throughout Iraq, the United States and its coalition partners will have an excellent prospect of ensuring the degree of security necessary for a successful transition to democracy. In essence, the goal for the U.S.-led peacekeeping force would be to ensure that no group or individual uses violence for political advantage. International security forces will reassure Iraq's Shi'a and Kurdish communities that repression at the hands of Iraqi Sunnis is at an end. Equally important, the presence of these foreign troops would reassure Iraqi Sunnis that the end of their monopoly on power does not mean their persecution and repression, minimizing their incentives to oppose the process. The presence of multinational troops could prevent small incidents from snowballing and thus could help create the expectation of peace within Iraq—an instrumental factor in making peace a reality.

Such a U.S.-led security force would likely affect all aspects of political transition profoundly and discourage, if not eliminate, most efforts to subvert the process by, most obviously, preventing the cancellation or disruption of elections and other elements of democratic institution-building. Preventing hate speech, warmongering, and chauvinism will be more challenging, but tremendous room for influence still exists. By ensuring domestic security and deterring foreign aggression, leaders will find playing on people's fears to gain power far more difficult.

The diplomatic dimension is relatively straightforward. The United States and other concerned powers should encourage Iraq's neighbors to facilitate peace and democratic transition in Iraq and, should this encouragement fail, deter them from intervening. Although autocracies such as the Gulf oil monarchies and other Arab states might be uncomfortable with U.S.-guided democracy in Iraq, stability in Iraq is the overwhelming priority for every single one of them. Thus, the argument that the alternative to democracy is probably not the Sunni strongman they may desire, but warlordism and civil war, will likely prove persuasive. Indeed, in conversations with officials from various Gulf states, we found surprisingly wide recognition of this fear.

Tehran, of course, would be highly concerned about a large U.S. military presence in Iraq and would prefer a pro-Iranian (or at least nonhostile) regime in Baghdad. The presence of a large U.S. troop component within the security force, however, would act as a strong deterrent to Iranian meddling, particularly given the poor condition of Iran's military. At least since Ayatollah Ruhollah Khomeini's death, Tehran has acted cautiously and tried to avoid provocations that might result in U.S. military action.

With Turkey, the situation is more complicated, but the United States still has considerable leverage. Even though relations became strained before the war began, the United States has tremendous influence with Turkey—economically, geostrategically, and as a result of their shared interests in the region. The Europeans possess great influence particularly because of Turkey's bid for membership in the European Union (EU), although skeptical Turks may question when this long-sought goal will ever become a reality. Washington also has enormous influence with the Kurds, who recognize that only the United States has the power and the will to protect their interests in a new, post-Saddam Iraq. The United States and the EU will thus be able to press both the

Kurds and the Turks to reach compromises short of warfare. By convincing the Kurds and others to respect Ankara's concerns regarding northern Iraq, the United States and the EU would greatly reduce Turkey's incentives to interfere in Iraqi politics. In fact, Turkey's readiness to intervene provides Washington with considerable leverage to ensure that the Kurds do not press for secession—because the Kurds understand that the United States will not defend them if they try to secede.

## The Singular Importance of the United States

Although the reconstruction of Iraq should be undertaken within a UN or some other international framework that reassures both the Iraqi people and the rest of the world, the United States nonetheless must actively lead the effort. If Washington shirks this responsibility, the mission will fail.

A security force composed mostly of allied troops or run by the UN in Iraq—as opposed to a strong command structure under UN auspices as was established in East Timor—would lack credibility. Iraq's neighbors, particularly Iran, might play off of fissures in the coalition's relationships to bolster their own influence. Internally, if control of the peacekeeping mission is split among different coalition members, different peacekeeping forces would employ different tactics and rules of engagement, allowing hard-liners in some sectors to foment discord.

Taking the reins of postconflict reconstruction in Iraq does not mean that the United States need retain large forces in Iraq forever. As soon as the security situation is calm and under control, the United States should place its operations under the UN's aegis (though not its control), hopefully as part of a larger international reconstruction effort for Iraq's political and economic sectors. This situation, in turn, should last for several years as the UN, nongovernmental organizations, and multinational security forces gradually devolve the functions of government to a new Iraqi regime—with security last on the list.[11]

Only when a new democratic government has demonstrated that it can govern should the international community, including the United

States, turn to a purely supportive role. Even then, the new regime may need U.S. help to ensure security. We can hope for a quick transition, but we should plan for a long one.

## WILL THE UNITED STATES BE WELCOME?

Critics of pursuing democracy in a post-Saddam Iraq further maintain that the United States will not be capable of playing the role outlined above because a hostile Iraqi people would soon compel U.S. forces to leave Iraq. In the immediate aftermath of Saddam's regime fall, the picture is mixed. Much of Iraq is politically quiescent or quietly pro–United States. In several parts of Iraq, however, angry demonstrations against the U.S. occupation have already occurred, leading critics to say that Iraqis are rejecting the U.S. presence.

We should not rush to judgment. One should recall that, before Operation Enduring Freedom and Operation Allied Force, conventional wisdom in the United States held that the highly nationalistic Afghans, Albanians, and others would not tolerate a long-term presence of outsiders. Today, however, these same people are in no hurry to have the foreigners depart.

The United States would be wise to secure a UN Security Council resolution authorizing a U.S.-led effort within the UN system because a resolution would allow both potential Iraqi leaders and Iraq's neighbors to feel that they are working at the behest of the international community rather than that of Washington. East Timor may be the best model for this. Australian forces ensured order and took the lead on many of the most important aspects of reconstruction, but all within a well-supported UN framework. To demonstrate U.S. goodwill, the United States should move quickly to aid international efforts to rebuild Iraq's infrastructure and help Iraq expand oil production to its full potential. Moreover, during occupation, the U.S.-led security force should work with Iraqis whenever possible. Policing will require local language and local knowledge just as much as it will require U.S. muscle.

The best means of ensuring that a U.S. presence is welcome in Iraq is to make winning over the Iraqi people the number one U.S. mission, even at the price of other important goals. Restoring Iraq's oil infrastructure and using profits to meet Iraq's needs rather than to cover the costs of occupation is one immediate way to generate goodwill. Force protection, while important, should come second to ensuring that intervening forces mingle with the population, visibly help build schools and repair roads, and otherwise take the inevitable risks that are part of fostering a healthy relationship.

## STAYING THE COURSE

A final argument against democratization for Iraq is that the United States' own lassitude will lead to an early withdrawal, leaving Iraq's democracy stillborn. The claim that the United States would not be willing to sustain a lengthy commitment has been made—and disproven—repeatedly. In his new history of U.S. decisionmaking about Germany after World War II, Michael Beschloss relays countless incidents in which senior U.S. policymakers, including President Franklin D. Roosevelt, asserted that the American people would not be willing to keep troops in Europe for more than one or two years. Beschloss quotes then-Senator Burton Wheeler (D-Mont.) charging that the American people would not tolerate a lengthy occupation of Europe, which he called a "seething furnace of fratricide, civil war, murder, disease, and starvation."[12] Similar statements are made about Iraq today by those who claim that the United States will not be willing to do what is necessary to help democracy flourish in Iraq.

In 1950, who would have believed that the United States would maintain troops in South Korea for more than 50 years? Before the U.S. intervention in Bosnia in 1995, many pundits claimed that occupying the Balkans, with its ancient ethnic and religious hatreds, would plunge the country into a quagmire, forcing the United States out, just as had happened in Lebanon and Vietnam. Yet, seven years later, U.S. forces are still in Bosnia. They have not taken a single casualty, and there is no public or private Bosnian clamor for them to leave. Furthermore, Iraq is far more important to the United States than Bosnia. Given the vital U.S. interests in a stable Persian Gulf, fears of U.S. fickleness seem sure to prove just as baseless for Iraq as they have for Germany, Japan, Korea, and Bosnia.

## The Strategic Importance of a Stable, Democratic Iraq

Full-blown democracy in Iraq offers the best prospects for solving Iraq's problems over the long term for several reasons. Democracy would provide a means for Iraq's ethnic and religious groups for reconciling, or at least create political mechanisms for handling, divisions by means other than force. It would create a truly legitimate Iraqi government—one that did not repress any elements of the Iraqi people but instead worked for all of them. For the first time in Iraq's history, the government would serve to enrich its citizenry rather than enrich itself at its citizenry's expense.

Failure to establish democracy in Iraq, on the other hand, would be disastrous. Civil war, massive refugee flows, and even renewed interstate fighting would likely resurface to plague this long-cursed region. Moreover, should democracy fail to take root, this would add credence to charges that the United States cares little for Muslim and Arab peoples—a charge that now involves security as well as moral considerations, as Washington woos the Muslim world in its war on terrorism. The failure to transform Iraq's government tarnished the 1991 military victory over Iraq; more than 10 years later, the United States must not make the same mistake.

## Notes

1. George W. Bush, remarks before the American Enterprise Institute, February 27, 2003, located at www.foreignpolicy.org (electronic version).
2. James Fallows, "The Fifty-First State?" *Atlantic*, November 2002, pp. 53–64, www.theatlantic.com/issues/2002/11/fallows.htm (accessed April 5, 2003).

3. Adam Garfinkle, "The New Missionaries," *Prospect* (April 2003), pp. 22–24.

4. Fallows, "The Fifty-First State?"

5. See Robert J. Barro, "Determinants of Democracy," *Journal of Political Economy* 107, no. 6, pt. 2 (December 1999): 158–183.

6. For detailed accounts of the effort to rebuild Bosnia, see Marchus Cox, "State Building and Post-Conflict Reconstruction: Lessons from Bosnia," *The Rehabilitation of War-Torn Societies*, January 2001 (project coordinated by the Centre for Applied Studies in International Negotiations); National Democratic Institute for International Affairs, "Europe: Central and Eastern: Bosnia-Herzegovina," www.ndi.org/worldwide/cee/bosnia/bosnia_pf.asp (accessed April 5, 2003) (updated June 2002); Bureau of European and Canadian Affairs, U.S. Department of State, "Summary of U.S. Government Policy on Bosnia," July 16, 1998, www.state.gov/www/regions/eur/fs_980716_bosqanda.html (accessed April 5, 2003).

7. For accounts of the effort to rebuild Kosovo, see Curt Tarnoff, "Kosovo: Reconstruction and Development Assistance," *CRS Report for Congress*, June 7, 2001; National Democratic Institute for International Affairs, "Europe: Central and Eastern: Yugoslavia: Kosovo," www.ndi.org/worldwide/cee/kosovo/kosovo_pf.asp (accessed April 5, 2003) (updated June 2002); Steven J. Woehrel and Julie Kim, "Kosovo and U.S. Policy," *CRS Report for Congress*, December 4, 2001; United Nations Interim Administration Mission in Kosovo, "UNMIK at a Glance," www.unmikonline.org/intro.htm (accessed June 25, 2002).

8. On democratization in Panama, see William L. Furlong, "Panama: The Difficult Transition towards Democracy," *Journal of Interamerican Studies and World Affairs* 35, no. 3 (autumn 1993): 19–64; Margaret E. Scranton, "Consolidation after Imposition: Panama's 1992 Referendum," *Journal of Interamerican Studies and World Affairs* 35, no. 3 (autumn 1993): 65–102; Margaret E. Scranton, "Panama's First Post-Transition Election," *Journal of Interamerican Studies and World Affairs* 37, no. 1 (spring 1995): 69–100; Karin Von Hippel, *Democracy by Force: U.S. Military Intervention in the Post–Cold War World* (Cambridge: Cambridge University Press, 2000).

9. This text may be found at http://memory.loc.gov/const/fed/fed_10.html (accessed February 26, 2003).

10. For the best description of this process, see Donald Horowitz, *Ethnic Groups in Conflict* (Berkeley, Calif.: University of California Press, 1985), pp. 395–440; Donald Horowitz, "Making Moderation Pay," in *Conflict and Peacemaking in Multiethnic Societies*, ed. Joseph Monteville (New York: Lexington, 1991), pp. 451–476; Richard Stubbs, "Malaysia: Avoiding Ethnic Strife in Deeply Divided Societies," in *Conflict and Peacemaking in Multiethnic Societies*, ed. Joseph Monteville (New York: Lexington, 1991), p. 287.

11. For more on postconflict reconstruction, see the series of six articles in "Nation Building's Successor," *The Washington Quarterly* 25, no. 4 (autumn 2002):

83–168; Council on Foreign Relations, "Guiding Principles for U.S. Post-Conflict Policy in Iraq," 2003 (the report of an independent working group cosponsored by the Council on Foreign Relations and the James A. Baker III Institute for Public Policy of Rice University); Rick Barton and Bathsheba Crocker, "Winning the Peace in Iraq," *The Washington Quarterly* 26, no. 2 (spring 2003): 7–22.

12. Michael Beschloss, *The Conquerors: Roosevelt, Truman and the Destruction of Hitler's Germany, 1941–1945* (New York: Simon and Schuster, 2002), p. 175.

**Dawn Brancati**

# Can Federalism Stabilize Iraq?

The United States devoted nine months to planning the war in Iraq and a mere 28 days to planning the peace, according to senior U.S. military officials. Much more time has to be invested in the peace, however, if the military achievements of the war are to be preserved and a stable democracy is to be created in Iraq. Establishing a governmental system that can accommodate Iraq's different ethnic and religious groups, previously kept in check by the political and military repression of the Saddam Hussein regime, is paramount to securing that peace. In the absence of a system uniquely designed toward this end, violent conflicts and demands for independence are likely to engulf the country. If not planned precisely to meet the specific ethnic and religious divisions at play, any democratic government to emerge in Iraq is bound to prove less capable of maintaining order than the brutal dictatorship that preceded it.

By dividing power between two levels of government—giving groups greater control over their own political, social, and economic affairs while making them feel less exploited as well as more secure—federalism offers the only viable possibility for preventing ethnic conflict and seces-

Dawn Brancati is a visiting scholar at the Center for the Study of Democratic Politics at Princeton University. The author would like to thank Jack Snyder for his comments and support; Rachel Bronson, Daniel Geffen, and Ruth Ben-Artzi for their regional expertise; and Brendan O'Leary for his constructive comments, which contrast with some of the views presented here.

The Washington Quarterly • 27:2 pp. 7–21.

sionism as well as establishing a stable democracy in Iraq. Yet, not just any kind of federal system can accomplish this. Rather, a federal system granting regional governments extensive political and financial powers with borders drawn along ethnic and religious lines that utilize institutionalized measures to prevent identity-based and regional parties from dominating the government is required. Equally critical to ensuring stability and sustainable democracy in Iraq, the new federal system of government must secure the city of Kirkuk, coveted for its vast oil reserves and pipelines, in the Kurdish-controlled northern region to assure that the Kurds do not secede from Iraq altogether.

For its part, the United States must take a more active role in advising Iraqi leaders to adopt a federal system of government along these lines. Such a system will help the United States not only to build democracy in Iraq but also to prevent the emergence of a Shi'a-dominated government in the country. Without this form of federalism, an Iraq rife with internal conflict and dominated by one ethnic or religious group is more likely to emerge, undermining U.S. efforts toward establishing democracy in Iraq as well as the greater Middle East.

## Dividing Lines in Iraq

By definition, democracy aims to provide representation and protection for the rights of everyone in society. Creating and sustaining such a system in Iraq, without opening the door to ethnic conflict, is no easy task. According to the former U.S. ambassador to the United Nations and chief negotiator of the 1995 Dayton accords, Richard Holbrooke, "To govern this country as a democracy would be very hard, since a true democracy would almost certainly lead to Shiite, Sunni, and Kurdish leaders who hold extreme positions. This would be worse than Bosnia, because the passions are much deeper, and the Bosnian war will not resume, whereas fighting between Sunnis, Shiites, and Kurds could easily begin any day if we aren't there."[1]

Specifically, establishing a democratic government in Iraq risks empowering identity-based parties, which, as the name alludes, represent only one ethnic, linguistic, or religious group in a country, and may suppress the

## Map I: Ethno-Linguistic Groups in Iraq

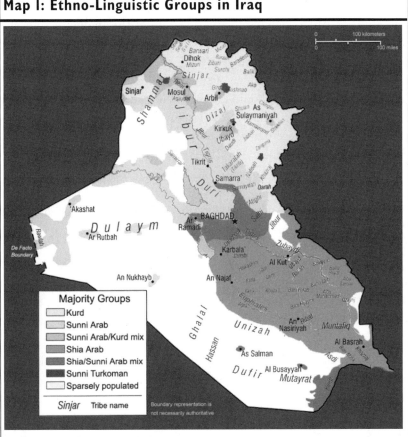

Source: *Iraq: A Country Profile* (Washington, D.C.: Central Intelligence Agency, 2003), www.lib.utexas.edu/maps/middle_east_and_asia/iraq_ethno_2003.jpg.

rights of other groups in the country. Three major identity groups are present in Iraq with a long history of strife among them. These groups are divided along ethnic and religious lines. Arabs are Iraq's largest ethnic group, comprising about 75 percent of Iraq's population and living primarily in the central and southern parts of the country, while Kurds comprise about 20 percent, living primarily in the north. Most Arabs are Muslims although they belong to two different sects of Islam: 55–65 percent of Iraqis are Shi'a Muslims, and 30–40 percent are Sunni Muslims.

The two sects' views of the Muslim leadership distinguish them from one another. Shi'as believe in the doctrine of the Imamate whereby leaders of the Muslim community should be descendants of the Prophet Muhammad and, thus, Ali ibn Abi Taleb, the son-in-law of the Prophet, should be the historical leader of the Muslim community. In contrast, Sunnis believe Muslims should choose their leaders based on their own attributes and do not support Abi Taleb. Although many other differences distinguish these two sects of Islam, they are rooted primarily in this basic disagreement.

Kurds are the second-largest ethnic group in Iraq and live primarily in the northern part of the country. In Iraq, ethnic and religious lines crosscut each other because both Arabs and Kurds are Muslims. Most Kurds are Sunni although some subscribe to the Yazidi religion, which is composed of elements of Christianity, Islam, and Judaism. Rounding out Iraq's ethnic map are Turkomans and Assyrians, with less than 5 percent of the country's population.

Relations between Arabs and Kurds have historically provided the greatest source of tension in Iraq. The Iraqi government has not only consistently excluded Kurds from positions of power but also tried to assimilate them into the country. As part of a program of Arabization, Saddam's government tried to assimilate non-Arabs by preventing them from publicly speaking in their own languages or being schooled in them and by pressuring them to adopt Arab names and to declare themselves as Arabs in official government documents, including identification papers and national censuses.

Saddam's regime combined these methods with the use of military force. The government specifically tried to undermine the Kurds' strength in the north by expelling them from the region and, in the process, razed thousands of Kurdish villages and killed hundreds of thousands of Kurds. More than 100,000 Kurds died in the infamous 1988 Anfal campaign alone, in which the Iraqi government used chemical weapons against them.[2]

Although ethnic tensions undoubtedly have been stronger, religious tensions have also been intense in Iraq, even beyond the Iran-Iraq War, when Iraqi Shi'as supported their Sunni-led government against Iran's Shi'a-controlled government. Even though the Shi'as are the country's largest religious group, the Sunnis have traditionally held more power. Even before Saddam came to power, Sunnis were favored in the country, with most Ba'th Party positions held by Sunnis as well as most of the top posts in the security forces. During his 24 years of power, Saddam deliberately favored the Sunnis and prevented Shi'as from practicing their own religion, arresting, expelling, or murdering clerics perceived as a threat to his power.

Following the Persian Gulf War in 1991, the Shi'as in the south, sometimes known as "the Marsh Arabs," tried to overthrow Saddam's regime. The Iraqi army retaliated, killing thousands of Shi'as as well as thousands of Kurds who separately rebelled against the regime. The government subsequently moved away from its secular foundation and attempted to nationalize religion, even establishing Sunni Islamic radio stations in Iraq, further increasing tensions between the two sects. When a prominent Shi'a cleric was executed by the regime in 1999, the Shi'as rose up again, this time in Basra. The government arrested and tortured thousands of Shi'as and even killed many—just how many remains unclear as the mass graves from the uprising are only now being uncovered.[3]

Although there are several different ethnic and religious groups in Iraq and a history of conflict among these groups, it is still possible to construct a stable democracy in Iraq for several reasons. Whatever their primary motivations, these groups have demonstrated support for federalism, and the fact that religious and ethnic cleavages in Iraq are indeed crosscutting could help moderate behavior and even help develop political parties across religious and ethnic lines—that is, as long as it is within the proper federal political structure.

## Common Ground

Ethnically diverse countries such as Belgium, Canada, India, Spain, and Switzerland have all constructed stable democracies through federalism. Tensions among Iraq's different ethnic and religious groups are no stronger or more volatile than tensions have been at one time or another in many of those countries. These tensions have even erupted into violence at various times in India, Spain, and Switzerland. Moreover, within the correct political framework, Iraq's crosscutting cleavages may conspire to make people behave more moderately. They may provide the basis for parties to mobilize groups across ethnic and religious lines, focusing politics on issues that are not ethnic or religious in nature, and may thereby defuse tensions. They may also promote more moderate policies on ethnic and religious issues. Whether Iraq is able to establish a stable democracy ultimately depends on the design of its system of federalism.

The Kurds are federalism's most zealous supporters in Iraq. Although some, including those who endorse federalism, want independence, most Iraqi Kurds are pragmatic and recognize that independence is not feasible given Turkey's adamant opposition to it. Turkey opposes Kurdish independence, fearing that it may spark a similar movement among Kurds in Turkey. Federalism is thus the Kurds next-best option, as it will give them control over many political and social issues that affect their lives as well as the ability to protect their identities against onslaughts they have experienced in the past.

Iraq's two main Kurdish parties, the Kurdistan Democratic Party (KDP) and the Patriotic Union of Kurdistan (PUK), have both endorsed federalism. According to Mas'ud Barzani, head of the KDP, federalism "will unite Iraq and solve its old and complicated problems" as well as "bolster Iraq's national unity and sovereignty."[4] Similarly, Jalal Talabani, PUK founder and secretary general, claims federalism will "protect the unity of Iraq" and ensure "the fulfillment of all the legitimate rights and demands of the people of Iraq."[5]

Federalism seems to be the system of choice for more than just the Kurds. In fact, all Iraqi leaders that opposed the regime before it collapsed have expressed their support for federalism in Iraq. The Iraqi opposition first voiced its support for federalism in December 2002 at the London conference of opposition leaders that included Kurds, Sunnis, and Shi'as. The members of the conference agreed that "[n]o future state of Iraq will be democratic if it is not federal at the same time in structure."[6] Federalism, they claim, is a necessary form of democracy because federalism protects the will of the minority against the will of the majority.

The U.S.-led coalition forces have voiced their support for federalism as well, allowing the Kurds to have their own semiautonomous region in the new Iraq while opposing independence for that region. The United States has not developed a concrete plan for federalism in Iraq, however, nor has it taken a position on the more controversial issues surrounding federalism, such as whether regional governments should have extensive power or whether Iraq should build the regional governments along or across ethnic and religious lines (although the Senate Foreign Relations Committee has discussed this point some). The U.S. government has also declined to take a position on whether the Kurds should control Kirkuk and has insisted, more broadly, that the Iraqi people should determine for themselves what system of government to adopt. Its position, or lack thereof, may be partially informed by the desire to allow Iraqis to decide how to govern their country themselves.

Clear opposition to federalism both within Iraq and in the Middle East region is also significant. Turkey, for example, fears that a federal system of government in Iraq that entitles the Kurds to their own regional government within Iraq and to control over Kirkuk's oil fields will encourage Iraqi Kurds to seek an independent state and, subsequently, lead the Kurds in Turkey to follow suit. Turkey's foreign minister, Abdullah Gul, has stated that Turkey will intervene militarily to prevent Kirkuk from becoming the capital of Iraq's Kurdish region.[7] When Kurdish forces entered the cities of Kirkuk and Mosul last March, Turkey even sent troops into northern Iraq to guarantee, according to Gul, "Iraq's territorial integrity."[8]

Iraqi minority groups in the northern part of the country also have reservations about establishing federalism in Iraq out of fear that the Kurds will discriminate against them in any Kurdish-dominated region that is created. Although the Kurdistan Regional Government (KRG), which was established under the protection of the no-fly zone created by the United States following the Persian Gulf War and is comprised of the two main Kurdish parties and a coalition of Christians and Assyrians, has promised to respect all people's rights, some minorities such as the Turkomans and Assyrians fear that a Kurdish regional government would harm their minority rights by protecting Kurdish identities and passing laws prohibiting non-Kurds from using their own language, practicing their own religion, or gaining rightful employment. The president of the Iraqi Turkoman Front, San'an Ahmad Agha, has warned, "If one group tries to favor itself over another ... it will lead to civil war. If there is a division, there will be an ethnic war."[9]

Despite their reservations, minority groups generally recognize the futility of opposing a federal government for Iraq, should the parliament adopt one. According to Agha, "Citizens have to comply with and accept whatever is ratified by the future parliament. If an act gains 99 percent of the votes, but there is a minority in the parliament with different opinions ... those with an opinion that falls into a minority have to comply with and accept the opinion of the majority."[10]

Its legitimate fear of imposing any form of government rather than allowing the Iraqis to choose a new government for themselves notwithstanding, the United States must actively promote federalism in the country. The failure to do so will prevent the United States from achieving its goal of creating a stable and democratic government in Iraq and may make Iraq more of a threat to U.S. security than it was before the war. Although what form of government to adopt ultimately will and should be the decision of the Iraqi people, U.S. officials must advise the Iraqi Governing Council to adopt federalism and must continue to assure Turkey that the United States does not support, and is willing to use political and economic incentives to discourage, Kurdish independence, should the Kurds decide to secede. By reassuring Turkey that the Kurds will not secede, the United States can make a federal system of government possible in Iraq.

The climbing number of casualties the United States has suffered since President George W. Bush declared major combat operations in Iraq over in early May 2003 has clearly enhanced the U.S. interest in turning Iraq over to the Iraqi people as soon as possible. Yet, a hasty turnover would be a grave mistake. The United States cannot transfer authority in Iraq until a new federal system of government has been established and until more than one democratic election has occurred without violence.

## Empowering the Positive, Eliminating the Negative

The most effective kind of federalism to ensure a stable, self-sustainable democracy in Iraq must be developed along the following lines.

### THE DIVISION OF POLITICAL AND FINANCIAL POWERS

First and foremost, federalism must be extensive in Iraq to ensure that the regional governments have considerable political and financial powers—an essential component for ensuring governmental protection for Iraq's various ethnic and religious groups and for preventing ethnic conflict and secessionism. Federalism has failed in countries such as Indonesia, Malaysia, and Nigeria precisely because it did not go far enough in granting regional autonomy. If regional governments are granted certain powers in principal but denied these powers in practice or given only modest powers in the first place, federalism is guaranteed to fail.

At a minimum, Iraq's regional governments should control language policy and education to enable the Shi'as and Kurds to protect their identities, which have been eroded in the past by the Iraqi government. The regional governments may also control other social, economic, and political issues such as health, unemployment, and intraregional trade, depending on the specific demands of different groups for autonomy, which are not yet apparent. The federal government should retain control, however, over issues affecting the entire country such as defense, foreign affairs, currency, citizenship, and infrastructure. Individual ethnic and religious groups in Iraq should also be integrated within a national military force with fair representation of all groups; allowing each region to have its own military force would make secession and ethnic conflict all the more likely.

Under the new federal system, Iraq's regional governments should also have considerable financial powers that allow them to legislate on economic policies that address needs specific to their region and to raise their own revenue so that they can pursue them. Without independent sources of revenue, the regional governments will remain dependent on the central government for funding. This will not only undermine their political autonomy but also prevent them from implementing the policies they create.

With most of Iraqi revenue coming from oil sales, the entire country should share in that revenue. If not, large disparities in wealth will develop across the country. The oil-rich regions, however, should receive a greater share of the oil revenue generated in Iraq because they produce more of this revenue in the first place and have incurred many externalities in the production of the oil, including the destruction of their local environment. Failure to compensate oil-rich regions for their oil could just as easily lead to future resentment as wealth inequalities might. Although it may be a fine line between the two extremes of regional control and national equitable distribution, some formula splitting the difference should be developed at the national level of government.

This kind of policy is consistent with the Kurds' demands. The Kurds want each of the country's regions to receive a portion of all the revenue in Iraq, including oil revenue, according to the size of its population. The Kurds' plan may not go far enough, however, to prevent the secession of Kurds from Iraq in the long term. If the Kurds do not receive a larger share of the oil revenue generated in Iraq than the size of their population warrants, they may decide to secede from the country in the future, should they find they do not have the money to finance the new policies and projects they devise.

The situation in Nigeria, also with abundant oil reserves, illustrates the potential problems the division of oil revenue could pose in a federal Iraq. Oil-rich regions in Nigeria have complained vociferously that they have incurred various economic and environmental costs in producing oil and, thus, deserve a greater share of the oil revenue. These demands have erupted into violence, with guerrilla groups even sabotaging oil pipelines to draw the attention of the national government. In response, the Nigerian government promised the oil-rich regions at least 13 percent more of the country's oil revenue than the oil-poor regions. Unfortunately, there are no checks in Nigeria on how this revenue is spent. So, intense and often violent competition for control of this revenue has occurred in the oil-rich region of the Delta as well as for control of the illegal bunkering of oil in the region.

Again, for its part, Turkey's opinion on just how much power should be allotted for the Iraqi regional governments centers around its fears of Kurdish attempts at secession. Turkey fears that giving the regional governments in Iraq too much political and financial power will bolster Kurdish interest in independence, even though the Kurds have expressed their support for staying within Iraq. Conflict is more likely to result, however, if the Kurds feel they are not given enough political and financial autonomy. When Iraq agreed to cede some autonomy to the Kurds in 1970, the Kurds rejected the plan because it did not give their regional government enough political power and did not include Kirkuk within their fold. Intense fighting ensued between the government and the Kurds when the government tried to impose its policy over the objections of the Kurds.

## REGIONAL BORDERS ALONG, NOT ACROSS, ETHNIC AND RELIGIOUS LINES

Although additional precautions will have to be taken to prevent identity-based parties from dominating the government, the borders of the regional governments in Iraq should be drawn along ethnic and/or religious lines so that the three major groups in the country have significant control over their own political, social, and economic affairs. Drawing Iraq's regional borders along, rather than across, ethnic and religious lines would create three distinct regional governments in Iraq in which the Kurds, Shi'as, and Sunnis each have a majority. The Kurds are particularly supportive of drawing Iraq's regional borders this way, as establishing a federal system of government divided along purely religious lines would divide the greater Iraqi Kurdish population into separate regions. The Sunnis would also benefit from such a scenario because they are outnumbered by Shi'as in the country and would be unrepresented in a centralized system of government where the largest groups in the country would have the most power.

Many scholars fear that drawing Iraq's regional borders along ethnic or religious lines will increase the likelihood of ethnic conflict and secessionism by strengthening ethnic and religious identities in the country. They point to cases of failed federations in the former Soviet Union, Czechoslovakia, and Yugoslavia as examples of what could result from drawing borders along ethnic and religious lines in Iraq. Yet, drawing regional borders along these lines in and of itself will not promote ethnic conflict or secessionism. Regional borders drawn along these lines in Belgium and Switzerland, for example, as well as others did not experience such misfortune. Rather, ethnic conflict and secessionism only become a real threat when identity-based parties dominate national and regional governments, as was the case in Czechoslovakia and Yugoslavia, and are able to reinforce ethnic and religious identities; use incendiary language to elevate tensions among groups; and turn all issues, even those only remotely related to ethnicity or religion, such as infrastructure and the environment, into questions of ethnicity and religion as well as autonomy from the federal government.

Banning identity-based parties outright is not the best way to rid Iraq of identity-based parties, as such an effort may jeopardize the democratic system as a whole. Instead, to prevent the emergence of identity-based parties effectively, the designers of the new federal system should construct the rest of Iraq's political system to encourage parties to widen their support bases. For example, adopting cross-regional voting laws would accomplish this by requiring parties to compete in a certain number of regions and to win a certain percentage of the vote in these regions to be elected to the federal government. Russia, Indonesia, and Nigeria have such cross-regional voting laws that have prevented identity-based parties from forming.

Iraq might also adopt a presidential system of government, a step currently supported by the Kurds and the Iraqi National Congress. Presidential systems of government are less favorable to regional parties because directly elected presidents need more cross-regional support to get elected than do prime ministers who are chosen by a parliament. Such design features would help prevent identity-based parties from forming in a national government even when each of the regions is comprised principally of one ethnic or religious group. Under a presidential system, parties would have to represent more than one ethnic and religious group if they are to have a certain amount of support in more than one region of the country.

Drawing Iraq's borders along ethnic and religious lines, however, may promote ethnic conflict by creating regional minorities within the subnational governments. As map 1 shows, creating completely homogenous regions in Iraq is impossible because Iraq's different ethnic and religious groups are intermixed in some areas of the country. Relocating these groups to different regions would also foster ethnic conflict or secessionism, as the partitioning of India did following World War II. By passing laws that discriminated against or ignored the demands of regional minorities, parties in regional governments such as Assam, Nagaland, and Mizoram have instigated ethnic conflict and demands by these minorities for separate regional governments in India.

In Nigeria as well, identity-based parties have attempted to expand the shari'a, a body of Islamic law, leading to conflict between Muslims and Christian Igbos in the north. To prevent the occurrence of such situations in Iraq, the national government must prohibit any laws that discriminate against other groups in the regional governments and allow grievances relating to discrimination to be brought before the constitutional court for redress.

The most often preferred alternative to drawing borders along ethnic and religious lines is to draw regional government borders across ethnic and religious lines in the hopes of weakening Iraqis' ethnic and religious identities.[11] Some have even suggested using the country's

## Map 2: Ethno-Linguistic Groups in Iraq's 18 Administrative Districts

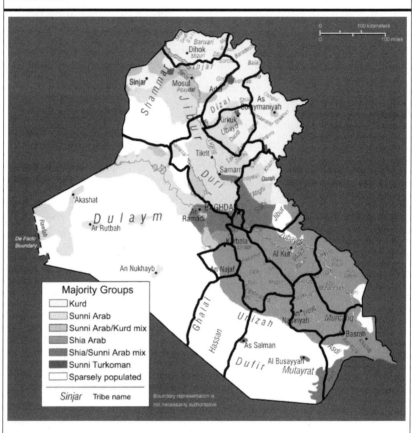

Source: *Iraq: A Country Profile* (Washington, D.C.: Central Intelligence Agency, 2003), www.lib.utexas.edu/maps/middle_east_and_asia/iraq_ethno_2003.jpg. Note: The ethnographic and administrative maps of Iraq are transposed on one another.

18 administrative districts as the borders of these new regional governments. Many Arabs, who support federalism, support this proposal. The Iraqi National Congress also supports dividing Iraq into several regions but not along its current administrative borders, which would underrepresent the Shi'a majority.

The greatest advantage in drawing Iraq's borders along ethnic and religious lines rather than across them is that this design is much more likely to prevent the dominance of identity-based parties. When regional borders are drawn along ethnic and religious lines, other institutions in a country, such as cross-regional voting laws and presidential systems of government, can prevent identity-based parties from dominating the government. With regional borders drawn across ethnic and religious lines, however, identity-based parties can arise because parties could compete throughout the country and represent only one ethnic or religious group in the country. The only way to prevent identity-based parties from dominating the government under this plan would be to ban them outright or to require parties to meet certain ethnic or religious quotas. Not only are both of these mechanisms undemocratic, they are also likely to meet strong opposition from the parties themselves.

Such is the situation in India, where the Bharatiya Janata Party (BJP) competes throughout India but only draws support from Hindus in the country. The BJP's pro-Hindu policies, which have included the razing of the Muslim mosque in Ayodyha and demands for a uniform civil code that eliminates special provisions for Muslims, have spawned significant conflict between Hindus and Muslims. Drawing regional lines across ethnic and religious lines might similarly lead to identity-based parties that represent Sunni Muslims, Shi'a Muslims, and Kurds in the country and that promote policies favoring their own groups and harming others. On the other hand, regional borders drawn along ethnic and religious lines, in conjunction with mechanisms such as cross-regional voting laws or presidentialism, can avoid such devastating consequences.

## KIRKUK

Finally, to diminish the likelihood of ethnic conflict and secessionism in Iraq, Kirkuk must be included in the Kurdish-controlled region that is created. The Kurds have a legitimate claim to this city. Kurds predominantly comprise the population of Kirkuk and would even more so had Saddam Hussein's regime not expelled them from the city and forced Arabs to take their place as part of its Arabization campaign. Moreover, Kurdish leaders have pledged to respect the rights of minorities in the city, which should allay the fears of minorities in the region. According to PUK leader Talabani, "We consider this city, Kirkuk, as a city of multinational fraternity because it is the city of Kurds, Turkomans, Arabs, and Chaldo-Assyrians. This city must be the symbol of fraternity of peoples of Iraq and of real Iraqi citizenship based on equality."[12]

Moreover, the Kurds are unlikely to accept any agreement in which Kirkuk is not included as part of a Kurdish-controlled region, as demonstrated by their inclusion of Kirkuk in the Constitution of the Iraqi Kurdistan Region, which was adopted by the KRG following the Gulf War and has governed the region ever since. The strength of the Kurds' attachment to the city was also demonstrated in their rejection of the 1970 autonomy agreement offered by the Iraqi government because it did not include Kirkuk in their region. If the Kurds are not given control over Kirkuk, they may not only reject any agreement that is presented to them but also may attempt to secede from the country and take Kirkuk with them.

Afraid that control of Kirkuk will avail the Kurds of the financial strength to declare an independent state, however, Turkey has indicated its intention to invade Iraq should the Kurds receive control over the city. Securing Kirkuk in the Kurdish territory will require assuring Turkey that the Kurds will not secede. In the short term, the United States may provide such a guarantee to Turkey based on the U.S. military presence in Iraq and opposition to the Kurds' independence. Another way to assure Turkey that the Kurds will not secede in the short term, or the long term for that matter, is to prevent the Kurds from controlling all the oil revenue generated in Kirkuk, which would greatly diminish the Kurds' apparent financial strength and thus lessen the likelihood of their declaring an independent state. As discussed earlier, such an arrangement would likely meet the approval of the Kurds as well; they have only requested a share of the oil revenue commensurate with the Kurdish proportion of Kirkuk's population.

## Not Just Any Federal System

The potential consequences of failing to design federalism properly and to establish a stable democracy in Iraq extend far beyond Iraqi borders. Civil war in Iraq may draw in neighboring countries such as Turkey and Iran, further destabilizing the Middle East in the process. It may also discourage foreign investment in the region, bolster Islamic extremists, and exacerbate tensions between Palestinians and Israelis. A civil war in Iraq may even undermine support for the concept of federalism more generally, which is significant given the number of countries also considering federalism, such as Afghanistan and Sri Lanka, to name just two. Finally, the failure to design and implement the kind of federalism that can establish a stable democracy in Iraq might undermine international support for other U.S. initiatives in the region, including negotiations for Arab-Israeli peace. Iraq's federal government must therefore be designed carefully so as to give regional governments extensive political and financial autonomy, to include Kirkuk in the Kurdish region that is created, and to limit the influence of identity-based political parties. The short- and long-term stability of Iraq and the greater Middle East depend on it.

## Notes

1. "Holbrooke Says U.S. Must Prepare for Long Stay in Iraq, Calls on Bush to Make Major Effort to Repair Ties with France," *Council of Foreign Relations*, April 18, 2003, www.cfr.org/publication.php?id=5871 (accessed January 4, 2004) (interview by Bernard Gwertzman).

2. Human Rights Watch, *Iraq's Crime of Genocide: The Anfal Campaign Against the Kurds* (New Haven: Yale University Press, 1995).

3. Andrew Clennell, "Mass Grave Found Near Kirkuk, Claims Kurdish TV Station," *Independent* (London), April 18, 2003.

4. "Kurdish Leader Barzani Believes Federalism Is the Answer," *BBC Worldwide Monitoring*, December 1, 2002.

5. "Iraqi Kurdish PUK Paper Praises President Bush's 'Endorsement' of Federalism," *BBC Monitoring International Reports*, March 8, 2003.

6. Conference of the Iraqi Opposition, *Final Report on the Transition to Democracy in Iraq*, November 2002, www.wadinet.de/news/dokus/transition_to_democracy.pdf

(accessed January 2, 2003) (amended by the members of the Democratic Principles Workshop).

7. Suna Erdem and Roland Watson, "U.S. Assures Turks that Kurds Will Withdraw," *Times* (London), April 11, 2003.

8. Mike Blanchfield, "Turks Enter Northern Iraq," *Gazette*, March 22, 2003.

9. Stefan Smith, "Iraqi Turkoman Leader Warns Kurdish Ambitions Could Spark Civil War," Agence France Presse, February 14, 2003.

10. "Turkoman Leader Reaffirms Commitment to Iraqi Territorial Unity," *BBC Worldwide Monitoring*, February 12, 2003.

11. "Guiding Principles for U.S. Post-Conflict Policy in Iraq," 2003, www3.cfr.org/pdf/Post-War_Iraq.pdf (accessed January 4, 2004) (report of an Independent Working Group Cosponsored by the Council on Foreign Relations and the James A. Baker III Institute for Public Policy of Rice University); Adeed Dawisha and Karen Lee Dawisha, "How to Build a Democratic Iraq," *Foreign Affairs* (May/June 2003): 36–50.

12. "Iraqi Kurdish PUK Leader Calls for Multi-Ethnic Administration for Kirkuk," *BBC Worldwide Monitoring*, April 14, 2003.

Jon B. Alterman

# Not in My Backyard: Iraq's Neighbors' Interests

The Bush administration's Middle East strategy has some rather expansive goals. Unwilling to content itself merely with eliminating the terrorist threat posed by Al Qaeda or forcing Saddam Hussein's regime from power, the administration has committed itself to creating a post-Saddam Iraq that will be an exemplar to the region: a nation that is strong, democratic, and free. As such, the administration is betting that the new Iraq will lead to the rise of liberty, freedom, and democracy in the Middle East; extinguish the flames of regional radicalism; and hold the key to resolving the Arab-Israeli conflict. In the words of Deputy Secretary of Defense Paul Wolfowitz, one of the chief proponents of Iraqi-led political change in the region, successful political change in Iraq is "going to cast a very large shadow, starting with Syria and Iran, but across the whole Arab world."[1] Sadly, the administration is betting on a long shot. Even worse, it undermines its own goals by talking about them so much.

Will unfolding events in Iraq improve conditions in the region? Unfortunately, the answer is probably not, and some of the biggest impediments to any resulting improvement come from Iraq's neighbors. Some

Jon B. Alterman is a senior fellow and director of the Middle East Program at CSIS. He wishes to thank Stephanie Denton and Kari Frame for their research assistance.

The Washington Quarterly • 26:3 pp. 149–160.

of them, such as Saudi Arabia and Turkey, are U.S. allies; others, for example, Iran and Syria, are not, but all these states share something in common: they find the U.S. vision for the future of Iraq and the region deeply threatening. Even more troubling, they have the means to keep that vision from coming to pass.

Regional states still play important spoiler roles in the Middle East. Their concerns cannot be brushed away, and the United States cannot intimidate them into slavish submission. Frustrating as it may be, broad and patient engagement is a surer way forward for the United States than rapid conquest. Bold and inspirational plans concocted in Washington may have their appeal in Georgetown salons, but in the fields of the Fertile Crescent, they are likely to turn arid long before they yield democratic fruit in Baghdad—or Cairo, Riyadh, or Tehran.

## The Reality of Democracy: All Things Considered?

This assessment does not argue that Arabs should be condemned to live under dictatorships nor that the U.S. government should seek a quick exit from involvement in Iraqi affairs. Few from within or outside the region would argue that the administration's vision of the Middle East is unattractive. The region's populations have too long suffered under governments that are authoritarian or worse; economic growth has been anemic while the youth unemployment rate has been high; and the people have been flirting with a radical rejectionism that threatens U.S. security but, even more fundamentally, threatens their own future. This rejectionism can take many forms, from the religious embrace of Osama bin Laden to a nationalist embrace of Palestinian suicide bombers, but it has two primary characteristics: an unrelenting sense of anger and a quixotic desire to overturn the existing order completely and replace it with an ill-defined utopian future.

When President George W. Bush said in February 2002 that "[a] new regime in Iraq would serve as a dramatic and inspiring example of freedom for other nations in the region,"[2] he was not setting his sights low. Although the task of establishing democracy in Iraq is not impossible, its enormity is impressive. In fact, several of the country's characteristics make it one of the more unlikely places to establish a strong democracy quickly that will inspire change throughout the Middle East. Consider:

• The people of Iraq have lived under a brutal dictatorship for a third of a century, during which dependence on authority has been nurtured and independent thought has been deadly. Changing mindsets will have to be an educational process that will take years and decades to accomplish.

• The Ba'th regime in Iraq accentuated sectarian, ethnic, tribal, and clan differences in Iraq as a means of maintaining political control. Through this system, the government was able to reward supporters and punish dissenters. Democracies, however, rely on shifting coalitions as voters give voice to their multiple identities. If Iraqis' political interests are based solely on their ethnic identity, the result will not be democracy but factionalism. Again, changing Iraqis' self-image will be a long-term process.

• The high-stakes battle for control between insiders and outsiders in Iraq is unlikely to be short lived. The professional expatriates who cursed the regime from London and Washington—in some cases for decades—will not retreat quietly. Neither will those who suffered under Saddam's regime forgo their rewards. Added to the mix, of course, will be mid-level Ba'thists who will seek to replicate the feat of those former Soviet officials who used their privileged positions in the *ancien régime* to profit when that regime crumbled.

Even if these formidable elements should prove surmountable over time, the most complicating factor in U.S. designs will remain the reality that not one of Iraq's neighbors shares the Bush administration's interests in establishing a strong and democratic state to serve as a beacon of hope and freedom to the region. Equally troubling, most of these countries have considerable experience stirring political pots beyond their borders, generally covertly and with full deniability. The boldness of the Bush administration's proclamation of its political goals for the region, then, is likely to have the opposite effect of the one intended. Rather than laying the groundwork for a democratic Iraq to inspire change throughout the Middle East, the U.S. government has only made democracy in Iraq and elsewhere even harder to achieve. A survey of the countries surrounding Iraq paints a daunting picture for would-be U.S. reformers there.

## Iran

First on the troubling list is Iran. Having lost hundreds of thousands of soldiers in an eight-year war instigated by Saddam, one would think that the Iranian government would celebrate his downfall. Although Iran's leaders will certainly not miss Saddam in many respects, Iran has also been perfectly content to live with the conditions of the last dozen years. A long-term U.S. troop presence in the Persian Gulf checked Iraqi aggression, and sanctions imposed on Iraq by the United Nations stymied Baghdad's ability to maintain its military power, let alone rebuild it. Far from exacerbating tensions, U.S. naval forces in the Gulf worked out an informal modus vivendi with their Iranian counterparts several years ago, and incidents of conflict are rare. In addition, popular discontent among Gulf Arabs about the U.S. troop presence in the region benefits the Iranians. As the primary Gulf government opposed to the U.S. presence, Iran is seen at least in part as the power balancing U.S. hegemony, not just as a threatening non-Arab power to the north.

Economically as well, Iran has benefited from the status quo. First, smuggling proceeds have provided a helpful source of revenue, especially for the Iranian Revolutionary Guard Corps, whose forces control some of the trade. Second, a struggling Iraqi oil industry has helped protect Iran's share of the global oil market and maintain stable and sometimes high prices for oil.

Change in Baghdad alters almost all these equations to the detriment of the Iranians. A strong Iraq in pursuit of better port access could seek Iranian territory, as Saddam did in 1980. Iranian smuggling revenues will plunge precipitously without the UN sanctions regime.

An economically open Iraq would lure international petroleum investment and increase production, both of which would prove detrimental to Iranian economic interests. Post-Saddam, U.S. occupation would put enemy troops around the Iranian border, meaning U.S. troops would be stationed not only to the west of Iran but also to the east (in Afghanistan) and to the south (in the Gulf). A free Iraq could embolden Iran's restive population to cast aside clerical rule. Finally, and perhaps most ominous, a U.S.-allied Iraq would become a platform from which the United States could pursue its attempt to win the trifecta: aiding regime change against the next member of the "axis of evil."

As Iran's rulers confront what they would likely see as existential threats, they have plenty of weapons in their arsenal. Iran's irregular forces can mount resistance against U.S. forces in Iraq, and the nation's deep involvement in Hizballah operations for two decades, combined with its support for Hamas, Palestinian Islamic jihad, and other groups, suggest that its ability to wage covert, low-scale warfare is robust. In addition, Iran has long-standing ties to a host of Iraqi parties and factions. For example, the Supreme Council for the Islamic Revolution in Iraq (SCIRI) is Tehran based and partly Tehran supported. SCIRI has formed common cause with some U.S.-backed groups in the past, but it has also sought at times to keep considerable distance between itself and the rest of the Iraqi opposition. Iran also has long-standing ties to the Patriotic Union of Kurdistan faction and its leader, Jalal Talibani. These relationships and others suggest that Iran has a long-term capability to influence the duration and intensity of political struggles within Iraq, if not always control their outcomes.

Reports have persisted that the United States and Iran struck some sort of accommodating deal over Afghanistan to prevent a clash. Perhaps, but striking a similar deal over Iraq would be much harder for several reasons:

- Afghanistan operates under a system that might best be called warlord federalism. The central government is exceedingly weak, and local warlords have maximal autonomy. As such, U.S. forces have generally been content to remain in the capital city of Kabul and pursue Al Qaeda remnants on the Pakistani border, while allowing the Iranians to build client-like relations in the western regions of the country. Two factors make it unlikely that Iraq will have such a decentralized government. First, the central government of Iraq con-trolled the country's main source of income, oil. Second, Iraq's neighbors, including the U.S. NATO ally Turkey, all have a strong preference for the territorial integrity of Iraq.

- The U.S. troop presence in Afghanistan is only a fraction of what it is likely to be in Iraq for some time to come. The United States en-tered Iraq with a far larger ground force than that with which it en-tered Afghanistan, and it has received far more international support for peacekeeping in Afghanistan than it is likely to receive in Iraq.

- The Iranians were desperate for a change from the Taliban regime, whose aggressive opium operations had led to the rise of heavily armed drug-running cartels along Iran's eastern border and had pro-moted an epidemic of heroin use in Iran. Iran had little to fear from the antebellum status quo in Iraq.

- The United States did not set regional political change as a measure of success in the Afghanistan operation.

## Saudi Arabia

Regime change in Iraq has topped Saudi officials' wish list for years. Saddam maintained a far larger army than Saudi Arabia, could easily reach Saudi cities with weapons of mass destruction, and had long been spewing anti-Saudi rhetoric. Yet, Saudi fears of political change within their own borders run deep, and the Bush administration's proclaimed political goals in Iraq have only exacerbated them.

Some quarters of the Saudi government remain deeply concerned about the direction of events in the kingdom. Public sympathy for bin Laden is rife, and the government is finding it exceedingly difficult to gain control over local charities, at least some of which are tied to groups that pursue acts of violence against civilians. In March 2002, unprecedented public protests erupted over Israeli military operations in the West Bank. Saudi Arabia has too few jobs for young Saudis and too few young Saudis with the skills needed to compete effectively on an international level. Although the situation in Saudi Arabia does not quite constitute the making of a revolution, conditions suggest that the status quo cannot be sustained indefinitely.

Crown Prince Abdullah has been trying to move the Saudi political system in the direction of reform for several years, and his efforts became more intense after the events of September 11, 2001. Clearly driven by the fact that so many of the September 11 hijackers grew up in the kingdom, Abdullah has pushed forward with efforts to reform the Saudi educational system, increase the number of young Saudis entering the workforce, and jump-start the economy.

In addition, Abdullah's language on the need for broader reform throughout the Arab world has become increasingly blunt, starting with his December 2001 statement at a Gulf Cooperation Council meeting. In January 2003, Abdullah floated an Arab reform initiative for Arab League action and also let it be known that he favored establishing an elected Chamber of Representatives in Saudi Arabia in six years.

However, Abdullah's moves are defensive, and he has to contend with an entrenched array of interests wedded to the status quo. He is cautiously seeking to adapt Saudi Arabia's system, careful neither to provoke undue resistance nor to open the floodgates of uncontrollable change. A political order in Iraq that would inspire Saudis to move for change in their own system would thus deeply threaten Saudi Arabia's current course of gradual reform.

Some might argue that Saudi politics move too slowly in any event, and an outside driver that compels change would be a constructive way to force the Saudis to move more quickly. From this perspective, forcing change in Saudi Arabia is the only way to ensure that the kingdom opens up and begins acting like a "normal" state rather than the unique monarchical theocracy that it is currently.

Rather than move more quickly toward reform in response to an external stimulus, however, the Saudis may instead seek to affect that stimulus. Threatened by republicanism in Yemen starting in the 1960s, Saudi Arabia supported royalist forces in the country for years. More recently, Yemenis have pointed to Saudi meddling in their internal affairs, accusing the kingdom of inciting southern secessionists in 1994 and of supporting the Islamist Islah ("Reform") Party today. Closer to home, Gulf politicians often talk of having to consider Saudi sensitivities as they plan for political reform in their own countries.

Although it is difficult to imagine that the Saudi government would go so far as to encourage individuals to kill U.S. officials in Iraq, it is not at all difficult to imagine that the Saudi government might take actions—or not take actions—that would have the effect of greatly complicating the establishment of a new, stable, and democratic political order in Baghdad. Were the Saudis to act, they would do so to prevent an undesirable outcome rather than to ensure a specific positive one, and they would almost certainly act largely through unofficial channels.

Another potentially complicating Saudi action would be to offer strong support to Islamist forces in Iraq who may oppose the U.S. government's goals there. Presumably, such support would be primarily financial, but it could also include providing teaching materials, training, and relief infrastructure. From the Saudi perspective, supporting Islamists in Iraq would prove beneficial in that it would spread Saudi political values: charity, adherence to authority, and the Saudi version of religious orthodoxy. The kingdom values these ideals in much the same way Americans value their understanding of individualism, freedom, democracy, and secular governance. Equally important, a shift toward Islamist politics in Iraq could serve Saudi interests by blunting U.S. enthusiasm for democracy in the Middle East, thereby eliminating a driver for change that the Saudis find threatening and difficult to control.

Yet another way that the Saudis could influence post-Saddam Iraq to their benefit would be to provide extensive support to Sunni Arab claimants to power at the expense of other, more numerous groups in the country. As such, Saudi clients could accentuate the sectarian nature of post-Saddam Iraq and further aggrieve groups such as the Shi'a, which are far more numerous than the Sunni Arabs but have often been unable to rise to power. Similarly, Saudi Arabia could find clients among Iraqi tribes with historic or ethnic ties to the Saudi kingdom, thereby ensuring that they could play a heightened role in the future of Iraq.

Saudi Arabia will not have any kind of veto over the political system in post-Saddam Iraq, but to the extent that Saudis see the situation there as affecting their own domestic political interests, they may seek to shape it. Because the Saudis' primary goal would be to limit the demonstration effect of Iraqi democracy on neighboring governments, their interests may directly conflict with some of the more expansive thinking in the U.S. government.

## Jordan and Syria

Jordan and Syria have fragile political systems under their respective new leaders. Both King Abdullah and President Bashar al-Asad have been trying to navigate the shoals of governance that their fathers had mastered over decades. Each new ruler benefited from the antebellum status quo in Iraq—Jordan through the cheap and discounted Iraqi oil it obtained aboveboard, and Syria through the Iraqi oil it smuggled under the table. Jordan has been trying valiantly to build close ties with the United States for the better part of a decade, and Syria appears periodically to be looking for ways to change its status as a pariah in the eyes of the United States.

For all these reasons, both of these countries are likely to be cautious. Yet, in their caution, they will almost certainly try to hedge their bets on Iraq's future. Although Jordan and Syria are unlikely to provide clear support to individual factions in Iraq, the leaders will probably show a willingness to tolerate Iraqi expatriates whom the United States might find unpalatable. Syria's alleged harboring of leadership families during the war was an early indication of this hedging, as was the departure of partisan fighters from Syria to Iraq. The bluntness of the resultant U.S. threats illustrates how few tools the United States has at its disposal when dealing with Syria, which is both unlikely to be fully compliant with the United States or provide it with a *casus belli*.

## Turkey

As a long-time NATO ally, Turkey may be a surprising obstacle to U.S. plans for democracy in Iraq. Turkey has intimate ties to Iraq through its own Kurdish community in Turkey's southeast and through its long-standing desire to project power into the Kurdish communities of surrounding states. The antebellum balance in northern Iraq was a delicate one—Turks and Kurds both benefited from having a more moderate buffer area on the Turkish border, and smuggling proceeds supported both sides. A unified, democratic Iraq, however, puts the whole Kurdish question into play.

How much autonomy from Baghdad will Iraq's Kurds enjoy, and will their transnational links with other Kurds increase or decrease? What happens to trade and to the smuggling proceeds that are so important to the economies of the region? Will Turkey be allowed to project more influence in Iraqi Kurdistan, or will Iraqi interests push Turkish interests back to the border? What will be the nature of Iraqi federalism, and what demonstration effect might it have on surrounding states? Will Turkey attempt to divide the Iraqi Kurds to keep them as a weak and fractured political force? None of these questions have been answered, but all will need to be.

The Turks inevitably will seek solutions favorable to Turkish interests, and those solutions may not be the same ones sought by their U.S. ally. U.S. policymakers are still smarting from the Turkish Grand National Assembly's refusal to allow attacks on Iraq out of U.S. bases in Turkey, highlighting rather clearly the extent to which U.S. and Turkish interests can differ on issues of regional security.

## Show Me the Money

One might argue that the desires of the surrounding states are irrelevant because the U.S. will to achieve military and political success in Iraq is so great, but is it? One can draw mixed conclusions from the U.S. record in Afghanistan. A highly touted January 2002 donor con-

ference in Tokyo attracted billions of dollars in pledges for Afghani reconstruction from around the globe, but converting the pledges to
dollars and euros has been an uphill battle. Indeed, a year after the fall
of the Taliban regime, Afghanistan's foreign minister described some
countries' records of disbursing their pledges as "very poor"[3]—and this
assessment came from a diplomat. In a meeting with the U.S. Senate
Foreign Relations Committee in February 2003, President Hamid Karzai
clearly indicated his concern that the United States might suffer from a
wandering eye, as solving problems in the next hot spot would diminish
U.S. attention toward Afghanistan. "Don't forget us if Iraq happens,"
Karzai pleaded with the committee.[4]

Karzai truly remains in dire need of help. More than a year after taking office, he controls little outside of Kabul, and regional warlords
have been ascendant throughout the country. Karzai has 3,000 troops
under his command, whereas between 100,000 and 700,000 members
of locally controlled militia groups roam the countryside.[5] Human Rights
Watch complains that, "[b]eyond Kabul, poor security, generalized crimi-
nality, and limited regard for basic human rights have marked the year
since the signing of the Bonn Agreement. ... The solution offered by
the U.S., to have warlords provide security outside of Kabul while the
international community trains a future Afghan army, has proven to be
a failure."[6]

In April 2003, Karzai's brother took the extraordinary step of coau-
thoring an op-ed in the *Washington Post* accusing the U.S. government
of backing Afghan warlords and putting Afghanistan squarely on the
path toward violence, poverty, corruption, and repression.[7] The Taliban
have indeed been routed, but it is difficult to argue that that regime has
been replaced by something looking much like a democracy. Rather, Afghanistan has returned to being Afghanistan—a country with a relatively cosmopolitan capital and a countryside controlled by tribal factions
whose allegiance can be easily rented but never completely bought.

The Balkans might be seen as a success story, but that situation differed from the one in Iraq currently in key respects. First, operations in
the Balkans enjoyed far broader international support than U.S. activi-

ties in Iraq have. U.S. troops did not always like conducting military operations with their NATO allies; however, those allies were there for the pedestrian and expensive tasks that required a large supply of personnel to provide policing, humanitarian assistance, and reconstruction. Europe was heavily committed to success in the Balkans from the beginning, while Europe's commitment to success in rebuilding Iraq is less clear.

Even more important, though, the Balkans benefited from a neighborhood that basically wanted the multilateral operation to succeed. Working to resolve internecine conflicts in the Balkans was difficult, but surrounding countries such as Austria, Hungary, and Italy did not seek to perpetuate conflict there. U.S. operations in Iraq have no such luxury.

There is little chance that U.S. activities in Iraq will turn into another Somalia. In that case, a weakly motivated United States committed troops to an international force with an ill-defined mission and unclear rules of engagement. U.S. troops became sitting ducks for attack, and the loss of 18 U.S. Army Rangers led to an ignominious retreat. Iraq could become another Beirut, however, where a highly motivated adversary was able to penetrate a single U.S. installation in 1982, cause catastrophic casualties, and force a change in U.S. strategy.

## Beyond Rhetoric: Building Political Partnerships

Regime change in Iraq unquestionably provides opportunities to provoke positive political change throughout the Middle East. An Arab democracy serving as a successful model could inspire populations throughout the region and provide a path for governments and populations to escape the mounting pressures under the current authoritarian systems in their homelands.

Under what conditions would such an effect be most likely? Many leaders in the Middle East have long viewed increased democratization as a threat and have acted to obstruct it. The Bush administration appears to have done little to mitigate that sense of threat. In fact, its rhetoric, both in background briefings and by well-connected proxies such as Richard Perle and James Woolsey, seeks to accentuate it. Consider the following quotation from an April 2003 speech by Woolsey, directed toward the governments of Egypt and Saudi Arabia:

> We want you nervous. We want you to realize that now, for the fourth time in 100 years, this country and its allies are on the march, and that we are on the side of those whom you, the Mubaraks, the Saudi royal family, most fear. We are on the side of your own people.[8]

Was Woolsey speaking for the administration? The individual that introduced him noted that day's *Washington Post* article floating his name as a potential administrator for Iraq. Woolsey clearly sought to give the impression that he was stating what the administration thought but could not say.

There are two problems with the sort of strategy for reform that Woolsey and some administration hawks appear to espouse. First, it motivates governments to block U.S. efforts to promote moderation and reform, even in cases when reform is in those governments' own interest. By putting regional governments on the defensive, statements such as Woolsey's make every effort at constructive interaction more difficult and thus make the kinds of obstruction described above more likely.

Equally troubling, Woolsey's words attract governmental obstruction while getting nothing in return. Middle Eastern populations are far more hostile to U.S. policy than they are to their own governments, and they doubt that the United States could possibly be serious about giving them a greater voice. When they do speak, they evince dismay over U.S. policy toward Israel and the Palestinians; resent American cultural dominance; and fear U.S. domination of their economies. No easy trade-off exists for the United States; it cannot quickly ditch unsavory governments to inspire their oppressed peoples. In fact, a strategy like the one Woolsey advocates is far more likely to result in the loss of the support of both the governments and the people of the Middle East, making the United States more of an isolated garrison state than a source of inspiration and hope.

By talking so boldly and optimistically about making Iraq into a democratic showcase, U.S. government officials effectively decrease the likelihood that Iraq will be such a model by highlighting the challenges a democratic Iraq will pose for the status quo in the region and thus energizing the defenders of the status quo to protect their interests. With every additional statement on how regime change in Iraq can catalyze democracy throughout the Middle East, Iraq's neighbors are prompted to concentrate on obstructing U.S. objectives in Iraq rather than on reforming their own systems. Such an outcome would prove lose-lose for the United States because it would impede reform both narrowly in Iraq and more broadly in the Middle East.

If the United States were serious about promoting political reform in the Middle East, a more promising course would be to exercise leadership that is practical more than rhetorical. The people of the region are skeptical of speeches, they are tired of them, and they have long ceased to find them inspiring. If the United States is to play a constructive role in effecting change in the Middle East, the government needs to do it by patiently and quietly building partnerships on the ground. Far more productive than all the rhetoric would be a subtler policy that, on one hand, builds a viable system in Iraq and, on the other, highlights how demographic and technological change, geopolitical shifts, and the ideological sterility of political debate in the region collectively ensure that political tools that have worked well in the past will prove far less effective in the future. The more U.S. officials strut and shout, the more they make the United States a target. Rather than inspiring democracy, they make it more likely that friends and adversaries in the region will move to protect their own interests, thereby frustrating those of the United States in the process.

## Notes

1.  Bill Keller, "The Sunshine Warrior," *New York Times Magazine*, September 22, 2002.

2.  Office of the Press Secretary, The White House, "President Discusses the Future of Iraq," February 26, 2003, www.whitehouse.gov/news/releases/2003/02/20030226-11.html (accessed April 20, 2003).

3.  Abdullah Abdullah, October 25, 2002, www.spa.gov.sa/CGI-BIN/spa_e_reslt2.asp?ser=564070.

4. Hamid Karzai, statement before U.S. Senate Committee on Foreign Relations, February 26, 2003, transcript from Federal News Service.

5. Ibid.

6. Human Rights Watch, "Afghanistan's Bonn Agreement One Year Later: A Catalog of Missed Opportunities," December 5, 2002, www.hrw.org/backgrounder/ asia/afghanistan/bonn1yr-bck.htm (accessed April 20, 2003).

7. Mahmood Karzai, Hamid Wardak, and Jack Kemp, "Winning the Other War," *Washington Post*, April 7, 2003, p. A15.

8. "Transcript: America, Iraq and the War on Terrorism, UCLA," www.avot.org/ stories/storyReader$141 (accessed April 20, 2003) (Woolsey speaking at UCLA Teach-In held by Americans for Victory over Terrorism).